A Slice of Life

ALSO BY BONNIE MARRANCA

Ecologies of Theatre
Theatrewritings
American Playwrights: A Critical Survey
(with Gautam Dasgupta)

AS EDITOR

Conversations on Art and Performance
Plays for the End of the Century
Hudson Valley Reader
American Garden Writing
Interculturalism and Performance: Writings from PAJ
American Dreams: The Imagination of Sam Shepard
The Theatre of Images
Theatre of the Ridiculous
Animations: A Trilogy for Mabou Mines

A Slice of Life

CONTEMPORARY WRITERS ON FOOD

EDITED BY

Bonnie Marranca

INTRODUCTION BY *Betty Fussell*

OVERLOOK DUCKWORTH
New York • Woodstock • London

First published in paperback in the United States in 2005 by
Overlook Duckwoth, Peter Mayer Publishers, Inc.
Woodstock & New York

WOODSTOCK:
One Overlook Drive
Woodstock, NY 12498
www.overlookpress.com
[for individual orders, bulk and special sales, contact our Woodstock office]

NEW YORK:
141 Wooster Street
New York, NY 10012

LONDON:
Gerald Duckworth & Co. Ltd.
Greenhill House
90-93 Cowcross Street
London EC1M 6BF

Library of Congress Cataloging-in-Publication Data

A slice of life : contemporary writers on food /
edited by Bonnie Marranca --1st ed.
p. cm.
1. Gastronomy–Literary collections. 2. Food--Literary collections
TX631.S56 2003   809'.933559--dc22   2003060983

Book design and type formatting by Bernard Schleifer
Printed in the United States of America
ISBN 1-58567-645-4
ISBN 0-7156-3412-7 (UK)
1 3 5 7 9 8 6 4 2

To my parents, Evelyn and Angelo Marranca,
for their good home cooking, lovingly served

and

To my favorite restaurant companions,
Stanley and Laura Kauffmann,
for their generosity of spirit

*Eroticism is the most intense passion and
gastronomy the most extensive.*

"At Table and in Bed," OCTAVIO PAZ

ACKNOWLEDGMENTS

Work on this food book opened up a wide new nework of acquaintances and resources, many of whom came to be generous and encouraging supporters of my work, through all its stages; Gloria Loomis who was the first to see that my concept for the book could become a reality and jump started the project for me; Nach Waxman of Kitchen Arts & Letters bookshop whose shelves yielded valuable source materials along with his comments on early versions of a table of contents; the James Beard Foundation Library, under the direction of Phyllis Issacson, which offered a bounty of writings on food to lose myself in and Linda Snow, librarian at the University of Texas, Dallas, who helped in preliminary research; Betty Fussell who enthusiastically took on the task of writing the book's Preface at a time when I was anxious to have a professional in the field respond to my work; the NYU Food Studies seminar where I have been introduced to many food writers and provocative areas of research in this growing field of scholarship; Antonio Attisani, in Turin, one of the former editors of *La Gola*, the Italian food and culture magazine which served as an early model for what I hoped would be the direction of food writing in this country; Cara DeSilva, whose editorial insights and generosity helped me in the last polishing stages of the manuscript; Peter Mayer and Caroline Trefler of The Overlook Press who have given me the opportunity to have the food book I wanted. I have many friends abroad (and their mothers) to thank for preparing special dishes for me or making sure I tasted local specialties, with the same gusto that they would urge me to see a certain performance or an architectural treasure I may have overlooked. I think they will recognize themselves in the pages of my Introduction.

CONTENTS

Contents

WHEN I HEAR THE WORD "market," I think food, not stocks. I've always loved food and growing up in an Italian family I took good home cooking for granted. It was several years before I realized that most Americans had been eating canned and processed food or TV dinners, while at home I was being nurtured on flavorful soups, spaghetti (before it became known as pasta), olive oil, fresh salads, dark green vegetables, and home-made pies and cookies. Both parents cooked and there always was—still is—plenty of good food available day or night.

Working on this book unloosed in me a flood of memories and images dealing with food. I can still recall my father driving me mornings to the bus stop for high school as I sat in the station wagon with a dish of peppers and eggs on my lap. I was frequently late for school but would never think of skipping breakfast. My father has always talked about his Neapolitan mother's cooking and the twenty-five loaves of bread and delicious pizza she made each week for a family of seven. And my mother, who opens nearly every conversation with a rundown of what meals she's prepared for the day, has now started to make the fried celery dish her own mother, an immigrant from Calabria, used to include every Thanksgiving until her death, in 1970. That's how long I have been talking about it. I can still remember the flavor of my grandmother's sauce, the color, and the way it looked in her dishes, which I now own. Surely, this is the stirring of "taste memory."

My food world was characterized by family drives in the evening to our favorite childhood stops for ice cream or lemon ice, hot dogs, root beer, and White Castle hamburgers. After school treats with friends included, not all on the same day, I might add, Ring Dings and Tastykake, Mexican hats, red licorice, peanut butter cups, Hershey fudgsicles, and cherry Cokes. When I later worked in a donut shop for a few months the best part of it was bringing home the leftovers after an all-night shift. My college roommate and I took over the kitchen in an A & W drive-in for a summer where we spent nights cooking and stuffing ourselves—in the days before any one was afraid of meat or fat—on California burgers, onion rings, French fries, and chili dogs. I remember the afternoon I had to work lunch hour alone and customer after customer ordered more hamburgers than I could manage on the grill. As they grew smaller and smaller I, half-panicked, half-convulsed with laughter at the shrinking burgers, imagined myself in a Lucy Ricardo routine. But, did anybody notice that what was slapped between squishy buns and smothered in garnishings was no bigger than a fifty-cent piece? Probably not—it still tasted swell.

These images always remained only a memory away, but if food be for thought, my own path to a book of food writings took many circuitous turns before settling down to the topic at hand. For the last twenty-six years, residing in New York City, I have been writing about theatre and editing a contemporary arts periodical that I co-founded, *PAJ: A Journal of Performance and Art*. My interests branched out in the late eighties, inspired by my living part of the year in the Hudson Valley. Once I had begun growing my own flowers and vegetables, it was not long before I decided to work on a gardening book. The result was *American Garden Writing*. Soon I took up another project, *A Hudson Valley Reader*, which collected several hundred years of writings by people who had lived in or traveled through the region. Now, my interests were becoming intertwined like a beautiful but uncontrollable ground cover. The "extracurricular" activities eventually influenced me to write a series of essays about what I called the "ecologies of theatre." There came to be no separation between my theatre work and the life I experienced in nature.

It was only a matter of time before a food book would suggest itself. From the start I had planned to organize a volume of writings which would include authors not known for writing about food. Even so, I was overjoyed to discover through my research an abundant choice of material, fascinating and sometimes little-known texts by novelists, poets, critics, and journalists who are already celebrated figures in the literary world and whose work has helped to shape contemporary cultural life. Their contributions to this book, along with those of professional food writers who explore the deeper meanings of food in societies every- where, demonstrate how much the writing life is rooted in the rituals of the everyday world, interfacing the private and the public, the local and the international. For a writer any subject can be the starting point for imaginative reflection on simple human acts that has a way of becoming the profoundest commentary on culture, history, or art. If the best food writing has the psychological and intellectual range of literature, what is also true is that writers bring the same literary inventiveness of the novel or poem to the casual essay and memoir.

For *A Slice of Life* I have gathered together a collection of individual pieces that accent the "writing" aspect of food writing, in its many personal and cultural inflections. Most of the individual contributions take the form of the personal essay that is usually created out of a writer's need to explore a special theme or simply to loll about in a meadow of paragraphs that exist for the pure pleasure of it. Putting thoughts to paper to see where they go. Chewing on sentences encrusted in memory. This is where the story of food begins.

For me, the world of food—its politics, customs, and aesthetics—started to unfold in a wider narrative as I began my travels through Europe. My first experience was as a college student living with a Danish family, in 1969, when I spent a semester at the University of Copenhagen. Here I was exposed to an entirely different cuisine—one based on butter, meat, cream, beer—that, historically, was set in opposition to the preference for olive oil, vegetables, bread, and wine in the Mediterranean diet, beginning with the defeat of the Romans by the "barbaric" tribes of the North in the medieval era. Returning many times since then I've been able personally to observe—and to taste—the gradual but steady intrusion, first of Mediterranean, then Asian cuisines, into the Nordic countries and across the European continent, olive oil and butter accommodating each other like the increasingly heterogeneous cultures of each country.

It was the great Dane, Isak Dinesen, who understood the sensual pleasure of food, creating in her story "Babette's Feast," a charming reflection on the true meaning of grace at the dinner table. But, there is another morsel from the Dinesen biography that is even more luscious, the passage in her memoir, *Out of Africa*, in which she describes how her Kikuyu servant Kamante named dishes after certain events of the day, like "the sauce of the lightning that struck the tree." Here, in one phrase, nature and culture were brought together in a fascinating poetics of the pre-literate mind.

Anthropology has become a strong current in contemporary food writing which is now often indistinguishable from travel writing. Likewise, cookbooks representing diverse ethnic cuisines appear regularly, even though they seem to share the same cultural ambitions. Take my word for it, few of them approach the literary charm of M. F. K. Fisher or Alice B. Toklas. Still, it is no longer enough simply to write a cookery book with recipes: they must come with anecdotes and family histories and photographs. This is an intriguing development over the last decade that is duplicated in the general public's interest in genres such as biography, the memoir, and documentary.

Where previously one could track the dreamworld of contemporary culture in film types such as journalists, investment bankers, or artists, now chefs—the latest celebrity species—are featured increasingly as characters in films centered in restaurants. A short list of them includes *Dinner Rush, Eat Drink Man Woman, Big Night, Tortilla Soup, Who's Killing the Great Chefs of Europe?, Mostly Martha*. Chef characters are written into current television advertising scenarios, too. The proliferating cookbooks and cable food shows, and expanded coverage in newspapers and magazines, when added to the popularity of cooking classes and designer cookware, all hype the new food culture. In SoHo, my Manhattan neighborhood, in the big glass windows of its restaurants, those dining out are simultaneously looking and being looked at, in a new kind of spectatorship. As a fanciful gesture super chef Daniel Boulud has even named a chocolate dessert after the opera singer Renée Fleming—"the diva Renée." If performance is the condition to which American culture seems increasingly to aspire, then it is no surprise to watch unfold in the variousness of its repertoire the new theatre of food.

The cost of a glass of wine and a dish of pasta in most New York restaurants has become, well, gastronomical, even as all too many diners leave their meals unfinished. Everywhere in urban cultures those with money to spare can afford to drink designer bottles of water all day or buy only organic food or obsess over the raw and the cooked, to salt or not to salt. The restless complexity of the diverse economies of gourmandism is insinuating itself into social life. Still, if nationwide, better-stocked supermarkets and an improved restaurant culture have transformed American eating habits, I am always surprised by the number of clerks at the checkout counters who don't know the names of ordinary fruits and vegetables.

American affluence and global tourism, accompanying the travels of foods across borders, offer to our tables a luxuriant way of dining. The return to the bourgeois idea of the comfortable "home" is reinforced in the culture by a growing emphasis on design, though the leisurely family meal itself is largely out of fashion. And, what of the idea of the "natural"? It changes in every era, like the idea of the "natural" actor. Americans like the pretense of *the natural* as if the complexity of stylization would contaminate the supposed order of their world. The same holds true of the disdain of the formal garden and preference for the untamed in nature, even as social life is more and more regulated.

What does all this eating and talk of food mean to our society? I can't help thinking that contemporary expressions of appetite have as much to do with spiritual hunger as self-gratification. The experience at table offers one of the few realms of privacy and intimacy in a culture of increasingly vulgarized public obsessions. It honors speech, direct communication—the face-to-face, not interface. Sharing a meal is a hands-on experience, not a virtual reality.

There are weekly declarations that the American public is growing more obese at the same time that many others refuse to eat or engage in other varieties of self-denial as equally compelling statements of self. Seeds, like birds and plants, are increasingly endangered, threatening the genetic diversity of our food supply. The Seed Savers Exchange in Iowa has been a growing force in the preservation of heirloom vegetable seeds, a project abandoned by the Department of Agriculture which favors the monoculture practices of big corporations that now control our food production and distribution.

Famine is worsening in the poorest countries of the world even as the rich have more and more of the world's food products at their disposal, in or out of season, and, especially in America, in larger and larger portions. Fast food accelerates abroad while, simultaneously, the Slow Food movement, started by the Italian Carlo Petrini to protect artisanal, regional foods, and culinary traditions from the onslaught of regulation and conformity, is gaining ground as a political force in the European community, impresssed by his ideal of "ecogastronomy." In Europe the outcry over genetically-modified food is loud and strong— they do not allow it on the continent except for animals—whereas in this country Americans don't seem to be bothered by the biogenetically-engineered products already sitting on store shelves. The bowl of fruit is no longer a still life. It has an ethics of production.

Food products are now subject to the same criticism as contemporary art: they are becoming less and less distinctive in order to travel more easily on the international market. As the varieties of consumption took on new meanings in cultural life over the decades so did the use of food in the culture and in the art world. In the post-war era Pop Art acted as both a critique of consumerism and a celebration of it: in Andy Warhol's soup cans and Coke bottles, Claes Oldenburg's food sculptures, and the kitchens of James Rosenquist and Roy Lichtenstein. Today, the visual arts increasingly incorporate food as image or object, opening up economic, sexual, and social themes that have long since departed from the earlier playful images of consumer culture and the processed foods industry. Few works of contemporary art have been so outspoken as Judy Chicago's installation *The Dinner Party*, which was just given a permanent home in the Brooklyn Museum. A triangular banquet table with place settings and ceramic floor text that documents the women throughout history who were and were not invited to the table, it uses the form of the dinner party to explore women's historical role in domestic and cultural space. Another kind of feminist art statement is posed by Janine Antoni, whose large chocolate sculpture in the shape of a cube, entitled *Gnaw*, has been featured in the new food journal, *Gastronomica*. Her bite marks are visible as gestures towards art history and her own relation to food. Chocolate, the floating signifier of the world, is a beloved ingredient in contemporary art.

Vic Muniz, the Brazilian artist, who now lives in Brooklyn, has created a series of *Pictures in Chocolate*. He uses Bosco, the chocolate syrup familiar from childhood, to depict a Freud in Bosco, a Charlton Heston as Moses in Bosco. To me, his most moving pictures are the *Sugar Children* series in which Muniz sprinkled sugar over the photographs of children of sugar plantation laborers and rephotographed them. The twice-removed image acts as a commentary on the geopolitics of production and consumption as well as on the political economy of identity. His photographs offer a visual equivalent to the kinds of socio-political histories of sugar, salt, spices, and cod that have been written recently, exploring the patterns of trade, migration, tourism, geography, and local politics that determine food production and distribution.

If the potato has also been the subject of a new food history, its more striking manifestation comes in the form of the Irish Hunger Memorial, a work of public art that was unveiled in Manhattan's Battery Park City in the summer of 2002. An installation the size of a quarter acre facing the Statue of Liberty, it recreates an abandoned Irish cottage, fallow potato fields and stone walls, also including native Irish plants in the site. But, the memorial goes beyond the remembrance of the Irish potato famine to underline the immensity of world hunger in displayed texts that are a part of it.

As the idea of history is expanded and reshaped in our time, situating previously marginal subjects in a contemporary context, it acknowledges more varied realms of human experience. Each new food history uncovers more secrets of the human race. Even casual examples of food writing by their very nature act as forms of narrative. To dine is a kind of performance where, from our place "setting," we exchange stories, debate ideas, and reveal our dreams, the unspoken settling temporarily in the silence between adverbs. Not surprisingly, many of the influential plays in the world repertoire take place in the kitchen or dining room. Here huge psychological dramas are served forth and characters devour one another or set themselves free in forked sentences. A certain brand of boiled-over British play of the late-50s, perfected by Arnold Wesker and John Osborne, and known as "kitchen sink realism," showed that all was not well in the family. Of course, Bertolt Brecht had already made the connection between theatre and eating when he disparaged the conventional stage as a "culinary theatre," as if the consumption of stale ideas during a performance were a form of bourgeois gluttony.

What is a dinner plate but a field of narrative that tosses back all kinds of images between servings, especially one's own. How full of meaning is the word "helpings" in the syntax of dining. For better or worse the dinner table is the center of the world, the family meal the source of the drama of the self. It is worth noting that the current renewed interest in storytelling and the anecdotal in various art forms— literary, visual, filmic—parallels the ascendency of restaurant culture. A meal becomes an event through the addition of good conversation and it has more often than not less to do with the food consumed than with the quality of companionship articulated. Even more so, the act of eating accompanied by a discussion of how the food was prepared, how it tastes—some cultures excel at this—is an instance of immense pleasure. Yet, everyone, at one time or another, has experienced the difficulty of swallowing angry words. The dinner table is one of the great settings of heartbreak.

In the best of circumstances, through the experience of food we make culture and contribute to the civilizing process, taking the measure of human activity in random acts of speech. Is it any wonder that the notion of "taste" describes both food and aesthetic judgment and that "palate" can mean both the roof of the mouth—what an image!— and the savor of the intellect?

All the more remarkable to learn of the profound meaning of food in extreme situations, such as a cookbook put together in a concentration camp or the American soldier in a Japanese prison who made his abject compatriot a birthday cake of rice, bananas, palm sugar, and limes. The Arctic explorer Ernest Shackleton's account of his starving men on Elephant Island notes that one of the books the men had on board the abandoned ship was a cookbook from which they read out recipes each night as they waited be be rescued, discussing them in detail, even suggesting improvements. Their diaries reveal a craving for carbohydrates. A world away, one of the most fascinating customs is the Thai funeral cookbook composed of recipes and anecdotes by a person before his or her death to be given to mourners at the funeral.

I have had occasion to travel abroad a great deal, having lived for at least several months at a time in Denmark, Italy, England, and Germany. One of my happiest trips was the spring, some years ago, when I was invited by Alitalia on a press junket to Umbria for what I imagined would be a theatregoing blitz, topped off by the Spoleto Festival. But, as it happened, the Europeans who joined our American group turned out to be food writers. We saw very little theatre but ate out way through the best restaurants in Umbria where I lost count of how many were named "La buca di San Francesco," as if a little plenary indulgence never hurt anyone. Only years later did I realize that this was a foreshadowing of my own divigations as a theatre critic. More recently, I was settled in Berlin for the better part of a year, the starting point for visits on the continent as far east as Warsaw and as far south as Seville, the varied foods offering their own chracteristic topographies on the dinner plate.

Bringing back special foods from abroad is one of the great pleasures of travel. Right now I have in my pantry a salami from the Marco Polo airport in Venice, pimientón from Madrid, a tube of Swedish salmon paste, sardines and a can of olive oil from Barcelona, porcini mushrooms from Bellagio, pumpkin oil from Graz, and a package of figs stuffed with walnuts and candied fruits that I just carried home from Cosenza. But, do you know what I've learned? None of these foods tastes the same in New York. Something is always missing. It has to do with the color of sunlight or the design of a window frame or birdsong—what we might call the *mise-en-scène* of a meal. Everything is different, starting with the pronounciation of vowels. Taste is both an activity and an engagement of the senses. It requires the attentiveness of one's entire being.

If favorite foods transported home don't seem the same when we return, neither do familiar foods from home taste the same in another country. Sometimes appetite mocks the traveler who has forgotten the cultural relativity of taste in distractions of the exotic. I recall the time my husband and I were walking down the street in Kathmandu and saw a sign that read, "Pizza." After several weeks on the Indian subcontinent, we couldn't resist. We walked up a narrow staircase and ordered one. We could almost taste it as we climbed the stairs. What arrived was round and doughy but the resemblance to pizza stopped there. When one's heart is set on a certain food craving overwhelms probability.

That truth was brought home to me again when two summers ago in Nova Scotia, we stopped by the side of the road to have a picnic lunch with our traveling companions, a couple from Sardinia. The sea and air and sun were glorious. After we had eaten, everyone looked forward to a cup of coffee, even though there was only a jar of instant with us. But not a drop of water was to be had anywhere. Our friends were so desperate that they simply opened the coffee jar and took a deep breath, temporarily satisfying themselves with the aroma of memory.

That, I came to understand, is the difference between desire and thirst.

When I realized that I had been returning from recent trips to Europe with notepads of recipes and observations on food, like the special candy in honor of St. Teresa made in Avila, or Modena's *Tortelli di zucca*, the idea of working on a book about food gradually drizzled its way into my thoughts. As a theatre critic, it occurred to me that reading recipes or writings about food, even listening to others extol the glory of meals enjoyed, is something like reading or hearing about a performance I had missed. It isn't always necessary to experience the event—sometimes it's better not to—because vicarious pleasure has its own deep connection to human experience when imagination takes hold. But, then, what I enjoy most about cooking is stirring as an occasion for letting my thoughts flow with the contents of the pan. And what I value is the exquisite pleasure of the last forkful, not the first.

Food has everything in the world to tell us about the mentalities of an age, its desiring tropes and geographies of taste, its contribution to the life of spectacle. Today, just as we have come to see natural history understood as part of the history of the world, the subject of food is now embraced as a history of humankind.

—Bonnie Marranca

January, 2003
New York City

INTRODUCTION:
EATING MY WORDS

FOOD IS NOT A SUBJECT in the way that the great subjects of literature like War, Love, Death, Sex, Power, Betrayal, or Honor are subjects. Neither is food an object, in the way that a Car, a Washing Machine, a Computer, a House are objects—generic commodities that we desire and consume. Rather, food is an action, more primal than speech and more universal than language. And for humans, there's the rub. While everything in the created universe eats, not everything speaks. Wind and water eat stone, night eats day, black holes eat light—silently. We find words to address these actions, but long before we ever arrived on the scene or said a word about it, every link in the terrestrial food chain, as in the cosmic chain, was chomping away and changing one thing into another. It's one of those givens we like to avoid because we don't fancy our table companions or dining conditions. We don't like to be reminded that if dung were not caviar to the dung beetle, the earth would be covered in shit.

Nor do we like to be reminded that we are steak tartare to worms or, if we thwart their slow munch, a grillade to flames. We want to be exempt, special, excused. We don't want to be reminded that in the game preserve staked out for us, we are flesh and blood like our fellow animals, subject to the same feeding frenzies but with inferior teeth. In terms of brains, we may be first among mammals, but we are mammals nonetheless, and as such we cannibalize our mothers in order to live. Each of us, no matter how noble his sentiments at a later stage of development, drinks mother's blood from the time he is a tiny egg clinging hungrily to a uterine wall. Long before speech, the drama of communication begins in the womb and is merely amplified with baby's first intake of breath that ends in a howl, acknowledging in premonitory outrage that life-long separation of the feeder from the fed. From birth on, what comes out of the mouth and what goes in are inextricably mingled because there is only the one orifice for both feeding and speaking, not to mention kissing. Was that a mistake in engineering or a brilliant subversion of human pretense?

Elias Canetti asks whether it wouldn't have been better to have one orifice for food and another for words. "Or does this intimate mixing of all our utterances with the lips, teeth, tongue, throat, all those parts of the mouth that serve the business of eating—does this mixing tell us that language and eating forever belong together, that we can never be nobler and better than we are?" But what if we ask the question another way? Does this intimate mixing of language and eating suggest that both are forms of knowledge and of communication, that ingesting what is outside us with lips, teeth, tongue, and throat is intimately related to excreting from within the cries, sighs, babbles, and prattles that are eventually transformed into words and sentences in the cauldrons of the human mind and imagination? Could we go further and suggest that the lineaments of the mouth lick into shape the very images that the mind of man conceives in his struggle to find sound bites and transmit them? The crunch of teeth biting into an apple shapes the image of the father of mankind, who hungers and thirsts after righteousness with actual lips and throat. Does not this intimate mixing suggest that the human animal is forever a bewildering compound of body parts and spirit sensors, a belcher of hymns, an angel that farts, and that wise eaters and speakers will savor the mixture?

For is not the mouth our primary mediator in distinguishing what is without from what is within, as we suck first our own and then other people's fingers and toes? We learn to see and to say "Mama" out of hunger, for both speaking and eating express similar actions of hungering, desiring, gathering, preserving, communing, laughing, fearing, loving, and dying in the long agon of separation and connection. Even a mouth eating in solitude—and silence—is engaged willy-nilly in discovering and communing with what is outside itself, which its hunger transforms by taking the outside literally in. We eat the world to know it and ourselves. If we fail to distinguish outside from in, we are stamped with a name and a story: Narcissus, hungering to eat himself, imaged in a pool, opened his mouth and drowned.

Eating, like speaking, reconnects through the imagination what reason has learned to disconnect through the senses. In this way, eating is a form of magic. When Shakespeare's Leontes discovers in *The Winter's Tale* that the statue of his Hermione is alive, he exclaims, "If this be magic, let it be an art lawful as eating." Eating, like speaking, mediates between opposite worlds, forging a bridge over the natal chasm between mind and body, images and substances, symbols and things that reason works hard to keep apart. Even as a noun, food suggests the action of ferrying meaning across species, across ontological continents, ensuring that despite the logic of appearances, you *can* turn a sow's ear into a silk purse through the "turn" of trope, or the "transfer" of metaphor, through speaking pictures, or images in action.

Food is always image and icon as well as substance. Semioticians explained decades ago how food, cooking, and eating create a tripartite language of their own through which a culture expresses itself, and this language dances between the literal and the figurative in the way that we usually expect of speech but not always of food. Despite laboratory analyses, mother's milk is never simply the sum of its biochemical or molecular parts, no more than a bottle of milk is. Who's holding the breast or the bottle or the baby, and where? Are mother and baby sitting on the grass in suburban sunshine or are they flat on a canvas surrounded by drapery and haloed cherubs? Are they on a railway platform herded into a cattle car by soldiers in uniform? Food always condenses a happening, a plot, which unfolds like any enacted drama in the spotlit present, surrounded by shadows of the past.

The most ancient originating plots in the Western world, in fact, hinge on the relation of food to language. Before the Madonna there was Eve, and before Eve there was Nin-ti, the Sumerian mother goddess whose story, told in the world's first written language, Sumer, is a food story. After the water god Enki ate eight of Nin-ti's magic plants, the goddess cursed eight of his bodily organs with death, then relented and restored the god to life. Nin-ti's name was a pun, which meant both "rib" and "to make live." In the language of Sumer, Eve's name also meant "rib," but the language and the food got muddled in the transition from Sumer to Hebrew, so that in the Hebrew story the lady Eve was given life by the rib of the man, whose death was caused by the woman's eating of a magic plant. Despite the gender and cultural reversal from mother goddess to father god, the paradox of the human animal remains intact: that which gives him life also kills him, and his tragedy is that he knows it.

Human life is so bound up with food—the sounds, textures, smells, tastes, emotions, ideas, and rituals of the one so meshed with the other—that to take a slice of life at any point is to cut into a full loaf, a pie, a roast, a terrine of meaning. Personal and cultural memories are so integral to eating and speaking that simply to name a food is to invoke the lifetime of a person—and a culture. We don't need Proust's madeleine. We have Twain's cornpone. Even when the nominal subject is a single food, such as coffee or oysters or beans, it is also about place and time and occasion and memory and need, just as it is about politics and economics and trade and war and religion and ceremony. While the first person singular is the instinctive voice in which to express our thoughts and feelings about food, the point of view will be as diverse as the position of the speaker: social critic, gardener, connoisseur, athlete, chef, housewife, farmer, dentist, historian, garbageman, politician, pastor, poet. All walks of life eat, in every corner of the world, whether in Nigeria, Bombay, Austria, Israel, Kyoto, or Iowa. Although attitude and tone of voice may play every key from rhapsodic to obscene, both the particularities of food and the universality of hunger keep the speaker, or writer, rooted in common ground.

Food, like language, forever unites the concrete with the universal, and a writer's attitude toward food will appear in how he manipulates the nervy relation between substance and symbol, jittery with dramatic tension, that dictates the behavior of us all. The materialist asserts the primacy of flesh: "*Erst kommt das Fressen, dann kommt die Moral,*" sings Brecht. The spiritualist denies or subjugates the flesh: "*I need nothing. I feel nothing. I desire nothing,*" writes Wole Soyinka in prison on the eleventh day of his fast. The ritualist transforms substance by symbol into rules of purity: Chitrita Banerji tells us that only *luchis*, a kind of fried bread, and cold vegetables may be eaten by the widows of Bengal. The sensualist translates substance and symbol alike into physical sensation: "The gamey taste and smell of ripened cheese is sexual, and provocative; the smell is maternal still, but now it is the smell of cyclical time," writes Paul Schmidt. The satirist mocks symbols by fabricating ridiculous substance: "The correct drink for fried bologna *à la Nutley, Nouveau Jersey*, is a 1927 Nehi Cola," writes Russell Baker.

Writings about food are necessarily as diverse as writings about any part of life and as illuminative of the things that matter because food is connected to everything. Homer, whether speaking of epic wars or journeys, never neglected food and drink. He specified in detail how to roast and salt the joint of meat and how to mix wine with water to invite the gods in. Greek gods ate and drank in the company of man long before Christians turned their God into cooked food to be eaten by men. That changed the nature of the feast, of course, although there was nothing new in gods who existed to be eaten. Think of Prometheus with his eternally gnawed, eternally renewed liver, wherein man's lips and tongue tasted forever the sour of cyclical time, the bitter of eternal hunger, the sweet of immortality, the salt of death.

In imaging the unavoidable and appalling fact that life eats life, the Ancient Maya invented a language in which men and gods were made of the self-same food in an eternal interchange of substance. A literal ear of corn growing in the fields was also the finely shaped head of the sacrificed young corn god with his hair of green leaves. To eat corn was to eat one's mother, father, sister, brother, and ancestor gods. Substance and symbol were so intimately mixed in the mouth of man that life and death were as mingled as body and soul, as eating and speaking. Maya speech wrapped the cosmos in a language of verbal and visual food puns, so that eating and speaking were alike actions of punning. To eat a kernel of corn, the substance of life, was to swallow a drop of blood, a sign of death. The Maya sign, or glyph, for bread abstracted the cornhusk wrapper and the ball of corn dough of an actual tamale, so that both speaker and eater alike shared in the bread's layered meanings of "sacred offering," "sacrificial blood," "something precious," "day." Every kernel of corn condensed the plot of the *Popul Vuh* and its hero, the sacrificed god Hunahpu, whose decapitated head in the calabash tree, after he and his twin brother outwitted the Lords of Death, impregnated Blood Woman who gave birth to man from her body of corn.

> And so then they put into words the creation,
> > The shaping
> Of our first mother
> > And father.
> Only yellow corn
> > And white corn were their bodies.
> Only food were the legs
> > And arms of man.
> Those who were our first fathers
> > Were the original men.
> Only food at the outset
> > Were their bodies.

Nothing else can do for man's mind and imagination what food does because it is the one and only thing that accompanies every single man, Maya, Christian, Muslim, Buddhist, on his journey from cradle to grave. If his first sound is a cry for milk, his last may be a whimper for sugared tea or a spoonful of Jell-O. Sans teeth, tongue, or throat, he still must open the veins of his body to the outside world to sustain life, whether or not he is conscious of that mechanized connection. His final image may not be of the loved face hovering over his bedside at all, but of a wished-for muffin or martini, as real and intense as the griever left behind.

Never underestimate the power of food to summon images and dictate lives in the here and hereafter. Why are the graves in almost every ancient culture stuffed with containers for food and drink to accompany the corpse on its journey between worlds? As in life, so in death, food remains our most faithful attendant on the ferry across the river Styx, giving comfort and sustenance to the frightened soul soon to swallow and be swallowed by a realm where outside and inside have no meaning and where that peculiar mixture of eating and speaking will vanish in the emptying out of appetite and the entering in of silence.

—BETTY FUSSELL

Place Settings

INTIMATE CUISINE

JOHN THORNE

SOMETHING HAS HAPPENED TO SUPPER.

I don't mean *dinner,* that special, slightly formal meal that we have friends over to and sometimes sit down to ourselves on special occasions, but the plain and casual feed that awaits us at end of day. I still look forward to it, but when I actually pull up to table, there's been a hesitant feeling somewhere inside me, a sense that something was no longer right.

All this must have been edging around in the back of my mind for some time, but I only became actually conscious of it the other night, watching one of those television ads where the family waits with bated breath for Dad's approval of a potent replacement for some or other thing Mom once made from scratch. But my sense of disquiet had nothing to do with the product. I realized I didn't believe in supper anymore, at least not that kind of supper.

With that realization came a sudden, happy feeling of relief. My relations with that meal have been troubled for a long, long time. I've always believed that home cooking means food simply and inexpensively made from cupboard staples. But I'm also aware that it mostly isn't—and how tempted almost every cook is to fall back into the waiting arms of the crowd of convenience foods that fill the supermarket shelves.

Not, of course, that some of those aren't better than others. Still, the fact that many cooks feel that they have no choice except to make meals scraped out of cans or defrosted from the freezer means that we are forced into playing a role we don't yet fully understand. After all, why should we—any of us—feel compelled to go on making more and more compromises in making a meal that shouldn't, and never did before, require it? We pay so much; we get so little back.

The usual argument, of course, is that these meals save us labor or time. But good, simple food from scratch can be set on the table almost as easily, so easily, really, as to make no difference. But—and this is the really important point—that food isn't the same as "supper" at all. When I cook for myself, I could easily make that kind of meal. But in my relationships, almost always, it hasn't seemed quite enough.

Instead, as best as I or the other could, we compromised or worked harder than was fair or sensible, to put real supper on the table.

The reason for this compulsion, I now realize, came from a sense of civility, of what in a family we sense is due the others. If that due is not paid, even for the best of reasons, it generates a sense of tension, of things not being right. The problem, however—for me, at least—is that this same unease has crept into ordinary supper as well.

What struck home so hard watching that television ad was the realization of how much we all eat supper as though we already were on television. Supper is such an incredibly public meal. Just as we were—many of us—brought up to wear clean underpants in case we got hit by a bus, we've also been trained to eat supper—to think of sup-per—as if at any moment the neighbors might shove their easy chairs up outside the picture window and settle down to watch the show.

Now, admittedly, this sense of public scrutiny was the flip side of the family's sense of self-esteem. It provided part of the cement that held things together. "Let them look!" it said. "They'll see us all around the table behaving ourselves, eating good stuff off polished plates, and none of us talking with our mouths full."

Nothing is wrong with this. It's just that the strain of providing this kind of theatre in our current relationships is starting to tell us some-thing. It's not so much that we don't want this at supper, but we hunger for something else very much more. And that hunger springs, not from the stomach, but from the heart.

Supper, after all, is our most social meal and, of all the day's con-tacts (apart, at least, from acts of love), perhaps the most needingly per-sonal one. And it isn't simply the growing impersonality of the food needed to make our familiar supper possible that distances the eaters at the table from one another, but the very shape of the meal itself.

Food, we need to remember, is communication as much as nutrition, and the message isn't simply what we pay for it, the care we put into mak-ing it, or even how nicely we serve it forth. It's right in there with the slices of boiled beef, mashed potatoes, green beans, lump of squash. That plain and homely food is awash with messages for us, talking all the time.

Only it's no longer saying what we need to hear. Its generous servings still speak of prosperity, its quality of good taste, its nutrition of education and concern, its very division into neat portions on the plate of respectability. But these aren't the things we now need most to say to each other. Outside in the world, things have changed. A public sense of family esteem no longer holds relationships together. Couples—married or not—and whole families, for that matter, now have to work hard to provide this for themselves.

The way that they work at this is to establish a sense of personal closeness, of a special caring and understanding that only comes from carefully nurtured attentiveness to each other's private self. What we now want to celebrate at supper is not civility but intimacy, and to do that, we have found an entirely different cluster of manners. Now we need a new way of eating—a new cuisine—to display it.

Intimacy . . . food. Brought into conjunction, our imagination immediately conjures a romantic occasion: caviar, dim lighting, a special vintage wine. And that's okay, I think; the intimate eating I have in mind flows from our desire to capture the special closeness such meals provide and bring it into the unromantic eating of the every day.

To accomplish this sense of needful privacy, intimate food must work in a very different way from the old-fashioned supper, which, even when painfully modernized, works best when it is—in form, if not content—almost identical to what is being eaten next door. Intimate food strives for another effect. Relaxed, uncomplicated, personal, it provides an oasis from our public selves and the pressures of outside demands by pushing the public world away. Mood matched to mood, candles are lit and shutters pulled shut, this time before—not after—the meal.

Because of its very personal qualities, intimate food may seem at first to share something of the unkempt carelessness of the solitary eater. A whole meal might be made of only appetizers, the meat served on, not with, the salad, the dessert eaten first. But, in fact, there is a style to this eating that springs directly from the claims of intimacy, twisting convention into off-centered patterns that mark them as our very own.

First, this is a cuisine of accommodation. Often, both partners work and neither wants to put the other to the task of an elaborate nightly meal. Supper must come together simply and easily out of what is at hand and by whoever has the chore or gets home first. And, since our days now follow eccentric rhythms, accommodation also means bending to meet the appetite that had no lunch, waiting for a suppertime that is suddenly delayed, or hurrying when the eaters must rush out directly after. Pasta, for instance, has become a mainstay of this kind of cooking because it can be so fresh, so quick, so adaptable to all these things.

Next, I think, it is a cuisine of spontaneity. Not that every meal must be impromptu, but there is always the sense that it springs, like good talk, from real attention and not a stock response. Politeness now demands not graciousness but mutual understanding, and supper has become a place where this is most pleasurably displayed. The golden melon on the fruit stand, the impulsive splurge on the first asparagus of the season, the sudden mutual craving for spareribs—intimate eating presupposes on both sides a willingness to meet a mood and join in, something that can't be done unless little risks are taken, desires voiced, contact made.

This, by the way, is also why one of the first reactions to this kind of eating is a feeling of vulnerability: we are too used, every one of us, to this idea of supper as something that is served us, from which we take our pleasure as we want, even to the point where one or the other must play the servant, at least before sitting down. But in intimate eating, it is not the stomach who is king, and especially not any particular stomach.

So, also, intimate eating is a cuisine of less. While there are many reasons for a general concern about overeating, in this instance it springs particularly from intimacy's need to share. And while no one can deny the satisfying closeness that comes from occasionally shared bouts of gluttony, in the long term it becomes a sort of mutual bribery, a substitute for something else.

Here, instead, selectivity has replaced surfeit as the accepted form of pampering: a few succulent slices of Westphalian ham for the slab of roast pork; the lustrous single chocolate truffle for the hot fudge sundae. Less on the table means the more we need—or should—offer the other in the pleasures of ourself.

W IS FOR WANTON

M. F. K. FISHER

❙❙❙ AND THE GREAT DIFFERENCE between the way a man eats, and has his doxy eat, when he plans to lead her to the nearest couch, and the way a woman will feed a man for the same end.

A man is much more straightforward—usually. He believes with the unreasoning intuition of a cat or a wolf that he must be strong for the fray and that strength comes from meat: he orders rare steak, with plenty of potatoes alongside, and perhaps a pastry afterward. He may have heard that oysters or a glass of port work aphrodisiacal wonders, more on himself than on The Little Woman, or in an unusual attempt at subtlety augmented by something he vaguely remembers from an old movie he may provide a glass or two of champagne, but in general his gastronomical as well as alcoholic approach to the delights of love is an uncomplicated one which has almost nothing to do with the pleasurable preparation of his companion.

A woman contemplating seduction, on the other hand, is wanton, and a wanton woman, according to the dictionary, is unchaste, licentious, and lewd. This definition obviously applies to her moral rather than her culinary side. Considered solely in connection with the pleasures of the table, a wanton woman is one who with cunning and deliberation prepares a meal which will draw another person to her. The reasons she does so may be anything from political to polite, but her basic acknowledgment that sexual play can be a sure aftermath of gastronomical bliss dictates the game, from the first invitation to the final mouthful of ginger omelet.

It is an agelong rumor, apparently fairly well founded, that the great procuresses and madams have always been the great teachers in *"la cuisine d'amour."* Such proficient pupils as Du Barry and the Countess of Louveciennes bear out this theory, and recipes ascribed to both of them are reprinted annually in various undercover publications dedicated to the somewhat dubious encouragement of libertinage.

Most of the culinary secrets told in them, at a high price and "in plain wrappers for mailing," lean heavily on the time-worn knowledge that dishes made with a great deal of mustard and paprika and other heating spices, and ones based on the generous use of shrimps and other fish high in phosphorus, are usually exciting to both human sexes but particularly to the male. Sometimes a more complicated significance, straight from Freud, is given to recipes thought of long before his day. The dish of eel innocently prepared for a gathering of good pastors by a former brothel cook, which Brillat-Savarin describes so lightly in his *Physiology of Taste,* is a perfect example of this: there is a phallic rightness about the whole thing, visual as well as spiritual, which has more to do with the structure of the fish than the possible presence of a mysterious and exotic spice.

In general, however, the great courtesans have paid less attention to the Freudian appearance of their kitchens' masterpieces, from what I can gather, than to the temperaments of the men they have willed to please. They have studied the appetites of their prey.

This is, in a way, a paraphrase of the old saying, "First catch your hare, then cook him": wolf or even goose can be substituted for the little wild rabbit.

Once caught, a human male is studied by the huntress as thoroughly as if he were a diamond. She looks at his ear lobes and his fingernails after he has eaten of rare beef, and if the former are plump and ruddy, arid the latter rosy pink, she knows his glands to be both satisfied and active. She analyzes his motor reflexes after he has downed a fair portion of jugged venison, and if instead of showing a pleasurable skittishness he yawns and puffs and blinks, she nevermore serves that gamy dish. She notes coldly, calculatingly, his reactions to wine and ale and heady spirits, as well as to fruits, eggs, cucumbers, and such; she learns his dietetic tolerance, in short, and his rate of metabolism, and his tendencies toward gastric as well as emotional indigestion. And all this happens whether she be a designing farm girl in Arkansas or a slim worldly beauty on the Cap d'Antibes.

Now I myself am neither of these. I have met a few famous madams, but for one reason or another have never discussed the gastronomy of love with them. I have read a great many books. I have watched a great many people, and fed them too. And here is how I would go about it, as of today, if I wanted to ensnare an average man and lead him, with proper discretion, to the marriage bed. (I say average. The truth is that I do not know a really average man, gastronomically or otherwise. A further complication is that I would quite probably be uninterested in one if ever I met him.)

Given the fact that I have found a male of about my own age, healthy, not too nervous, fairly literate, in other words, one I would like to have cleave unto me for reasons of pleasure if not reproduction: I would soon discover his likes ("First catch your wolf..."), and more gradually his dislikes, the deep-seated kind based on the fact that his grandmother made him eat cold turkey one day when it thundered, and his father once called stuffed goose's neck rattlesnake meat, and that sort of thing.

By then I would know what he thought he admired and what he *really* did. If he fancied himself as a bored diner-out I would gradually tease and excite him by bewilderment, and serve him what he thought he hated, in a quiet, lonely room. If he thought he could not possibly eat anything with onion in it I would prove my own control of the situation without his knowing it and prepare a few artful dishes to lead him to realize that he now loved what he had most abhorred. If he hated company I would insinuate two or three or even five arresting characters into his prandial pattern.

In other words I would quarrel with him, on a celestially gentle plane.

I would placate his early inhibitions, and flatter his later ones, and in the end I would have educated him without pain to the point where some such menu as the following would culminate in the flowering of mutual desire, whether social, financial, or impurely intramural:

Good Scotch and water for him, and a very dry Martini for me.

A hot soup made of equal parts of clam juice, chicken broth, and dry white wine, heated just to the simmer.

A light curry of shrimps or crayfish tails. The fish must be peeled raw, soaked in rich milk, and drained, and the sauce must be made of this milk, and the fish poached for at best six minutes in the delicately flavored liquid. This is a reliable trick.

Rice for the curry, and a bland green salad—that is, with a plain French dressing containing more than its fair share of oil.

A dessert based on chilled cooked fruits, with a seemingly innocent sauce made of honey, whole cinnamon, and brandy, poured over and around them at boiling point and allowed to chill.

By preference I would serve a moderately dry champagne, from the curry on through the last course. If I had no champagne I would produce a bottle of some light chilled wine like a Krug Traminer, since it would be stimulating without going dead once swallowed, as most of the beers and ales do which might superficially seem more desirable. I would serve coffee in great moderation, to put it bluntly, lest it dampen the fire with cold reason.

Thus, depending on the man, the surroundings, and the general conditions of light and shade, I would go about my business—in a time-honored gastronomical fashion which indeed has much of the wanton and therefore unchaste about it, more in the telling than in the dreamed performance, but which still need not be either lewd or vulgarly licentious, at least in one woman's lexicon.

1

Here it seemed a good time, and place, to consult a few friends whose amorous experience was admittedly wider than my own. Instead of asking their opinions on aphrodisiacal gastronomy, however, I managed to astound them by demanding the reverse side: the dishes, meals, drinks, which had proved most likely to dismay them, couchward.

It was agreed, and in my own timid way I must concur, that there is no true whip to love except the need itself, which needs no whip. That is, if two people wish, hope, plan, to be together, they need have no fear of what they must eat first, and indeed no interest in it. Provided they do not eat and drink too much, which there is little risk of their doing if the other hunger be urgent and strong enough, they are as it were impervious to the throes of postprandial digestion. They can eat lobster, rarebit, oysters, tenderloin, and even cold pudding, and will arise undismayed.

On the other hand, flickering passion that must be fanned by a deliberate conglomeration of spices, perfumes, shaded pink candelabra, muted gypsy music, and stretched satin underpinnings, is in a delicate state, most easily nourished and strengthened by the frank admission that autosuggestion is more important than proteins, temporarily at least. This form of hypnosis, no matter how delicious its results, was not what interested me in my naive census-taking: I wanted to know what would most quickly and completely down my aides.

One said overeagerness for something too long wanted, which I pointed out to him had no necessarily gastronomical connotation, to which he replied that when he was nine he yearned for a Christmas orange more than ever he had since for a woman, and that when he finally got it and bit into it he was as sick as a little pig.

I had no answer to this Jesuitry, so I turned with genteel determination toward a more forthright lover of fair ladies. He supported the theory that nothing can stop true passion, but that an unfortunately chosen dish can form a distinct hazard in the smooth path toward its consummation. When urged, he sketched in with discreet brevity the picture of a male invited by a female to sup with her; he arrived shaved and laved, dallied hopefully over a predinner drink or two, and then was sat down before the one thing in the world he most actively loathed the thought of eating, in his case okra (another and another of my helpers spoke up: avocados, one said in vicarious anguish, kidneys said another). Love hopefully turned to lust, and then lust itself dwindled.

Early training forbade my further questions. but as I am somewhat impatient of such sad, adamant prejudices, I cannot help wondering if a strong enough passion might not surmount even a detested flavor, the okra or avocado, even the kidneys en brochette or in a crisp little artful pie. It seems to me that if a mature, otherwise sensible man turned res-olutely from me because he was served with something his mother or his governess had shuddered away from a generation earlier, I would feel myself none too irresistible and would, quite candidly, look elsewhere.

Such surmises, happily, are neither my meat nor my poison, and I can only hope, with all possible philosophy, that fewer and fewer of my fellow men will need to retreat from battle with some such excuse as the look, taste, or smell of a dished overture to another equally basic form of nourishment. I have watched youths and maidens, physically beauti-ful no matter how boring otherwise, lap up with catlike wisdom a few loathsome hamburgers at a drive-in before going bluntly into the hill country under the moon. I have also watched, perhaps with more curiosity because of the perverse quality of the outcome, producer and star, who would eagerly consent to being billed as satyr and nymph but would more aptly qualify as tired-old-dyspeptic and faded-dope, seat themselves in a good restaurant with all the refined smirks, pattings, and ocular caresses of an expurgated page from *Nana,* and then nibble this, sip that, with the deliberate sly caution of children who have been promised that if they wash the front steps every Saturday they will get their heart's desire for Christmas.

I doubt that they ever do, and a dingy hint of suspicion in even the most amorous, oysterish eye, the coyest café smile, strengthens that doubt.

No matter what shrewd compound from an old whore's cookery book might be produced for them, or for their likes in any walks of life; no matter what revivifying wine or tonic water could be poured for them; no matter, in the end, what spiced essences they spilled upon themselves in the hope of future flames, it would be futile if there was no hunger or lust stronger than their physical ennui, their worldly exhaustion. Something beyond gastronomical boundaries must then take over: the pharmacopoeia of passion.

This special medal has its other side. A wanton woman who could knowingly lead a man toward bed might just as easily, according to my talkative advisers, turn him away from it; and perhaps a whole dictionary of non-love should be written, about how to prepare this and that food most sure to stem desire—kidneys, okra, and avocado, all of them sur canapés d'hier-soir. I myself, imagining one man I would like to woo, can easily invent a menu that would floor him like a stunned ox, and turn him, no matter how unwittingly on his part, into a slumberous lump of masculine inactivity. It is based on what I already know of his physical reactions, as any such plan must be.

I would serve one too many Martinis, that is, about three. Then while his appetite raged, thus whipped with alcohol, I would have generous, rich, salty Italian hors d'oeuvres: prosciutto, little chilled marinated shrimps, olives stuffed with anchovy, spiced and pickled tomatoes—things that would lead him on. Next would come something he no longer wanted but could not resist, something like a ragout of venison, or squabs stuffed with mushrooms and wild rice, and plenty of red wine, sure danger after the cocktails and the highly salted appetizers. I would waste no time on a salad, unless perhaps a freakish rich one treacherously containing truffles and new potatoes. The dessert would be cold, superficially refreshing and tempting, but venomous: a chilled bowl of figs soaked in kirsch, with heavy cream. There would be a small bottle of a Sauterne, sly and icy, or a judicious bit of champagne, and then a small cup of coffee so black and bitter that my victim could not down it, even therapeutically.

All of this would be beautiful fare in itself and in another part of time and space. Here and now it would be sure poison—given the right man. I would, to put it mildly, rest inviolate.

What a hideous plan!

It could be called:

HOW TO UN-SEDUCE

(recipe above)

CHOPSTICKS

ROLAND BARTHES

A<small>T THE</small> F<small>LOATING</small> M<small>ARKET</small> in Bangkok, each vendor sirs in a tiny motionless canoe, selling minuscule quantities of food: Seeds, a few eggs, bananas, coconuts, mangoes, pimentos (nor to speak of the Unnamable). From himself to his merchandise, including his vessel, everything is *small*. Occidental food, heaped up, dignified, swollen to the majestic, linked to a certain operation of prestige, always rends toward the heavy, the grand, the abundant, the copious; the Oriental follows the converse movement, and tends toward the infinitesimal: the cucumber's future is not its accumulation or its thickening, but its division, its tenuous dispersal, as this haiku puts it:

> *Cucumber slices*
> *The juice runs*
> *Drawing spider legs*

There is a convergence of the tiny and the esculent: things are not only small in order to be eaten, but are also comestible in order to fulfill their essence, which is smallness. The harmony between Oriental food and chopsticks cannot be merely functional, instrumental; the foodstuffs are cut up so they can be grasped by the sticks, but also the chopsticks exist because the foodstuffs are cut into small pieces; one and the same movement, one and the same form transcends the substance and its utensil: Division.

Chopsticks have other functions besides carrying the food from the plate to the mouth (indeed, that is the least pertinent one, since it is also the function of fingers and forks), and these functions are specifically theirs. First of all, a chopstick—as its shape sufficiently indicates—has a deictic function: it points to the food, designates the fragment, brings into existence by the very gesture of choice, which is the index; but thereby, instead of ingestion following a kind of mechanical sequence, in which one would be limited to swallowing little by little the parts of one and the same dish, the chopstick, designating what it selects (and thus selecting there and then *this* and nor *that),* introduces into the use of food not an order but a caprice, a certain indolence: in any case, an intelligent and no longer mechanical operation. Another function of the two chopsticks together, that of pinching the fragment of food (and no longer of piercing it, as our forks do); to *pinch,* moreover, is too strong a word, too aggressive (the word of sly little girls, of surgeons, of seamstresses, of sensitive natures); for the foodstuff never undergoes a pressure greater than is precisely necessary to raise and carry it; in the gesture of chopsticks, further softened by their substance—wood or lacquer—there is something maternal, the same precisely measured care taken in moving a child: a force (in the operative sense of the word), no longer a pulsion; here we have a whole demeanor with regard to food; this is seen clearly in the cook's long chopsticks, which serve nor for eating but for preparing foodstuffs: the instrument never pierces, cuts, or slits, never wounds but only selects, turns, shifts. For the chopsticks (third function), in order to divide, must separate, part, peck, instead of cutting and piercing, in the manner of our implements; they never violate the foodstuff: either they gradually unravel it (in the case of vegetables) or else prod it into separate pieces (in the case of fish, eels), thereby rediscovering the natural fissures of the substance (in this, much closer to the primitive finger than to the knife). Finally, and this is perhaps their loveliest function, the chopsticks *transfer* the food, either crossed like two hands, a support and no longer a pincers, they slide under the clump of rice and raise it to the diner's mouth, or (by an age-old gesture of the whole Orient) they push the alimentary snow from bowl to lips in the manner of a scoop. In all these functions, in all the gestures they imply, chopsticks are the converse of our knife (and of its predatory substitute, the fork): they are the alimentary instrument which refuses to cut, to pierce, to mutilate, to trip (very limited gestures, relegated to the preparation of the food for cooking: the fish seller who skins the still-living eel for us exorcises once and for all, in a preliminary sacrifice, the murder of food); by chopsticks, food becomes no longer a prey to which one does violence (meat, flesh over which one does battle), but a substance harmoniously transferred; they transform the previously divided substance into bird food and rice into a flow of milk; maternal, they tirelessly perform the gesture which creates the mouthful, leaving to our alimentary manners, armed with pikes and knives, that of predation.

FRANCS AND BEANS

RUSSELL BAKER

As chance would have it, the very evening Craig Claiborne ate his historic $4,000 dinner for two with thirty-one dishes and nine wines in Paris, a Lucullan repast for one was prepared and consumed in New York by this correspondent, no slouch himself when it comes to titillating the palate.

Mr. Claiborne won his meal in a television fund-raising auction and had it professionally prepared. Mine was created from spur-of-the-moment inspiration, necessitated when I discovered a note on the stove saying, "Am eating out with Dora and Imogene—make dinner for yourself." It was from the person who regularly does the cooking at my house and, though disconcerted at first, I quickly rose to the challenge.

The meal opened with a 1975 Diet Pepsi served in a disposable bottle. Although its bouquet was negligible, its distinct metallic aftertaste evoked memories of tin cans one had licked experimentally in the first flush of childhood's curiosity.

To create the balance of tastes so cherished by the epicurean palate, I followed with a *pâté de fruites de nuts of Georgia,* prepared according to my own recipe. A half-inch layer of creamy-style peanut butter is troweled onto a graham cracker, then half a banana is crudely diced and pressed firmly into the peanut butter and cemented in place as it were by a second graham cracker.

The accompanying drink was cold milk served in a wide-brimmed jelly glass. This is essential to proper consumption of the pâté, since the entire confection must be dipped into the milk to soften it for eating. In making the presentation to the mouth, one must beware lest the milk-soaked portion of the sandwich fall onto the necktie. Thus, seasoned gourmandisers follow the old maxim of the Breton chefs and "bring the mouth to the jelly glass."

At this point in the meal, the stomach was ready for serious eating, and I prepared beans with bacon grease, a dish I perfected in 1937 while developing my *cuisine du dépression.*

The dish is started by placing a pan over a very high flame until it becomes dangerously hot. A can of Heinz's pork and beans is then emptied into the pan and allowed to char until it reaches the consistency of hardening concrete. Three strips of bacon are fried to crisps, and when the beans have formed huge dense clots firmly welded to the pan, the bacon grease is poured in and stirred vigorously with a large screwdriver.

This not only adds flavor but also loosens some of the beans from the side of the pan. Leaving the flame high, I stirred in a three-day-old spaghetti sauce found in the refrigerator, added a sprinkle of chili powder, a large dollop of Major Grey's chutney and a tablespoon of bicarbonate of soda to make the whole dish rise.

Beans with bacon grease is always eaten from the pan with a tablespoon while standing over the kitchen sink. The pan must be thrown away immediately. The correct drink with this dish is a straight shot of room-temperature gin. I had a Gilbey's, 1975, which was superb.

For the meat course, I had fried bologna *à la Nutley, Nouveau Jersey.* Six slices of A&P bologna were placed in an ungreased frying pan over maximum heat and held down by a long fork until the entire house filled with smoke. The bologna was turned, fried the same length of time on the other side, then served on air-filled white bread with thick lashings of mayonnaise.

The correct drink for fried bologna *à la Nutley, Nouveau Jersey,* is a 1927 Nehi Cola, but since my cellar, alas, had none, I had to make do with a second shot of Gilbey's 1975.

The cheese course was deliciously simple—a single slice of Kraft's individually wrapped yellow sandwich cheese, which was flavored by vigorous rubbing over the bottom of the frying pan to soak up the rich bologna juices. Wine being absolutely *de rigueur* with cheese, I chose a 1974 Muscatel, flavored with a maraschino cherry, and afterward cleared, my palate with three pickled martini onions.

It was time for the fruit. I chose a Del Monte tinned pear, which, regrettably, slipped from the spoon and fell on the floor, necessitating its being blotted with a paper towel to remove cat hairs. To compensate for the resulting loss of pear syrup, I dipped it lightly in hot-dog relish, which created a unique flavor.

With the pear I drank two shots of Gilbey's 1975 and one shot of Wolfschmidt vodka (non-vintage), the Gilbey's having been exhausted.

At last it was time for the dish the entire meal had been building toward—dessert. With a paring knife, I ripped into a fresh package of

Oreos, produced a bowl of My-T-Fine chocolate pudding which had been coagulating in the refrigerator for days and, using a potato masher, crushed a dozen Oreos into the pudding. It was immense.

Between mouthfuls, I sipped a tall, bubbling tumbler of cool Bromo-Seltzer, and finished with six ounces of Maalox. It couldn't have been better.

SWEDISH FOOD

EMILY PRAGER

IT WAS IN 1984 THAT I had my first foreign sale and traveled to Stockholm. I was a brand new fiction author then andthe idea of having my book translated into another language and published in a foreign land was really too wonderful to be true. I was prepared to love Sweden, its people, its flora and fauna, even its book critics, but what I never suspected was the adoration I would feel for Swedish food.

It began at the Castle Hotel, a small establishment on a little side street right off Stockholm Harbor. In the tiny breakfast room, its wall adorned with portraits of great American jazz musicians, I ate my first smoked trout paste on flat bread. I remember it was in a little round, jam-like tin, and it tasted divine, both salty and sweet at the same time. I was just trying it, you understand, I didn't like fish all that much. So the fact that I loved the flavor took me by surprise. I determined then and there to be ecumenical and to sample whatever Swedish fish delicacies might come my way.

I think I should mention that I was never a big eater, nor a food aficionado. I always ate to live and though I enjoyed it, I would never have classed dining as one of my main pleasures. But perhaps that is exactly why I took to Swedish food. It is, as international cuisines go, entirely . undemanding and pleasing at the same time.

I remember walking into a Russian tea shop in Gamla Stan, the old town, an area of Stockholm that dates from medieval times and has cobbled streets and shops that sell clothes custom-made from reindeer skin. As Sweden is a neighbor of Russia, this tea shop was quite authentic and in its center a huge samovar hissed and dispensed tea. An old Russian woman in a babushka was serving luncheon foods.

I perused a glass case that contained open-face sandwiches of ham and salmon and then I saw what I wanted to try—a prawn and mayonnaise salad on thin wheat bread with half a hard boiled egg and a sprig of dill. I paid for it, brought it back to my table and took one bite. I had found my perfect food.

When I think of Swedish cuisine four adjectives come to mind: fresh, light, healthy and pretty, the four things most important to me in comestibles. I hate heavy sauces and complicated recipes of the type that are all the rage these days in Manhattan restaurants. You can take your shitake mushrooms with a walnut and feta mousse over a bed of Basmati, away. Thanks.

But those tiny fresh shrimp with a bit of homemade mayonnaise, half a fresh boiled egg and the sylvan taste of dill—a concoction that looks like a scoop of peppermint ice cream—that was heaven to me and, joy of joys, to the Swedes as well. Prawn salad is the hamburger of Sweden and even at a cocktail party where I was introduced to all the book critics, I ate those sweet prawns and inhaled the faint pickly scent of dill.

It interested me that a people who live in such a cold climate eat so lightly. But to offset the lightness of their foods, they often have dollops of cream or fruit sauces on the side. Even Swedish meatballs, which I ordered one night in a restaurant with a gorgeously ornate domed ceiling, were light and tasty, tiny, too, with a fresh cream gravy. You really haven't lived until you've eaten Swedish meatballs with a sauce of just-picked cloud berries. It is the best combination of sweet and meat on Earth.

When I returned from Sweden I mourned the food like a lost lover. I was unhappy with American lunch food after that and even considered moving to Stockholm for a while so that I could have the prawn salad that I craved. But I didn't and, as the years passed, the romance dimmed and I had all but forgotten it.

Then one day I received a catalogue in the mail from a new Swedish-owned store that was opening in New Jersey. It was called IKEA and sold household goods. Its opening spelled a new era in shopping—actually leaving New York City to shop, which few did before IKEA and many do now.

I rented a car and drove to New Jersey to have a look.

Memories of Sweden flooded over me as I walked through the store—the faint Viking overtones in the designs, the spare, organized white and cream birch wood rooms, the whimsical combination of monarchical touches—crowns, bed curtains, fur throws—along with the sensible socialist prices.

At last, hungry from shopping, I went up to the cafeteria and grabbed a tray. As I filed past the glass cases, I suddenly saw my long lost love, prawn salad on a slice of wheat bread with half a hard boiled egg. I did a double take. Could it be?

Swedish food, the entire cafeteria was Swedish food. Swedish meatballs with lingonberry sauce, grilled cold salmon with sour cream. I couldn't believe my good fortune. They even had sparkling currant juice which is like the best of champagne without the alcohol.

I filled my tray and took a seat by the windows which overlooks Newark Airport. SAS planes were taking off even as I scooped the fresh prawns and fresh mayonnaise into my mouth.

Suddenly I could see the sun glinting off the water of Stockholm harbor and I could smell the fresh clean air. I could feel the velvet seats of the opulent movie theatre where I saw a six hour version of *Fanny and Alexander*. I could hear the hiss of the samovars and the sound of Russian being spoken.

And now, every few months, when the pressure gets too great, I find someone with a car and make them drive me to IKEA. Any IKEA will do. They all serve Swedish food. And while I eat lunch, I remember what it was like to be a young author whose first book of fiction has just been published abroad.

HOLIDAY MEALS

DAVID MAS MASUMOTO

M Y MOTHER BLAMES CAMP for her limited cooking skills. She was the youngest child of Japanese immigrants and entered Gila River Relocation Center as a young teenager. For four years she never washed rice, peeled a carrot, or cooked an egg. No one taught her how to plan a meal, shop for and purchase ingredients, or prepare a breakfast, lunch, or dinner. No one passed down family recipes during that time. The Sugimoto women never prepared a homemade feast for their clan. Mom does not recall even eating many meals with her mother. Baachan Sugimoto had become a widow while in camp and knew she'd have to work to support herself and the family, so she secured a job in the mess hall, mostly serving food and cleaning up, saving money for an uncertain future. Mom knew how to pick grapes and spread them on raisin trays better than how to make a sauce or soup base. Only later, along with many other Nisei women, did she take cooking classes at the Buddhist church, learning how to make *sushi* and properly set an American holiday table.

Mom tried her best to provide our family with traditional Thanksgiving and Christmas dinners. She'd lay out cookbooks and magazine menus on the kitchen counter in order to prepare the turkey or ham and the other customary dishes of mashed potatoes, stuffing, and pumpkin pie. In addition, she set out a bowl of cranberry sauce with the turkey or applesauce for the ham. By dinnertime, our table looked like a Norman Rockwell painting, except that the smiling faces with rosy cheeks were Japanese-American.

But there the similarity ended. Dad enjoyed white rice with his holiday meal and politely passed on the rolls and buns, shiny with glazed butter. We complimented Mom's picture-perfect feast with green tea instead of wine, toasting the occasion with Japanese ceramic teacups and loud slurps of the hot liquid. We *never* ate the cranberries or apple-sauce with our meats. We considered the fruits to be desserts and found it confusing to consume them as a sauce or condiment. We knew what a holiday table was supposed to look like, but no one told us how it was supposed to be eaten.

My grandparents never developed an appetite for American foods. Neither *baachan* cooked for the holidays. They both felt more comfortable in the fields than in the kitchen. I remember once Baachan Masumoto going out to work on Christmas Day. Mom made us delay opening our gifts until Baachan returned home for lunch. Then when we attacked the presents, tearing the paper and tossing the ribbon aside, Baachan sat by herself. She had no presents for any of her children or grandchildren. Instead she carefully folded the sheets of colorful paper and gently rolled the ribbon for future use. In the afternoon, while we were lost in our new toys and games, she slipped outside to work. Only now do I realize her subtle gift was her own labor as she'd prune one more vine and dig out one more weed. With the future harvests, I'd realize the fruits of her offerings.

While we were growing up, our holiday celebrations were very simple. Ordinary events were never overshadowed by gluttonous dinner tables. In elementary school, just before Christmas vacation, all of the kids would march into the auditorium, where boxes of oranges and some hard candy were stacked. We were given a paper bag and instructed to take one orange along with a handful of sweets. A nearby citrus grower had donated the produce to our school, a holiday gift to kids who had little money to spare, an act of kindness during a season of giving. Ironically, many of the farm-worker parents of my classmates may well have harvested these oranges; their invisible fingerprints flavored each fruit with both pride and shame. It was a special event. My friends and I pondered whether to eat the orange at school or take it home to share with family. Today I still consider a simple orange as part of my holiday feast.

Marcy's family holidays come from Wisconsin—our two clans are separated by thousands of miles and two cultures from opposite sides of the world. We are Japanese and Buddhist, they are German and Lutheran or Catholic. We grow raisins and peaches in the heat of California, they work a small dairy through Wisconsin's demanding seasons. Yet we share a sense of tradition. Homegrown foods are an essential ingredient for holiday meals—they are part of being a close family. I realized my wife's family truly appreciated me when her Grandma Rose started asking for "Mas's raisins" for her Christmas baking. My farm and my produce had finally become part of their family holiday table.

My farm not only provides me with a livelihood, it also nourishes family and community traditions. Growing raisins and peaches becomes an asset during the holidays, especially when my mother-in-law discovers she now has an endless supply for her cooking. Raisins are part of her family's special recipe for turkey stuffing, and seeing those tiny black morsels mixed with the bread, celery, and seasoning makes me feel welcomed. In addition, my dried peaches go well with her Christmas tradition of fruit stollens served alongside their holiday oyster stew. Raised on seafood, I find an affinity with the oysters and please my in-laws by asking for seconds. I ask about the meaning of this ritual, as I don't normally associate seafood with the holidays.

"Why, it's the tradition!" is their answer, followed by another ladleful of stew into my bowl.

They sometimes take traditions to extremes. They often raise their own holiday turkeys—poor old tom can be seen walking around in their yard, his head bobbing up and down, back and forth, with his overconfident strut. The next day he joins us for dinner in a different form! Perhaps, though, I take this sense of family—and family pets—a bit too seriously.

On the other hand, holiday turkeys always created a problem for my own family. The men were given the "honor" of carving the grand bird, but none of us knew quite how to do it. We had no grandfathers to pass down their techniques and favorite knives, no role models to watch and imitate as we grew up. Dad sometimes started the task, studying the pictures in an old *Joy of Cooking*. But standing with family around, hungrily eyeing the meal we had anticipated all day, enticed by the aromas—this was not the time nor the place to learn a new ritual. Dad would give up and pass the bird to Mom. She then carried it back into the kitchen, where we heard her whacking and tearing the creature into tiny shreds, as if she were preparing strips for a *teriyaki* sauce or *okazu*/stir-fry.

At the age of thirty-five I reluctantly begin to learn how to carve, prompted by my frantic wife when she hosts the family holiday dinner. "Here," she says, thrusting the golden brown bird into my hands. I imagine her adding, "It's time you became a man." So I venture into new territory, my in-laws scrutinizing my rite of passage as I nervously stand before "their" bird. By now, though, I have learned a valuable lesson about family—how to defer gracefully to an older generation and let them show me how it's done. They quickly accept their familial roles. My father-in-law sharpens an old knife by whipping it up and down a sharpening steel. My mother-in-law tugs the drumstick up and down, testing to see if the turkey is properly done. She begins to grin as it works loose and looks up to a smiling husband as he leans over, knife glistening razor-sharp. Now all parties celebrate quite contentedly.

Japanese customs also find their way into our holidays. One annual celebration held at the end of the year is making *mochi*. Mochi is made from sticky steamed rice that is pounded and kneaded into a doughy cake. We eat it fried and seasoned with soy sauce or add it to traditional Japanese soups and stews. On cold winter nights, I boil the *mochi* and sweeten it by sprinkling on a mixture of sugar and soy powder.

We make *mochi* once a year, often hundreds of pounds at a time. This requires much help and many hands. A special sweet rice is first distributed to a dozen households, and for several days the grains are soaked, drained, and resoaked in water. Early on the *mochitsuki/mochi* -making day, the men rise early and build fires with old grape stumps and redwood stakes. The smoke hugs the earth, then wanders upward to blend with the winter fog. To keep warm, the men hug themselves and rock back and forth, shifting from one foot to the other. I can see their breath when they exhale.

They begin to cook batch after batch of rice. The steam seeps upward through a series of four flat wooden boxes, each with a thick portion of the white grains. The bottom box cooks the fastest, and is then refilled with uncooked rice and set atop the stack. The initial rice is often slightly overcooked, as some of the kernels may have browned because of the uneven temperature of the dancing flames before the fire settles into glowing embers. The men often treat themselves to a break-fast bowl of hot rice with tea and *umeboshi*/pickled plums, smacking their lips with the sharpness of the vinegary flavor.

With the next batch, the freshly cooked and steaming rice is dumped into a stone urn. A skilled team then pounds it with a wooden mallet, a team leader kneeling and quickly flipping the rice between whacks, blending the grains and gradually forming a huge ball of rice dough. A modern method has also been introduced, requiring less teamwork and timing: electric grinders mash the sticky grains together, creating a smooth paste while avoiding smashed fingers.

Finally, a line of hands must be ready to mold the hot dough into small two-or-three-inch flat cakes. An elder pulls a small lump from the ball and quickly passes it down a long table to a row of kneaders. Fingers pull at the dough, still steaming hot if the timing has been pre-cise, stretching the outer skin until an even, smooth texture is created, pinching it together and creating an invisible seam on the bottom. As the rice cools, a glassy surface coats each cake.

In Japan, extended family gather for this holiday event. In America, only a few families were large enough to make *mochi* on their own. The required extra hands of aunts, uncles, and cousins remained in Japan. As a result, making *mochi* instead became a community function— neighbors, churches, and social clubs gathered as extended family. I often joined a church group to make *mochi* or our family partnered with a Japanese-American neighbor.

I wonder what new dishes will find their way onto my family's holiday tables of the future. Traditions must evolve—otherwise they become acts without meaning, fossils from dead civilizations, relics of a past that only remind us of where we were, not where we're going. Whether we like it or not, we're in continual pattern of updating family recipes. I toast the future, when my children will find ways to break through cultural barriers. My daughter wants to leave *manju,* a Japanese sweet cake, for Santa at Christmas. She says he must be getting tired of cookies all the time.

I smile when I see a new variation on a theme—like the time a young Yonsei (fourth-generation Japanese American) who grew up "very American" tried to follow tradition by bringing a rice dish to a Japanese community potluck. I still laugh to myself when I think of her placing "rice crispy treats" on the table alongside the *sushi,* fried rice, and *nigiri*/rice balls. Despite some of the whispers from the older women, the young woman saw nothing wrong with her effort; she fulfilled her commitment while working full-time and being a single parent. I admired her creativity.

One day I may see a near-vegetarian holiday feast, as some of my wife's cousins eat more lightly and have given up the heavy meat-and-potatoes meals of their childhood. Yet I can also see a plate of summer sausage on the table, especially if it's venison from the annual deer hunt in Wisconsin. A rite of passage—a son's or grandson's first deer—will continue to become part of the feast, just as it has been for generations.

Our foods will help place us. My children, who will have the opportunity to know their grandfathers from both sides of the family, will never have to apologize for the diversity of our holiday recipes. They will recall the simple *nigiri* my mom makes for them by rolling rice into a cylinder shape and wrapping it with a strip of *nori*/seaweed. They will laugh and retell the story of Marcy's first experience with *mochi,* eating a lump of it at a holiday meal of *ozoni*/soup. She chewed and chewed the sticky mass and finally attempted to swallow it in a single gulp. It became lodged in her throat, and for a moment she could not breathe, then it slipped down past her windpipe. I joke that she simply choked on Japanese culture. "And almost died," she retorts. "But I survived."

Marcy and I still plan to continue the Japanese tradition of celebrating New Year's Day with an open house. Plates of *teriyaki* chicken, *sushi,* and *somen* salad, along with symbolic dishes—long *soba*/buck-wheat noodles for long life, *kuromame*/black beans for good luck, and herring for virility and the blessings of many children—fill the table as we host dozens of guests. My aunts and Mom are grateful for us continuing the tradition—they grew weary of all the cleaning and cooking that needed to be done. Initially the relatives made most of the Japanese food, not quite trusting my wife. But as with most customs, time has a way of overcoming prejudices, so that now they trust her skills. We are the new generation of Japanese Americans.

Throughout the day, guests will come by and visit as we welcome the new year with a toast of *sake.* I find myself repeating, "What better way to begin the year than with family and friends in celebration?" With our farmer relatives and neighbors, we are able to forget the disappointments of the past year and look forward to the new with our naive optimism. In keeping with Japanese traditions, we also serve everyone salmon. We tried precooking some one year, but found it awkward when served cold. Other years we used canned salmon, but that didn't seem right. I don't know how it's prepared in Japan, but for American palates, we found smoked salmon to work the best. Each year when I repeat the Japanese saying about why we serve salmon—"It's the one fish that always returns home"—I'm still greeted with warm smiles and comforting silence. We then know the new year has begun properly.

HOW TO EAT IN FLIGHT

UMBERTO ECO

A SIMPLE JOURNEY BY AIR a few years ago (round trip to Amsterdam) cost me in the end two Brooks Brothers neckties, two Burberry shirts, two pairs of Bardelli slacks, a tweed jacket bought in Bond Street, and a Krizia waistcoat.

All international flights observe the commendable ritual of serving a meal. But, as everyone knows, the seats are narrow, the tray likewise, and the ride is sometimes bumpy. Furthermore, the napkins offered by airlines are skimpy and, if you stick one inside your collar, it leaves your abdomen vulnerable, whereas if you unfold one in your lap, your chest is exposed. Common sense would suggest that the foods served should be compact, not the kind that make spots. It is unnecessary to resort to vitamin tablets. There are such compact foods as breaded veal cutlet, grilled meat, cheese, french fries, and roast chicken. Spot-making foods include spaghetti with abundant, American-style tomato sauce, eggplant parmesan, pizza straight from the oven, and piping hot consommé in little bowls without handles.

Now, a typical in-flight menu comprises some long-cooked meat smothered in brown gravy, generous portions of tomato, vegetables finely chopped and marinated in wine, rice, and peas with sauce. Peas are notoriously elusive—not even the greatest chefs can produce petits pois farcis—especially if, deferring to the insistence of Miss Manners, the consumer is determined to eat the peas with his fork rather than the more practical spoon. Don't tell me that the Chinese are worse off. I can assure you it is easier to grip a pea with chopsticks than to pierce it with a fork. It is also pointless to rebut that the fork is used to collect the peas, not to pierce them, because forks are designed for the sole purpose of dropping the peas they pretend to collect.

Furthermore, peas in flight are duly served only when there is turbulence and the captain turns on the "fasten seat belts" sign. As a result of this complex ergonomic calculation, the peas have only two alternatives: either they roll down your shirtfront or they fall on your fly.

As the ancient fabulists taught us, to prevent a fox from drinking out of a glass, the glass must be tall and slim. Glasses on planes are short, squat, rather basin-like. Obviously, any liquid will spill, obeying the laws of physics, even when there is no turbulence. The bread is not a French baguette, which you have to tear with your teeth even when it's fresh, but rather a special friable roll which, the moment it is grasped, explodes in a cloud of fine powder. Thanks to the Lavoisier principle this powder vanishes only in appearance: on debarking, you will find that it has all accumulated under your behind, managing to stain even the seat of your trousers. The dessert tends to the meringue genre, and its fragments mix with the bread, or else it dribbles over the fingers immediately, when the napkin is already steeped in tomato sauce and hence unusable.

True, you still have the perfumed towelette: but this cannot be distinguished from the little envelopes of salt, pepper, and sugar, and so, after you have put the sugar in the salad, the towelette has already ended up in the coffee, which is served boiling hot and in a heat-conducting cup filled to the brim, so that it may readily slip from your seared fingers and blend with the gravy that has now congealed around your waist. In business class the hostess pours the coffee directly into your lap, hastily apologizing in Esperanto.

Airline quartermasters are certainly enlisted from the ranks of those hotel experts who adopt the only type of pot that, instead of pouring the coffee into the cup, scatters eighty percent of it on the sheet. But why? The most obvious hypothesis is that they want to give the traveler an impression of luxury, and they assume he has in mind those old Hollywood movies where Nero always drinks from broad-brimmed goblets that spatter wine on his beard and his chlamys, or the pictures where a feudal lord gnaws a haunch of meat that smears grease on his lacy shirt, as he embraces a courtesan.

But why, then, in first class where the space is ample, do they serve compact foods, like Russian caviar on buttered slices of toast, or smoked salmon or lobster chunks with a drop of oil and lemon? Is it perhaps because in the films of Luchino Visconti, when the Nazi aristocrats say "shoot him," they pop a single, compact grape into their mouth?

WRITING IN RESTAURANTS

JAY PARINI

O NE ALWAYS IMAGINES THAT writers need the solitude of a mountain cabin for creative work, with nothing in the background but the occasional birdcall or snapping twig. One thinks of Thoreau hidden among the foliage at Walden Pond or Robert Frost in his little log cabin in Ripton, Vermont, or—a more extreme example—Marcel Proust buried in his cork-lined study. After all, the merest knock of an unexpected visitor from Porlock brought to a halt the ferocious spell of Coleridge in the midst of writing "Kubla Khan" (or so he claimed). On the other hand, the Left Bank of Paris has always been a favorite spot for writers such as Hemingway or Sartre, both of whom seemed to thrive in the noisy atmosphere of cafes.

For twenty years, I've devoted nearly every morning of my life to writing, and—like most writers, I suspect—having the right place to work has been terribly important to me. As a graduate student at the University of St. Andrews in Scotland in the seventies, I found a tea shop where I could sit undisturbed for hours on end with books and manuscripts piled up around me. The tea came in shiny metal pots, and the waitress—her name was Fiona—freshened the pot every hour or so. A large plate of scones was always on the table, and you paid only for what you ate. It was a sleepy and, I suppose, unprofitable enterprise—as a business—but for me it provided just the right amount of distraction. I sat there every morning for nearly seven years, composing innumerable college essays, a doctoral thesis, a book of poems, and an unpublished novel in that poorly ventilated but homey tearoom.

When I took my first teaching job, at Dartmouth College in New Hampshire, I was given faculty housing in a quaint faculty apartment building just off campus. A bachelor, I needed a minimum of space—a bedroom with a study seemed positively luxurious. I fitted out the study

with a big oak desk, a typing table, a glass-fronted bookcase, filing cab-
inets, a telephone—the works. Then I sat down to work.

But I couldn't work. It was just too damn quiet. So I wandered
uptown, a few blocks away, where I discovered a restaurant called Lou's
on the main street in Hanover. It was modeled on the old-fashioned
American diner, and I confess to an inordinate fondness for diners. They
call up in me an inexpressible nostalgia for a past I never had, a society
in which everyone gathered over coffee to chat about everything and
nothing, a place where romances kindled, where good humor flourished, and any job could be put off till another day. (I still make a point
of stopping at diners whenever I'm even remotely in the market for a
sandwich or a cup of coffee on the road.)

Lou's became, for me, the ideal study. I arrived every morning at
eight or so, carrying my spiral notebook and assorted texts. I never varied my diet: cups of coffee with dry English muffins (and a scoop of
peanut butter at the side, for protein). Lou, the elderly owner of the
place, took a liking to me, and he made sure that a particular booth at
the back was always empty when I got there. The waiters too became
friends; they never had to ask what I wanted. They just brought it. And
I would sit there for two or three hours writing poems, scribbling academic articles, underlying my copy of *Paradise Lost,* whatever. I wrote
three books in that booth, and I don't think any would have made it
into print without Lou's hospitality.

What I liked about Lou's was the distant clatter of dishes, the purr
of conversation, and the occasional interruption of a friend. Restaurants
provide a kind of white noise, but—unlike real white noise—the sound
is human. Noses are blown. People cough. You're reminded of the world
of phlegm and digestion. And you feel connected. There is also a strange
but unmistakable connection between cooking and writing—writing,
like cooking, is a bringing together of elemental substances for trans-
mutation over a hot flame. It seems fitting that writing and cooking
should be going on simultaneously under the same roof.

As people are quick to point out, writing is a desperately lonely
activity; although writing in restaurants doesn't exactly solve that problem, it somehow softens it. Surrounded by people you don't necessarily
have to interact with, you feel free to concentrate. Once I'm involved in
the tactile process of writing—the pleasurable transference of emotions
and ideas into language—I find that I don't really have to worry about
concentration. If I can't concentrate, it means I'm working on the
wrong thing or I probably didn't get enough sleep the night before.
Whatever the reason for not writing, I don't blame the restaurant.

Restaurant society is still a human web, and if any part of the web is disturbed, the whole fabric shakes. I was fully aware of who else was sitting in Lou's. Every public eating place has its regulars, and the regulars are a right-knit group, loyal to their spot; they often don't even know each other by name, but they depend upon the tacit assumption of shared good feeling—toward each other as well as toward the place itself. After a year or so, I pretty much knew by name everyone who ate frequently at Lou's. And we often shared the high and low points of our lives. When I got married, for instance, the regulars at Lou's all signed a card of congratulations. I even attended the funeral of an elderly gent who had never said a word to me but who sat for three years in the adjoining booth for at least half an hour every morning. Until the funeral, I had known him only as Herb, the man who liked underdone boiled eggs with a side of dry toast.

As a novelist, I found my time in Lou's an indispensable part of my education. Like Zola, I soon found that local hangouts offer an unbelievably transparent window on any community. Lou's was classless, which meant that taxi drivers, window washers, insurance salespeople, haberdashers, dentists, and professors sat cheek by jowl over coffee and homemade donuts. Looking up from my work, I could take in an array of conversation and dialects, and I learned a great deal about how the United States works from that little booth. I became, alas, a world-class eavesdropper, often scribbling overheard conversations in my notebook and, at a later date, including versions of these dialogues in my fiction.

When I left Hanover in 1982, one of my biggest fears was that I'd never find another place to work that was nearly as cozy. But this was not the case. We moved to Middlebury, a small Vermont town just across the Green Mountains. There we bought a small house from which I could easily walk uptown, where Middlebury offered a dazzling array of alternatives to Lou's. I eventually settled upon an ice cream parlor and soda fountain straight our of Norman Rockwell that goes by the unlikely name of Calvi's. Located on the village green, Calvi's has proved ideal for verse composition. An array of newspapers and magazines lines the left wall. The soda fountain dominates the right, presided over by a large brown photograph of the current owner's grandfather, the Calvi who founded the establishment in the late nineteenth century. In the back are booths and tables, with the stuffed heads of antlered moose and elk staring balefully off the walls. In good weather, one can sit on the screened-in porch off the back that somewhat perilously overhangs Otter Creek and its roaring waterfall—a kind of mini-Niagara that might be thought of as Middlebury's centerpiece. The roar of that waterfall is white noise squared.

Calvi's is sleepier than Lou's, by far. It is dark in the back, and the waiters (who always wear soda-jerk jackets in the old style) are so unobtrusive that one has to stand on the table and dance to get a coffee refill. I don't care anymore. There is just enough clatter to reassure me, and I have found the regulars as interesting and friendly as those at Lou's. I have taken devotion so far as to make Calvi's the setting for a long quasi-philosophical poem about appearance and reality called "At the Ice Cream Parlor."

In the poem, meaning no harm, I refer to the "tacky plastic spoons" that might be considered the hallmark of this particular establishment. I was talking about the relationship between any given plastic spoon and the Platonic ideal of Spoon—one of the great subjects of Western metaphysics, if you will. Assuming—correctly—that Mr. Calvi himself would probably not have read the poem (published in a 1988 book of mine called *Town Life*), a well-intentioned neighbor of mine provided him with a photostat. The padrone found that his gaze stuck upon the fateful adjective: *tacky*. I suspect it will take years—perhaps decades— for me to live down that untoward epithet.

Apart from the vaguely social aspects of writing in restaurants—the delicious sense of being alone within a communal context—there is a further advantage. In a public place, one doesn't normally use a writing machine more complicated than a pencil. In the age of word processing, diners are an ideal place for the rediscovery of this remarkable product of our civilization. The pencil is surprisingly efficient, in fact. You can delete what you don't like with a quick horizontal stroke that both rids you of the unwanted phrase and simultaneously preserves the deletion—just in case it was better than the revised version, which is often the case. Also the strange visceral connection between hand and brain is somehow lost in the subliminal click of keyboards and the computer screen's unyielding gaze. Furthermore, one misses the slight rustle of paper, the smell of freshly sharpened pencils or wet ink, the ancient and alluring texture of text making.

The habit of writing in restaurants has the added advantage of making one's vocation highly portable. In 1985 I spent a sabbatical year in Italy, for instance, and I found myself quickly adapting to the local scene through my connection to one particular café. We were living in a lovely village south of Naples that happened to be rich in cafés. The Sirena [mermaid] was a café-bar on the chief promenade that looked our over the old harbor front, with the Mediterranean winking in the middle distance—almost too perfect. It occurred to me almost immediately that this must be the best place in the world for a writer to work. Seated at one of its dozen or so tables, I could take in the baroque spectacle of Italian town life with ease. Eating a fresh pastry and drinking a foamy cup of cappuccino, the muse seemed never too far away. (This was, of course, before the advent of notebook computers.)

My wife, Devon, is also a writer, but her love of the typewriter has usually kept her our of my restaurants. In Italy, however, our little villa on a cliffside overlooking the sea quickly proved inhospitable as a place to work; it was just too damp and cold, especially in winter. So we both made our way to a café (usually separate ones) in the morning, me with my notebook and pencil, she with her battery-operated portable typewriter. After a couple weeks, the owner of the café where Devon worked—an elderly man whom everyone called Nono—insisted that she actually keep her typewriter behind the bar so that she didn't have to lug it into town every morning.

I wrote most of a book of poems in Amalfi, and when I pick up that volume, I can smell the cappuccino and taste the almond-flavored pastry. I can hear the clinking of cups and low murmur of Italian chatter. It's the same with all my books or essays, even my book reviews. I remember exactly where I wrote them, in what diner or restaurant, truck stop, bar, or country inn. Every word is redolent of some particular cuisine, some idiosyncratic atmosphere that I'll have made temporarily into a kind of home. My only worry is that, in a future filled exclusively with Burger Kings and Kentucky Fried Chickens, both of which clog their atmospheres with canned music, I will have to change professions. The muse cannot stand Muzak.

MY MOTHER'S BLUE BOWL

ALICE WALKER

VISITORS TO MY HOUSE are often served food—soup, potatoes, rice—in a large blue stoneware bowl, noticeably chipped at the rim. It is perhaps the most precious thing I own. It was given to me by my mother in her last healthy days. The days before a massive stroke laid her low and left her almost speechless. Those days when to visit her was to be drawn into a serene cocoon of memories and present-day musings and to rest there, in temporary retreat from the rest of the world, as if still an infant, nodding and secure at her breast.

For much of her life my mother longed, passionately longed, for a decent house. One with a yard that did not have to be cleared with an ax. One with a roof that kept out the rain. One with floors that you could not fall through. She longed for a beautiful house of wood or stone. Or of red brick, like the houses her many sisters and their husbands had. When I was thirteen she found such a house. Green-shuttered, white—walled. Breezy. With a lawn and a hedge and giant pecan trees. A porch swing. There her gardens flourished in spite of the shade, as did her youngest daughter, for whom she sacrificed her life doing hard labor in someone else's house, in order to afford peace and prettiness for her child, to whose grateful embrace she returned each night.

But, curiously, the minute I left home, at seventeen, to attend college, she abandoned the dream house and moved into the projects. Into a small, tight apartment of few breezes, in which I was never to feel comfortable, but that she declared suited her "to a T." I took solace in the fact that it was at least hugged by spacious lawn on one side, and by forest, out the back door, and that its isolated position at the end of the street meant she would have a measure of privacy.

Her move into the projects—the best housing poor black people in the South ever had, she would occasionally declare, even as my father

struggled to adjust to the cramped rooms and hard, unforgiving qualities of brick—was, I now understand, a step in the direction of divesti-
ture, lightening her load, permitting her worldly possessions to dwindle
in significance and, well before she herself would turn to spirit, roll
away from her.

She owned little, in fact. A bed, a dresser, some chairs. A set of liv-
ing-room furniture. A set of kitchen furniture. A bed and wardrobe
(given to her years before, when I was a teenager, by one of her more
prosperous sisters). Her flowers: everywhere, inside the house and outside. Planted in anything she managed to get her green hands on,
including old suitcases and abandoned shoes. She recycled everything,
effortlessly. And gradually she had only a small amount of stuff—mostly
stuff her children gave her: nightgowns, perfume, a microwave—to
recycle or to use.

Each time I visited her I marveled at the modesty of her desires. She
appeared to have hardly any, beyond a thirst for a Pepsi-Cola or a
hunger for a piece of fried chicken or fish. On every visit I noticed that
more and more of what I remembered of her possessions seemed to be
missing. One day I commented on this.

Taking a deep breath, sighing, and following both with a beaming
big smile, which lit up her face, the room, and my heart, she said: Yes,
it's all going. I don't need it anymore. If there's anything you want, take
it when you leave; it might not be here when you come back.

The dishes my mother and father used daily had come from my
house; I had sent them years before, when I moved from Mississippi to
New York. Neither the plates nor the silver matched entirely, but it was
all beautiful in her eyes. There were numerous paper items, used in the
microwave, and stacks of plastic plates and cups, used by the scores of
children from the neighborhood who continued throughout her life to
come and go. But there was nothing there for me to want.

One day, however, looking for a jar into which 'to pour leftover
iced tea, I found myself probing deep into the wilderness of the overstuffed, airless pantry. Into the land of the old-fashioned, the outmod-
ed, the outdated. The humble and the obsolete. There was a smoothing
iron, a churn. A butter press. And two large bowls.

One was cream and rose with a blue stripe. The other was a deep,
vivid blue.

May I have this bowl, Mama, I asked, looking at her and at the blue
bowl with delight.

You can have both of them, she said, barely acknowledging them,
and continuing to put leftover food away.

I held the bowls on my lap for the rest of the evening, while she watched a TV program about cops and criminals that I found too horrifying to follow.

Before leaving the room I kissed her on the forehead and asked if I could get anything for her from the kitchen; then I went off to bed. The striped bowl I placed on a chair beside the door, so I could look at it from where I lay. The blue bowl I placed in the bed with me.

In giving me these gifts, my mother had done a number of astonishing things, in her typically offhand way. She had taught me a lesson about letting go of possessions—easily, without emphasis or regret—and she had given me a symbol of what she herself represented in my life.

For the blue bowl especially was a cauldron of memories. Of cold, harsh, wintry days, when my brothers and sister and I trudged home from school burdened down by the silence and frigidity of our long trek from the main road, down the hill to our shabby-looking house. More rundown than any of our classmates' houses. In winter my mother's riotous flowers would be absent, and the shack stood revealed for what it was. A gray, decaying, too small barrack meant to house the itinerant tenant workers on a prosperous white man's farm.

Slogging through sleet and wind to the sagging front door, thankful that our house was too far from the road to be seen clearly from the school bus, I always felt a wave of embarrassment and misery. But then I would open the door. And there inside would be my mother's winter flowers: a glowing fire in the fireplace, colorful handmade quilts on all our beds, paintings and drawings of flowers and fruits and, yes, of Jesus, given to her by who knows whom—and, most of all, there in the center of the rough-hewn table, which in the tiny kitchen almost touched the rusty wood-burning stove, stood the big blue bowl, full of whatever was the most tasty thing on earth.

There was my mother herself. Glowing. Her teeth sparkling. Her eyes twinkling. As if she lived in a castle and her favorite princes and princesses had just dropped by to visit.

The blue bowl stood there, seemingly full forever, no matter how deeply or rapaciously we dipped, as if it had no bottom. And she dipped up soup. Dipped up lima beans. Dipped up stew. Forked out potatoes. Spooned out rice and peas and corn. And in the light and warmth that was *Her*, we dined.

Thank you, Mama

ONE

NIGELLA LAWSON

"DON'T KNOCK MASTURBATION," Woody Allen once said: "it's sex with someone I love." Most people can't help finding something embarrassingly onanistic about taking pleasure in eating alone. Even those who claim to love food think that cooking just for yourself is either extravagantly self-indulgent or a plain waste of time and effort. But you don't have to belong to the drearily narcissistic learn-to-love-yourself school of thought to grasp that it might be a good thing to consider yourself worth cooking for. And the sort of food you cook for yourself will be different from the food you might lay on for tablefuls of people: it will be better.

I don't say that for effect. You'll feel less nervous about cooking it and that translates to the food itself. It'll be simpler, more straightforward, the sort of food you want to eat.

I don't deny that food, its preparation as much as its consumption, is about sharing, about connectedness. But that's not all that it's about. There seems to me to be something robustly affirmative about taking trouble to feed yourself—enjoying life on purpose rather than by default.

Even in culinary terms alone there are grounds for satisfaction. Real cooking, if it is to have any authenticity, any integrity, has to be part of how you are, a function of your personality, your temperament. There's too much culinary ventriloquism about as it is; cooking for yourself is a way of countering that. It's how you're going to find your own voice.

One of the greatest hindrances to enjoying cooking is that tense-necked desire to impress others. It's virtually impossible to be innocent of this. Even if this is not your motivation, it's hard, if you're being honest, to be insensible to the reactions of others. As cooking for other people is about trying to please them, it would be strange to be indifferent to their pleasure, and I don't think you should be. But you can try too hard. When you're cooking for yourself, the stakes simply aren't as high. You don't mind as much. Consequently, it's much less likely to go wrong. And the process is more enjoyable in itself.

When I cook for myself, I find it easier to trust my instinct—I am sufficiently relaxed to listen to it in the first place—and, contrariwise, I feel freer to overturn a judgment, to take a risk. If I want to see what will happen if I add yogurt or stir in some chopped tarragon instead of parsley, I can do so without worrying that I am about to ruin everything. If the sauce breaks or the tarragon infuses everything with an invasive farmyard grassiness, I can live with it. I might feel cross with myself, but I won't be panicked. It could be that the yogurt makes the sauce or that the tarragon revitalizes it. I'm not saying that cooking for seven other people would make it impossible for me to respond spontaneously, but I do think it's cooking for myself that has made it possible.

Far too much cooking now is about the tyranny of the recipe on the one hand and the absence of slowly acquired experience on the other. Cooking for yourself is a way of finding out what you want to cook and eat, rather than simply joining up the dots. Crucially, it's a way of seeing which things work, which don't, and how ingredients, heat, implements, vessels, all have their part to play. When I feel like a bowl of thick, jellied white rice noodles, not soupy but barely bound in a sweet and salty sauce, I'm not going to look up a recipe for them. I know that if I soak the noodles in boiling water until they dislodge themselves from the solid clump I've bought them in, fry two cloves of garlic with some knife-flattened scallions and tiny square beads of chopped red chili in a pan before wilting some greens and adding the noodles with a steam-provoking gush of soy and mirin, with maybe a teaspoon of black bean sauce grittily dissolved in it, it will taste wonderful, comforting, with or without chopped coriander or a slow-oozing drop or two of sesame oil. I can pay attention to texture and to taste. I know what sort of thing I'm going to end up with, but I'm not aiming to replicate any particular dish. Sometimes it goes wrong: I'm too heavy-handed with the soy and drench everything in brown brine, so that the sweet stickiness of the rice sticks is done for, and there's no contrast; I might feel, when eating, that the chili interrupts too much when I'm in the mood to eat something altogether gentler. These aren't tragedies, however. And, frankly, most often I get satisfaction simply from the quiet putting together of a meal. It calms me, which in turn makes me enjoy eating it more.

But cooking for yourself isn't simply therapy and training. It also happens to be a pleasure in itself. As most women don't have lives now whereby we're plunged into three family meals a day from the age of nineteen, we're not forced to learn how to cook from the ground up. I don't complain. Nor do I wish to make it sound as if cooking for yourself were some sort of checklisted culinary foundation course. The reason why you learn so much from the sort of food you casually throw together for yourself is that you're learning by accident, by osmosis. This has nothing to do with the culinary supremacism of the great chefs or those who'd ape them. Too many people cook only when they're giving a dinner party. And it's very hard to go from zero to a hundred miles an hour. How can you learn to feel at ease around food, relaxed about cooking, if every time you go into the kitchen it's to cook at competition level?

I love the open-ended freedom of just puttering about in the kitchen, of opening the fridge door and deciding what to cook. But I like, too, the smaller special project, the sort of indulgent eating that has something almost ceremonial about it when done alone. I'm not saying I don't often end up with the au pair special, a bowl of cereal, or its street-princess equivalent, the phone-in pizza. But I believe in the rule of "Tonight Lucullus is dining with Lucullus."

Eating alone, for me, is most often a prompt to shop. This is where self-absorption and consumerism meet—a rapt, satisfyingly convoluted pleasure. The food I want most to buy is the food I most often try not to eat—a swollen-bellied tranche of cheese, a loaf of bread. These constitute the perfect meal. A slither of gorgonzola or coulommiers sacrificed on the intrusive and unyielding surface of a cracker at the end of dinner is food out of kilter. Just bread and cheese is fine to give others if you've shown the consideration of providing variety. But I want for myself the obsessive focus of the one huge, heady *baveuse* soft cheese, or else a wedge of the palate-burning hard stuff, a vintage Cheddar or strong blue—too much, too strong. If I'm eating a salty blue cheese, its texture somewhere between creamy and crumbly, I want baguette or a bitter, fudge-colored *pain au levain*; with Cheddar, real Cheddar, I want doughier white bread—whichever, it must be a whole loaf. I might eat tomatoes with the bread and cheese, but the tomatoes mustn't be in a salad, but left whole on the plate, to be sliced or chopped, *à la minute*. But, then, I love the takeout-shop equivalent of the TV dinner.

I am pretty keen on the culinary ethos of the Greasy Spoon, too—bacon sandwiches, fried-egg sandwiches, egg and bacon sandwiches, sausage sandwiches; none requires much in the way of attention and certainly nothing in the way of expertise. Even easier is a sandwich that on paper sounds fancier, a fab merging of diner and gourmet-store cultures. Get a large portobello mushroom, put it in a preheated 400°F oven stemmed and covered with softened butter, chopped garlic, and parsley for about 20 minutes; when ready, and garlicky, buttery juices are oozing with black, cut open a soft roll, small ciabatta, or chunk of baguette even, and wipe the cut side all over the pan to soak up the pungent juices. Smear with Dijon mustard, top with the mushroom, squeeze with lemon juice. Sprinkle some salt, and add some chopped lettuce or parsley as you like; think of this as a fungoid—but, strangely, hardly less meaty—version of a steak sandwich. Bite in, with the juices dripping down your arm as you eat.

There are other memorable, more or less noncooking solitary suppers: one is a bowl of good canned tomato soup with some pale, undercooked, but overbuttered toast (crusts off for full nostalgic effect); another, microwave-zapped, mustard-dunked frankfurters (proper frankfurters, from a delicatessen, not those flabby, adulterated things from the supermarket). The difficulty is that if I have them in the house, I end up eating them while I wait for whatever I'm actually cooking for dinner to be ready. And my portions are not small to start off with. Two defenses, other than pure greed: I hate meagerness, the scant, sensible serving, and if I long to eat a particular thing, I want lots of it. I don't want course upon course, and I don't want excess every day. But when it comes to a feast, I don't know the meaning of enough.

Cooking for two is just an amplification of cooking for one (rather than the former being a diminution of the latter). To tell the truth, with my cooking and portion sizes, there isn't often a lot to choose between them. Many of the impulses that inform or inspire this sort of cooking are the same: the desire to eat food that is relaxed but at times culinarily elevated without loss of spontaneity; the pleasures of fiddling about with what happens to be in the fridge; and, as with any form of eating, the need to make food part of the civilized context in which we live.

LINGUINE WITH CLAM SAUCE

My absolutely favorite dinner to cook for myself is linguine with clams. I have a purely personal reason for thinking of fish, of any sort, as the ideal solitary food because I live with someone who's allergic to it. But my principle has wider application: fish doesn't take long to cook and tastes best dealt with simply, but because it has to be bought fresh needs enough planning to have something of the ceremonial about it. I don't know why *spaghetti alle vongole* (I use linguine because I prefer, here, the more substantial, more resistant, and, at the same time, more sauce-absorbent tangle they make in the mouth) is thought of as restaurant food, especially as so many restaurants ruin it by adding tomatoes. I have to have my sauce bianco.

The whole dish is easy to make. It is, for me, along with a steak béarnaise, unchallengeable contender for that great, fantasy Last Meal on Earth.

15	littleneck clams, well rinsed and scrubbed	2	tablespoons olive oil
⅓	pound linguine	½	dried red chili pepper or pinch dried red pepper flakes
	salt	⅓	cup white wine or vermouth
1	garlic clove, minced or finely sliced	1-2	tablespoons chopped parsley

To further cleanse the clams of their sand, put them to soak in a sinkful of cold water to which you've added 1 tablespoon of baking soda. Allow to soak 1 hour.

Heat water for the pasta. When the water comes to the boil, add salt and then the linguine. Cook the linguine until nearly but not quite ready; you're going to give them a fractional amount more cooking with the clams and their winy juices. Try to time this so that the pasta's ready at the time you want to plunge it into the clams. Otherwise drain and douse with a few drops of olive oil.

In a frying pan with a lid into which you can fit the pasta later, fry the garlic gently (it mustn't burn) in the olive oil and then crumble in the red chili pepper or add the pepper flakes. Add the clams to the pan. Pour the wine or vermouth over and cover. In 2 minutes, the clams should be open. Add the pasta, put the lid on again, and swirl about. In another minute or so, everything should have finished cooking and come together; the pasta will have cooked to the requisite tough tenderness, absorbed the salty, garlicky, winy clam juices, and be bound in a wonderful, almost pungent sea syrup. But if the pasta needs more cooking, clamp on the lid and give it more time. Chuck out any clams that have failed to open.

Add half the parsley, shake the pan to distribute evenly, and turn into a plate or bowl and sprinkle over the rest of the parsley. Cheese is not grated over any pasta with fish in it in Italy (nor indeed where garlic is the predominant ingredient, either) and the rule holds good. You need add nothing. It's perfect already. Serves 1.

Taste Memory

THE QUEST FOR PIE

MICHAEL DORRIS

*O*NE OF THE SEMINAL BOOKS of my childhood was *Mickey Sees the U.S.A.*, a travel extravaganza in which Mickey, Minnie, and the two nephews, Morty and Ferdy, set out in a red convertible and traverse the country. Every place they pass offers adventure, new sights, tasty treats—the ultimate all-American family vacation on wheels.

That was awhile ago—so far in the past that Disneyland didn't yet exist as a promotional destination—but the high concept of that fictional journey took root in my imagination and informed each subsequent family outing. We had relatives scattered from Tacoma to Miami, from New York to San Francisco, from Tensed, Idaho, to Henderson, Kentucky, and every summer my mother, my aunt, and I managed to visit some of them. (Occasionally my cousin Frank would join us, but not for the long hauls. He had a tendency to become carsick, and once my aunt had to bathe his forehead in milk from the thermos just to distract him until we reached a picnic grounds.)

I was too young to drive, of course, so I became the navigator. In deep winter I would begin to clip coupons from the *National Geographic*, soliciting maps and lodging brochures from the tourist bureaus in states along our potential routes. These packets, as they were invariably labeled, arrived in impressively lumpy envelopes, extolling the "enchantment" of New Mexico, the "surprises" of Missouri, the "discovery" potential of New England. Sometimes, once I had learned to type, I wrote letters to accompany the clippings, broadly hinting that I had more than just a passing interest in this or that region and was in fact contemplating relocation. This line of correspondence yielded even more substantial harvests of mail when the respective state offices of economic development got into the act. For one heady week in 1959 I received, absolutely free, a daily subscription to the Fort Worth *Star-*

Telegram, forever establishing in my mind a loyalty to that plucky city in its underdog rivalry with Dallas—which was apparently above wooing my business.

Over the spring I would cull through my colorful stash, making shortlists of state parks, petting zoos, and inexpensive motels that promised heated, kidney-shaped swimming pools. I mail ordered a wonderful little device that looked like a cross between a ball point pen and a thermometer—by merely adjusting a setting to correspond to the scale of a map and running the creaking metal wheel on the tip along the route of any highway, one got an instant reading of the approximate mileage involved. Then it was a matter of simple arithmetic. The distance from starting point A to destination B divided by fifty miles an hour (my family's average speed) times eight hours a day (their joint endurance capacity behind the wheel) equaled the range of my accommodations search.

There was a limit, however, to the discretion I enjoyed. I was, after all, a child, a passenger, and my mother and aunt—the women who drove the car and paid the bills—had their own priorities that any proposal of mine necessarily had to incorporate. And those were, in a word, pie.

Looking back, I realize now that each of our journeys could quite accurately be described as a quest for pie. For instance, like experienced surfers who chart odd itineraries (Laguna to Capetown by way of The Big Island) in order to snag a reliable wave en route, I always had to include Paoli, Indiana, in any cross-country trip. There was a café off the square in that placid hamlet where was served, according to my mother the connoisseur, a lattice crust like no other. Woven in intricate patterns across a sea of blueberry or peach, each segment was crisp and melting, studded with just the right amount of sugar, laced with a subtle jolt of almond extract, and browned to perfection. If I brought us through Paoli too soon after a major meal, we might order our twenty-five-cents-apiece slices for the crust alone, reluctantly leaving the fruit on the green plastic plates.

An innocuous-looking lunch counter in New Ulm, Minnesota, was the polar opposite: a decent pastry, nothing to complain about, but a truly spectacular chess or lemon or coconut cream within. The baker wouldn't tell, but my grandmother back home, upon hearing my aunt describe the airy yet smoothly substantial and satisfying volume of the filling, put her money on whipped egg whites and a dash of mace. No amount of research was too exhaustive in pursuing the solution to so important a mystery, and that was fine with me.

(New Ulm was also the site of my favorite motel in the world: a swimming pool, a playground, and a fully made bed that folded down from a door in the wall—for eight dollars a room. I always finagled it so we hit town just as the sun was about to set, and consequently in New Ulm we ate pie for dinner and then again for breakfast.)

The pie map of the United States bears little resemblance to standard demographics. The New Yorks and Clevelands and Milwaukees are mostly etched in light print, marked with tiny dots, while the big black circles and capital letters are reserved for BRATTLEBORO, Vermont, TYLER, Texas, SHELBY, Montana, and HAYS, Kansas. There are other features as well: on the west side of an invisible line, running roughly correspondent to the Appalachians, people prefer their doughnuts with icing. The South is The South when you leave a restaurant and instead of "good-bye" the waitress pleads, "Come back," unless it's New Orleans and she croons, "Enjoy." The hallmark of the Midwest is "Have a good one," answered by "You betcha," and an all-you-can-eat salad bar with at least one hundred items, most of them encased in Jell-O. The Rocky Mountain states feed in pure volume, no matter what the course—the byword there is "Refill?"—whereas the Pacific Rim overdoes it with fruit, as in a wedge of orange on the plate next to your pizza.

A culinary relief map of the country pretty much inverts the standard topological zones. Rather than the vaguely camel-back shape of North America (the humps represented by the two major north-south mountain ranges), portion size translates into more of a hammock effect. Sea level becomes the highest instead of the lowest part, and major sags and droopings are found inland from the coast. The state of Utah, for instance, constitutes the sleeping giant's hip, for it's a place that compensates an arid and rather Spartan environment by distributing ten-cents-a-pop soft ice cream machines at the exit door of most restaurants with large parking lots. Nebraska, home of a particularly high-density food called potato meatloaf (offered at rest stops beckoning from the endless interstate 80), accounts for the mid-depression of the continent, and the old South—arbitrarily centered in Gadsden, Alabama, birthplace of the bottomless grit—is its lolling head, which, as any chiropractor will tell you, is the heaviest part of the body.

European tourists, with their effete tradition of teeny-tiny glasses of no-ice Coca-Cola, must be flabbergasted by the proffering of "20 oz. Thirst Busters" at each K-4 convenience store in the. western steppes, and Japanese honeymooners, coining from a context of hundred-dollar steaks, must believe they've found paradise in the hefty "full-pound burgers" of rural Texas. Dietary largesse is patriotic, an entitlement protected, coterminal with individual ownership of automatic weapons, by the Constitution. We fought Iraq for the right to drive-thru an emporium boasting thirty-six oil-based flavors of frozen nondairy dessert. We celebrate Christmas with Federal-Expressed boxes of the world's weightiest Oregon pears or Idaho potatoes or California onions, or by sending each other baskets, their overflowing contents of dense Edams and Goudas barely contained by protective cellophane, shipped from Wisconsin—a state whose highway signs proclaim, more often than historic markers or scenic vistas, simply CHEESE. Less specific, but no less commanding, is the banner permanently overhanging Tower City, North Dakota, visible for miles in any direction, shouting FOOD, and followed by an enormous arrow pointing straight down to the rich, loamy landscape.

For Americans of a certain age and class, food is the punctuation of life, a commercial break between those bothersome segments of work or play that require the use of our hands, thus prohibiting their availability for unwrapping, unpeeling, or defrosting. Eating certifies leisure, the coffee 'n' Danish break a defiance of the time clock, the snack a voluntary intrusion into a routine not of our own making. And yet eating is also a kind of defensible duty, a recreation we can shrug off as a need, excuse ourselves for, indulge in with some righteousness. Researchers tell us that diners' pupils narrow to pinpoints when plates are set before them. Our beings concentrate, focus, rivet to the task at hand. We need to eat, we tell ourselves. Our parents mandated it, and they were happy when we complied. Food made us good. It made us grow. Unlike masturbation or pleasure reading or a midmorning nap, determined consumption carries a cultural cachet of respect, equaled only, on occasion, by refraining from eating, an appositive ingestive practice during which, if anything, our minds are even more firmly fixed on what's not for dinner. We read cookbooks as literature, copy and exchange exotic recipes, devote on the average (if we can afford it) one technology-laden room of our homes for the sole purpose of food storage and preparation, and another, plus deck or patio, for its display prior to disappearance. We support an entire industry of pressure-sealed leftover containers because we invariably prepare more of everything than we need.

What is this obsession with jumbo helpings? Is it the aftershock of the Great Depression, a kind of chipmunk drive to hoard unto and into ourselves so that in the event of lean days we can feed off our own stored fat—the ultimate convenience: we don't even have to leave home or microwave! Is it an assertion of Manifest Destiny, the ultimate reward for the transoceanic migration of our starving ancestors? Do we eat "because it's there"? Certainly for most of us the urge to stuff normally arises from habit, not from hunger. Early on we were initiated into the cleanplate club by a ritual that culminated in a swipe of every eating surface with Wonder bread, a final lip-smack cleansing of each utensil, the lick of fingertip so that no available morsels escaped our digestive tract. Is it an instinctive urge toward bulk-signifying power, a thumbed nose at death, an insistence on closure before the hunt begins afresh?

Once food has been elevated to the category of symbol, it begins to serve other, quasi-existential functions. Pie, for my mother, is much more than pie. It's the icing on the doughnut of a life challenged with disappointments in love and expectation, an affordable, slightly illicit luxury, a thing for which her addiction is coyly confessed. Pie has served as a staple of barter in her dealings with the universe—raised, as she was, in a complex Roman Catholic economy of indulgences and leveraged buyouts. The standard microsystem was fairly straightforward: three hundred days' grace in the afterlife for the trifling price of a whispered ejaculation, more for a whole rosary or a novena. Attending mass on the first Friday of each of nine consecutive months purchased an insurance policy that guaranteed a happy death. Remaining resolutely still during the reading of the long gospel of Palm Sunday or Easter sprung the soul of your choice from purgatory on early parole.

Good works produced results, and there was no more potent form of good works than sacrifice, no sacrifice more expensive than one involving abstention from the thing most cherished. Abraham anted up Isaac. St. Elizabeth of Hungary abdicated her royal throne. St. Teresa, obviously on my family's wavelength, forewent all nourishment save a daily communion wafer.

It's little wonder that my mother's devotion to pie became a valuable commodity, her own personalized bargaining chip with a shrewd divinity so omniscient that no over-weighting of the scale or inflated price gouging would ameliorate. Pie, like the coin of the realm, came in various denominations, depending on my mother's sliding preference. Value was purely subjective, and all contracts were accepted or rejected on a single best-bid basis—no haggling allowed. In my mother's metaphysical accounts payable department, apple and cherry were nickels and dimes, the stuff one threw on (or, more accurately, took off) the table in exchange for the finding of lost car keys, but God *knew* how much she loved her pecan. When she negotiated to forego it voluntarily for, say, six months in reciprocation of my receipt of a college scholarship, it was a serious offer He couldn't ignore. My aunt once saved herself and an entire busload of other tourists from vaulting over the guardrail of a twisting Mexican highway by eliminating, curve by treacherous curve, every type of liquor, nut, and cake from her future diet. There was something my grandmother wanted enough to warrant her giving up all candy—for life—at the age of forty-two, but she would never tell me what it was. Obviously, "no publicity" was part of the deal.

At the other end of the spectrum from deprivation lies submission, and my family, in extremis, has been known to combine the two: not eating potato chips, for instance, is all the more negotiable when supplemented by a contract to consume salad without dressing. For every declined satin negligé among the major food groups, there's a hairshirt waiting to be donned, and doing with can easily double the value of doing without. But if comestibles are the hard currency of immortal transaction, they're also clearly the reward for virtue. Dinner is to a day what dessert is to dinner.

Such philosophizing is a perfectly respectable way to wile away the minutes between breakfast and brunch. Think about the issue intensely enough, however, and the automatic biological response is hunger—an insight that is no stranger to the fast-food industry, whose roadside advertisements must convey, in staccato shorthand, a metalanguage that can be scanned, judged, and braked for by people hurtling past at seventy miles per hour. Inevitably in transit, where having enough fuel is an ever-present concern, there's a spillover from gas tank to stomach, and thus the vocabulary of a menu must communicate more than simple information, especially to a target audience. No type of vehicle is more desirable than a station wagon or van, preferably one that carries a suction-cupped yellow window message announcing "Child on Board." Not only do such chariots transport multiple hungry passengers, but they are likely to be in the thrall of juveniles who experience no hesitation in making a snap decision. In casting their net for such prey, restauranteurs lay a double bait. To the recently literate young they dangle, "Fried!" and to the long-suffering parents they whisper, "Relief."

"Homemade" is a basic code word of such establishments, along with "Family Style" and "E-Z Access," but these phrases are subtle substitutes and stand-ins for their true meanings: doubleburgers, grilled cheese, and peanut butter. "Don't wormy," parents are assured. "They won't gag. And we won't complain when they spill their drink." In many of these establishments, pictographs replace writing on the laminated menus. Standardized, no-surprises photographs beckon diners seeking the reassurance of a homogenized national cuisine. Adults are lured by the supposed economy of "platters," with their suggestion of balanced nutrition coupled with volume, and proprietors compete against each other with ingenious "extras." "Boy Have We Got Chicken!" brags a Country Kitchen in Great Falls, Montana, whereas a Denny's in Bellevue, Washington, simply exclaims, "Canadians!" Certain nouns, masquerading as other grammatical forms, are especially in evidence—*country, purveyor, family, kitchen, dining*—and ersatz icons implanted into decor ("antiqued" or quilted wall hangings, oak-grain coat hooks, and wood-burned slogans) also contribute to a sense of the predictable and familiar "away from home."

Exceptions to this type of lingo often signal promising gastronomic finds, for even as a chef might err on the billboard, being slightly off the mark in comprehending the lowest common denominator, so too might the side dishes retain a regional or individualistic signature. "Egg Roll and Barbecue Take Out" could spell disaster, but at least it will probably be a memorable one. "Live Bait and Ice Cream" indicates a particular sensibility. The old-fashioned word "café" is often a plus, especially when it lacks an accent mark, is preceded by the cook's first name, and graces a cement block building surrounded, at 6:00 A.M., by a semicircle of parked police cruisers and pick-up trucks bearing in-state license plates. Once inside, listen for a bell attached to the door, look for day-of-the-week specials listed on a blackboard in illegible penmanship, and keep an eye out for real plants in the windows. If actual herbs or tomatoes are growing outside, settle yourself upon a round stool at the lunch counter. And if the owner confesses, with some pride, that the well-scrubbed stains on the baby high chair upholstery were made by her very own grandchildren, contemplate permanent residence. You may have stumbled into an eatery where children are regarded as people with smaller appetites amid not as a separate, cholesterol-crazed subspecies.

It's the kind of joint Mickey and Minnie were always pulling into during their journey of forty years past, the Americana of Frank Capra faces, bottomless cups of coffee, and in-the-booth jukeboxes with selections drawn from local favorites rather than MTV. It flourished when geography meant more than a printout of bills from the same motel chain, when the Mississippi River divided—except for Pittsburgh—the radio stations whose call letters began with a "W" from those that started with a "K," when every small town produced its own version of a newspaper reporting its own slant on the news.

And it still exists.

In 1986, Louise and I drove a Dodge Caravan across the country with one son and four daughters to visit my grandmother. We probably appeared to be the ideal demographic—the nuclear family feeding group—but in our hearts we were Kerouac, ready to be transformed by the bizarre, the offbeat, the unknown. We eschewed major highways and fine family dining that provided crayons with the placemats, and we set our radar detectors for homemade curtains in the windows of establishments with names like "Betty's." We spent a night in the Atlasta Motel because it advertised "in-room clock radios" and "heat."

Late one afternoon we came by chance upon the cafe of our dreams in an otherwise undistinguished little town in the Pacific Northwest. A mimeographed sheet, tucked between the salt amid pepper shakers, informed us that a "pie war" was presently under way with a rival establishment, one block down Main Street, and as a result a slice from any of the sixteen varieties made fresh on the premises that morning could be had for only thirty-five cents. So confident was the baker that he invited us to sample the competition (naturally, at the same price), then return and get our money back if his was not better. For me, it was Paoli squared—Parsifal had found the holy grail.

DON'T SQUEEZE THE TOMATOES!

CHARLES SIMIC

A NEIGHBOR CONFESSED TO ME recently, "Maybe once or twice in my life I tasted a truly perfect tomato." Then he proceeded to describe in all the lascivious detail the glories of a vine-ripened, just-picked tomato. I knew precisely what he was talking about, so I just kept nodding enthusiastically. What struck me listening to him is how rare and memorable the experience he was eulogizing is. Here was someone who lives in the country, who loves Italian food and buys tomatoes year round, making fussy distinctions between a ripe and a truly ripe fruit. Perfection in a tomato seems to be as elusive and causes as much lyrical excess as Romantic love. "No wonder they were called love apples by our ancestors," I said to my neighbor, and he readily agreed. There was something positively sinful about such pleasure. It would have been more appropriate if naked Eve had bitten into a beefsteak tomato, or even better into an "early girl." A God who frets over his tomato plants makes more sense than the one who says, please don't touch my apple tree.

Thinking about apples and tomatoes, I was reminded of my childhood. Every August my mother would bring from the country baskets full of tomatoes to make sauce. There'd be tomatoes in the kitchen and every other room, tomatoes on book shelves, on tables, and even on her grand piano. Who could resist biting into them? I'd devour them the way one devours an apple. I'd take a bite, sprinkle salt on the deep red pulp and then take another voracious bite. Of course, since the tomatoes were very ripe, the juice would run down my chin and onto my clothes. My mother had a brilliant solution. She'd make me strip naked and sit in the bathtub with a salt shaker and a supply of tomatoes. When I was through "making a pig of myself" in her words, I'd yell and she would come and turn the shower on and wash me off.

Biting into a ripe tomato like that is still something I love to do, although these days I remain fully dressed and only lean over the kitchen sink. One night I caught my reflection in the window above the sink. The face of a happy madman, I thought: my lips smeared, my chin and the nose dripping; the half-eaten tomato in one hand, the salt shaker in the other. It's the tongue licking the lips that knows how good life can get, it occurred to me.

These memories came back to me while I was reading recently about a new species of super tomato being concocted by genetic engineers in California. The so-called FLVR SAVR Tomato, soon to be in your local market, is tailored not to rot. Its producers claim that "it resists spoilage and can be shipped at a tasty, red-ripe stage." In short, a miracle to equal turning water into wine! The gene that causes the ordinary tomato to turn soft is eliminated scientifically. The FLVR SAVR, one imagines, remains on the vine caressed by the golden sunlight until it reaches perfection of ripeness. It is then harvested with maternal care and travels and arrives at your local supermarket in immaculate condition as if it were picked minutes ago. The skin is so thin, so firm and delicate, you'll have to use your sharpest knife to slice it properly. The moment you do, that rich, fresh tomato smell will hit your nostrils. You will be in paradise. Your wife will grab a slice and you'll grab one too. Mmmmmmmm, is what you'll both say together, and then you'll give each other a long, sloppy kiss.

"It sounds to me like that square tomato perfect for shipping they dreamed up a few years ago," is what my wife actually said. But I wasn't dissuaded. A perfect tomato interests me in both its culinary and its metaphysical aspect. In Aristotelian terms, I believe, something is perfect when it has actualized and realized its specific form. In other words, it has fulfilled its nature and found its truth. St. Thomas Aquinas sought to prove the existence of God from the degrees of perfection to be observed in the world. How close is it to divine perfection? is the question he asked. A ripe tomato out of season is a marvel. A deathless tomato is a blasphemy.

All the ramifications of this are nicely illustrated in Hawthorne's famous story "The Birth Mark." His hero Alymer, if you remember, killed his divinely beautiful spouse in the process of removing her slight imperfection, the tiny birthmark she had. "The pale philosopher," as Hawthorne calls him, concocted an elixir for her to drink. It worked. Briefly, he beheld her in her flawless beauty, but then his wife dropped dead. The lesson Hawthorne wants us to draw is this: it is the fatal flow of humanity to stick its nose where it doesn't belong. Alymer, like many of us, was a philosophical idealist who denied the commonsense view that imperfection is our lot. For him the intellect was supreme, the mind was godlike, the earth could be remade into a lost Eden. He didn't make a pact with the devil in the story, but he might as well have. All the smart alecks of his kind are, of course, direct descendants of Dr. Faustus. He would have understood instantly the urge to redesign the tomato in the lab.

From the culinary aspect, the temptation is perhaps even greater. I remember one viciously cold January, many years ago, when we discovered some fabulous Israeli tomatoes here in New Hampshire. Ordinarily, hothouse tomatoes, if that's what they were, are a huge disappointment. They look good but have no taste. These Middle East tomatoes were nothing like that. They appeared in a small country store where we occasionally stopped to get gas and buy milk. Reasonably priced, tasty, ripe, it boggled the mind how they got there. Obviously someone found it profitable to fly them over that great distance. As we ate them, we imagined ancient prop planes dragged out of junk yards to be flown across the Mediterranean and the Atlantic with a load of these tomatoes. Drunks fired by major airlines, Laos and Vietnam veterans accustomed to suicide missions—how else could these tomatoes be so cheap? They were available just that one dark winter, and then, like a vision from the Arabian Nights, they vanished, never to be seen again.

The tomato craze is of a relatively recent date. I asked my students recently if the Founding Fathers ate spaghetti with tomato sauce. Most of them were not sure, but a few said with complete confidence that they did. I ask such bizarre questions from time to time in order to test their general knowledge of history and determine how close it has approached the absolute zero. In any case, the tomato plant supposedly originated in Peru, although the word *tomatl* is Aztec from the root "toma," meaning to swell, grow plump, hence toma-tl, the plump thing. Wherever it actually came from, we know for certain that the Spaniards brought it to Europe in the 16th century. It was planted in Spain, Portugal, Italy, France, England as an ornamental, but it took a couple of centuries until some unknown benefactor of future humanity actually bit into it and liked what he tasted. Mystery veils that all-important event. Like most everything else in cookery, it must have been an accident I leave you to imagine in all its wonderful details.

For example, I read once in a medieval Byzantine book on winemaking the story of how the old Greeks learned to make wine less alcoholic. According to the author, the wine they drank in ancient Greece was so heavy that one would get an instant hangover after one goblet. Impossible to do philosophy with such a head. All they were really capable of is putting on armor and banging each other over the head with a heavy sword. Then one day a couple of friends were drinking wine on a terrace overlooking the sea; Suddenly it started to rain and they ran inside the house for cover, leaving their goblets outside. It was only a brief shower so they were back on the terrace almost immediately. But when they tasted the wine, they were amazed by how light, how pleasant it tasted. And that's how the Greeks learned to add water to their wine and with suddenly cleared heads started-to ponder the nature of the universe.

As for the tomato, we are pretty sure the Italians improved it. Thomas Jefferson brought it from Europe and planted the first tomatoes on these shores in 1781, but he never ate them. An Italian painter in Salem, Massachusetts, in 1802, we learn, did that. His neighbors must have been horrified. After all, they still had not properly gotten over the witchcraft trials.

"Tomata," as it was called and spelled then, slowly became familiar in the course of the 19th century. The February 1835 issue of *Harvey's American Gardener's Magazine* reports that tomatoes are being used in salads. There are preserving directions, recipes for tomato soup, and most important of all, recipes for ketchup in early 19th century cookbooks.

Is America imaginable without ketchup? Even these days in restaurants in Europe it is not uncommon for waiters to bring a bottle of ketchup to the table, without being asked to, after realizing their customers are American. It's surprising, therefore, to learn that until very recently there were still people in this country who believed that tomatoes are poisonous and that they even cause cancer. The tomato plant, of course, is a relative of the deadly nightshade, so the fear has some basis.

No more. Now every market sells canned and fresh tomatoes. The greasiest greasy spoon throws a chunk or two into the mixed salad. Of course, the difference between that tomato and the real thing is like the difference between reading about sex in a high school pamphlet and actually doing it. Bred to withstand the steel fingers of the harvester, picked green, artificially reddened in ethylene gas chambers, this generic tomato is chewy, sour, flavorless, and can be bounced like a ball. If there's an ideal of unsavoriness, this has to be it. No amount of zesty salad dressing, spices or salt improves it much. We accept this poor substitute because we never stop longing for the real thing.

Gene-splicing, however, is scary. "Some thirty genetically engineered foods are waiting to be placed on the market," says *The New York Times*. We know farmers have been crossbreeding plants since the early days of agriculture to bring out certain agreeable characteristics, but it took years to accomplish the slightest change. Genetic engineering works relatively fast. What's even more remarkable, it can combine plant genes with animal genes; so, for example, a lobster can be cross-bred with a tomato if one desires to make the tomato withstand cold to the degree that a lobster can.

"What if I'm allergic to lobster," says a friend of mine, "and I get the same reaction when I eat the new tomatoes?"

"It'll be like biting into a Frankenstein monster," says another deep pessimist I know.

Personally, I'm still—after three generations—a child of peasant culture. I put both elbows on the table. I break bread with my hands. I talk with my mouth full. Reading about a low-cholesterol pig "being worked on" in Princeton, New Jersey, worries me to no end. How big is it gonna get if there's no fat on it at all? A colleague at the university told me about a scientist who grew a six-foot rooster by experimenting on its pituitary gland. What a crow it must have had! I hear it was slow and awkward, and ended up being killed by a mutt who did not care for its looks.

If my father were alive today, he too would have been attracted and repelled by the promise of this new tomato. In his view, which I share completely, a salad of ripe tomatoes is one of the glories of life. First of all, it smells good. There are onions in it, hot green peppers, basil and olive oil. It's a simple dish, but to do it properly the proportions have to be just right. Too much of this, too little of that, and it's not quite the same thing. This is an art of nuance in which the senses of taste and smell reign supreme. Generalizations, abstractions, in the form of recipes, measuring cups, and spoons have no place here. The tongue is more subtle than the word. Like the poets, it doesn't believe in a single meaning. Stick your face in the bowl, my father advised.

To do complete justice to such a salad, one must have a loaf of coarse Italian or French bread on the side. The bread makes the wine taste better and is needed to wipe the bowl clean in the end. That wonderful mixture of oil, onion, herb, and tomato juice beats any elixir Alymer and his kind can come up with.

My wife objects. She prefers the more elegant French way of making the salad in which the tomato is not sliced into chunks but into thin slices which are then laid on the plate and sprinkled with freshly made vinaigrette. I remember once being told in a small neighborhood restaurant in Paris that tomato in vinaigrette was the only thing they had in the way of an appetizer. I was disappointed, but not after I tasted what they brought me. There were only four slices on the plate and they were exquisitely flavored. I sipped a light rosé and wiped the plate with bread under the approving gaze of the fat proprietor.

The moment the subject of good tomatoes comes up, memory starts its parade: Jersey tomatoes sold on the streets of New York, roadside stands in New England and California. Late summer feasts in back-yards and restaurants with a garden. Tomatoes posing alone. Tomatoes with anchovies, with tuna, with sliced cucumbers, with black olives, with young mozzarella, with poached fish, with capers, with potatoes, with eggplant, with sausages. Tomatoes in various pasta sauces. All the Provencal, Greek, Sicilian, and Spanish casseroles. Hearty minestrones. Pots of steaming bouillabaisse and other Mediterranean fish stews. Gold gazpachos with bottles of well-chilled white wine.

Cucina e Nostalgia is the title of a gastronomic memoir by a master Italian chef, Alfredo Viazzi, published some years ago. That describes the way we all talk about food. In every inspired conversation about a meal, there is a longing to savor once again that delicious last drop, that piquant morsel of some gorgeously prepared dish and bring back that long-ago day when we were truly happy in the company of a few friends or some hover.

NOSTALGIA IS NOW, the producers of the FLVR SAVR should have shouted from the rooftops! Instead, they said, "The data demonstrate that the FLVR SAVR tomato is as safe and nutritious as the currently available fresh tomatoes." Not everybody was convinced. A certain Mr. Jeremy Rifkin has recently formed a group called the Pure Food Campaign which has declared war on the FLVR SAVR. Environmental groups are understandably concerned about the potential consequences of altering the biological make of foods by cell-cloning or moving genes from animals into plants. Reuters reported last October that "1,000 U.S. chefs have announced that they'll boycott bioengineered food." A thousand chefs all wearing chefs' hats and shaking their wooden spoons at us is nothing to take lightly.

"I will not sacrifice the entire history of culinary art to revitalize the biotechnology industry," declared Rick Monner, executive chef at the Water Club Restaurant. Yes, of course, but then there's Rebecca Goldburg, a senior scientist with the Environmental Defense Fund, who said that, unlike Rifkin, her group is not opposed to all genetically engineered foods.

I'm as wary of scientists in the kitchen as my grandmother was of men, but what if this tomato is harmless and simply tastes great? There's genetically engineered Florida corn which my green grocer tells me is already on the market and doesn't taste bad. Also, what if foods can be made more nutritious and the need for nasty pesticides and chemical fertilizers is eliminated at the same time?

Being of two minds, I figured, why not conduct a quick poll of my own? Have my own private Donahue show with a few friends and neighbors whose taste buds and good sense I trust?

What I heard is not exactly what I expected. Here's a sampling of their views:

"I put cow shit on my tomatoes and it doesn't prevent me from eating them."

"It's hard to believe they didn't have tomatoes in Roman orgies."

"Just another product of body-builder mentality."

"Tomato juice is the best cure for hangovers."

"It's the rot in the fruit that makes it taste good. You can't get rid of one without getting rid of the other."

"Be sure to see Attack of the Killer Tomatoes."

"I'd like to know when was the first rotten tomato thrown at a performer?"

"The sad truth is that we Americans have forgotten that even a tomato has a soul."

"I remember a chicken that told fortunes," somebody's mother said, to which the rest of us shouted, "what the hell does that have to do with tomatoes?"

JOSEPH WECHSBERG

SOME RESTAURANTS ON THE European continent still carry on along the lines of the highest gastronomical tradition, but practically not one of them is located in the vast, bleak area behind the Iron Curtain. No meal can be perfect if the ingredients that go into it aren't, and in the countries under Soviet domination it is impossible to obtain perfect ingredients. Often it is impossible to obtain any ingredients at all. People in Czechoslovakia, Poland, Rumania, and Hungary liked to eat well; the best restaurants in Prague, Warsaw, Bucharest, and Budapest ran a close second to the best restaurants in France. But now food is rationed in all these places. It is no longer a question of getting good food, but of getting any food at all.

Even if some of the great restaurants were still in existence, the number of potential patrons of good food would be close to zero. Europe's gourmets have always belonged to what were once the privileged classes—aristocrats, capitalists, diplomats, prosperous artists, and professional people. All of them have been "eliminated" in the Soviet orbit. As for the inevitable new rich—Communist Party leaders and black-marketeers—they don't seem to care or know anything about truly good food. Consequently, that formerly great epicurean institution, the European restaurateur who made an art of his profession, creating new dishes and inspired variations of old ones, is now almost extinct in a large part of the Continent.

Perhaps the last practicing representative of this great art in the vast, unepicurean Iron Curtain territory was Charles Gundel. A native of Budapest, Gundel—the name is pronounced "Goon-del," with the accent on the first syllable—contributed more to the fame of Hungarian cooking than any other man and is ranked by connoisseurs all over the world in a class with such restaurateurs as Escoffier and Fernand Point.

I met Gundel one evening in 1948 when I had dinner at one of the two restaurants he then operated in Budapest, in Városliget, or City Park. The restaurant occupied the ground floor of a solid two-story building surrounded by a garden that in summer was used for outdoor dining. Cream-colored curtains in the windows, plain white lights, an inconspicuous entrance, and soft music conveyed a nostalgic sense of Old World atmosphere rather than of contemporary flashiness.

As I entered, an elderly doorman with a bushy hussar mustache uttered a reverent: *"Alázatos szolgája. Jó napot kivánok"* ("Your humble servant. Good day"), which is still a familiar greeting in Budapest, Communists or no Communists. He apologized for his awkward bow, explaining that this was one of his rheumatic days, and led me to a patriarch in charge of the cloakroom. This old man was apparently too decrepit to do any work, but he had two assistants, agile boys of a mere seventy years or so, who relieved me of my hat and topcoat and wished me good appetite.

I was then taken in tow by a faultless maître d'hôtel, for whom a small army of no less faultless captains, waiters, and busboys stood aside. He guided me to a table not far from a seven-man gypsy band— two violins, a viola da gamba, a cello, a bass fiddle, a tamboura (big bass guitar), and a cimbalom (dulcimer). The *primás,* by way of tuning, expertly gave his men the D, not the A, as do the phony, Westernized gypsies in Paris and New York night clubs.

Food and music don't ordinarily mix well, I think, each being too important in its own way; but as the evening progressed I found that Gundel's gypsy band did not intrude upon my enjoyment of what was served me. The musicians played their rhapsodic songs in a hauntingly soft way, ending each piece with a sad, lingering, instrumental outcry . . .

It's not always easy to tell an authentic gypsy fiddler from a phony. Some impostors fool you with trills, ornamentations, rubati, and caprices in minor key that sound almost like the real thing. They play intervals less than a half tone and make sudden transitions, from C to E major or A-flat major, which are characteristic of genuine gypsies. I've often tried the gypsy tricks on my violin. It seems so easy: the constant use of the augmented second in melodic progression; a lot of improvisations; odd harmonies and sharp rhythms. But when I tried, it didn't sound exciting—just bad.

The gypsies at Gundel's were no phonies. I watched the *primás* as he put his fiddle up to his chin and started to play. He began with a deceptively simple melody, playing mostly alone. Now and then he was accompanied by the cimbalom. One by one, the others came in and the mood of the song changed. It became more primitive, violent. The structure was simple enough: they were doing variations on the leader's theme. Sometimes they would fall back, while the *primás* would perform virtuoso tills and ornamental notes, fast scales, and doubling notes. Then the orchestra would unite in a general wailing song, and the leader would play a recitative in parlando style, pleading, singing, and sobbing on his instrument.

It was an extraordinary performance. The *primás* held the bow with his whole right fist—which would have killed my old violin teacher. He played false notes and committed all major violin crimes. He would never have made the beginners' class at any music school. But he and his men were *real* and they created a genuine mood. They seemed as essential a part of Gundel's restaurant as the little busboys, the faint scent of wine and good food, the comfortably spaced tables, the mirrors and lights, the gleaming silver, and the fresh flowers on the tables.

The maître d'hôtel handed me the menu. It was printed in Hungarian and French, except for one line of English in small type along the right-hand margin. This read: "12% will be added to the amount of the bill, and 10% taxes, and in the evening 5% music.

While I was pondering this, a heavily built man appeared, bowed in a courtly, though not at all deferential, manner, introduced himself as Charles Gundel, and welcomed me to his restaurant. He looked just like the description of him given to me by some Hungarian friends of mine who are now living in New York and who become melancholy at the mere mention of his name—a massive, towering, oaklike man of great dignity, with a deeply lined face, a bald head, and an enormous double chin that half covered his black butterfly tie. He wore thick-lensed glasses, a black single-breasted suit, and an old-fashioned silver-gray waistcoat.

I introduced myself, in turn, and said that I brought him greetings from my friends, who had been faithful clients of his for many years. He smiled benevolently at this and said that he would be glad to help me choose my dinner.

My friends had warned me expressly against ordering dishes that were listed on the menu. "If you want to be respected, ask for something that's not on the bill of fare," one of them had said.

Gundel discreetly inquired about my health, digestion, and eating preferences, and then suggested that I start with *Balatoni fogas à la Rothermere*, made after a recipe that he had created in honor of Lord Rothermere.

"Just the filet of the fish, boiled in a *court bouillon* made with white wine, then covered with *sauce hollandaise* and topped off with a crayfish *pörkölt*, a ragout in a thick paprika sauce," he said. He made a circle with thumb and forefinger, closed his eyes, and shook his head slowly, and for a moment there was an expression of ethereal delight on his face.

"You can't get a better *fogas* than the one that comes from our Lake Balaton," he went on. "This fish, called *Lucioperca sandra,* is white and more tender than its brother in the Danube. Life is easier for the *fogas* in the soft, calm waters of the lake than in the swiftly flowing Danube, where he has to fight against the strong current and overdevelops his muscles. And the velvety sand of the lake whitens his skin."

Gundel gave me a questioning look. I nodded, overwhelmed by the avalanche of information.

"Afterward, how about a filet of hare?" he asked. "Larded with bacon, grilled *à l'anglaise,* and served with *sauce béarnaise?* Or perhaps the national specialty, breaded goose liver ?"

Before I could answer, he shook his head and said: "Might be too heavy for you, though. Let me order you a veal cutlet done in the Pittsburgh style. We call it that because we first made it for the Mayor of Pittsburgh, when he came here some fifteen years ago. A cutlet of veal filled with a purée of *foie gras* and served with *sauce Périgueux.* A little rice to go with it, and perhaps an endive salad sprinkled with fresh, chopped chives and tarragon leaves, which I was fortunate enough to find in the market this morning."

I murmured assent to all this, at which Gundel turned to the maître d'hôtel, who had been standing respectfully a short distance behind him, and gave him the order, speaking softly in the technical jargon of his profession, like one doctor conversing with another in front of a patient, and underscoring a few fine points with gestures of his big, expressive hands. The maître d'hôtel hurried away.

"Suppose you try one of our Hungarian wines with your meal," Gundel said to me. "Egri Bikavér, perhaps—Bull's Blood, that is. It is a red, tart, mellow, aromatic wine, *genre Bordeaux,* with just the right proportion of tannin."

He wished me good appetite and said he would like to talk to me later. "I am particularly glad that you are from New York," he told me. "My oldest son is a neighbor of yours there. He is in charge of the restaurant in the Great Northern Hotel."

I asked him to sit with me while I dined, but he refused.

"Please enjoy your dinner in solitude," he said. "I'll be back."

Twice while I was enjoying my dinner Gundel came by, and both times he stopped to inquire whether everything was all right. He nodded in a matter-of-fact way when I replied that this was the best meal I had had during six months of traveling about the Continent. For dessert he suggested fresh peach compote, or pancakes filled with ground walnuts, sugar, and raisins and covered with chocolate cream. I chose the latter.

He sat down at my table while I was having a *barack* (dry apricot brandy) and *espresso* coffee, strong and black, served in a small glass. It was past ten o'clock now, and hardly a third of the tables had been occupied.

Gundel sighed deeply. "Our prices are regulated by the government, and we don't charge more than the other comparable places in town," he said, "but there just aren't enough people left here who can afford to spend the money it takes to buy a good dinner."

A complete meal at Gundel's, with a bottle of wine, would run to about a hundred forint, approximately eight and a half dollars at the official rate of exchange, or about half the weekly salary of a white-collar worker. Gundel's guests, he said, were mostly government big shots, foreign diplomats, hard-currency tourists, and local black-marketeers. Occasionally one of the former habitués of the place—an impoverished bank manager possibly, or a dismissed government minister—would sell one of his last Persian rugs and spend a good share of the money on an evening at one of Gundel's restaurants, pointing up the old Hungarian proverb: "We are poor, but we live well."

Such fleeting indulgence in high life was not without danger. An agent of the Gazdasági Rendörség, the feared Economic Police, might happen into the restaurant, in which case he would almost surely visit the lavish spender the following morning and inquire about the source of his sudden wealth. No matter how reasonable the explanation, there was always the chance that it would be considered unsatisfactory, and, if so, serious charges would be laid against the splurger.

"It's getting so I'm always amazed when anybody comes in at all," Gundel said. "In time, I suppose, there won't be any guests, and that will be the end of it."

He gave a resigned shrug. Thirty-eight years of violent ups and downs had given him a philosophical attitude toward the vicissitudes of life. Since 1910, the year he became a full-fledged restaurateur in Budapest, Gundel had been, as he put it, "through two world wars, two inflations, two occupations, two revolutions, and one counterrevolution." In 1918 he was catering, in the grand manner, to a Habsburg archduke, and the following year he was serving the wild-eyed followers of the Communist Bela Kun.

"They would eat only the white stems of asparagus, because they considered the green tips inedible," Gundel said. "After them came

Horthy and the White Terror, and we had guests who ordered roast goose and ate only the wings and legs, because they thought the breast wasn't good enough."

During the Horthy regime Gundel became what amounted to official caterer to the Hungarian government. Ten years ago he was catering to the then King Carol of Rumania, and in 1947 he catered to Ana Pauker of Rumania, who seemed much less of a connoisseur than her royal predecessor.

"I've been called a symbol of continuity through chaos," Gundel said. "Only a little over three years ago, during the three-month battle for Budapest, this place was a stable for Wehrmacht horses. Where we sit now, I saw a horse fall down and die. Practically everything I owned vanished—rugs, mirrors, curtains, linen, glassware, silverware. Shameful! I used to own enough gold plates and gold knives and forks and spoons to serve a hundred and twenty people. Where are they today? Only the chinaware was left. My great collection of rare cookbooks was burned. Some of them were five hundred years old and contained the oldest known Hungarian recipes. Also among them was a very valuable cookbook of Roman times, in an English translation by a physician of Queen Elizabeth. But the worst loss of all was the wines."

Gundel's eyes grew moist. He called a captain and asked him to bring one of the establishment's prewar wine cards. It was an eighteen-page booklet on parchment paper, arranged by categories—wines *en carafe, vins blancs du pays, vins rouges du pays,* Bordeaux wines, Burgundy wines, Rhine and Moselle wines, Tokay wines, dessert wines, Hungarian *vins mousseux,* French champagnes, cognacs, and liqueurs, as well as beers and mineral waters.

Next to the name of each of the Hungarian wines were some numerals and letters, which, Gundel explained, were for the guidance of his foreign guests. A key card with corresponding numerals and letters accompanied each wine list, and from it a customer could ascertain the precise degree of sweetness or dryness, fullness, and flavor of the wines offered. A white wine from the Badacsony district, for example, called Badacsonyi Kéknyelü, was marked "7.III.a.," meaning that it was extra dry, full-bodied, and aromatic. A white wine called Kecskeméti Edes Furmint, from the Royal Hungarian State Cellars in Budafok, bore the marking "1.III.a.b.," meaning that it, too, was full-bodied and aromatic, and, in addition, *fin,* but sweet.

I asked about the Tokay wines on the list. Gundel took off his glasses, closed his eyes and rubbed them with the palm of his hand, as if he were trying to bring back memories.

"Here we say that Tokay is the wine of kings and the king of wines," he told me gently. "It has nothing artificial in it. You drink it just as it comes from grapes grown in the volcanic soil of the Tokay district, in the northeastern part of the country—an ideal natural blend of bouquet, alcohol, and sugar. There are four principal kinds of Tokay wine. Tokay Aszu is a wine that is graded on a basis of how many butts of dried-on-the-vine grapes went into its making. The more dried grapes, the sweeter the wine, and the types are numbered from one to six. Next comes Muscatel Aszu, made of muscat grapes. Then there is Szamorodni—the name meant 'born by itself' in ancient Hungarian—a wine with a sugar content that varies according to climatic conditions. Thus there are both dry and sweet Szamorodni. Finally, there is Essence of Tokay, the rarest of them all. To make Essence, one must wait until the grapes are dry on the vine. The grapes must never be pressed. The sheer weight of them brings forth just a little juice, which in due time matures into a heavy, sweet, liqueur-like wine that makes one think of honey. It is a wine that can be kept almost forever. At the time of the war, we still had a few bottles labeled 1811, the year Napoleon Bonaparte prepared to march on Moscow." He fell silent.

"How much did a bottle cost ?" I asked.

"About twenty dollars a half liter," he replied. "I recall, too, that we had some other choice vintages—1815 and 1866, and an especially fine one of 1854. That must have been one of the greatest Tokay years. Who drank those wines that were in our cellars? A lot of soldiers, I would guess, who were already intoxicated before they broke the heads off those precious bottles."

He sighed and put his glasses back on.

"I'm sorry," he said. "The memory of those old treasures always makes me sentimental. You know what Pope Benedict XIV wrote about some casks of Tokay that had been sent to him by Empress Maria Theresa? 'Blessed is the soil which produced thee, blessed is the queen who sent thee, and blessed am I who may enjoy thee.'"

Gundel turned the pages of the old wine list. "We also had some fine Bordeaux and Burgundy wines," he said. "I remember a Château Cos-d'Estournel 1928 and a great Puligny-Montrachet 1929."

Gundel and I counted up and found forty-eight liqueurs listed, among them Dreher's cherry brandy, Gessler's Altvater, Zwack's Unicum and Paprika, Fratelli Branca's Fernet Branca, Campari Bitter, Jourdes's Cordial Médoc, and Pernod's absinthe. For abstainers there were twenty-six mineral waters—Vichy, Karlsbader, Salvator, Apollinaris, Biliner, and so on.

* * *

Good food and good drink have been Gundel's chief interest in life for as long as he can remember. He was born in Budapest in 1883, and his first recollection is of hanging around the kitchen and wine cellars of the Erzherzog Stefan, a hotel that was owned by his father. In his middle teens he set out to learn the profession of hotel and restaurant management in the famous cities and resorts of western Europe. He worked in Neuchâtel, and then in Frankfurt am Main, where he met the famous Swiss hotelman César Ritz, who was impressed by his ability and took him on to Paris and then London.

"Monsieur Ritz was a great man," Gundel said feelingly. "He always used to tell me: 'Charles, be creative and inspired about new sauces and new ragouts, but remain old-fashioned about your table arrangements.'"

Two or three years later Gundel was home on a visit when his father became ill, and he felt that he ought to remain in Budapest to help out at the hotel. Its restaurant was noted for its cuisine, and with reason; Gundel, who remembers in detail the menus of distinguished dinners he has served the way Toscanini remembers scores, told me with particular enthusiasm about a luncheon party given there on his parents' wedding anniversary in 1903, when he was twenty. The meal consisted of *potage Windsor,* cold sturgeon with *sauce rémoulade,* saddle of venison with *sauce Cumberland, punch à la Romaine,* Styria *capon à la broche,* salad, compote, *parfait de noces,* patisserie, fruit, and cheese.

One of the jobs entrusted to the young Gundel was doing the daily buying at the market. There he frequently met an-other young hotel-man, Josef Marchal, whose father, Edouard Marchal, had once been *grand chef* at the court of Napoleon III. In 1860 the elder Marchal had been sent by Napoleon as a "present" to Alexander II, Tsar of Russia; he had later made his way to Budapest, where he bought the Hotel Queen of England and settled down.

"Edouard Marchal deeply influenced a whole generation of Hungarian chefs," Gundel told me. "He taught them to use fewer spices and fewer fats, and, in general, how to make lighter dishes that would please an international clientele. When his son became manager of the new Palace Hotel in Lomnicz, a resort in the Tatra Mountains that was fashionable among Austrian aristocrats and British and American millionaires, I became his assistant. The hotel had an annex a few kilometers away, which was managed by Margaret Blassutigh, the sister of Josef Marchal's wife. Everybody assured me that she was an energetic and pretty girl, just the right wife for me. I replied that I wouldn't go near the place. I didn't like the idea of other people picking out a wife for me. Well, you know how it is. One Sunday afternoon I sneaked over, because I was so curious. I had to admit that the place was in first-class shape. I talked a little shop with Margaret, and, first thing I knew, we were engaged. We got married in 1907. Then I took the Palace Hotel over and we stayed on, running it for three years, until our third child was born."

In 1910 Gundel and his family moved to Budapest, where he bought a once well-known but by then run-down restaurant called the Wampetits. It was in this restaurant that I was dining. Gundel renamed it after himself, and hired musicians and singers, and later whole symphony orchestras and opera companies to entertain his guests. There were partitioned sections in one part of the garden for private open-air parties and a terrace for socially and otherwise prominent folk.

"People with good food and wine manners would in due time graduate to the terrace," Gundel said. He seems to look back on this era as the golden period of his life.

The end came abruptly when the First World War broke out. Gundel, after engaging a manager to help his wife run the restaurant, served forty-four months in the army, most of the time with the rank of captain and as executive officer of a battalion. He now feels that through inattention to his duties he may have contributed to the collapse of the Austro-Hungarian monarchy, for he spent most of his time in the kitchen of the officers' mess, trying to drill some sense into the cook, a stubborn Czech who before the war had been a taxidermist in Prague.

"That's the way he cooked, too," Gundel said, shuddering at the recollection.

Gundel returned to Budapest after the war and guided his restaurant through the various revolutions that swept the country. In 1926, while continuing to operate the City Park establishment, he took over the restaurant in the St. Gellért Hotel, at the foot of St. Gellért Mountain on the opposite side of the town.

The St. Gellért was a vast complex of thermal springs, parks, gardens, terraces, playgrounds, and two big swimming pools, one enlivened by artificial waves, the other by invigorating air bubbles that were forced up through the floor of the pool. The restaurant itself contained spacious banquet rooms for large gatherings, small chambers for private parties, a beer tavern, and two public dining-rooms, one with a dance orchestra and the other with a gypsy band.

Gundel called in a brother of his named François and his old friend Josef Marchal to assist him with this huge enterprise. At the St. Gellért he often had as many as twenty private parties and two or three banquets a night. A banquet might be served for as many as nine hundred people. Importers of sea food sold more of their wares to Gundel's restaurants than to all the other restaurants in Budapest combined.

Within a few years Gundel's reputation had become international. When King Victor Emmanuel of Italy visited Hungary in 1937, the government opened up the banquet hall of an old castle for him in the ancient coronation city of Székesfehérvár and asked Gundel to equip and staff it and to provide a meal there. This association with royalty made Gundel sought after by nearly all Hungarian aristocrats who could afford entertaining on a feudal scale. But Gundel emphasized that in spite of the volume of his business in those years he never lowered his standards.

"We were lucky in having first-class personnel," he told me. "Every once in a while I would send my chefs, *souschefs,* and maîtres d'hôtel to France to brush up a little. The French are our masters, unsurpassed."

He gravely shook his head and kept a respectful silence in honor of the French masters. After a while he said: "Our payroll was quite large for a place like Budapest, which, after all, has never been a very big city. Here at the City Park restaurant alone I had a steady crew of sixty-five waiters and busboys, and the basic crew in the kitchen consisted of a head cook, two butchers, two cold men, three pastry cooks, a roast man, a *saucier,* an *à-la-minute* cook, and two specialists in Hungarian dishes. We also had a few women working here, one specializing in *Wiener Schnitzel,* one in hot pastry and strudel, a vegetable woman, a cheese woman, and, during the summer months, two girls for fruit. Of course, there would always be a number of apprentice cooks and various other helpers around, too.

Gundel thought diligence, a little luck, and a continuous study of what people like are responsible for success in the restaurant business.

"The work of a competent restaurateur doesn't begin with keeping an eye on the kitchen," he said. "He must go to the market himself to get the best there is. Even then the outcome is often doubtful. It is difficult to make something good out of second-class materials, but it is quite easy to spoil first-class ones. People often appreciate a superb meal without quite realizing what makes it better than another meal of apparently much the same sort. You can't distinguish between fresh fruits and the very freshest ones unless you have eaten, let us say, wood strawberries, newly picked in a sunny glade, or tasted a ripe apricot straight from the tree. Yet it is this almost imperceptible difference between fresh and freshest that is all-important. That is why even during my most prosperous years I made it a habit to do all the marketing myself. Every morning at eight I would go to the market with a list of our needs that my chef had compiled the evening before. In addition, I would always buy whatever seemed to be exceptionally good that day—new asparagus, perhaps, or some outstandingly beautiful apples, or fresh *süllö,* as young *fogas* is called, or *kecsege,* a fish that looks something like sturgeon and is very tasty, hot or cold, and has no bones at all.

"Beef is always a problem for the one who buys. It must be aged, but it mustn't be frozen. Did you ever take meat from a freezer and watch it thaw out? The little bit of pink juice that has formed under it is now lost, and that little bit makes so much difference in the taste! We used to get beef from steers that had been fed on sugar-beet mash, but they aren't feeding cattle that way any more."

His marketing done, Gundel would proceed to the St. Gellért and busy himself in his office until noon. Then he would make the rounds of the kitchens and dining-rooms. At one thirty he would drive over to inspect his City Park place.

"Your customers should always know that you are on hand," he said to me. At three o'clock, he went on, he would sit down to lunch with his family, and then, after a short nap, spend the rest of the afternoon at a business meeting or a funeral. He has always been a zealous pallbearer.

"In the years just before the second war, it seemed to me that almost every day one of my old guests was buried," he said.

By six o'clock Gundel would be back at the St. Gellért, and later in the evening he would go to the City Park restaurant. It was a busy life, but he found time for discussions with his chefs, in the course of which many new delicacies were developed.

"Only a genius like Escoffier actually invented dishes," he said with what I gathered was excessive modesty. "You don't *invent* a dish by spreading mint sauce over a pork roast. All we did was make new variations on classical recipes."

Most people associate paprika with Hungarian cuisine, but I noticed that there were only two or three paprika dishes on Gundel's menu.

"The French influence," he said when I asked him about this. "For years now, we have been using fewer and fewer condiments. Above all, we have cut down on the use of paprika. Few Hungarians today realize that paprika, the Hungarian national spice, was hardly used at all in this country a century ago. In Hungarian cookbooks of the early nineteenth century, there is scarcely any mention of it. It isn't a native Hungarian plant, either. Columbus brought one variety of it to Spain from America. When the Turks overran Hungary, early in the sixteenth century, they brought with them another variety, some think from India. Today in our cooking we use paprikas that aren't too hot but are sweetish and piquant rather than sharp, and much milder than cayenne pepper or curry. Good paprika has a certain sugar content. It mustn't be overheated or the sugar content will turn too quickly into caramel and both the color and the flavor will be spoiled. Most foreigners call all dishes that contain paprika *gulyás.* We Hungarians divide paprika dishes into four varieties: *gulyás, pörkölt, tokány,* and *paprikás.* "

He looked at me inquiringly through the thick lenses of his glasses and said: "I am not boring you?"

I assured him that I was glad to learn about paprika dishes from the greatest living authority on the subject.

He nodded absently. *"Gulyás,"* he continued, "is prepared by cooking together finely chopped onions, cubes of potatoes and meat, green peppers and tomatoes, caraway seeds, garlic, salt, and paprika, and sometimes a dough that is nipped *off,* bit by bit, between the forefinger and thumb. The meat used is beef, and there is plenty of gravy, almost like a soup. *Pörkölt* also contains finely chopped onions, paprika, and meat, but in bigger pieces and from fatter animals—veal, mutton, game, pork, goose, and duck. For *tokány* the meat is usually cut in lengthwise pieces. It may contain sweet or sour cream, or no cream at all, mushrooms, asparagus tips, and, parsley roots. As for *paprikás*—the finest of them all, to my taste—it is made of fish, fowl, lamb, or veal, and either sour or sweet cream, or a mixture of both."

Two men and a woman came in and were seated at a table near us. They were, Gundel said, Americans, and one of the men was with the United States Legation. He rose, went over to greet them, and asked what they would like.

The woman said: "Oh, a steak, I suppose, medium rare, and one of the men said: "Same for me. French fries, please, and a couple of vegetables." The other said: "Same here."

Gundel recoiled, but only slightly, and relayed the order to a captain. Then he came back to my table.

"They're fine people, generous and kind," he said. "Unfortunately, they never learned to eat. They just feed themselves. I must say, though, that I did have some American guests here occasionally, between the two wars, who appreciated good food. In fact, one of the great banquets of my career was given on June 12, 1931, in honor of a number of American businessmen, or maybe they were hotelmen. I have forgotten which, but I have not forgotten the menu."

Gundel stared up at the ceiling, like a high priest summoning divine inspiration, and said: "Cantaloupe, chicken consommé *au tokai, vol-au-vent Aurora,* saddle of venison *rôti à l'anglaise* with *sauce béarnaise,* a salad *de primeurs,* strawberries *à l'Anthéor,* hot savories, *petits fours.*"

He lowered his eyes and came back to earth. "Don't be deceived by the simple names. I've never been in the habit of giving fancy names to dishes. The chicken consommé, for instance, had nothing in common with the chicken consommés that one finds on most menus. A classic chicken consommé must have a distinctive flavor, and it takes a good chef to prepare one. The *vol-au-vent Aurora* was made with a ragout of crayfish and *sauce Cardinal.* Only a thoroughly trained chef can do it properly. And the salad *de primeurs!* Americans would probably call them fresh young garden vegetables. My son Charles sometimes sends me menu cards from New York, where, it seems, they use the word 'fresh' with everything. As if in a good place it should be considered necessary to point out that the food is fresh! Also, I am told, 'fresh' does not necessarily mean fresh in America. Here, when we say 'fresh,' we mean, of course, vegetables that are served the very same day they come out of the garden... But I'm becoming garrulous. Forgive me. There are not many guests these days who are interested in the fine points of good cooking."

He gave a deep sigh. "That banquet, for instance! It was one of those memorable affairs that don't happen any more. I can only quote from Berchoux:

> *Il se mettait à table au lever de l'aurore,*
> *L'aurore en revenant l'y retrouvait encore."*

Gundel raised his hands in a gesture of despair and said: "People are too busy in these times to care about good food. We used to spend months working over a *bonne-femme* sauce, trying to determine just the right proportions of paprika and fresh forest mushrooms to use.

"And take carp. Over in America carp isn't too popular a fish. People don't like that muddy taste. Well, I've always maintained that carp can be very good. We would put live carp taken from still lakes into screened tanks and lower them into the Danube and leave them there for two weeks. The current would wash away that muddy taste, and in the end the carp were delicious."

Gundel got up and said he would be back soon, he had to look after his guests. I sat there sipping my *barack,* listening to the gypsy musicians. The music became louder and faster now, and some of the guests began to hum and to tap the floor. The gypsies were not playing music: they were telling each other stories on their instruments, funny and sad stories, tales of love and heroism and compassion and hatred. When they stopped, I nodded to the *primás* and he came over and had a *barack* with me. He was a black-haired, mustachioed man with high cheekbones and the saddest eyes I'd seen in a long time. I asked him where he had learned his melodies.

"On our wanderings," he said. "We hear a song and play it again. It's very much like telling an anecdote. You don't always tell it the same way. You make your changes and then people hear it from you and add their own changes and exaggerations, and when the story comes back to you, you hardly recognize it. We play *lasser* (slow) or *friss* (fast), and we count either *üf* (three) or *dört* (four)." He always used Turkish words when he talked of his music. He liked to talk music all the time, but he couldn't read a single note; none of his men could. They had never heard of triplets or diminished-seventh chords. Once they had heard Suppé's *Light Cavalry,* and in no time they rearranged the piece and played their own version of it. Everybody thought it was swell, but no one recognized it.

"We miss the right mood now," the *primás* said, sadly glancing at the almost empty dining-room. "We gypsies play best when we *feel* the music. We need dim lights, the perfume of beautiful women, the drinks and whispered voices and tears in the eyes of our listeners. To be able to excite others, we must be excited ourselves. And now—"

He didn't finish the sentence, gave me a sad nod, and returned to his orchestra. A moment later he took up one of their sad, haunting songs.

Gundel came back to my table after a while with a photograph of a group of youngsters—six boys and five girls.

"My children," he said, and there was real pride on his face. "Eleven of them, and I also have seventeen grandchildren. You must go and see my son Charles when you get back to New York. He used to help me here. He was expert at making, among other things, a delicious dessert called *rétes,* a strudel with extremely thin dough. In 1939 he went over, accompanied by a staff of four cooks and five waiters, to manage the Hungarian Pavilion at your World's Fair. I understand they did quite well, though they served a number of strange concoctions, like a drink they called a Pishta. They made it of blackberry liqueur, brandy, orange juice, lemon juice, and seltzer. And then there was something, called the Attila Cup, made out of Hungarian *mousseux,* Bull's Blood, curaçao, fruit, mint, and sugar."

Gundel reflected gloomily on these formulas, and then shook himself like a wet dog.

"When war came," he said, "Charles and his nine companions stayed on in New York. They found good jobs there, all of them. Charles later managed a restaurant called Hapsburg House and then one called the Caviar. You must go and see him at the Great Northern when you get back. Two of my other sons were not so fortunate. Franz was taken prisoner by the Russians. He did not return home until last year, and then I put him in charge of the St. Gellért restaurant. Josef, after being taken hostage by the Germans, was confined for many months in a displaced-persons camp in Germany.

"People sometimes ask me whether my children were brought up on fancy Gundel food. Naturally, they were not. They had to eat whatever came to the table, and most of the time the food was strictly middle-class. Only once in a while, on Christmas or Easter, there would be something special. It's nice to have so many children, but in times like these I worry about them."

During the German occupation Gundel's City Park place was patronized almost exclusively by generals and colonels of the Wehrmacht and the S.S. at lunch and dinner, but late in the evening some of his many Jewish friends who were hiding out would sneak in through a back door for a quick meal in the kitchen. In the course of the Russian siege the St. Gellért Hotel, which had also been a favorite of Hitler's officers, was bombed and partially burned out, while the City Park restaurant underwent its conversion into a stable.

Gundel and his wife were permitted to stay on in a tiny room in the cellar of the City Park place. Gundel lost eighty pounds during the siege and came, he said, to look "almost normal." While the battle of Budapest was still going on, he began talking to contractors about yanking the horse stalls out of his City Park restaurant and making it into a dining-room again. He also set about collecting glassware, mirrors, and pots and pans wherever he could find them, and succeeded in reopening both his restaurants not long after the Red Army marched in.

Hungarian government officials immediately found Gundel's establishments highly acceptable places for the entertainment of their Russian liberators. The people of Budapest were near starvation; in the last weeks of the siege they had grown so hungry that they ate some of the animals in the Municipal Zoo.

It was impossible to get much food in the city. The peasants in the surrounding countryside didn't want to sell what little they had in return for badly inflated paper money. Gundel hired a cart and drove out to their farms to bargain. He traded the few shoes, shirts, and bits of jewelry he had left for butter, flour, eggs, and meat. His lifetime savings, two and a half million pengö, which had made him a rich man, had disappeared.

The only guests in his restaurants were Russian officers, and; later, a sprinkling of British and Americans. By February 1, 1946, a not very lavish meal at a Gundel restaurant cost over a million pengö, or what it would take a Budapest worker a month to earn. (For an American, it was only $1.66.) On the City Park restaurant menu of January 6, 1946, a cold *fogas* with *sauce tartare* was listed at 80,000 pengö; on February 3, at 130,000; on May 12, at 350,000; on July 15, at 26,000,000.

On August 1, the day the currency was stabilized and the forint was introduced as the new unit of currency, at the rate of one to 400,000,000,000,000,000,000,000,000,000,000 pengö, Gundel customers were charged twelve forint, or a dollar, for a *fogas*. Today the price has gone up to fifteen forint.

"Our bookkeeper, poor fellow, almost went crazy," Gundel told me. "Here, let me show you." He called a captain and instructed him to bring one of the ledgers that showed the firm's financial transactions during the inflation period.

Gundel opened the book at random. On June 24, 1946 the restaurant had taken in the improbable amount of 30,382,752,000,000,000 pengö, and at that, Gundel said, he was going farther and farther into the red. The value of the pengö dropped so rapidly that frequently he lost a small fortune between eight in the morning, when he bought food at the market, and early afternoon, when he sold it. Perfidious customers would come in, enjoy a good meal, and then "discover" that they didn't have enough money with them to pay for it.

"They would pay the bill three days later, when the amount wouldn't buy a ride on a streetcar," Gundel said. "We'd always thought the inflation was bad after the First World War, when English workers and clerks could and did come to live at the St. Gellért like millionaires on their old-age-pension checks, but during that period prices went up only twelve thousand per cent. This time it was astronomical."

Gundel closed the book and asked the waiter to bring him the guest-book. It was a bright, leather-bound volume that might well have served as the basis for a *Who Was Who* of Europe between the wars. It seemed as if every tourist, painter, banker, singer, diplomat, king, ex-king, musician, politician, and fellow restaurateur on the Continent, and many from elsewhere, had been a Gundel guest.

Gundel was most impressed by the tributes and signatures of playwrights, poets, and novelists. Like a great many other Hungarians, he liked to think of himself as something of a writer. He has written essays on Hungarian food and Tokay wines, a highly diverting cookbook, and two other books: *The Art of Entertaining* (1938), a practical guide for hostesses, and *The Profession of Entertaining* (1940), a compendium of tips for the ambitious restaurant-owner.

Perhaps the most notable of all the scribblings in Gundel's guest-book is a poem that John Galsworthy wrote one night after a dinner at Gundel's. It is called "The Prayer" and reads:

> *If on a spring night I went by*
> *And God were standing there,*
> *What is the prayer that I would cry*
> *To him? This is the prayer.*
>
> *O Lord of Courage grave,*
> *O Master of this night of spring,*
> *Make firm in me a heart too brave*
> *To ask Thee anything!*

The gypsy musicians were playing another sad tune, and for a while Gundel said nothing, listening to the melodies of the distant past. Then a distinguished-looking elderly man in a shabby suit entered the dining-room. Gundel excused himself and hurried over to him. As the new-comer sat down at a near-by table, Gundel remarked that it seemed like ages since he'd seen him here.

The man nodded sadly, saying something about the bad times, and Gundel agreed, nodding equally sadly. Both men sighed, and then Gundel said: "And now I ask you what will be your pleasure? A pheasant *aux choux rouges*? Or a veal cutlet, as in the old days? Dipped in egg and flour, covered with mushrooms and finely shredded ham, sprinkled with . . ."

Last year, Gundel's restaurants were nationalized. Now Hungary's Communist commissars entertain their honored guests at Gundel's. The name has remained, but nothing else has. The food is bad. Gundel himself was permitted to leave. He lives in quiet retirement somewhere in Austria.

MEATLESS DAYS

SARA SULERI

I HAD STRONGLY HOPED THAT they would say sweetbreads instead of testicles, but I was wrong. The only reason it had become a question in my mind was Tillat's fault, of course: she had come visiting from Kuwait one summer, arriving in New Haven with her three children, all of them designed to constitute a large surprise. As a surprise it worked wonderfully, leaving me reeling with the shock of generation that attends on infants and all the detail they manage to accrue. But the end of the day would come at last, and when the rhythm of their sleep sat like heavy peace upon a room, then Tillat and I could talk. Our conversations were meals, delectable, but fraught with a sense of prior copyright, because each of us was obliged to talk too much about what the other did not already know. Speaking over and across the separation of our lives, we discovered that there was an internal revenue involved in so much talking, so much listening. One evening my sister suddenly remembered to give me a piece of information that she had been storing up, like a squirrel, through the long desert months of the previous year. Tillat at twenty-seven had arrived at womanhood with comparatively little fuss—or so her aspect says—and her astonishing recall of my mother's face has always seemed to owe more to faithfulness than to the accident of physiognomy. "Sara," said Tillat, her voice deep with the promise of surprise, "do you know what *kapura* are?" I was cooking and a little cross. "Of course I do," I answered with some affront. "They're sweetbreads, and they're cooked with kidneys, and they're very good." Natives should always be natives, exactly what they are, and I felt irked to be so probed around the issue of my own nativity. But Tillat's face was kindly with superior knowledge. "Not sweetbread," she gently said. "They're testicles, that's what *kapura* really are." Of course I refused to believe her, went on cooking, and that was the end of that.

The babies left, and I with a sudden spasm of free time watched that organic issue resufface in my head—something that had once sat quite simply inside its own definition was declaring independence from its name and nature, claiming a perplexity that I did not like. And, too, I needed different ways to be still thinking about Tillat, who had gone as completely as she had arrived, and deserved to be reproached for being such an unreliable informant. So, the next time I was in the taut companionship of Pakistanis in New York, I made a point of inquiring into the exact status of *kapura* and the physiological location of its secret, first in the animal and then in the meal. Expatriates are adamant, entirely passionate about such matters as the eating habits of the motherland. Accordingly, even though I was made to feel that it was wrong to strip a food of its sauce and put it back into its bodily belonging, I certainly received an unequivocal response: *kapura,* as naked meat, equals a testicle. Better, it is tantamount to a testicle neatly sliced into halves, just as we make no bones about asking the butcher to split chicken breasts in two. "But," and here I rummaged for the sweet realm of nomenclature, "couldn't *kapura* on a lazy occasion also accommodate something like sweetbreads, which is just a nice way of saying that pancreas is not a pleasant word to eat?" No one, however, was interested in this finesse. "Balls, darling, balls," someone drawled, and I knew I had to let go of the subject.

Yet I was shocked. It was my mother, after all, who had told me that sweetbreads are sweetbreads, and if she were wrong on that score, then how many other simple equations had I now to doubt? The second possibility that occurred to me was even more unsettling: maybe my mother knew that sweetbreads are testicles but had cunningly devised a ruse to make me consume as many parts of the world as she could before she set me loose in it. The thought appalled me. It was almost as bad as attempting to imagine what the slippage was that took me from nipple to bottle and away from the great letdown that signifies lactation. What a falling off! How much I must have suffered when so handed over to the shoddy metaphors of Ostermilk and Babyflo. Gosh, I thought, to think that my mother could do that to me. For of course she must have known, in her Welsh way, that sweetbreads could never be simply sweetbreads in Pakistan. It made me stop and hold my head over that curious possibility: what else have I eaten on her behalf?

I mulled over that question for days, since it wantonly refused to disappear after it had been posed: instead, it settled in my head and insisted on being reformulated, with all the tenacity of a query that actually expects to be met with a reply. My only recourse was to make lists, cramped and strictly alphabetical catalogues of all the gastronomic wrongs I could blame on my mother; but somehow by the time I reached *T* and "tripe," I was always interrupted and had to begin again. Finally it began to strike me as a rather unseemly activity for one who had always enjoyed a measure of daughterly propriety, and I decided that the game was not to be played again but discarded like table scraps. For a brief span of time I felt free, until some trivial occasion—a dinner, where chicken had been cleverly cooked to resemble veal—caused me to remind my friends of that obsolete little phrase, "mutton dressed up as lamb," which had been such a favorite of my mother's. Another was "neither flesh nor fowl," and as I chatted about the curiousness of those phrases, I suddenly realized that my friends had fallen away and my only audience was the question itself, heaving up its head again and examining me with reproach and some scorn. I sensed that it would be unwise to offer another list to this triumphant interlocutor, so I bowed my head and knew what I had to do. In order to submit even the most imperfect answer, I had to go back to where I belonged and—past a thousand different mealtimes—try to reconstruct the parable of the *kapura*.

Tillat was not around to hear me sigh and wonder where I should possibly begin. The breast would be too flagrant and would make me too tongue-tied, so I decided instead to approach the *kapura* in a mildly devious way, by getting at it through its mate. To the best of my knowledge I had never seen *kapura* cooked outside the company of kidney, and so for Tillat's edification alone I tried to begin with the story of the kidney, which I should have remembered long ago, not twenty-five years after its occurrence. We were living in Lahore, in the 9-T Gulberg house, and in those days our cook was Qayuum. He had a son and two daughters with whom we were occasionally allowed to play: his little girl Munni I specially remember because I liked the way her hair curled and because of all the times that she was such a perfect recipient of fake *pan*. *Pan*, an adult delicacy of betel leaf and nut, can be quite convincingly replicated by a mango leaf stuffed with stones: Ifat, my older sister, would fold such beautifully simulated *pan* triangles that Munni would thrust them into her mouth each time—and then burst into tears. I find it odd today to imagine how that game of guile and trust could have survived even a single repetition, but I recollect it distinctly as a weekly ritual, with us waiting in fascination for Munni to get streetwise, which she never did. Instead, she cried with her mouth wide open and would run off to her mother with little pebbles falling out of her mouth, like someone in a fairy tale.

Those stones get linked to kidneys in my head, as part of the chain through which Munni got the better of me and anticipated the story I really intend to tell. It was an evil day that led her father Qayuum to buy two water buffalo, tethering them at the far end of the garden and making my mother beam at the prospect of such fresh milk. My older brother Shahid liked pets and convinced me that we should beam too, until he and I were handed our first overpowering glasses of buffalo milk. Of milks it is certainly the most oceanic, with archipelagoes and gulf streams of cream emitting a pungent, grassy odor. Trebly strong is that smell at milking-time, which my mother beamingly suggested we attend. She kept away herself, of course, so she never saw the big black cows, with their ominous glassy eyes, as they shifted from foot to foot. Qayuum pulled and pulled at their white udders and, in a festive mood, called up the children one by one to squirt a steaming jet of milk into their mouths. When my turn came, my mother, not being there, did not see me run as fast as I could away from the cows and the cook, past the vegetable garden and the goldfish pond, down to the farthermost wall, where I lay down in the grass and tried to faint, but couldn't.

I knew the spot from prior humiliations, I admit. It was where I had hidden twice in the week when I was caught eating cauliflower and was made to eat kidney. The cauliflower came first—it emerged as a fragrant little head in the vegetable garden, a bumpy vegetable brain that looked innocent and edible enough to make me a perfect victim when it called. In that era my greatest illicit joy was hastily chewing off the top of each new cauliflower when no one else was looking. The early morning was my favorite time, because then those flowers felt firm and crisp with dew. I would go to the vegetable patch and squat over the cauliflowers as they came out one by one, hold them between my knees, and chew as many craters as I could into their jaunty tightness. Qayuum was crushed. "There is an animal, Begum Sahib," he mourned to my mother, "like a savage in my garden. *Maro! Maro!*" To hear him made me nervous, so the following morning I tried to deflect attention from the cauliflowers by quickly pulling out all the little radishes while they were still pencil-thin: they lay on the soil like a pathetic accumulation of red herrings. That was when Munni caught me. "*Abba Ii!*" she screamed for her father like a train engine. Everybody came running, and for a while my squat felt frozen to the ground as I looked up at an overabundance of astonished adult faces. "What are you doing, Sara *Bibi*?" the driver finally and gently asked. "Smelling the radishes," I said in a baby and desperate defiance, "so that the animal can't find the cauliflower." "Which one?" "The new cauliflower." "Which animal, *bibi ji*, you naughty girl?" "The one that likes to eat the cauliflower that I like to smell." And when they laughed at me, I did not know where to put my face for shame.

They caught me out that week, two times over, because after I had been exposed as the cauliflower despoiler and had to enter a new phase of penitence, Qayuum the cook insisted on making me eat kidney. *"Kirrnee,"* he would call it with a glint in his eye, *"kirrnee."* My mother quite agreed that I should learn such discipline, and the complicated ritual of endurance they imposed did make me teach myself to take a kidney taste without dwelling too long on the peculiarities of kidney texture. I tried to be unsurprised by the mushroom pleats that constitute a kidney's underbelly and by the knot of membrane that holds those kidney folds in place. One day Qayuum insisted that only kidneys could sit on my plate, mimicking legumes and ignoring their thin and bloody juices. Wicked Ifat came into the room and waited till I had started eating; then she intervened. "Sara," said Ifat, her eyes brimming over with wonderful malice, "do you know what kidneys do?" I aged, and my meal regressed, back to its vital belonging in the world of function. "Kidneys make pee, Sara," Ifat told me, "That's what they do, they make pee." And she looked so pleased to be able to tell me that; it made her feel so full of information. Betrayed by food, I let her go, and wept some watery tears into the kidney juice, which was designed anyway to evade cohesion, being thin and in its nature inexact. Then I ran out to the farthermost corner of the garden, where I would later go to hide my shame of milking-time in a retch that refused to materialize.

Born the following year, Tillat would not know that cautionary tale. Nor would she know what Ifat did when my father called from Lady Willingdon Hospital in Lahore to repeat that old phrase, "It is a girl." "It's a girl!" Ifat shouted, as though simply clinching for the world the overwhelming triumph of her will. Shahid, a year my senior, was found half an hour later sobbing next to the goldfish pond near the vegetable garden, for he had been banking on the diluting arrival of a brother. He must have been upset, because when we were taken to visit my mother, he left his penguin—a favorite toy—among the old trees of the hospital garden, where we had been sent to play. I was still uncertain about my relation to the status of this new baby: my sister was glad that it was a girl, and my brother was sad that it wasn't a boy, but we all stood together when penguiny was lost.

It is to my discredit that I forgot this story, both of what the kidney said and what it could have told to my still germinating sister. Had I borne something of those lessons in mind, it would have been less of a shock to have to reconceive the *kapura* parable; perhaps I'd have been prepared for more skepticism about the connection between kidneys and sweetbreads—after all, they fall into no logical category of togetherness. The culinary humor of kidneys and testicles stewing in one another's juices is, on the other hand, very fine: I wish I had had the imagination to intuit all the unwonted jokes people tell when they start cooking food. I should have remembered all those nervously comic edges, and the pangs, that constitute most poignancies of nourishment. And so, as an older mind, I fault myself for not having the wits to recognize what I already knew. I must have always known exactly what *kapura* are, because the conversation they provoked came accompanied with shocks of familiarity that typically attend a trade of solid information. What I had really wanted to reply, first to Tillat and then to my Pakistani friends, was: yes, of course, who do you think I am, what else could they *possibly be?* Anyone with discrimination could immediately discern the connection between *kapura* and their namesake: the shape is right, given that we are now talking about goats; the texture involves a bit of a bounce, which works; and the taste is altogether too exactly what it is. So I should have kept in mind that, alas, we know the flavor of each part of the anatomy: That much imagination belongs to everyone's palate. Once, when my sisters and I were sitting in a sunny winter garden, Tillat began examining some ants that were tumbling about the blades of grass next to her chair. She looked acute and then suddenly said, "How very sour those little ants must be." Ifat declared that she had always thought the same herself, and though I never found out how they arrived at this discovery, I was impressed by it, their ability to take the world on their tongues.

So poor Irfani, how much his infant taste buds must have colored his perception of the grimness of each day. Irfan was born in London, finally another boy, but long after Shahid had ceased looking for playmates in the home. It now strikes me as peculiar that my parents should choose to move back to Pakistan when Farni was barely a year old, and to decide on June, that most pitiless month, in which to return to Lahore. The heat shriveled the baby, giving his face an expression of slow and bewildered shock, which was compounded by the fact that for the next year there was very little that the child could eat. Water boiled ten times over would still retain virulence enough to send his body into derangements, and goat's milk, cow's milk, everything liquid seemed to convey malevolence to his minuscule gut. We used to scour the city for aging jars of imported baby-food; these, at least, he would eat, though with a look of profound mistrust—but even so, he spent most of the next year with his body in violent rebellion against the idea of food. It gave his eyes a gravity they have never lost.

Youngster he was, learning lessons from an infant's intuition to fear food, and to some degree all of us were equally watchful for hidden trickeries in the scheme of nourishment, for the way in which things would always be missing or out of place in Pakistan's erratic emotional market. Items of security—such as flour or butter or cigarettes or tea— were always vanishing, or returning in such dubiously shiny attire that we could barely stand to look at them. We lived in the expectation of threatening surprise: a crow had drowned in the water tank on the roof, so for a week we had been drinking dead-crow water and couldn't understand why we felt so ill; the milkman had accidentally diluted our supply of milk with paraffin instead of water; and those were not pistachios, at all, in a tub of Hico's green ice cream. Our days and our newspapers were equally full of disquieting tales about adulterated foods and the preternaturally keen eye that the nation kept on such promiscuous blendings. I can understand it, the fear that food will not stay discrete but will instead defy our categories of expectation in what can only be described as a manner of extreme belligerence. I like order to a plate, and know the great sense of failure that attends a moment when what is potato to the fork is turnip to the mouth. It's hard, when such things happen.

So, long before the *kapura* made its comeback in my life, we in Pakistan were bedmates with betrayal and learned how to take grim satisfaction from assessing the water table of our outrage. There were both lean times and meaty times, however; occasionally, body and food would sit happily at the same side of the conference table. Take, for example, Ramzan, the Muslim month of fasting, often recollected as the season of perfect meals. Ramzan, a lunar thing, never arrives at the same point of time each year, coming instead with an aura of slight and pleasing dislocation. Somehow it always took us by surprise: new moons are startling to see, even by accident, and Ramzan's moon betokened a month of exquisite precision about the way we were to parcel out our time. On the appointed evenings we would rake the twilight for that possible sliver, and it made the city and body both shudder with expectation to spot that little slip of a moon that signified Ramzan and made the sky historical. How busy Lahore would get! Its minarets hummed, its municipalities pulled out their old air-raid sirens to make the city noisily cognizant: the moon had been sighted, and the fast begun.

I liked it, the waking up an hour before dawn to eat the prefast meal and chat in whispers. For three wintry seasons I would wake up with Dadi, my grandmother, and Ifat and Shahid: we sat around for hours making jokes in the dark, generating a discourse of unholy comradeship. The food itself, designed to keep the penitent sustained from dawn till dusk, was insistent in its richness and intensity, with bread dripping clarified butter, and curried brains, and cumin eggs, and a peculiarly potent vermicelli, soaked overnight in sugar and fatted milk.

And if I liked the getting up at dawn, then Dadi completely adored the eating of it all. I think she fasted only because she so enjoyed the *sehri* meal and that mammoth infusion of food at such an extraordinary hour. At three in the morning the rest of us felt squeamish about linking the deep sleep dreams we had just conducted and so much grease—we asked instead for porridge—but Dadi's eating was a sight to behold and admire. She hooted when the city's sirens sounded to tell us that we should stop eating and that the fast had now begun: she enjoyed a more direct relation with God than did petty municipal authorities and was fond of declaiming what Muhammad himself had said in her defense. He apparently told one of his contemporaries that *sehri* did not end until a white thread of light described the horizon and separated the landscape from the sky. In Dadi's book that thread could open into quite an active loom of dawning: the world made waking sounds, the birds and milkmen all resumed their proper functions, but Dadi's regal mastication—on the last brain now—declared it still was night.

I stopped that early rising years before Tillat and Irfan were old enough to join us, before Ifat ran away to get married, and before my father returned to ritual and overtook his son Shahid's absent place. So my memories of it are scant, the fast of the faithful. But I never lost my affection for the twilight meal, the dusky *iftar* that ended the fast after the mosques had lustily rung with the call for the *maghrib* prayer. We'd start eating dates, of course, in order to mimic Muhammad, but then with what glad eyes we'd welcome the grilled liver and the tang of pepper in the orange juice. We were happy to see the spinach leaves and their fantastical shapes, deftly fried in the lightest chick-pea batter, along with the tenderness of fresh fruit, most touching to the palate. There was a curious invitation about the occasion, converting what began as an act of penance into a godly and obligatory cocktail hour that provided a fine excuse for company and affability. When we lived in Pakistan, that little swerve from severity into celebration happened often. It certainly was true of meatless days.

ISRAEL—FORGING A NATIONAL STYLE
WITH GEFILTE FISH AND COUSCOUS

CLAUDIA RODEN

When I first went to Israel, more than twenty years ago, to see my relatives and to find out what was happening in the kitchen, people would say, "Please don't write anything bad," or "Why don't you write a sexy novel instead?" Visitors then always complained about the food and had praise only for Arab restaurants, most of which were mere kiosks at the back of gas stations. They would ask, "What happened to all the foods from all those different countries?" This year, friends were keen to take me to wonderful new restaurants, to make me try new products and to talk about cooking. But when I asked about trends I was told, "It's for you to find out and to tell us," as though an outsider was better able to discern.

Since the establishment of the state, everything has changed constantly, as we should expect from a new land of immigrants from more than seventy countries where each new wave of settlers has brought something new. Culinary trends are sometimes contradictory. They have to do with the economic and political situation, with the direction the food industries take, the fruits the kibbutzim decide to grow, the fish that are farmed. Trends also depend on the mix of population, on who works in the kitchens of the land, who sells food in the street, and who is in the business of catering for weddings and bar mitzvahs. Moreover, ideology is involved. In the early days of the state, the Diaspora and its food was something to be forgotten, but now it is back in a big way.

What you can see is a longing for a national cuisine so that, as Israelis say, "we can feel at ease at each other's tables." Thirty years ago, an Israeli writer expressed the view that: "We will be near to becoming one nation when we can sit at each other's tables without feeling unease or strangeness. Liking each other's foods is a big step

towards liking each other." It is part of the need for cohesion in this eth-
nically mixed society, where cooking in the home is a mosaic acquired
in the four corners of the world—where Eastern European food is considered "Jewish" and the rest "ethnic" and where Arab street food such
as falafel, hummus, babaghanouzh, shakshouka, and Moroccan cigars
is considered Israeli. Only turkey schnitzel, which is the main food
eaten regularly by everybody, and not shared with neighboring Arab
countries, is identified as purely Israeli.

Trendy chefs and food writers try to create a new Israeli cuisine
using Biblical ingredients such as honey, figs, and pomegranates;
indigenous foods, like prickly pears and chickpeas; and Israeli produce,
like avocado, citrus, mango, and cream cheese, which the national fruit
and dairy boards are promoting. They use French. Italian, and Chinese
techniques, and flavors from the ethnic communities. They do so with
an eye on *The New York Times'* food pages and *Gourmet* magazine and
the latest fads an California. America's appeal is powerful, and it is easier for Israelis to identify with a young country of emigration. They call
what they are doing "melting-pot" cooking and "fusion cuisine."

There is another kind of "fusion cuisine" which develops by itself
and has nothing to do with fads and fashions. One example is the
falafel in pita now offered by vendors with a choice of salads and pickles and peppery relishes such as the Yemeni zhoug and Moroccan haris-
sa. A new hybrid, which I found at an Ethiopian snack bar near the old
Tel Aviv bus station, is the "Jerusalem mix"—a chopped-up mixture of
fried chicken giblets and offal—flavored with the fiery-hot spices of
Ethiopia. One could say that much of the food produced in the army,
hospitals, schools, and institutional cafeterias can be classed as "fusion
cuisine." A disgruntled hotel food-and-beverages manager called what
has developed in the kitchens of the land "a horrible mishmash of what
cooks learn from each other, usually when they are in the army."

The mishmash is a far cry from the cooking of one of the first established Jewish communities in Palestine, which was made up of families
from Syria, Lebanon, and Turkey, who came to be known as the
"Jerusalem aristocracy." They were highly sophisticated about food and
possessed a wide repertoire of delicacies on which they lavished much
time, starting sometimes to prepare on Sunday for the following Sabbath.
Their dishes—pies like sambousak, pasteles, and borekas, vegetable
gratins and stuffed vegetables, rice and bulghur pilafs, delicately flavored
with herbs and spices and aromatics like tamarind, sour pomegranate
syrup, and flower waters—are now considered Jerusalem classics.

Apart from these Oriental Jews, established long before the creation
of the state of Israel, there were those who came to Palestine to die, and

ultrareligious Ashkenazi communities who came for a pious life. The Zionist *halutzim* (pioneers), who migrated from Russia and Poland at the beginning of the century to start the first kibbutzim, or cooperative settlements, brought with them a deep sense of mission and socialist ideology, and they founded Israel as a puritanical society with the ideals of the simple life. The bread, olives, cheese, and raw vegetables which they ate at 9 A.M., after they had been working for four hours in the fields, was the basis of the famous kibbutz breakfast, which in its more opulent form is standard fare in all hotels in Israel today. The self-service consists of many types of cheese, soft and hard; pickled and smoked herring; yogurt, leben, and sour cream; olives and hard-boiled eggs, served up with a variety of breads and accompanied by fresh orange juice and coffee. Tomatoes, cucumbers, and scallions are served whole for everyone to create his or her own salad. There are also a variety of prepared salads including grated carrot, peppers, and cole slaw, and omelettes, eggplant purees, hummus, and pickles, followed by compotes of figs and plums and fresh fruit. These "kibbutz foods" have become a national institution and have been adopted by Israelis for their light everyday evening meals as well as for breakfast. The puritanical legacy is expressed today as a profound distaste for the Israeli enthusiasm for food, seen as "conspicuous consumption" and "oral fixation."

The early pioneers and the first immigrants from Europe to the newly established state were happy to abandon the "Yiddish" foods of Russia and Poland as a revolt against a past identity and an old life. Zionism's early desire had been to leave the shtetl behind and to break with everything it stood for. The new state lived by a vision of the future and looked with distaste at the foods that represented exile and martyrdom. There was no place in the Promised Land for food that smelled of persecution and anti-Semitism. Anyway, it was not suitable in the hot Mediterranean climate.

The new Hebrew type, the antithesis of the old passive Jew, looked for his identity in the Bible, and it was assumed that the Yemenites and Oriental Sephardim were closest to the early Jews of Biblical times. The European immigrants learned from the old, established Sephardim how to use the local produce, especially vegetables such as zucchini, peppers, eggplant, and artichokes, which were new to them. The food of the local fellahin (villagers) and Bedouin Arabs had a strong appeal for the early Zionists. They were shepherds and dressed like the Biblical figures depicted by nineteenth-century painters, and represented their forefathers in appearance and way of life. Arab and Oriental food like hummus and falafel, both of which are based on the indigenous chickpea, exerted a powerful pull on the young. It was very tasty and cheap, and it was offered by street vendors, at a time when eating a cheap snack on the go was becoming a way of life.

The first ten or more years after the establishment of the state in 1948, when the country was isolated and at war with all her neighbors, have left their mark in the kitchen. Many refugees lived in absorption camps; apartments were small and sometimes had three families sharing. People cooked on tiny oil stoves in pots called "sirpella" (we called them *casseroles palestiniennes),* which are still used today to save on fuel. There were no refrigerators, only iceboxes, and at mealtime dining tables had to be dragged from under school books and sewing. The Tzena period, as it is called, was a time of rationing, of making do from nothing, from what you got with coupons. And dose memories of the Holocaust were not conducive to inspired cooking. A legacy of those times of scarcity and austerity is a repertoire of mock or simulated foods which are the popular butt of humorists. They were ingenious ways of making something out of something else—chopped liver from eggplant, applesauce from zucchini, radish jam as a substitute for cherry jam, semolina pudding instead of whipped cream, and turkey as a substitute for veal schnitzel or for lamb in kebabs. Restaurants at the time also served an ubiquitous fish "fillet"—an unidentifiable compressed fish mixture imported from Norway—nondescript "white" cheese, yogurt and salad, bean-and-vegetable soup, mushy pasta with a little goulash. You only went to the restaurant if your mother was sick and there was nothing to eat in the house. Pioneers and volunteers never went; by their standards, only decadent people spent time in restaurants.

Part of the normalization process in the late 1970s—explained as the euphoria of finally emerging from the trauma of deprivation and austerity and the constant threat of war into a new affluence with greater travel facilities and the peace with Egypt—was an explosion of interest in food, from French cuisine and the exotic dishes of China, Hawaii, and Bali, to cooking with wine and herbs and healthy vegetarianism. Eating out in restaurants became a popular recreation.

At home today, people still on the whole eat according to their background. In street markets, as in the frozen and chilled food sections in the supermarket, you see a variety of foods of different origins. You find Bulgarian yogurt-and-cucumber salad and Bulgarian palamida (marinated bonito), Iraqi kubba and Syrian kibbeh, Turkish borek, Yemeni flaky and spongy breads and hot peppery zhoug, Moroccan cigars, Polish lokshen pudding, Russian piroshki, Hungarian blintzes, and Viennese tortes. Every group of immigrants has made an impact, and the repertoire of foods at people's disposal is forever growing.

The greatest impact has come from the large Sephardi migration, and most particularly from Morocco, which forms the largest single ethnic group. The Sephardim are seen as knowing and caring more about food. A young Moroccan cook explained: "The Ashkenazim are more concerned with getting on, studying and going to university. We want to enjoy our life. We like to keep the family together round the table with friends chatting and joking. The mother cooks so that the children come back on Shabbath, even when they are married."

For years, the kitchens of the land—from the army, schools, and hospitals to restaurants and hotels—have recruited their staff from the working-class population of Oriental Jews, from countries like Morocco, Tunisia, Turkey, Iraq, Kurdistan, and Yemen, and Israeli Arabs. Caterers too are from the Middle East. But despite its predominance, North African and Oriental food is seen as low-class, poor food. As Israelis often complain, it is the poor Sephardim who settled in Israel, while the rich and educated have gone elsewhere.

When I express my appreciation of Moroccan dishes to some of my Israeli friends, they look surprised, to say the least. The truth is that the cooking standards of Moroccan immigrants have deteriorated in Israel more than in other countries. One catering manager explained it in this way: "The cooks have rejected their mothers' cooking, because they see it as part of a humiliating backward culture. Yet, after learning the basics at the army catering school, they fall back on what they vaguely remember from home." In the early days of their massive immigration, the Sephardim were labeled backward and primitive. It was believed that the way to transform them into modern Israelis was to make them forget their backward Oriental past and assimilate them into the dominant Ashkenazi culture. The "melting-pot" policy was at the expense of Sephardi cultural pride and identity. It has a lot to answer for in the state of the kitchens.

Things have changed now. Intensive attempts are made to restore the lost pride of all the ethnic communities by reviving and disseminating their rich cultural heritage. The media make much of ethnic foods. Women's magazines and radio announcers ask people to send in recipes from their old hometowns and children are encouraged to bring their mothers' special dishes to share at school. Although it is still not fashionable for trendy restaurants to admit to Arab and Oriental influences, "Mediterranean" styles are in and young chefs visit their parents' old homelands to rediscover the more refined dishes.

The Diaspora has become fashionable, with a revival of interest in roots in old homelands and a strong nostalgia for the past. While Israelis are struggling to define themselves, confronted daily by the questions of their rights to the land and of who is a Jew, they have felt the need for an older cultural heritage to fall back on. Young people are rediscovering their roots through the Jewish writers of America and a revival of Yiddish music, theatre, and food. Gefilte fish, cholent, kishke, tzimmes, and lokshen pudding are "in," imbued with the charm of nostalgia and sentimentality. Once you found these dishes in the big hotels catering for American tourists; now the trendy cafés that offer "Jewish food" are places where the young congregate.

Like other aspects of cultural heritage, the food is being decided by the new generation. People look at each other's food when they get together on Friday nights and when they eat at weddings and bar mitzvahs. As one caterer told me, they have to offer an enormous selection, because their clients choose an enormous list so that "everybody will be satisfied." There has to be everything—from gefilte fish and latkes to Moroccan cigars and stuffed vine leaves.

Israelis love food and, judging by how busy the vendors are all day, they eat all the time. National insecurity is given as one reason for the constant noshing or grazing. Another is the traditional Eastern European idea of good mothering by constant feeding, immortalized in the old joke about the Jewish mother who presses food on her offspring to induce guilt, and in the refrain of a seventies song that translates, "Danile, Danile, eat your bananile!" Who knows? Things change so fast, by the time this book [*The Book of Jewish Food*] comes out, Israel might be on the gastronomic tourist map.

PLIGHT DU JOUR

JAY JACOBS

M OST AMERICAN FOOD WRITERS attribute their putative expertise to their early exposure to the definitive cookery of a parent or mentor— usually a mother or household domestic who specialized in regional or some sort of ethnic fare. I had no such exposure. My father and mother fancied themselves an epicure and a cook, respectively. Both were mistaken. My old man inhaled Russian caviar, Cuban cigars, old cognac, and ripely odoriferous French and Italian cheeses on the rare occasions when he was solvent, but his tastes were formed solely by the market value of his choices, and if potatoes had been priced at twenty dollars an ounce, he'd have scoffed down the spuds just as ostentatiously. A dedicated philanderer, he spent as little time as possible in the bosom of his family (thereby sparing himself my mother's cooking) before cutting out for good when I was in my late teens, and my memory of him is largely olfactory. A self-styled inventor among other things, he spent his infrequent sessions at home in the kitchen, where he cooked up noisome batches of chemicals and reeking paraffin mixtures in his bootless attempts to perfect a fire-retardant paint and a hard-boiled egg with an infinite shelf life. His scheme for the latter was to stock vending machines with the immortal hen fruit and install the machines in gin mills across the nation, with a fair proportion of which he was intimately familiar.

My mother, a freelance fashion illustrator, sometime photographers' model, and erstwhile companion of assorted bohemians in her native Greenwich Village, could boil water without noticeably diminishing its flavor, but that was about the extent of her culinary skills. During my early tadpolehood, she specialized in what might be termed audiovisual cuisine. The first meals I can remember with any clarity took the form of storybook landscapes, with castles of mashed potato, forests of spinach, stepping-stone paths of sliced carrot, and gardens of topiary broccoli, all overcooked to a uniform grayness (her style was sculptural, rather than painterly), with a voice-over narration by the author. Every meal was a novella, rich in incident but short on flavor.

Gastronomically, life took a turn for the better during my tenth and eleventh years, which were spent in the Pocono Mountains of eastern Pennsylvania. Having deposited his family on a farm there one summer, my father decided to prolong our visit indefinitely while he conducted a dalliance in New York with a young woman who, it was rumored, was a redhead, a communist, and the mother of his bastard son. (I never was able to determine which of the charges most incensed my mother, but I suspect it was the first. She herself remained raven-haired, and proud of it, until her death in her early seventies.)

The owners of the farm rented a few rooms to summer guests, who were fed, family-style, three times a day. It was at the communal table that I tasted, actually tasted, food for the first time. Honest-to-God, dirt-scratching chickens were killed every Sunday for dinner, and great heaping platters of flapjacks were served every morning with home-cured ham or bacon, eggs fresh from the hen-house, butter churned an hour earlier, and foaming milk still udderwarm and redolent of cow. Sweet corn was picked while the pot boiled, and tomatoes were sliced and eaten while they still smelled of sun and vine. Behind the barn was a vast thicket of raspberries, and I'd devour handfuls of fruit on the spot, like a young bear, lacerated by thorns and bitten mercilessly by the mosquitoes that swarmed there. I gathered cool peppery watercress from the shallows of the creek and was paid a dime a bushel for the elderberries I picked, which I assumed were named for the female elders who made wine from them.

On the farm, I got my first lessons not only in how real foods smelled and tasted, but in the genesis and nurture and the often brutal realities of their production and preparation for the kitchen. I'd been told from infancy that hens laid eggs, cows gave milk, and bacon came from pigs. As a city kid, however, I'd seen less evidence in support of these fables than in support of the Tooth Fairy or Santa Claus. My knowledge of most of the foods I'd eaten was made up of abstractions so confusing that, in an attempt to find out something about egg production at age six or seven, I had asked, How many chickens [meaning to say eggs] get laid in a week?" It wasn't until the onset of puberty that I learned what my parents had found so hilarious about a simple slip of the tongue.

During that summer, I learned to milk the cows, gather the eggs, feed the stock, and skin whatever eels I caught, after nailing them by their heads to the barn door. I witnessed the beheadings of the Sunday chickens and wondered for some years thereafter whether Marie Antoinette had flapped around in a bloody circle when the blade fell on her neck. I became intimate with chicken shit, cow flop, and slop buckets and learned respect for their usefulness in the food cycle.

Between chores and play, I'd hang around the kitchen, where the women of the farm spent the better part of their daylight hours putting up the next winter's provisions as the summer wore on. Happily immersed in the sweet steamy fug that built up as hundreds of pounds of fruit were converted to jams and jellies, I was given the job of slipping peaches from skins loosened by a brief bath in boiling water. I lugged case after case of quart Mason jars from a storeroom to the kitchen, where they were sterilized and filled with stewed tomatoes, beans, corn, and various pickle relishes, later to be arrayed in gleaming rows in the dark cellar pantry. As summer waned, cabbage was shredded, salted, and weighted in earthenware crocks for a long winter's supply of sauerkraut, and tubers were stored in the root cellar. From time to time, when the sweet sultry air of the kitchen began to cloy, I'd wander off to the icehouse, toss a couple of burlap sacks over a frozen block, and drowse in a cooler season, inhaling the clean aromas of earth, lake water, and wet sawdust.

Summer's end changed the tempo and texture of life on the farm. The other boarders were gone (including a kid my age named Billy Steeper, who had never tired of reminding me that a wooded hill on the property was steep but he was Steeper), and the kitchen increasingly became the focus of activity as the days grew shorter and cooler. I was enrolled in a one-room schoolhouse some two miles through woods and fields from the farm and adjacent to a general store that stocked a maddeningly comprehensive assortment of penny candies. My school days began with light chores and the usual hearty breakfast. Then I'd be handed my lunch box (invariably packed, like everyone else's, with a ripely fartable egg sandwich) and sent off to dawdle through terrain exploding with pheasant and partridge.

Lessons began after allegiance to the flag was pledged and the morning's hymn—"The Old Rugged Cross," "Rock of Ages," or the like—was sung by the entire student body, whereupon sliding partitions were closed, separating grades two through five, and the hours until midday recess ticked interminably by.

Recess impelled a mad rush to the general store, where forty-odd kids would jostle for position at the candy counter, each clutching a penny or two and stooping before the bowfront glass in agonies of indecision. There were licorice ropes in red and black and nonpareils and jawbreakers; gummy red Indian-head coins and the inch-high chocolate figurines then universally known as "nigger babies" and Hershey's Kisses in bright foil sprouting tissue umbilical cords; rock candy (both crystalline and amber) and peanut brittle and sour balls; marzipan bananas that tasted disconcertingly like castor oil and colored sugar dots stuck on yard-long strips of paper and crinkly foil cups with peanut butter fillings; sugary green peppermint leaves and cayenne-charged red devils and candy corn and a near-infinitude of other delights. Decisions were taken and changed as many as a dozen times by each kid before the irrevocable choice was made; finally, in a poignant ritual altogether new to me, each child would return to the schoolyard and solemnly present what had been chosen to another.

Much later, it seemed obvious that the recess exchange of penny candies was an acting-out in microcosm of the prevailing ethos of the region during the Depression. The sharing of food by people who had little else to share amounted to a way of life in the Poconos, as it probably did in much of rural America at the time. Farmers who could afford a few rounds of shot would parcel out their bounty of game to the entire community, and people who were seldom able to put butcher's meat on the table would regularly feast in season on squirrel, rabbit, venison, bear, partridge, quail, and pheasant. When the women of the area gathered in a farmhouse parlor for the weekly quilting bee, they'd bring covered dishes along, and marvelous cakes and pies and homemade candy. My own contributions were windfall hickory nuts and black walnuts, gathered on the way home from school and cracked open with a hammer on an iron stove lid.

The gastronomic high point of the season was Halloween, when everyone in the region turned up at dusk in Stroudsburg, the nearest town of any size, where trestle tables laden with food ran end to end along the length of the main drag and communal gluttony continued long past everyone's normal bedtime. As I remember the scene, it was straight out of Pieter Brueghel the Elder's Peasant Wedding, with the addition of half-naked young bucks, painted up as Indian braves, who pounded huge war clubs against the macadam, setting off the light explosive charges loaded in the club heads.

We left the farm toward the end of the year, with several months' board unpaid, and relocated to the smaller of Stroudsburg's two hotels. It was a momentarily wrenching break for me to be cut off from an extended family (with whose only daughter, eight years my senior, I thought I had fallen eternally in love) and what had seemed an idyllic existence. Life in town soon took on an allure of its own, however, although the food didn't measure up to the other compensatory pleasures. Breakfast was provided by the hotel, but otherwise my mother exercised her meager culinary talents on a hot plate in our rooms. Our meals seemed pathetically inadequate after months of sumptuous feeding on the farm; indeed, they were pretty awful. My mother was the only cook I've ever known who regularly resorted to canned potatoes. An occasional piece of donated game and the odd few slices of baloney excepted, the only meat I can recall eating during our stay in Stroudsburg was the hotel's breakfast bacon, most of my share of which was snaffled up by Skinny Brand, an impoverished farm kid who went miles out of his way to join me in the dining room on his way to school.

Having defaulted on our hotel rent (as he had on our farm board) for months on end, my father was reluctantly compelled to resume some semblance of familial responsibility. Temporarily forsaking his red-haired mistress and their rumored child, he turned up in Stroudsburg one weekend, packed us into the car, and drove us to New York, where he had rented an apartment on the extreme Upper West Side, somewhere on the outskirts of Newfoundland. Perhaps because I detested the neighborhood, my memories of life there are rather spotty.

My best friends and only social dining companions of that period were Johnny Bloomer and Mario Gangi. Johnny, an Irish janitor's son, subsisted exclusively on potatoes, eating them three times a day, boiled, at home, and roasting them over street bonfires between meals. The roasted spuds, known as mickeys, were filched in wholesale lots from the neighborhood greengrocers, who unwittingly abetted the thieves by providing them with fuel in the form of discarded fruit crates. The roasting of mickeys did not require the culinary genius of an Escoffier. The potatoes were simply tossed into the fire and left there until thickly encrusted with charcoal. Mickey connoisseurs were readily recognizable by their blackened lips and teeth, their blistered fingers, and their smoky aroma. Thanks to the flavorlessness of my mother's cooking, the taste memory of those mickeys is one of the very few I can summon up from that time of my life. In retrospect, their charred sapor seems as delectable as the hot paving tar kids chewed in rural Pennsylvania.

Mario Gangi was an uncommonly handsome kid with huge liquid brown eyes and wavy black hair. These features looked even better on his sister, who also had breasts that left me sick with desire. Mario and I occasionally played ball after school. One afternoon, when he had neglected to bring his glove, we went to get it at his family's apartment. His mother, an immigrant from Naples, insisted that we have something to eat before we left. Classically, she exhorted us to *"Mangia, mangia"* as she served up heaping plates of *pollo alla cacciatore*. It was the most savory food I'd ever put in my mouth, and it introduced me to a culinary genre with which I've since conducted a passionate love affair.

The wholesome, hearty food of the Poconos had been a revelation of sorts, with its straightforward, uncomplicated flavors of earth and air and sunshine and rainwater, but Signora Gangi's dish, a commonplace in the Italian repertory, invested eating with dimensions I'd never suspected. Judiciously applied quantities of gently sauteed garlic, unknown to the Pennsylvania Dutch, lent subtle pungency to the orchestration, as did olive oil, oregano, rosemary, mushrooms, tomatoes, and onions. The dish resonated with a vibrancy I could no more have imagined than I could a previously unknown color. It contrasted textures and aromas I'd never before experienced; it was the mucilaginous product of elderly, flavorsome flesh, gently braised on the bone until it fell away at the touch of a fork, releasing clouds of seductive perfume. Decades and thousands of meals after the fact, it remains the most affecting dish I've ever experienced and the one I try to replicate when in dire need of elemental maternal comfort. Mario Gangi lived in a roach-infested cold-water tenement flat. I envied his startling good looks, his beautiful sister's disturbing presence, and his mama's chicken cacciatore more than I ever have envied anyone else's more generally coveted blessings. If some parsimonious fairy godmother offered me just one of the usual three wishes, I guess I'd go for the chicken.

MEAT

SALLIE TISDALE

I WENT TO THE BUTCHER'S several times a week as a child. Meat was always in my life. The butcher shop was just down the street from our house, past the old, squat Carnegie Library, the Elks Club, the Groceteria, the bakery, and the big stucco fire department with its long driveway. I loved the Meat Market best; it was orderly, with the hushed front room encased in windows. The floor was golden oak, shiny and clean, facing a horseshoe of white metal display cases curving away like the fabric of space. The air held the scent of clean skin.

I would lay my hot cheeks against the cool glass and gaze at the meat inside: flaccid steaks, roasts, and sausages in neat rows like tile or shingles laid atop each other in patterns of soft red, pink, and maroon. I knew the textures—they were my textures. I liked to examine the down on my legs, the way the irises of my eyes opened and closed when I turned the light above the bathroom mirror off and on, the intricate maze of my belly button. I pulled scabs off and chewed them, and licked the ooze that followed. The rump roast in the glass case made a delicate curve, the curve of my own pliable buttocks. Me, but not me.

I was an inscrutable child, I think, a puzzle to my mother, who had had a girl's youth of starch and oxfords. I threw off the nice things she wrapped around me. My feet are still hard and rough, jerkied from the dry days spent wandering my little town, dashing over the softened asphalt in summer, wrapped in hardy boots in the cold.

On panting summer days the basement beckoned, crowded and lifeless, the air cool, musty, and dim after the glazed sunlight. No one would find me there, if anyone cared to look. Most of the small basement was filled with a freezer, which my mother, one in a long line of carefully organized women, kept always filled as a hedge against catastrophe. (Distantly, my mother's voice at the top of the stairs: "Shut the freezer!"—trailing off into words I didn't bother to hear.) Its heavy white lid seemed to lift from the stiff latch with relief, and swing up so that a waft of the freezer's queer fog blew in my face. My taut, tanned skin could breathe again in the damp. There was often a whole side of beef in the freezer at a time, broken up among the TV dinners and the quails of bean soup and the ice cream. Each cut was wrapped in white freezer paper, and labeled with a red wax crayon in strange abbreviations: "FLK STK 4 #" and "P CHOPS - 6." The irregular, heavy packets sat in the cold trough like a haphazard pile of white rocks littered with food.

The ancient grass skirt my father had brought home from the War hung on one wall, its clackety tendrils yellow with age. He kept a safe there, too, tucked inside a rough cavity torn by hammers from the cement foundation. Here were the dusty boxes of Christmas tree lights, the empty jam jars, a bike frame, a trunk, the lethal table saw I was never to touch. My silences were sometimes the silence of the lost, the wandering, but they could be deliberate and ungiving, too. I would lean on a post beside the freezer and fade half away from the world gazing at my father's old toy train, wrecked against a tiny hillside.

There was never a meal without meat; every afternoon the house filled with the scents of frying oil and roasting flesh. The long dining table leaned towards my father's end, anticipating the heavy cuts on the platter beside him—the pot roast, the round roast beef, the piles of rust-colored chops dripping juice. He carved. At Thanksgiving he leaned over the enormous turkey to get a good purchase, the double blades of the electric carving knife slicing in a noisy blur. When he lost his temper at the table, voices suddenly raised, a hand out to swat, to knock aside a complaining child, he forgot the knife sometimes, holding it out in front like a Samurai, as he bellowed at us three children. On quiet nights we squabbled for drumsticks, thick hamburger patties, the fatty end of the roast. I always had the chicken's back with its fat, heart-shaped tail that my grandmother called the pope's nose, and when we were done our plates were littered with the rags of bones.

My father was a volunteer fireman; it was his one great victory. Like all the firemen, he had a closed-circuit radio with its own codes and shrill calls, so we could follow the progress and crises of each fire from a distance. The town had a siren for everyone else, and its long whooing call was as sweet as the coo of a dove to me. Every few weeks, the alarm would sound during dinner, and he would move so fast, so instinctively, that time seemed to stand still: the knife or fork or bite of food falls to the table, his chair scrapes back along the floor, we children scoot close to the table out of his way as he thunders past, "Goddammit!" trailing him out the back door, the door slams and seconds later his pickup roars out of the driveway. My mother listens to the radio, we go get our books, because when my dad is gone my mother lets us read at the table. Afterwards, she takes us to the Richmaid for ice cream.

Buying meat was like this every time: I am with my mother, an efficient, plain woman with the smell of academics around her. She much preferred reading to cooking, but she cooked every day. The butcher, Mr. Bryan, is my father's best friend. He stands behind the counter, a tall jolly man with a hard round stomach covered in a white apron streaked with blood. He has saved his best meat for my mother, kept it apart for her inspection: a pot roast, a particular steak, perhaps giblets saved for her special dressing, the hard nubbins of chicken hearts and kidneys, the tiny livers purple-red like gems in his palm.

Now and then Mr. Bryan went to the back of the store and brought my mother something really special: a whole beef heart, balanced like a waxy pyramid on his hands, or a cow's tongue, one of my favorite things. Sometimes I would come into the kitchen in the middle of the morning and find a tongue set out waiting for the pot, an enormous apostrophe of flesh covered in pale papillae. Tongue takes forever to cook, boiling for many hours on the stove, and it filled the kitchen with a tender mist and steamed the windows gray. When it was done, my mother sliced the tongue as soft as angel cake into thin, delicious strips unlike anything else, melting, perfumed. When all the rest of the world wouldn't bend, flesh would bend. That was what flesh was.

Mr. Bryan spreads his hands full of meat on stiff wax paper out to my mother, as though making an offering, and at her nod lays the flesh upon the scale. Together, with hardly a word, they watch the red needle pass the delicate cross-hatch of numbers, roll up, linger, stop; he murmurs the price, which goes into a monthly account book, and wraps the meat in careful white bundles, along with a pile of bones for our dog.

I wait, and smell the blood rising from the sawdust spread across the floor behind the counter.

"I've got something for you." Mr. Bryan has a little bottlebrush mustache, a Hitler mustache, coarse and black. He leans over the counter and holds out his two huge hands in fists, his hairy hands and big round sausage fingers hiding a surprise. His arms are like my father's arms, thick and powerful and tanned dark brown, his hands are my father's hands, workmen's hands, and he waggles them in front of me like a magician.

Abracadabra! I grab for the wiener he has hidden: "Which finger do you want?" he laughs with a big Santa Claus belly laugh, the sausage balanced in his knuckles. I laugh politely, too, and finally grab it and retire silently to a corner. The sphincter on each end is like my old aunt's mouth I am sometimes forced to kiss, a dark center with radioles of pinched wrinkles. Inch by inch, beginning here, I peel the shiny pink skin off with my teeth. I eat the spongy mulch slowly, sucking its sweet and salty juices like a popsicle, transfixed by the window, watching the steady, slow passage of people outside in the glare.

Sometimes I would do little errands with my father. He was a weary man, infinitely restless. He always went through back doors, never the front, and so I learned to walk in like I belonged everywhere: the hardware store where I could plunge my arms up to the elbow in bins of nails, letting the sharp edges bite a little, and the sporting goods store where I could study the rows of staring animal heads that circled the room, and the Elks Club, and the lumber yard. Then he'd have another snort, and get back in his old pickup and drive two blocks to the next brief chat, the next chore.

My father liked foods no one else in the family ate. He made his own rich soups, his own jerky. He liked the gifts of game my grandfather would bestow at times, the big cuts of purplish venison, the whole ducks with their peculiar, wild taste. He liked tripe, fresh jalapeño peppers, horseradish, Limburger and feta cheese, Rocky Mountain oysters: foods strong and biting, with a certain presence, foods unmistakably here. I was the only one who'd share his little treats with him, and this strange intimacy bound us across the table when nothing else held us near. The two of us sitting alone at the big dining table with a pot of steamed clams between us and little bowls of melted butter, shucking the sweet tidbits out with a clatter of forks. For him I ate what only he would eat, the far corners of flesh: pickled pig's feet, elk, brains, sweetmeats. I was proud to eat these things. It made me less a daughter, and more a son.

With my father it was like this: He parks his truck in the alley and we enter the Meat Market through the unmarked alley door. The floor in the back of the market is gritty with fine yellow sawdust, streaked with blood; it grips my shoes like flypaper and piles up along the walls in little drifts. On the tables, the big block tables too heavy to move, knives and saws, pikes and hooks striped with blood. A slab of beef hangs in the hall, ready to be sliced into the day's steaks, and while the men talk over my head I sidle up close beside it, sniffing its fragrance, stroking its soft, waxy fat. I don't listen to the men because I know they won't say anything important.

At the very back of the Meat Market is the walk-in freezer, behind a huge shiny door with a silver handle as big as a car jack. One of the assistant butchers steps past me and opens it, and a breath of moist air escapes like a faint snow, almost maternal. Inside in the dim light I can see the rows of beef sides, pierced by huge hooks, the ribs bumpy and the fat dangling. There are yellow chickens hung like underwear on a line, and whole gutted pigs with giant snouts.

I know what this means now, these dead by the hundreds and thousands that haunted my days. I saw the carcasses, the knives, I licked the blood off my fingertips. But then I was very young. The world was solid, the world was what it was, and nothing more. It had no ghosts, no God. No dead pigs and trussed chickens just the meat my mother cooked for supper while my father ducked out back for a quick drink before we ate. I watch the man walk among these objects hanging in the frigid air, brushing them gently with his shoulder so they sway a little in the breeze of his passing, and I wait for the quiet conversation of the smiling men to end, and hope Mr. Bryan will give me a wiener.

Mr. Bryan, of course, was a fireman, like all my father's friends, and his kids were fire brats like me and sat beside me on the fussy rows of hose when we rode the trucks in the parades. The fire department turned a hundred years old the day before I was born, and by then my father had been fighting fires for years.

Now and then I was taken to the fire department on one of my father's little errands, entered its high ceilings and its echoes and wandered among the stately, patient trucks. I could peek underneath them, and examine the long rows of turnout clothes, stiff rubberized overalls and Wellington boots smelling of oil and smoke. I loved fires and their pure destruction. I loved the prescribed movements of ritual and chaos that were the same every time. For years I wanted to be either a nun or a fireman, and the fact that I was neither Catholic nor a man bothered me. I just trailed after the firemen whenever I could. I often could. I was very free to come and go, and willing to walk miles if need be to find the circled trucks and milling men, to come in close beside the whirling lights and listen to the urgent, murmured voices and the dashing spray of foam water, hissing down into the heat.

In late August when the afternoons were close with heat, the fire department had a barbecue for the families. Mr. Bryan provided the meat and the huge steaming barbecue grill with its electric spit. We all gathered in the farthest corner of the big city park near my home, where the shade was thick and cool, and you could hear the thwack of tennis balls in the nearby courts. The men stood around in small clumps, holding beers, laughing, basting the huge joint of beef. The spit turned heavily with a fluctuating whir, and the juice dribbled off the blackened flesh and landed spitting in the coals.

It was forbidden to drink in the park, but the firemen did it; even some of the firemen's wives, like Mrs. Bryan, whom I always thought a little notorious and outspoken. My mother just smoked, one cigarette after the other, leaning forward over a picnic table to make a point to one of her friends, another fireman's wife. I climbed a nearby pine tree and spread myself around the trunk, hidden in its needles, and practiced saying out loud the unsavory insults I learned from my peers. They were mostly flesh words. Skin-and-bone words, animal words: Chickenshit. Wienie. Horse's ass. And later, the rest of the flesh, all that was sliced off at the butcher's when we weren't looking: Prick. Pussy. Cunt.

When Mr. Bryan pronounced the beef ready, with his deep and hearty chortle, I quickly slid out of the tree and lined up to eat. I held out my plate for a gentle slap of rare meat cut very thin, the pink juices draining through the thin paper plate onto my hand. I added sweet baked beans, potato salad, garlicky French bread, and chocolate cake, and begged my mother for one more soda, just one more. The smoke swirled around and around my head.

After the picnic we drove up to the huge municipal swimming pool, ours alone for the afternoon. One useless white-nosed lifeguard stayed behind. The crowd of full-bellied men in swimming trunks would have knocked each other aside for the chance to rescue someone; it would make the day complete. I lay baking in the sun and imagined drowning, dropping into the water, lost; I am saved by firemen, raised up sputtering from the water by a host of hard, stout hands that pull me up and out and into the cathedral of sun in one motion.

The lifeguard with his poker face scans the crowd, ignoring the flirting girls. The air is filled with the bright sounds of splashing water, the muscular double bounce of the diving board, hollering boys, singsong children's cries. The firemen even drink beer on the swimming pool deck, a sin so great and marvelous I fall backward into the water with joy. My brother scrambles to the top of the high dive and blasts off into a cannon ball, tucked and spinning, hitting the hard blue water with a wanton splash.

I wash the sticky pitch and sauce away without a thought. The sweat is gone, the juices gone, dried up by the sun and rinsed away by the chlorine scent of the pool. We stay while the flat empty sky turns from chalk blue to ivory to black, our little voices carried off like vapor, until the men and women lean back to watch the stars appear, and I rest my own sleek head in the breast of water, and sink away.

* * *

You will think me disingenuous if I tell you now that I didn't know what meat was. I couldn't know, the shift from cow to beef is a shift so monumental and sudden that it's hard to conceive. Perhaps small children cannot know this even when they are witnesses, and I was never a witness. I have never seen an animal slaughtered for meat. And if you had leaned over me when I was four or five or six, and suggested I eat an animal, I might have struck out with shock. I loved animals more, and more easily, than I loved my parents. I held my old dog, a dour, mongrel Lab, for hours in my room sometimes, telling him what I couldn't tell; I was weak with him because he kept that secret. I loved horses, goats, deer, and the cattle chewing stupidly by the backroad fences; in my bedroom I kept lizards, snakes, chameleons, and a rat, and that was all my mother allowed. And it was my mother who one day told me where meat came from, as though it were the most natural thing.

I was about seven when I asked, that age when one begins to see the depth of betrayal in the world, that one can't really count on things after all. And my mother answered, yes, the chicken we ate for dinner was the same as the chickens down the street I would cluck at through the fence, the ones with the thick white feathers that filled the breeze. That the peeled skin of the wieners Mr. Bryan gave me were loops of intestine washed clean, and their pulp a ground mash of bodies and bones. That the unbelievable objects had a name, a face, a history, the sweet and salty taste was the taste of blood, the same as my blood. It came all at once, like a blow, that pickled pigs' feet was not a colorful metaphor but the very thing, that I had eaten a *pig's* foot, and much more.

I lived on bare noodles and peanut butter sandwiches for a long time after that. I wouldn't allow her to spoon the sausage-flavored spaghetti sauce onto my plate. A few years later, it seemed less important, the resistance too hard. Perhaps I had had other surprises: it's hard to remember whole sections of those years. I've gone years without eating meat as an adult, and years when I was too tired not to eat whatever I found in front of me. And lots of times when I craved flesh, when I broiled and roasted, made scratch gravy and giblet dressing like my mother's or sat at my long dining table with a pot of steamed clams clattering against my fork, times when I longed for the irreducible flavors of meat, to be full of meat. And I will even now find myself knocked flat sometimes when I see meat in front of me and realize what I'm doing. It is a heart-felt knowledge—that word, like all those other words for sudden understanding—it is visceral, gut-level, organic. I hold the steak with a fork and begin to cut a slice and my stomach turns upside down; it feels as if I'm cutting my own flesh off and that I'll choke to death upon it, like a prisoner fed his own treacherous, boiled, tongue.

One shock after another. Breasts and hips and hair, more of the pleasures and debts of flesh. I began to bleed several days a month, and when I sat to pee the smell rose up yeasty and rich. I found furtive darting touches: I found lips, saliva, tongues, sweat, fingers. My dog decayed from the inside out, and stank and stumbled and licked the mysterious lumps under his fur. I traced his ribs so near the surface the day before he died. Then my mother yellowed and thickened and wept and died and my father's big arms hung loose and his black hair turned gray. He took his snorts out back in the garage. I knelt between the knees of a boy a little older than myself, and took his penis in my mouth, and smiled not with pleasure or appetite, but with triumph behind the curtain of my swaying hair. I moved out to the fleshy edges of things, and finally I grew wings like angel wings, and I flew away.

The word *butcher* comes—a long way down the years—from the word *buck*. He-goat. They are set aside, butchers, into their own unions, their own neighborhoods, their own bars, set aside. I don't know if it means anything that besides Mr. Bryan my father's closest friend was the undertaker: it may not mean anything more than the limits of a small town. But I think of the Butcher's Mass, their special blessing, and the *shehitah* of the Jews. The *Shohet,* the slaughterer who must be pious and above reproach, must be as swift and painless as he can be in the killing, murmuring a benediction near the animal's ear and following with a graceful stroke across the throat. I think of Mr. Bryan's cleaver.

The Meat Market burned down on a hot day under a blank blue sky. It was apocalypse. It was a great fire.

I stood at the end of the alley and watched the flames spurt out the back door in gouty bursts. I heard a shriek of metal inside, and guessed the white metal cooler had turned red and ignited its own frost. The smoke billowed out the back door in a cottony black cloud, and I clapped my hands. Men in turnouts and boots rushed past and paid me no attention, and I could see my father paying out the hose from the pumper with great speed.

The meat burned: the water washed it clean. I learned later that Mr. Bryan had inherited the Meat Market from his father, and he'd secretly hated it all those years, going home at night with the stink of blood on his hands and hair. He is still jolly and thick-fingered, and he still comes by to see my father, who is tired and gruff and without cheer. They have been retired from fires, too old to go into the heat and pull things out. For myself, I know you can't be cleansed until you know how dirty you really are. I still live far away, still seek salvation from my many sins.

RESTAURATION: THE ART OF EATING RETURNS TO RUSSIA

LEON ARON

W HEN I LEFT MOSCOW for the United States in 1978, the humorists in the city of my birth were fond of circulating a true story about a Politburo member's daughter who, having come down with food poisoning, was greeted at the Kremlin hospital by her mother's reprimand: *Ty s'ela shto-to v gorode?!* "You've eaten something in the city, haven't you?!" Supplied weekly with enormous food parcels from secret depots, the top party bosses, their children, their servants, and, in the finely calibrated order of seniority, the rest of the nomenklatura—from the military brass and Central Committee staffers to propagandists, writers, journalists, and movie directors—considered suspect anything sold in stores.

At the time, however, Moscow was still better off than the rest of the country, where meat appeared in stores twice a year: around the anniversary of the "Great October Socialist Revolution" on November 7 and "Labor Solidarity Day," May 1. During the rest of the year, one could purchase (with a valid ration coupon) a monthly allotment of "meat products," which in the heyday of glasnost, in 1988, a Soviet newspaper described as 500 grams (about a pound) of "cooked sausage" and 300 grams (11 ounces) of "smoked sausage." In the late 1980s, along with milk and cheese, meat was available at semi-privatized "farmer's markets," but to buy in required monthly food outlays of at least 150 rubles—an astronomical sum in a country where one third of the citizens lived on less than 100 rubles a month (then about $10).

By that time Moscow's relative prosperity, sustained by robbing the rest of the country, had collapsed under the assault of hundreds of thousands of hungry visitors from the provinces, where, as a Russian newspaper columnist put it, children had to be told "what was meat and what, in theory, could be done with it." Every day the commuter trains, called *kolbasnye elektrichki,* or sausage trains," disgorged the foragers at the capital's seven train stations. In the 1970s an underground joke circulated about a Moscow Jew, who, when asked why he was emigrating, said: "I am tired of holidays: bought sausage—a holiday; found toilet paper—a holiday; got to buy shoes—holiday again. I long for a dreary, non-festive existence." By the fall of 1991, the collapsed state-owned economy had left behind absolutely bare shelves of grocery stores, bread lines around the block, and sacks of potatoes on the balconies of Moscow residents preparing for famine.

Today, the joke has lost its point, and the Moscow Jew would be hard-pressed not to find a party. The streets are brightly lit; the shop windows, inviting. The sidewalks, no longer littered with cigarette butts, are scrubbed clean. At every major Metro station there are gorgeous roses for sale, reportedly trucked in from Holland and flown in from Honduras. The flow of cars is thick and furious, and Audis, BMWs, and Toyota Land Cruisers no longer turn heads. Moscow women, who used to beg their male bosses to bring back a pair of panty hose from a trip abroad, now sport European fashions and haircuts. Metro riders are no longer morose and rude; smiles and jokes are suddenly common. It seems that everyone has a cell phone.

The shift to a more open economy has given rise to a post-Communist middle class, which consists of the young, the college-educated, and the residents of large cities. The tastes and preferences of this modest but energetic and increasingly self-confident population account for all manner of new trends sweeping Russia in the past decade.

The stifling ownership of everyone's livelihood and tastes by an impoverished, corrupt, and autarkic state has gone the way of *Pravda,* the jamming of foreign broadcasts, compulsory classes of political education, and awful clothes. Nowhere is the metamorphosis as vivid and as easily discernible, even to a casual tourist, as in the national gastronomic renaissance. That gastronomy has been ahead of many other areas of life in the speed and robustness of recovery is due to the fact that the Russian table was always one place where the state receded. The kitchen was a substitute for the public square, the table talk a surrogate for free political discourse. In the long run, liberty creates wealth everywhere, but in Russia it has repaid the debt to the table a hundredfold.

An amazing abundance and variety of food is now available in Moscow. Snack bars and kiosks dispensing not only Russian but Mexican, Japanese, Chinese, Greek, and Middle Eastern fare dot the same sidewalks on which crowds of shabbily dressed men and women, weighed down by bags and bundles, used to shuffle silently and sullenly from store to store in search of food. Menus, cookbooks, lunch counters, and home pantries brim with items discovered after an eighty-year hiatus: pineapple and kiwi, asparagus, squid and baby-octopus salad, frogs' legs, or pizza. People everywhere in the city walk around munching on *shawarma,* which every New Yorker will instantly recognize as a species of gyro: chicken or lamb sliced off a hot rotating cone, wrapped, falafel-like, in either pita or flat Georgia *lavash* and dipped in spicy yogurt.

In Moscow's new gastronomic universe everything has to be fresh and hot. Between appointments on my last visit I found myself, a ten-ruble bill in hand, in front of a kiosk selling *chebureki,* the large Crimean meat pasty. "And heat it up, will you?" an older woman in a white kerchief ordered the vendor. The latter complied by putting the pie in a microwave oven. Inspired by the intrepid babushka, I overcame the inbred fear of Russian salesclerks and requested that my order be warmed as well. Quite apart from being its own virtue, the courage paid handsomely in gastronomic terms when the first bite through the thick chewy skin revealed a hot and smooth meatball of lamb and beef with garlic and parsley in an aromatic gravy.

Will collapses at the sight of *vypechka*—freshly baked goods, sold for a few rubles on street corners, outside all major Metro stations, and, of course, in bakeries that seem to grace every other block: puff pastry *(sloyki)* and danishes *(vatrushki)* with fillings of cheese or prunes or poppy seeds; buns with raisins; tarts with apricots, apples, or blueberries; meringue cookies, éclairs, almond rings (my favorite), napoleons (vanilla-flavored cream between four or five layers of very thin and flaky puff pastry), rum babas, large muffins *(keksy),* or sochniki: hefty little bricks of sweet cottage cheese surrounded by a crumbly dough shell.

All of the former nomenklatura delights now are to be found in ordinary grocery stores *(gastronomy)*—like the Razumovskiy *gastronom* near a friend's apartment in a quiet residential neighborhood on Leningradskoye Highway close to the Airport Metro. In addition to the abundance displayed on the counters, products available from the store's supplier include fifty-four kinds of sausages and nineteen hams, ranging in price from 18 to 146 rubles a kilo (30 cents to $2.43 a pound), and such exotic concoctions as veal sausages, the Sicily with olives or the Lyonnaise with mushrooms, and the precious holiday treats of my childhood: the delicate, smooth, and aromatic *doktorskaya* and the hard, peppery, fat-speckled salami *servelat* at the equivalent of $1.60 and $2.50 a pound, respectively. *Servelat* used to be available either in snack bars set up at polling places on "election" days to attract "voters" or during the week before New Year's Eve (officially, there was no Christmas in Soviet times), and, along with oranges, bananas, or apples, was among the best gifts one could bring to a friend's house. Among the sixteen kinds of cheeses the *gastronom* displays are the hard, piquant, light-yellow *poshekhonskiy;* the round and softer *gollandskiy* wrapped in red wax; the slightly salty and viscous Georgian *sulguni;* and feralike *brynza.* The breads vary from the fat, white, all-wheat ellipses of *bulki* (which, with soft butter, are the best pedestal for caviar) to darker hues of rye to the dense, crusty, and round *orlovskiy* and the black, pungent *borodinskiy* studded with caraway seeds.*

The Razumovskiy carries, among former rarities, smoked or cured sturgeon *(osetr, beluga,* and *sevryuga)* and salmon *(syomga, gorbusha, keta,* and *nerka)* for between 31 and 75 rubles for 100 grams (or $1–$2.50 for three and a half ounces). Caviar now can be bought in almost every shop, and the price is fairly low. Caviar in small tins and glass jars with metal lids ranged from salmon's red (ripe and briny) at 99 rubles for a 113-gram can ($3.20 for 4 ounces) through *osetr's* small and firm kernels (300 rubles, or $10) to the luscious, silvery-gray *beluga* at 500 rubles ($16). Except for holidays, fish was virtually absent from the Russian diet in Soviet times.

For those in need of a serious dessert—for an evening tea at home or, following the tradition, a gift to bring to a dinner party—there are torte kiosks. Chocolate, cream, or soufflé or filled with nuts, layered with waffles, or any combination thereof, these round, square, or log-like concoctions with names like *adagio, polyot* ("flight"), *ptich'e moloko* ("birds' milk"), *shchelkunchik* ("nutcracker"), *stratosfera, kapriz* ("caprice"), and *nezhnost'* ("tenderness") weigh between one and four pounds each and cost between 32 and 280 rubles ($1–$9). One of the kiosks near the Airport Metro sold fifty-seven varieties.

Nearby, Azeri vendors sell homegrown tomatoes, cucumbers, honeydew melons, apples, watermelons, large southern cherries *(chereshni),* as well as imported pineapples, oranges, and bananas. Bananas were the impossible dream of every Moscow child of my generation (most Soviet children outside the city didn't know what a banana was), the ultimate prize our mothers captured once or twice a year after queuing for hours. They were often green and small, and turned black with rot within a few days. No matter: we loved their exotic shape and sweet mushy flesh, which was like nothing else we had ever had. Now they sell for less than 50 cents a pound, and children do not yell and drag their mothers toward the stalls, and no one is surprised or even especially pleased at

---

*In 2001, for the first time since the late 1920s, Russia had enough grain not only to feed its people and cattle without millions of tons of American, Canadian, and Argentine wheat but to export at least 5 million tons.

their availability. People buy one or two at a time and, children and grownups alike, eat them casually while walking and irreverently throw the beautiful yellow skins into sidewalk trash cans.

Another national craving is also now amply supplied by the market: between August and October no Moscow grocery store is complete without mushrooms. There are tall and firm *podberyozoviki* ("the ones under a birch tree") in dark-brown bonnets; all-white *gruzdi* ("the heavy ones"); saffron milk caps, or *ryzhiki* ("little red ones"); yellow *maslyata* ("little buttery ones"); chanterelles *(lisichki,* or "little foxes"); and, of course, the noblest fungi of the Russian forest and a dream of every mushroom-picker: the squat, fleshy, tawny-brimmed *belyie* ("the white ones") on a chubby white stem.

Some mushrooms are used in soups; others are fried in butter with scallions and potatoes, or stewed in sour cream, flour, and parsley and then baked in pies, or salted and marinated to form one of the three best accompaniments to vodka. (The other two are herring and pickles. To make the latter, sprinkle cucumbers with grated horseradish and sliced garlic, layer with dill and currant leaves, and cover with hot salt-water.) The mushroom season having begun early last summer because of unusually heavy rains and cool weather, the Razumovskiy offered half a dozen ready-to-eat mushroom salads: in sour cream or olive oil, and with beets, carrots, and potatoes.

Like the sudden abundance of food, the transformation in the way it is consumed has been nothing short of dramatic. Dull and heavy, like Russians' lives, food used to be gorged on—after months of relentless foraging and hoarding—on birthdays, the November 7 anniversary of the Revolution, and New Year's Eve, and drowned in vodka. The rest of the year, the food was meager but the vodka still plentiful. It was the shortage of food and the cheapness of vodka, which contributed up to one fifth of the state budget both in czarist and Soviet times, that were responsible for the stereotype of Russia as a nation of depressed drunks.

More and better food and the appearance of colorful beer bars, especially the ubiquitous Zolotaya Bochka ("Golden Barrel") chain, are likely to change this stereotype. Whetted by the opening of the market to imports, Russia's thirst for beer has increased by leaps and bounds since 1991. After 1998, when most Russians could not afford the imports because of the ruble devaluation, 1,500 private breweries filled the market with domestic brands, with the Zolotaya Bochka brand among the most popular. For the first time in history, Russians started to drink more beer than vodka—a development immensely beneficial for the national health, the public order, and the life expectancy for Russian men, for whom alcoholism was among the leading causes of death.

The new casualness in acquiring food and the appreciation of taste and freshness are Russian gastronomic trends that were merely interrupted in 1917. Classic Russian literature and classic Russian cuisine were born and reached their golden age at about the same time—between, approximately, 1830 and 1890—and the former has compiled a marvelous record of the latter. Here, for instance, is the "gentleman of average means" from Gogol's *Dead Souls,* who ordered ham at the first tavern on the road; suckling pig at the next stop; a "chunk of sturgeon or sausage with onions" farther down the road; and finished on sterlet soup with *rasstegai*—round, open, literally "unbuttoned," fish pies with filling exposed in the center—and *kulebyaki*—multilayered puff-pastry pies, stuffed with rice, mushrooms, onions, or baked salmon and dripping with melted butter.

Chekhov gave Russian literature its first gastronomic martyr: the midlevel bureaucrat Semyon Petrovich Podtykin, ambushed by cruel fate after what seemed to him an interminable wait for an Easter meal. At last the housekeeper-cook carries into the dining room a tall stack of *blini.* The hot, thin pancakes are beautiful: crisp on the bottom, white, porous, and soft, "like the shoulder of a merchant's daughter." Semyon Petrovich tears off the top two round sheets, douses them in hot melted butter, and slowly spreads caviar. Spots uncovered by the caviar are covered with sour cream. He looks with an artist's pride on his succulent canvas, pauses yet again to survey the table covered with *zakuski* (hors d'oeuvres), adds a slice *of syomga,* then a sardine and a sprat; rolls the *blini* into a tight tube, drinks a shot of vodka, sighs in anticipation—and, in an object lesson to all perfectionists, dies of apoplexy.

The flowering of classic Russian cuisine coincided with the rapid economic expansion and explosive growth of the middle class in the aftermath of Alexander II's liberal reforms. Moscow offered culinary delights to suit every taste and almost every wallet. For a few kopecks street vendors sold pies and *blini, kalachi* (white rolls), fried buckwheat *kasha* , or smoked sturgeon with horseradish and vinegar, to be washed down with hot *sbiten'* (a mead drink spiced with cardamom and nutmeg) in the winter and *kvas* (Russia's national nonalcoholic drink, made from rye bread fermented with sugar) in the summer.

Filippov's bakery produced kopeck buns, loaves, and warm little pies, *pirozhki* (the word deriving from the Russian *pir,* or "feast"), with meat, rice, mushrooms, cottage cheese, or raisins. For five kopecks one could buy pies big enough to provide, with a cup of tea, a hearty

Russian breakfast. The official purveyor to the St. Petersburg court, Filippov bought only the best rye grain from Tambov Province and sent inspectors to watch over the milling. Frozen by a secret method, his *kalachi* were shipped all over Russia, thawed in wet towels, warmed, and served, according to witnesses, "hot and aromatic."

Muscovites were notorious *traktir*goers, and in the capital there were thousands of these tavernlike forerunners of restaurants. The poor would pay kopecks for a bowl of *shchi* (cabbage soup) with meat and porridge. In the frigid winter, the ubiquitous coachmen (*izvozchiki*) would warm themselves at roadside *traktiry* with a pot of tea, fried pork, giblets with pickled cucumber, smoked catfish, and a loaf of bran bread.

Gurin's and Egorov's, the best in the long line of great Moscow *traktiry,* fed the city gourmands between 1850 and 1890. Gurin's was renowned for, along with its food, the largest organ in Moscow, and people flocked there to listen to the music. Located at the end of the present-day Okhotny Ryad street, Egorov's set the national standard of excellence for *blini*, which were served right off the huge wooden spatula all day long, plain or with caviar, smoked fish, or a score of other fillings, and for *rasstegai* adorned, in the center of the top layer, with the crown jewel of a glistening slice of roasted sturgeon or baked turbot's liver. In the seafood restaurant on the second floor, wealthier customers drank their sterlet *ukha* (fish broth) next to a giant tank of live fish.

Some of Europe's leading chefs worked in Moscow in the second half of the nineteenth century. One of them, the Frenchman Olivier, who owned the expensive and fashionable Hermitage, gave his name to the hearty salad of meat, potatoes, eggs, pickles, peas, scallions, and mayonnaise without which to this day no festive Russian table, no matter how exalted or poor, is complete.

Waiting on tables in the best Moscow *traktiry* was a much sought-after profession. According to Vladimir Gilyarovskiy's *Moskva i Moskvichi* ("Moscow and Muscovites"), an apprenticeship began with dishwashing and was followed by six months in the kitchen (to remember "all the sauces") and four years as a busboy. A successful graduate was required to purchase the uniforms, consisting of six shirts and trousers of expensive Dutch linen, to be kept "white as fresh snow" and free of wrinkles.

All was lost when the last vestiges of private enterprise disappeared in the early 1930s. Taken over by the state, a few good restaurants lingered for years, most conspicuously the one at the Union of Soviet Writers on Povarskaya, or Cook's, Street. Yet by the mid-1930s, in the *The Master and Margarita*, Mikhail Bulgakov mourned the restaurant's decline: "Do you remember sterlet in a silver saucepan, cut into pieces and interlaced with lobster tails and fresh caviar?" he asked wistfully.

"Or eggs filled with pureed mushrooms and served in tiny cups? And how about blackbird filets—with truffles? Of quail à la Genoa?"

No major Soviet Russian author wrote in praise of fine food after that.

A decade after the end of the relentless Soviet deprivation, incompetence, universal thievery, and daily indignities—the world Nabokov called "so shoddy, so crabbed and gray"—the Russian capital seems to have been remade into one of Europe's best (and best-hidden) gastronomic destinations. The change in taste, decor, and service is even more startling than the availability of food. Outside of the *stolovye* ("dining rooms") of the high nomenklatura (closed to ordinary mortals), meals were equally awful in the glitzy Metropol or Natsional (which catered to foreigners, their KGB minders, and "official Russians") and in the "cafés" and "restaurants" for the masses—except that in the former the execrable food was dispensed with servility in kitschy chic, while in the latter it was ladled out in rudeness and squalor. All this has been replaced by cleanliness, politeness, good training, competence, and, in many cases, polish and even panache.

Of course, far from all of Moscow's more than 4,000 restaurants are within the middle-class range. For those who, following Dr. Johnson, wish to smile with the wise but feed with the rich (that is, the 5 percent with monthly incomes of over $3,500), there are several dozen superb establishments. Among them are Tsarskaya Okhota ("Czar's Hunt") in Zhukovka, near Stalin's favorite dacha, where in 1997 Boris Yeltsin entertained French president Jacques Chirac; the CDL, in the former headquarters of the Union of Soviet Writers; the Sirena, Moscow's best seafood restaurant, which serves lobsters, oysters, crabs, and giant shrimp in a hushed, wood-paneled decor as enormous sturgeon swim under the glass floor and sea creatures frolic behind the glass walls; and the Savoy, the Grand Imperial, Le Romanoff, the Metropol, and the Grand Opera—with their cavernous dining rooms, crystal chandeliers, silver cutlery, and floor-to-ceiling mirrors.

A step below this grandeur are restaurants that middle-class Muscovites enjoy on special occasions. Across Tverskaya Street from Pushkin Square is Café Pushkin, an example of an intense but tasteful quest for authenticity that characterizes Moscow dining today. The restaurant is housed in a typical early-nineteenth-century Moscow building, quite a few of which miraculously have survived the Soviet decay and demolition. The inside looks very much like a Moscow museum: parquet floors, mirrors fogged with age in heavy bronze frames, a patina of fine cracks on the marble stairs and the walls, a medium-size dining room under a thirty-foot ceiling, and a wide staircase with cast-iron banisters leading to the second-floor library. But all is an illusion: the restaurant is barely four years old and was built from scratch on an empty lot within five months.

The Pushkin offers the mainstays of Russian cooking: *kvas* and *sbiten'*; suckling pig with apple gravy (as a cold appetizer); *blini* with *osetr* and salmon caviar; mutton Hussar, "stewed in beer for more swagger," as the menu describes it, and baked with mushrooms into a pie; beef Stroganoff; chicken giblets with mushrooms in rye-bread "pots"; salmon and sturgeon (grilled, stewed, or jerked), *pel'meni* (dumplings) with beef, pork, veal, salmon, or mushrooms; and catfish "baked into a potato puree under a spinach sauce." Appetizer and soups are between $6 and $9, and most entrees are between $10 and $23, with the most expensive—saddle of lamb accompanied by vegetables—at $29.50.

It being July, my hosts (up-and-coining lawyers in their early forties) and I ordered the summer classic of chilled kvas-based soup, *okroshka*. Thinly sliced scallions, radishes, beef, potatoes, boiled eggs, and cucumbers, dill, a dollop of sour cream, and a touch of horseradish blended harmoniously, each ingredient true to its character and texture. Marinated Baltic sprats were delicate, their sharp briny taste balanced by an accompanying vinaigrette of potatoes, beets, onions, dill pickles, eggs, and mayonnaise. The entrées were faultless: golden-brown veal cutlet à la Pozharsky (a famous nineteenth-century Russian chef, who made the dish from wild game) and crisp grilled sturgeon.

Both in the fare and the setting Beloye Solntze Pustyni, or BSP ("White Sun of the Desert"), on Neglinnaya Street is as far from the lean elegance of the Pushkin as St. Petersburg is from Bukharator Samarkand. It dazzles with brilliant colors and pampers shamelessly. The restaurant is a festive blend of a Central Asian *chai-khana* (teahouse) and a movie set. The film that gave the restaurant its name is an irreverent tragicomedy about the Russian civil war, set on a barge marooned on Turkestan's Caspian shore. The movie miraculously made it past the censors in the late 1960s and became a cult hit. The dining room is wrapped in red, gold, and black Persian carpets: on the floor, over the whitewashed clay walls, and on the seats. Female servers wear gold, red, and mauve paisley silk tunics over baggy silk trousers, *sharavari*, and matching embroidered skullcaps. Life-size papier-mâché soldiers crouch behind a Maxim machine gun. A few feet away swarthy white-bearded elders smoke hookahs on wooden boxes inscribed ОПАСНО: ДИНАМИТ! ("DANGER: DYNAMITE!").

In the center of the room, circling an enormous tree trunk, is a *dastarkhan:* a prix-fixe collection of at least two dozen hot and cold Central Asian dishes, including such standards as *lagman* (noodles-and-lamb stew); *manty* (large lamb dumplings); *shashlyki* of sturgeon, lamb, and chicken; tender and pungent sausage *kazy,* and baked eggplant stuffed with nuts. The patrons' tables are constantly resupplied with clear, cool, tart pomegranate juice and hot, flat white bread extracted with long-handled wooden spatulas from the ovens through openings in the walls. *Plov* (pilaf), which is the heart and the obligatory dish in every meal, never stops cooking in the iron cauldrons hung over a low fire, where the rice is steamed with chunks of lamb shoulder or leg, carrots, onions, hot red pepper, and saffron. Although sauteed in lamb fat instead of olive oil and considerably more pungent than risotto, the classic *plov* is as much a product of constant stirring. Solemnly borne by two sous-chefs, the giant clay pot of *plov* was placed on a wooden pedestal next to our table and ladled onto the plates by the chef himself, a strapping Uzbek in a monumental starched toque.

In post-Soviet Russia, as in any other country, the backbone of the national cuisine, however, is to be found not in the almost theatrical elaborateness of the Pushkin or the BSP but in places that are "neither chic nor sordid," in A. J. Liebling's immortal classification: the restaurants where a meal is not an event but an uncomplicated and affordable pleasure. An entrée in scores of such places in Moscow rarely exceeds the equivalent of $12. Muscovites stop by after work for a bit of smoked salmon or pickled Baltic Sea herring, marinated mushrooms, fresh *kholodetz* (pork or veal in aspic), a plate of pel'meni, *pirozhki* with a cup of chicken or beef bouillon, a bowl of borscht or fish broth, a cup of tea—and, often, listen to live jazz or romantic Russian ballads.

The Bochka ("Barrel") serves pigs roasted on a spit, veal brains with mushrooms in a pot, and grilled salmon. The Oblomov, named after Ivan Goncharov's great nineteenth-century novel, features waitresses and waiters in crinolines and tails and a giant of a maître d' in luxurious muttonchops and a morning coat who converses with customers in Fyodor Chaliapin's deep bass. Those tormented by nostalgia for their Soviet youth may avail themselves of the New Vasyuki (the name is from the hilarious 1928 satire *The Twelve Chairs,* by Il'ya Il'f and Evgeniy Petrov), on whose menu one finds "The union of the sword and the plough": two plump pieces of sturgeon with black and red caviar inside and a side of fried potato shavings under cream sauce.

A more elaborate retro gastronomic experience is offered by Club Petrovich, named after the main character of a popular cartoon strip: a plumber who is an incorrigible *sovok* (*Homo sovieticus*)—petty, cunning, thoroughly corrupt, and fiercely competitive for meager Soviet amenities. The theme appealed to Russian P.R.-niks—a hardboiled and cynical lot— and the place became the hangout *(tusovka)* of ad-men and -women, imagemakers, and political-campaign managers. Its walls covered with original black-and-white photographs of Soviet movie stars and hanging toilet plungers, the restaurant is a combination of a crummy communal apartment and a *kontora* (office): the Soviet shrine and the citadel of sadistic petty bureaucrats on whose bribe-induced mercy untold millions of hapless tenants threw themselves with their tales of leaking roofs, burst sewer pipes, cold radiators, and rusty drinking water. The menu is delivered in the Soviet bureaucrat's indispensable carrying case: a thick, cardboard folder with tassels *(papka)* stained with imitation grease. Served by generous platefuls, the retro food—*sosiski* (fat frankfurters), *bitochki* (small steaks), *grechnevaya kasha* (boiled buckwheat groats), *lapsha* (noodles), *kupaty* (crisp fried sausages stuffed with spicy mincemeat)—is incomparably fresher and better-tasting than the Soviet original but perfectly recognizable.

Still, the most memorable Moscow meal was at Shinok ("Tavern"), Number 2, 1905 Revolution Street, where dinner requires a serious commitment of time and effort. To come here for lunch is a strain and a waste of food designed to be consumed leisurely.

Babel, Isaak Emanuilovich Babel—you gourmand, Jewish cavalryman, admirer of Maupassant and seeker after Flaubertian perfection, rotund little bon vivant in steel-rimmed glasses; you who compared your life to "a meadow in May, the meadow on which women and horses wandered"—where was your soul that night? Your fierce, voracious and restless soul, which left your body in the basement of the Lubyanka in January 1940 after the customary midnight shot in the back of the head, like hundreds of thousands of other "enemies of the people" swept out in Stalin's Great Purge?

We ate cold stuffed fish with horseradish, like the one your grandmother served on Saturday nights in Odessa—the dish of which you wrote that it was "worth converting to Judaism for." We drank a toast to your Aunt Bobka, in whose jam strudel and poppy-seed pie you tasted "the heart of our tribe, the heart so good at struggle"—and our strudel and our pie were just as stirring.

And Babel's was not the only ghost looking down on us. The fabulous food was a medium of communing with another son of the fat and fecund soil of the Russian empire's southern rim: Russia's strangest genius, a depressive and anti-Semite, who produced some of the funniest pages of the Russian literary canon; a passionate patriot who loved

Russia from "the beautiful faraway" of an apartment on Rome's Via Sistina above the Spanish Steps; a gourmand who called the stomach his "noblest inner organ," left unmatched descriptions of Russian and Ukrainian food, and starved himself to death. Gogol was there with Babel, like Jewish tavern owners, *shinkari,* and their Ukrainian and Russian customers—and occasional pogrom murderers—who had been through four centuries of mutual need and loathing.

Behind the glass wall next to our heavy dark table, two milk-white goats, a red horse, and a spotted pig chewed and slept and walked about attended by a woman of ample proportions in the Ukrainian folk dress of a bright red jacket and a full green skirt with a few inches of linen petticoat showing below the hem, and the customers ate and drank, as they did—minus the glass partition—in Gogol's *Evenings near the Village of Dikan'ka.*

Here were all the requisite dishes, as if prepared by Pulkheria Ivanovna of Gogol's *Old World Landowners* for her perennially hungry husband or by lascivious Khavronya Nikiforovna from *Sorochinskaya Fair* for her cowardly lover: *syrniki* (cottage-cheese pancakes), *pampushki* (rolls), *galushki,* irregularly shaped pieces of dough, white and slippery, served hot with sour cream, known as *klyotski* in the Russian-Jewish version, and *vareniki,* ravioli-like large dumplings stuffed with fruit or cheese and served with either sour cream or sweet fruit sauce. *Vareniki* were served in small earthenware crocks—"little pots," Gogol wrote, "with lids sealed by wax or grease lest some mouthwatering creation of the old tasty cuisine lose its flavor."

Our Shinok waiter put on the table a tall cold pitcher of *kvas* beaded with moisture. Recalling, again, Gogol's *Evenings* we had asked for an elaborate pear-and-blackthorn-berries version. They had it.

Zakuski, hors d'oeuvres, continued to arrive: the velvety *forshmak*—a soufflé of herring soaked in milk overnight to take away the salt and baked with eggs, onion, and breadcrumbs—with roast potatoes, followed by *pirozhki.* Unlike the Moscow variety—oval, flaky, layered, and uniformly browned—these gifts of southern Russia were perfectly round brown cupolas on white bottoms. Faced with a choice of nine different stuffings, I recalled Gogol's *Old World Landowners* and ordered two with liver and two with buckwheat and cabbage, sauteed with onions and dill.

Appearing in solemn silence, the king of Russian soups, steaming borscht, heralded the end of the appetizer prelude. The classic borscht's inimitable bouquet of flavors comes from the harmonious multiplicity of ingredients that are sautéed together in animal fat and sprinkled with lemon juice and a dash of sugar before being ladled into beef bouillon fortified with potatoes: cabbage, carrots, onions, peppers, garlic, tomato paste, tomatoes, and bay leaf. Potatoes, sour cream, and a few pinches of deep-fried flour together produce the thick, almost chewy, but creamy and fluid texture. Our borscht was strong and dark purple, with floating islands of beef and potatoes. It was accompanied by hot *pampushki,* but we asked for black rye bread and garlic cloves to rub against the crust instead of those gentle rolls.

If borscht is the king and stuffed fish the queen, the prince of the traditional southern Russian (and Jewish) tables is undoubtedly *kislo-sladkoe zharkoye,* a sweet-and-sour beef stew. A species of *tzimmes* (generic Yiddish for sweetened meat-and-vegetable stews), the beef is dressed with tomato paste, carrots, and onions. The key to the dish is the elusive and precarious balance between sugar (or honey) and lemon juice. (The sweet side also may be fortified with prunes and apricots; and the sour, with vinegar.) Here, too, the Shinok passed with flying colors: served piping hot, under a thick, dark orange sauce, the cubed brisket was tender but fully textured.

The tea came with an apple strudel of cinnamon, nuts, and raisins; *pirog s makorn* (poppy-seed pie); and *smetannik* (a sour-cream-and-jam pie). All were freshly baked, their slightly moist interiors harboring the intense sweetness and spice that over the centuries have fortified the Russian-Jewish heart against disasters.

The dessert was accompanied by the homemade digestive *nalivka,* in its most popular—cherry—version. The juiciest fruits are mixed with the best vodka and plenty of sugar and allowed to stand for at least a month before straining. I found the Shinok's concoction stronger and not as sweet as my Grandpa Abram's homemade version but just as flavorful. "We do not drink vodka," Grandpa Abram used to declare to the bitterly disappointed Russian porters, painters, or plumbers claiming the customary glass of vodka upon the completion of a job. *"Vot nalivka , pozhaluysta!"* ("But, by all means, please help yourself to the *nalivka!"*)

I silently dedicated the few last drops of vodka to the memory of my grandmothers, Sima Shvartz and Roza Atlas, who had forged delectable masterpieces out of the poverty and strain of Soviet existence.

The next evening, the last of my trip, walking with an old friend and his nine-year-old son along Pyatnitskaya Street in Zamoskvorech'e—Moscow's sedate residential district, populated before 1917 by well-to-do merchants and today home to less important embassies—we saw four tables on the sidewalk. The small restaurant inside, with white curtains on the windows and cheerful Gobelins on the walls, looked like a Moscow apartment.

After a short July shower, the air was fresh and cool. In the soft bluish dusk, a sudden burst of light from the sidewalk signaled a small but safe harbor of friendship and intimacy. What I thought was possible only on the edge of a sleepy piazza in Rome's Trastevere or on a narrow street on Paris's Left Bank was suddenly part of Moscow.

The marquee read Soosy Poosy—the cooing of a Russian parent over a baby. A children's café? No, no, laughed a beautiful young woman. "It's just that we are trying to be like your family's apartment. Also we are a family restaurant: I wait on tables, my parents cook. Are you coming in?"

Full of beer, jambalaya, fried shrimp, and oysters from the Louisiana American Steak House up the street, where waiters wore tight jeans and toy silver guns in holsters, we had to decline.

"Prikhodite k nam koga-nibud." "Come see us sometime," the woman called out. *"Pridyom. Pridyom, ob'yazatel'no pridyom."* "We will be back. We certainly will," I promised.

GERALD ASHER

"WHAT WAS THE BEST wine you ever tasted, the one you always remember?" It's a question I'm often asked when someone newly introduced first realizes how I spend much of my waking time. How to answer? I think I'm expected to château-drop, to say something glamorous about a Margaux '53, a Cheval-Blanc '47 or a Mouton-Rothschild '45—a monumental wine, by the way, still flamboyantly vigorous when poured for me at a dinner at Mouton itself a couple of years ago. (There's a real château-drop for you.)

But how does anyone compare that Mouton-Rothschild with a Cheval-Blanc '47, last tasted in the 1970s, to decide which was "better"? And what would be the point anyway? Such wines are almost always impressive, and usually memorable. But that isn't the same thing as "always remembered," is it? In any case, one's memory of a wine is rarely a mere abstraction of aroma and flavor. Often it seems to reflect so well a particular context that later we are never quite sure whether we remember the circumstances because of the wine or the wine because of the circumstances. At times the two can even be ludicrously at odds.

Not long ago, while helping a friend clean up an apartment from which the removal men had taken his furniture just hours before, I came across a bottle of Barossa Valley Cabernet Sauvignon, a 1981 from the Hill-Smith estate, overlooked by the packers. We were tired and more than ready to stop. Fortunately, one of us had a corkscrew and there were paper cups in a kitchen cupboard. We sat on the floor, our backs to the wall. The wine was more than remarkable: it was sleek and patrician and elegant beyond anything I'd expected. At that moment, it was the most delicious wine in the world . . .

When mountains labor to bring forth a mouse, that can be memorable, too. In the 1960s, when my company in London imported and

distributed the wines of Henri Maire—an important but highly promo-
tion-driven wine producer in the Jura, in eastern France—I was asked,
at short notice, to arrange a small dinner at a distinguished restaurant
(my choice) for a few distinguished guests (my choice). The principle
dish (Henri Maire's choice), prepared by none other than Raymond
Oliver, at the time still reigning at Le Grand Véfour, was to be flown
over from Paris hours before the event.

The object was to show—in London and Paris simultaneously and
with precisely the same, dish—a wine that Henri Maire had shipped in
barrel around the world. In the eighteenth century it had been a custom
to send certain sherries to and from the tropics in the hold of sailing
ships; the journey was thought to age fortified wines advantageously.
Names of certain blends—Fine Old East India, for example—still allude
to the practice. The wine Henri Maire had chosen to be despatched for
two years before the mast, so to speak, was an Arbois rosé. He called
it Vin Retour des Iles and proposed to offer it to his numerous guests at
the Grand Véfour (and to my much smaller group in London) to
demonstrate—I think—that Arbais rose was serious wine and not to be
confused with the pretty tipples in designer bottles then increasingly
popular at restaurant lunch tables.

I chose to hold my dinner in a private dining room at Prunier's on
St. James's Street. Simone Prunier, a consummate restaurateur, was a
resourceful woman of limitless discretion, and I knew I could rely on
her to pull together what seemed to me to be an adventure fraught with
risk. We knew nothing of the dish to be sent from Paris except that it
was to be *marcassin* (young wild boar) accompanied by a sauce. It
would need only to be reheated.

We composed a menu around this dish: champagne and canapés to
greet the arriving guests; a plain poached turbot with hollandaise
(Prunier's, after all, was renowned for its fish but we didn't want to
upstage Raymond Oliver); cheeses from the Jura area—the Franche-
Comté—to follow the *marcassin;* and a sumptuous pineapple ice, to be
brought to the table packed inside the original fruit, enveloped in a veil of
finely spun sugar. I selected Henri Maire wines for the fish and the cheese
that would allow the special bottling of rosé every chance to be the star.

The dish, transported expeditiously by Air France from restaurant door
to restaurant door, was something of an anticlimax: I can describe it only
as minced wild-boar patties in a brown sauce. Unfortunately, the wine
offered neither compensation nor distraction. Henri Maire had decided, at
the last minute, that there was barely enough Vin Retour des Iles for the
swelling number of his guests at the Grand Véfour and therefore none—not
a single bottle—was sent to London. I was asked to serve the standard

Arbois rosé instead. I have to say, it was a perfectly satisfactory wine. But it was not, as Dr. Johnson once said of a perfectly satisfactory dinner, what you would ask a man to. Least of all at Prunier's.

Who knows what vinous perspectives the actual Vin Retour des Iles might have opened up for us? In a brief but charming new book, *La légende du Vin*, subtitled (in French, of course) *A Short Essay of Sentimental Enophilia,* Jean-Baptiste Baronian, French novelist, essayist, critic and editor, says that those who appreciate wine find in every glass a trace of a history, of a civilization, and of a gesture that bind together a time and a place.

A few years ago I tasted, on an exceptional occasion in California, the 1771 and 1791 vintages of Château Margaux. Both wines were a vibrant strawberry color and astonishingly fresh; their bouquet was extravagantly scented. In the eighteenth century, wine, like fruit, was bottled for preservation, not aging, and it was common practice to perk the aroma of red Bordeaux with powdered orrisroot, the rhizome of iris. It was used then, as it still is (but in perfume, not in wine) to contribute a scent of violets. In any case, both wines were made before Cabernet Sauvignon, with its distinctive pungency and dense garnet color, had replaced Malbec as the principal grape of the Médoc.

With Fragonard, Couperin and Beaumarchais as touchstones, anyone speculating on how an eighteenth-century French wine tasted back then would imagine something with very much the delicacy, the luminosity, and the perfumed intensity of those wines. I confess, though, that foremost in my own mind as they slipped down my throat was the thought that I was drinking—in Los Angeles, the quintessential twentieth-century city—wines made by men alive in Bordeaux at the time of the American and French Revolutions. Just to look at Chardin's painting of a bowl of raspberries can be an eighteenth-century experience. But in absorbing alcohol converted from fruit sugar two centuries earlier, I was actually sharing calories transmitted in solar energy that had also warmed the faces of Thomas Jefferson and Marie-Antoinette.

But *most* memorable of my life? Were it not that people casually met might assume I was making fun of them, I would in fact explain that it was, and still remains, unidentified. I drank it at a mountain inn near the Simplon pass in the early summer of either 1962 or 1963. From 1955 until 1970 I spent weeks on end visiting suppliers all over Europe to taste and select the wines my firm brought to London. For much of that time there were neither *autoroutes* nor *autostrade,* and I drove a Triumph TR4 (which I'd had refinished in deep Burgundy red instead of its original British racing green) to get myself quickly from place to place. Well, that was the rational explanation at any rate.

I'd spent the night at Sion, in the Swiss Valais, after an evening of *raclette*—molten slivers of the local cheese draped over hot potatoes—and the cooperative's Fendant, a flowery white wine with which we were having a modest success in England. I was on my way to Verona, and had set off early to be sure of reaching Milan by evening.

There was little traffic on the road—the Simplon is more often used as a rail route—and by noon I was high in the Alps with the Swiss-Italian border behind me. It was early June, and for most of the way wildflowers were scattered along the roadside. At the higher altitudes, drifts of snow still lay dazzlingly white in the midday sun. The exhilaration of the climb—the TR4 would respond with its distinctive soft roar as I changed through the gears on those endless, steep turns—the crisp air, the brilliant light, and the grandeur of the mountains, made me feel I was on top of the world. And I almost was, literally. But I was also hungry and had many curving miles ahead of me to Domodossola, where I planned to stop for a late lunch.

Then an inn appeared. It was small, but comfortably appealing. The deliciously simple set lunch of sautéed veal scallops and buttered noodles with a salad of green beans was typical of what one finds in the mountains. My glass was filled with a light red wine poured from a pitcher, left on the table. I was relaxed, carefree, and happy. Oh, how ruby bright that wine was; it gleamed in the sunlight. I remember clearly its enticing aroma—youthful but with a refinement that surprised me. The wine was sweetly exotic: lively on my tongue, perfectly balanced, and with a long, glossy finish. It was the sort of wine that Omar Khayyam might have had in mind for his desert tryst. The young woman who had poured it for me was amused when I asked what it was. It was, she said, vino *rosso*.

I sat there trying, without success, to put my finger on the grape. It was probably one of those sub-Alpine varieties already then disappearing into odd pockets of vineyard in remote valleys—Bonarda perhaps, or Ruchè. Or perhaps it was, more conventionally a Brachetto, a Freisa or a Grignolino, any one of which was likely to show more than its usual appeal if grown near that altitude. Whatever it was, the wine had been made with uncommon care. It was exquisitely graceful.

I shall always remember that wine, though I have never learned what it might have been. Italian friends have suggested Vercelli, from the Novara hills, just a way farther south; and others, Valtellina, farther east. No wine I've tasted since from either has come close.

But the pleasure in any wine is subjective: we each bring something to what is there in the glass and interpret the result differently. Perhaps, on that June day more than thirty years ago, I had contributed an extra-large dose of well-being. Who can say?

Theatres of Food

NATURALLY

MICHAEL POLLAN

I. SUPERMARKET PASTORAL

ALMOST OVERNIGHT, THE amount and variety of organic food on offer in my local supermarket has mushroomed. Fresh produce, milk, eggs, cereal, frozen food, even junk food—all of it now has its own organic *doppelgänger*, and more often than not these products wind up in my shopping cart. I like buying organic, for the usual salad of rational and sentimental reasons. At a time when the whole food system feels somewhat precarious, I assume that a product labeled organic is more healthful and safer, more "wholesome," though if I stop to think about it, I'm not exactly sure what that means. I also like the fact that by buying organic, I'm casting a vote for a more environmentally friendly kind of agriculture: "Better Food for a Better Planet," in the slogan of Cascadian Farm, one of the older organic brands. Compared with all the other food in the supermarket, which is happy to tell you everything about itself except how it was grown, organic food seems a lot more legible. "Organic" on the label conjures a whole story, even if it is the consumer who fills in most of the details, supplying the hero (American Family Farmer), the villain (Agribusinessman) and the literary genre, which I think of as "supermarket pastoral." Just look at the happy Vermont cow on that carton of milk, wreathed in wildflowers like a hippie at her wedding around 1973.

Look a little closer, though, and you begin to see cracks in the pastoral narrative. It took me more than a year to notice, but the label on that carton of Organic Cow has been rewritten recently. It doesn't talk about happy cows and Vermont family farmers quite so much anymore, probably because the Organic Cow has been bought out by Horizon, a Colorado company (referred to here, in proper pastoral style, as "the Horizon family of companies"). Horizon is a $127 million public corporation that has become the Microsoft of organic milk, controlling 70 percent of the retail market. Notice, too, that the milk is now "ultra-pasteurized," a process the carton presents as a boon to the consumer (it pushes the freshness date into the next millennium), but which of course also allows the company to ferry its milk all over the country.

When I asked a local dairyman about this (we still have one or two in town) he said that the chief reason to ultrapasteurize—a high-heat process that "kills the milk," destroying its enzymes and many of its vitamins—is so you can sell milk over long distances. Arguably, ultra-pasteurized organic milk is less nutritious than conventionally pasteurized conventional milk. This dairyman also bent my ear about Horizon's "factory farms" out West, where thousands of cows that never encounter a blade of grass spend their days confined to a fenced dry lot, eating (certified organic) grain and tethered to milking machines three times a day. So maybe Organic Cow milk isn't quite as legible a product as I thought.

I wasn't sure if the farmer had his facts straight (it would turn out he did), but he made me wonder whether I really knew what organic meant anymore. I understood organic to mean—in addition to being produced without synthetic chemicals—less processed, more local, easier on the animals. So I started looking more closely at some of the other organic items in the store. One of them in the frozen-food case caught my eye: an organic TV dinner (now there are three words I never expected to string together) from Cascadian Farm called Country Herb: "rice, vegetables and grilled chicken breast ships with a savory herb sauce."

The text-heavy box it came in told the predictable organic stories—about the chicken (raised without chemicals and allowed "to roam freely in an outdoor yard"); about the rice and vegetables (grown without synthetic chemicals); even about the carton (recycled)—but when I got to the ingredients list, I felt a small jolt of cognitive dissonance. For one thing, the list of ingredients went on forever (31 ingredients in all) and included such enigmas of modern food technology as natural chicken flavor, high-oleic safflower oil, guar and xanthan gum, soy lecithin, carrageenan and natural grill flavor, this last culinary breakthrough achieved with something called "tapioca maltodextrin." The label assured me that most of these additives are organic, which they no doubt are, and yet they seem about as jarring to my conception of organic food as, say, a cigarette boat on Walden Pond. But then, so too is the fact (mentioned nowhere on the label) that Cascadian Farm has recently become a subsidiary of General Mills, the third biggest food conglomerate in North America

Clearly, my notion of supermarket pastoralism has fallen hopelessly out of date. The organic movement has become a $7.7 billion business:

call it Industrial Organic. Although that represents but a fraction of the $400 billion business of selling Americans food, organic is now the fastest-growing category in the supermarket. Perhaps inevitably, this sort of growth—sustained at a steady 20 percent a year for more than a decade—has attracted the attention of the very agribusiness corporations to which the organic movement once presented a radical alternative and an often scalding critique. Even today, the rapid growth of organic closely tracks consumers' rising worries about the conventional food supply—about chemicals, about additives and, most recently, about genetically modified ingredients and mad cow disease; every food scare is followed by a spike in organic sales. And now that organic food has established itself as a viable alternative food chain, agribusiness has decided that the best way to deal with that alternative is simply to own it. The question now is, What will they do with it? Is the word "organic" being emptied of its meaning?

II. THE ROAD TO CASCADIAN FARM

I don't know about you, but I never expect the bucolic scenes and slogans on my packaged food to correspond to reality (where exactly is Nature's Valley, anyway?), but it turns out the Cascadian Farm pictured on my TV dinner is a real farm that grows real food—though not quite the same food contained in my TV dinner.

Cascadian Farm occupies a narrow, breathtaking shelf of land wedged between the Skagit River and the North Cascades in the town of Rockport, Wash., 75 miles northeast of Seattle. Originally called the New Cascadian Survival and Reclamation Project, the farm was started in 1971 by Gene Kahn with the idea of growing food for the collective of environmentally-minded hippies he had hooked up with in nearby Bellingham. At the time, Kahn was a 24-year-old grad-school dropout from the South Side of Chicago who, after reading *Silent Spring* and *Diet for a Small Planet*, determined to go back to the land, there to change "the food system." That particular dream was not so outrageous in 1971—this was the moment, after all, when the whole counterculture was taking a rural turn—but Kahn's success in actually achieving it surely is: he went on to become a pioneer of the organic movement and did much to move organic food into the mainstream. Today, Cascadian Farm's farm is a General Mills showcase—a P.R. farm," as its founder freely acknowledges—and Kahn, erstwhile hippie farmer, is a General Mills vice president and a millionaire. He has become one of the most successful figures in the organic community and also perhaps one of the most polarizing; for to many organic farm-

ers and activists, he has come to symbolize the takeover of the movement by agribusiness.

"Organic is becoming what we hoped it would be an alternative to,"
says Roger Blobaum, who played a key role as a consumer advocate in
pushing Congress to establish the U.S.D.A.'s fledgling organic program.
"Gene Kahn's approach is slowly but surely taking us in that direction. He's
one of the real pioneers, but there are people now who are suspicious of
him." Kahn is apt to call such people "purists," "Luddites," "romantics"
and "ideologues" who have failed to outgrow the "antibusiness prejudices"
of the 60s. He'll tell you he's still committed to changing the food system—
but now from "inside." Few in the movement doubt his sincerity or commitment, but many will tell you the food system will much sooner change
Kahn, along with the whole meaning of organic.

On an overcast morning not long ago, Kahn drove me out to
Rockport from his company's offices in Sedro-Woolley, following the
twists of the Skagit River east in a new forest green Lexus with vanity
plates that say "ORGANIC." Kahn is a strikingly boyish-looking 54,
and after you factor in a shave and 20 pounds, it's not hard to pick his
face out from the beards-beads-and-tractor photos on display in his
office. Back in the farm's early days, when Kahn supervised and men-
tored the rotating band of itinerant hippies who would show up to
work a day or a week or a year on the farm, he drove a red VW Beetle
and an ancient, temperamental John Deere. Kahn lived in a modest
clapboard farmhouse on Cascadian Farm until 1993. Now he lives in a
McMansion high in the hills overlooking Puget Sound.

Like a lot of the early organic farmers, Kahn had no idea what he was
doing at first and suffered his share of crop failures. In 1971, organic
agriculture was in its infancy—a few hundred scattered amateurs learning by trial and error how to grow food without chemicals, an ad hoc
grassroots R. & D. effort for which there was precisely no institutional
support. Though it did draw on various peasant-farming models, modern-day organic agriculture is a relatively novel and remarkably sophisticated system with deep roots in the counterculture. The theoretical roots of
organic agriculture go back a bit further, principally to the work of a
British scientist by the name of Sir Albert Howard. Based on his experiments in India and observations of peasant farms in Asia, Howard's 1940
treatise "An Agricultural Testament" demonstrated the connection
between the health of the soil and the ability of plants to withstand diseases and pests. Howard's agricultural heresies were praised in the pages
of *The Whole Earth Catalog* (by Wendell Berry) and popularized by J.I.
Rodale in *Organic Gardening and Farming* magazine—which claimed
700,000 readers in 1971, one of whom was Gene Kahn.

But the word "organic" around 1970 connoted a great deal more than a technique for growing vegetables. The movement's pioneers set out to create not just an alternative mode of production (the farms) but of distribution (the co-ops and health-food stores) and even consumption. A "countercuisine" based on whole grains and unprocessed ingredients rose up to challenge conventional industrial "white bread" food. ("Plastic food" was an epithet you heard a lot.) For a host of reasons that seem risible in retrospect, brown food of all kinds (rice, bread, wheat, sugar) was deemed morally superior to white. Much more than just lunch, organic food was "an edible dynamic" that promised to raise consciousness about the economic order, draw critical lines of connection between the personal and the political. It was also, not incidentally, precisely what your parents didn't eat.

Such was dinner and the dinner-table conversation at Cascadian Farm and countless other counterculture tables in the early 1970s. As for an alternative mode of distributing food, Kahn recruited a hippie capitalist named Roger Weschler to help him figure out how to sell his strawberries before they rotted in the field. Weschler had helped found something called the Cooperating Community, a network of Seattle businesses committed to ecological principles and worker self-management A new offshoot, Community Produce, began distributing the food grown at Cascadian Farm, and Weschler and Kahn set out, in the unembarrassed words of Cascadian Farm's official corporate history, "to change the world's food system." Twenty-nine years later, Weschler is still at it, operating a produce brokerage devoted to supporting family farmers. And Kahn? Weschler, who has lost neither his scraggly black beard nor his jittery intensity, told me that by going corporate, his old friend "has made a very different choice."

If Kahn were the least bit embarrassed by the compromises he has made in his organic principles since those long-ago days, he would surely have rewritten his company's official history by now—and never sent me to interview Weschler. But as we walked around the farm talking about "how everything eventually morphs into the way the world is," it seemed clear that Kahn has made his peace with that fact of life, decided that the gains outweighed the losses.

In time, Kahn became quite a good farmer and, to his surprise, an even better businessman. By the late 70s, he had discovered the virtues of adding value to his produce by processing it (freezing blueberries and strawberries, making jams), and once Cascadian Farm had begun processing, Kahn discovered he could make more money buying produce from other farmers than by growing it himself. During the 80s, Cascadian Farm became an increasingly virtual sort of farm, processing and marketing a range of packaged foods well beyond the Seattle area.

"The whole notion of a 'cooperative community' we started with gradually began to mimic the system," Kahn recalled. "We were shipping food across the country, using diesel fuel—we were industrial organic farmers. I was bit by bit becoming more of this world, and there was a lot of pressure on the business to become more privatized."

That pressure became irresistible in 1990, when in the aftermath of the Alar scare, Kahn nearly lost everything—and control of Cascadian Farm wound up in corporate hands. In the history of the organic movement, the Alar episode is a watershed, marking the birth pangs of the modern organic industry. After a somewhat overheated "60 Minutes" exposé on apple growers' use of Alar, a growth-regulator that the Environmental Protection Agency declared a carcinogen, middle America suddenly discovered organic. "Panic for Organic" was the cover line of one newsweekly, and, overnight, demand from the supermarket chains soared. The ragtag industry wasn't quite ready for primetime, however. Kahn borrowed heavily to finance an ambitious expansion, contracted with farmers to grow an awful lot of organic produce—and then watched in horror as the bubble of demand subsided along with the headlines about Alar. Kahn was forced to sell a majority stake in the company—to Welch's—and set out on what he calls his "corporate adventure."

"We were part of the food industry now," he told me. "But I wanted to leverage that position to redefine the way we grow food—not what people want to eat or how we distribute it. That sure as hell isn't going to change." Kahn sees himself as very much the grown-up, a sober realist in a community of unreconstructed idealists. He speaks of selling out to Welch's as "the time when I lost the company" but doesn't trouble himself with second thoughts or regrets; in fact, it was all for the best. "Welch's was my business school," he said. Kahn seems to have no doubt that his path is the right path, not only for him but for the organic movement as a whole: "You have a choice of getting sad about all that or moving on. We tried hard to build a cooperative community and a local food system, but at the end of the day it wasn't successful. This is just lunch for most people. Just lunch. We can call it sacred, we can talk about communion, but it's just lunch."

In the years after the Alar bubble burst in 1990, the organic industry recovered, embarking on a period of double-digit annual growth and rapid consolidation, as mainstream food companies began to take organic—or at least, the organic market—seriously. Gerber's, Heinz, Dole, ConAgra and A.D.M. all created or acquired organic brands. Cascadian Farm itself became a miniconglomerate, acquiring Muir Glen, the California organic tomato processors, and the combined company changed its name to Small Planet Foods. Nineteen-ninety also marked the beginning of federal recognition for organic agriculture: that year, Congress passed the Organic Food Production Act. The legislation instructed the Department of Agriculture—which historically had treated organic farming with undisguised contempt—to establish uniform national standards for organic food and farming, fixing the definition of a word that had always meant different things to different people.

Settling on that definition turned out to be a grueling decadelong process, as various forces both within and outside the movement battled for control of a word that had developed a certain magic in the market-place. Agribusiness fought to define the word as broadly as possible, in part to make it easier for mainstream companies to get into organic but also out of fear that anything deemed not organic would henceforth carry an official stigma. At first, the U.S.D.A., acting out of longstand-ing habit, obliged its agribusiness clients, issuing a watery set of stan-dards in 1997 that, incredibly, allowed for the use of genetic modifica-tion, irradiation and sewage sludge in organic food production. But an unprecedented flood of public comment from outraged organic farmers and consumers forced the U.S.D.A. back to the drawing board, in what was widely viewed as a victory for the movement's principles.

Yet while the struggle with agribusiness over the meaning of the word "organic" was making headlines, another, equally important struggle was under way at the U.S.D.A. between Big and Little Organic, and this time the outcome was decidedly more ambiguous. Could a factory farm be organic? Was an organic cow entitled to dine on pasture? Did food addi-tives and synthetic chemicals have a place in organic processed food? If the answers to these seem like no-brainers, then you, too, are stuck in an out-dated pastoral view of organic. Big Organic won all three arguments. The final standards, which will take effect next year, are widely seen as favor-ing the industry's big players. The standards do an admirable job of set-ting the bar for a more environmentally responsible kind of farming, but as perhaps was inevitable, many of the philosophical values embedded in the word "organic" did not survive the federal rule-making process.

Gene Kahn served on the U.S.D.A.'s National Organic Standards Board from 1992 to 1997, playing a key role in making the standards safe for the organic TV dinner and a great many other processed organic foods. This was no small feat, for Kahn and his allies had to work around the 1990 legislation establishing organic standards, which pro-hibited synthetic food additives. Kahn argued that you couldn't have organic processed foods without synthetics. Several of the consumer representatives on the standards board contended that this was precisely the point, and if no synthetics meant no organic TV dinners, then TV dinners were something organic simply shouldn't do.

Joan Dye Gussow, a nutritionist and an outspoken standards-board member, made the case against synthetics in a 1996 article that was much debated, "Can an Organic Twinkie Be Certified?" She questioned whether organic should simply mirror the existing food supply, with its highly processed, salted and sugary junk food, or whether it should aspire to something better—a countercuisine. Kahn responded with market populism: if the consumer wants an organic Twinkie, then we should give it to him. As he put it to me on the drive back from Cascadian Farm, "Organic is not your mother." In the end, it came down to an argument between the old movement and the new industry, and the new industry won: the final standards simply ignored the 1990 law, drawing up a "national list" of permissible additives and synthetics, from ascorbic acid to xanthan gum.

"If we had lost on synthetics," Kahn told me, "we'd be out of business."

Kahn's victory cleared the way for the development of a parallel organic food supply: organic Heinz ketchup (already on the shelves in England), organic Hamburger Helper, organic Miracle Whip and, sooner or later, organic Twinkies. This is not a prospect everyone relishes. Even Kahn says: "I'm not looking forward to the organic Twinkie. But I will defend to the death anyone's right to create one!" Eliot Coleman, a Maine farmer and writer whose organic techniques have influenced two generations of farmers, is repulsed by the whole idea: "I don't care if the Wheaties are organic—I wouldn't use them for compost. Processed organic food is as bad as any other processed food."

III. THE SOUL OF A NEW TV DINNER

Small Planet Foods's headquarters in Sedro-Woolley occupies a downtown block of 19th-century brick storefronts in this faded and decidedly funky logging town. The storefronts have been converted into loftlike offices designed in the alternative-capitalist style: brick walls, air ducts and I-beams all in plain sight—no facades here. Since every day is dress-down day at Small Planet Foods, Friday is the day everybody takes his or her dog to work. I spent a Friday in Woolley, learning the ins and outs of formulating, manufacturing and selling an organic TV dinner.

Steve Harper, Small Planet's chief food scientist, described the challenge of keeping a frozen herb sauce from separating unappetizingly (instead of modified food starch, organic food scientists rely on things like carrageenan, a seaweed derivative, to enhance "freeze-thaw stability") and explained the algorithm governing the relative size and population of chicken chunks (fewer bigger chunks give a better "quality perception" than a larger number of dice-size cubes). He also explained how they get that salty processed-food taste right inside a chicken chunk: marinade-injecting hypodermic needles.

If Harper is responsible for the "recipe" of a Cascadian Farm TV dinner, it falls to Mary Shelby, the company's vice president for operations, to get the meal "cooked." Shelby, who came to Small Planet after a career in operations at Birds Eye, handles the considerable logistics involved in moving three dozen ingredients on time to the co-packing plant in Alberta, Canada, where they are combined in a microwaveable bowl. He described an elaborate (and energy-intensive) choreography of ingredients, packaging and processes that takes place over a half-dozen states and two countries. Fresh broccoli, for instance, travels from a farm in the Central Valley to a plant in Sanger, Calif., where it is cut into florets, blanched and frozen. From California, the broccoli is trucked to Edmonton, Alberta, there to meet up with pieces of organic chicken that have traveled from a farm in Petaluma, Calif., with a stop at a processing plant in Salem, Ore., where they were defrosted, injected with marinade, cubed, cooked and refrozen. They don't call it processed food for nothing.

Most everyone I met at Small Planet Foods expressed a fervently held belief in the value of organic farming. There was a politics to their work, and if they had had to compromise certain ideals in order to adapt their products to the mainstream food system, all this was in service to a greater good they seemed never to lose sight of: converting the greatest number of acres of American farmland to organic agriculture. The solitary exception to this outlook was a vice president for marketing, the man most responsible for developing Cascadian's new slogan, 'Taste You Can Believe In." R. Brooks Gekler is a marketing star at General Mills who was installed at Small Planet Foods immediately after the acquisition. A year later, Gekler, a handsome, well-spoken New York University M.B.A., was still something of an outsider at Small Planet Foods. "There are people here who regard me as the Antichrist," he joked. I think it was around the time he explained to me, apropos of his colleagues, that "some principles can be an obstacle to success" that I understood why this might be so.

"I came here to help the company identify its consumer target," Gekler explained crisply, "which is different from what they believed." In marketing parlance, Small Planet (like the rest of the organic industry) had traditionally directed its products toward someone called "the true natural"—a committed, activist consumer. True naturals are the people on whom the organic food industry has been built, the outwardly directed, socially conscious consumers devoted to the proposition of "better food for a better planet." But while their numbers are growing—true naturals now represent about 10 percent of the U.S.

food market, as a large proportion of Gen X'ers join their ranks—the future of organic, General Mills says, lies with a considerably larger group of even more affluent consumers called the "health seekers." It is to this group that Cascadian Farm is targeting its new TV dinners.

Health seekers, who today represent about a quarter of the market, are less "extrinsic"—that is, more interested in their own health than that of the planet. They buy supplements, work out, drink wine, drive imported cars. They aren't interested in a countercuisine, which is why Cascadian's new line of frozen entrees eschews whole grains and embraces a decidedly middle-of-the road "flavor profile."

The chief reason the health seeker will buy organic is for the perceived health benefits. This poses a certain marketing challenge, however, since it has always been easier to make the environmental case for organic food than the health case. Although General Mills has put its new organic division under the umbrella of its "health initiatives" group, "organic" is not, at least officially, a health, nutrition or food-safety claim, a point that Dan Glickman, then secretary of agriculture, took pains to emphasize when he unveiled the U.S.D.A.'s new label in December: organic, he stressed, is simply "a production standard."

"At first, I thought the inability to make hard-hitting health claims"—for organic—was a hurdle, "Gekler said when I asked him about this glitch. "But the reality is, all you have to say is 'organic'— you don't need to provide any more information." These particular consumers—who pay attention to the media, to food scares and to articles like this one—take their own health claims to the word.

Suddenly the genius of Cascadian Farm's new slogan dawned on me. "Taste You Can Believe In": meaningless in and of itself, the slogan "allows the consumer to bring his or her personal beliefs to it," Gekler explained. While the true natural hears social values in the phrase "Believe In," the health seeker hears a promise of health and flavor. The slogan is an empty signifier, as the literary theorists would say, and what a good thing that is for a company like General Mills. How much better to let the consumers fill in the marketing message—healthier, more nutritious, no pesticides, more wholesome, sustainable, safer, purer—because these are controversial comparative claims that, as Gekler acknowledged, "make the conventional food industry very uncomfortable."

Before I left his office, I asked Gekler about his own beliefs— whether or not he believed that organic food was better food. He paused for a long time, no doubt assessing the cost of either answer, and deftly punted.

"I don't know yet."

IV. DOWN ON THE INDUSTRIAL ORGANIC FARM

No farm I have ever visited before prepared me for the industrial organic farms I saw in California. When I think about organic farming, I think family farm, I think small scale, I think hedgerows and compost piles and battered pickup trucks. I don't think migrant laborers, combines, thousands of acres of broccoli reaching clear to the horizon. To the eye, these farms look exactly like any other industrial farm in California—and in fact the biggest organic operations in the state today are owned and operated by conventional mega-farms. The same farmer who is applying toxic fumigants to sterilize the soil in one field is in the next field applying compost to nurture the soil's natural fertility.

Is there something wrong with this picture? It all depends on where you stand. Gene Kahn makes the case that the scale of a farm has no bearing on its fidelity to organic principles and that unless organic "scales up" it will "never be anything more than yuppie food." To prove his point, Kahn sent me to visit large-scale farms whose organic practices were in many ways quite impressive, including the Central Valley operation that grows vegetables for his frozen dinners and tomatoes for Muir Glen.

Greenways Organic is a successful 2,000-acre organic-produce operation tucked into a 24,000-acre conventional farm outside Fresno; the crops, the machines, the crews, the rotations and the fields were indistinguishable, and yet two very different kinds of industrial agriculture are being practiced here side by side.

In place of petrochemical fertilizers, Greenways's organic fields are nourished by compost made by the ton at a horse farm nearby. Insects are controlled with biological agents and beneficial insects like lacewings. Frequent and carefully timed tilling, as well as propane torches, keeps down the weeds, perhaps the industrial organic farmer's single stiffest challenge. This approach is at best a compromise: running tillers through the soil so frequently is destructive to its tilth, yet weeding a 160-acre block of broccoli by hand is unrealistic.

Since Greenways grows the same crops conventionally and organically, I was interested to hear John Diener, one of the farm's three partners, say he knew for a fact that his organic crops were "better," and not only because they hadn't been doused with pesticide. When Diener takes his tomatoes to the cannery, the organic crop reliably receives higher Brix scores—a measure of the sugars in fruits and vegetables. It seems that crops grown on nitrogen fertilizer take up considerably more water, thereby diluting their nutrients, sugars and flavors. The same biochemical process could explain why many people—including the many chefs who swear by organic ingredients—believe organic produce simply tastes better. With less water in it, the flavor and the nutrients of a floret of organic broccoli will be more concentrated than one grown with chemical fertilizers.

It's too simple to say that smaller organic farms are automatically truer to the organic ideal than big ones. In fact, the organic ideal is so exacting—a sustainable system that requires not only no synthetic chemicals but also few purchased inputs of any kind and that returns as much to the soil as it removes—that it is most often honored in the breach. Yet the farmers who come closest to achieving this ideal do tend to be smaller in scale. These are the farmers who plant dozens of different crops in fields that resemble quilts and practice long and elaborate rotations, thereby achieving the rich biodiversity in space and time that is the key to making a farm sustainable.

For better or worse, these are not the kinds of farms Small Planet Foods does business with today. It's simply more efficient to buy from one 1,000-acre farm than 10 100-acre farms. Indeed, Cascadian Farm the corporation can't even afford to use produce from Cascadian Farm the farm: it's too small. So the berries grown there are sold at a roadside stand, while the company buys berries for freezing from as far away as Chile.

The big question is whether the logic of an industrial food chain can be reconciled to the logic of the natural systems on which organic agriculture has tried to model itself. Put another way, Is "industrial organic" a contradiction in terms?

Kahn is convinced it is not, but others both inside and outside his company see a tension. Sarah Huntington is one of Cascadian's oldest employees. She worked alongside Kahn on the farm and at one time or another has held just about every job in the company. "The maw of that processing plant beast eats 10 acres of cornfield an hour," she told me. "And you're locked into planting a particular variety like Jubilee that ripens all at once and holds up in processing. So you see how the system is constantly pushing you back toward monoculture, which is anathema in organic. But that's the challenge—to change the system more than it changes you."

One of the most striking ways Small Planet Foods is changing the system is by helping conventional farms convert a portion of their acreage to organic. Several thousand acres of American farmland are now organic as a result of the company's efforts, which go well beyond offering contracts to providing instruction and even management. Kahn has helped to prove to the skeptical that organic—dismissed as "hippie farming" not very long ago—can work on a large scale. The environmental benefits of this educational process shouldn't be underestimated. And yet the industrialization of organic comes at a price. The most obvious is consolidation: today five giant farms control fully one-half of the

$400 million organic produce market in California. Partly as a result, the price premium for organic crops is shrinking. This is all to the good for expanding organic's market beyond yuppies, but it is crushing many of the small farmers for whom organic has represented a profitable niche, a way out of the cheap-food economics that has ravaged American farming over the last few decades. Indeed, many of the small farmers present at the creation of organic agriculture today find themselves struggling to compete against the larger players, as the familiar, dismal history of American agriculture begins to repeat itself in the organic sector.

This has opened up a gulf in the movement between Big and Little Organic and convinced many of the movement's founders that the time has come to move "beyond organic"—to raise the bar on American agriculture yet again. Some of these innovating farmers want to stress fair labor standards, others quality or growing exclusively for local markets. In Maine, Eliot Coleman has pioneered a sophisticated market garden entirely under plastic, to supply his "food shed" with local produce all winter long; even in January his solar-heated farm beats California on freshness and quality, if not price. In Virginia, Joel Salatin has developed an ingenious self-sufficient rotation of grass-fed livestock: cattle, chickens and rabbits that take turns eating, and feeding, the same small pasture. There are hundreds of these "beyond organic" farmers springing up now around the country. The fact is, however, that the word "organic"—having entered the vocabulary of both agribusiness and government—is no longer these farmers' to redefine. Coleman and Salatin, both of whom reject the U.S.D.A. organic label, are searching for new words to describe what it is they're doing. Michael Ableman, a "beyond organic" farmer near Santa Barbara, Calif., says "We may have to give up on the word 'organic,' leave it to the Gene Kahns of the world. To be honest, I'm not sure I want the association, because what I'm doing on my farm is not just substituting materials."

Not long ago at a conference on organic agriculture, a corporate organic farmer suggested to a family farmer struggling to survive in the competitive world of industrial organic agriculture that he "should really try to develop a niche to distinguish yourself in the market" The small farmer replied: "I believe I developed that niche 20 years ago. It's called 'organic.' And now you're sitting on it."

V. Gene Kahn Visits the Mothership

In March, I accompanied Gene Kahn on one of his monthly visits to the General Mills headquarters, a grassy corporate campus strewn with modern sculptures in the suburbs outside Minneapolis. In deference to

Fortune 500 etiquette, I put on a suit and tie but quickly realized I was overdressed: Kahn had on his usual khakis and a denim work shirt embroidered with a bright red Muir Glen tomato. When I said something, Kahn told me he makes a point of not changing his clothes when he goes to Minneapolis. I get it: an organic farmer in an embroidered work shirt is part of what General Mills was acquiring when it acquired Small Planet Foods. Yet this particular organic farmer is presumably a far sight wealthier than most of his new corporate colleagues: when General Mills bought Small Planet Foods for an estimated $70 million, Kahn still owned 10 percent of the company.

Together, Kahn and I toured General Mills's Bell Technical Center, a sprawling research-and-development facility where some 900 food scientists, chemists, industrial designers and nutritionists dream up and design both the near- and long-term future of American food. This was Kahn's first visit to the facility, and as we moved from lab to lab, I could see his boyish enthusiasm mounting as he collected new ideas and business cards.

In the packaging-design lab, even before Arne Brauner could finish explaining how he engineered the boxes, bowls and cups in which General Mills sells its products, Kahn asked him, "Has there ever been a completely edible packaging for food?" Brauner rubbed his chin for a moment.

"The sausage. That was probably the first."

Kahn now told him about the bowl in which Cascadian Farm sold its frozen entrees. Plastic would have turned off the organic consumer, he explained, so they were using coated paperboard, which isn't readily recyclable. Would it be possible, Kahn wondered, to make a microwaveable bowl out of biodegradable food starch? Brauner said he had heard about a cornstarch clamshell for fast-food burgers and offered to look into it. Kahn took his card.

Kahn had another, more off-the-wall request for Perry May, the man in charge of General Mills's machine shop. This is where engineers and machinists make the machines that make the food. Kahn asked Perry if his shop could help develop a prototype for a new weeding machine he had dreamed up for organic farmers. "It would be an optical weeder with a steam generator on board," Kahn explained. "The scanner would distinguish between a weed and a corn plant, say, and then zap the weed with a jet of hot steam." May thought it might be doable; they exchanged cards.

"I feel like a kid in a candy store," Kahn told me afterward. "Organic has never had these kinds of resources at its disposal."

On the drive back from Bell, Kahn grew positively effervescent about the "organic synergies" that could come from General Mills's acquisition of Pillsbury, a $10.5 billion deal now awaiting F.T.C.

approval. Pillsbury owns Green Giant, and the prospect of being able to draw on that company's scientists (and patents) has planted agronomic fantasies in the fevered brain of the former farmer: broccoli specifically bred for organic production ("We've never had anything like that!"); an organic version of Niblets, Green Giant's popular proprietary corn; carrots bred for extra vitamin content. In fact, Kahn got so worked up spinning his vision of the industrial organic future that he got us lost.

So this was how Kahn proposed to change the American food system from within: by leveraging its capital and know-how on behalf of his dream. Which prompts the question, Just how does the American food system feel about all this? As Kahn and I made the rounds of General Mills's senior management, he in his work shirt, I in my suit, I tried to find out how these tribunes of agribusiness regarded their new vice president's organic dream, exactly how it fit into their vision of the future of food.

The future of food, I learned, is toward ever more health and convenience—the two most important food trends today—at no sacrifice of taste. "Our corporate philosophy," as one senior vice president, Danny Strickland, put it, "is to give consumers what they want with no trade-offs." Organic fits into this philosophy in so far as the company's market research shows that consumers increasingly want it and believe it's healthier.

The acquisition of a leading organic food company is part of a company-wide "health initiative"—along with adding calcium to various product lines and developing "functional foods" like Harmony, a soy-and-calcium-fortified cereal aimed at menopausal women. When I asked Ian Friendly, the sharp, young executive in charge of the company's health-initiative group, if this meant that General Mills believed organic was more healthful than conventional food, he deftly shifted vocabulary, suggesting that "wellness' is perhaps a better word." Wellness is more of a whole gestalt or lifestyle, which includes things like yoga, massage and working out. It quickly became clear that in the eyes of General Mills, organic is not a revolution so much as a market niche, like menopausal women or "ethnics," and that health is really a matter of consumer perception. You did not have to buy into the organic "belief system" to sell it. When I asked Strickland if he believed that organic food was in any way better, he said: "Better? It depends. Food is subjective. Perceptions depend on circumstances."

I got much the same response from other General Mills executives. The words "better food," uttered so unself-consciously in Sedro-Woolley, rang in their offices like a phrase from a dead language. Steve Sanger, the company's chairman, said: "I'm certain it's better for some people. It depends on their particular beliefs." Sheri Schellhaas, vice president for research and development, said, "The question is, Do consumers believe organic is healthier?" Marc Belton, a senior vice president for cereals and the executive most responsible for the Small Planet acquisition, put it this way. "Is it better food? . . . You know, so much of life is what you make of it. If it's right for you, it's better—if you feel it's better, it is."

At General Mills, it would seem, the whole notion of objective truth has been replaced by a kind of value-neutral consumer constructivism, in which each sovereign shopper constructs his own reality: "Taste You Can Believe In." Kahn understands that there is no percentage in signing onto the organic belief system, not when you also have Trix and GO-Gurt and Cinnamon Toast Milk and Cereal Bars to sell, yet, as he acknowledged later, contemporary corporate relativism drives him a little nuts.

Old-fashioned objective truth did make a brief reappearance when Kahn and I visited the quality-assurance lab deep in the bowels of the Bell center. This is where technicians grind up Trix and Cheerios and run them through a mass spectrometer to make sure pesticide residues don't exceed F.D.A. "tolerances." Pesticide residues are omnipresent in the American food supply: the F.D.A. finds them in 30 to 40 percent of the food it samples. Many of them are known carcinogens, neurotoxins and endocrine disrupters—dangerous at some level of exposure. The government has established acceptable levels for these residues in crops, though whether that means they're safe to consume is debatable: in setting these tolerances the government has historically weighed the risk to our health against the benefit—to agriculture, that is. The tolerances also haven't taken into account that children's narrow diets make them especially susceptible or that the complex mixtures of chemicals to which we're exposed heighten the dangers.

Harry Leichtweis, a senior research analytical chemist at General Mills, tests for hundreds of different chemical compounds, not only the 400 pesticides currently approved by the E.P.A. but also the dozens of others that have been banned over the years as their dangers became known. Decades later, many of these toxins remain in the soil and continue to show up in our food. "We still find background levels of DDT and chlordane," he explained. Now the lab tests Small Planet Foods's products too. So I asked Leichtweis, who is a pale, rail-thin scientist with Coke-bottle specs and no discernible affect, if organic foods, as seen from the perspective of a mass spectrometer, are any different.

"Well, they don't contain pesticide."

Leichtweis had struck a blow for old-fashioned empiricism. Whatever else you might say about an organic TV dinner, it almost certainly contains less pesticide than a conventional one. Gene Kahn was beaming.

VI. Local Farm

My journey through the changing world of organic food has cured me of my naïve supermarket pastoralism, but it hasn't put me off my organic feed. I still fill my cart with the stuff. The science might still be sketchy, but common sense tells me organic is better food—better, anyway, than the kind grown with organophosphates, with antibiotics and growth hormones, with cadmium and lead and arsenic (the E.P.A. permits the use of toxic waste in fertilizers), with sewage sludge and animal feed made from ground-up bits of other animals as well as their own manure. Very likely it's better for me and my family, and unquestionably it is better for the environment. For even if only 1 percent of the chemical pesticides sprayed by American farmers end up as residue in our food, the other 99 percent are going into the environment—which is to say, into our drinking water, into our rivers, into the air that farmers and their neighbors breathe. By now it makes little sense to distinguish the health of the individual from that of the environment.

Still, while it surely represents real progress for agribusiness to be selling organic food rather than fighting it, I'm not sure I want to see industrialized organic become the only kind in the market. Organic is nothing if not a set of values (this is better than that), and to the extent that the future of those values is in the hands of companies that are finally indifferent to them, that future will be precarious.

Also, there are values that the new corporate—and government—construction of "organic" leaves out, values that once were part and parcel of the word but that have since been abandoned as impractical or unprofitable. I'm thinking of things like locally grown, like the humane treatment of animals, like the value of a shorter and more legible food chain, the preservation of family farms, even the promise of a countercuisine. To believe that the U.S.D.A. label on a product ensures any of these things is, as I discovered, naive.

Yet if the word "organic" means anything, it means that all these things are ultimately connected: that the way we grow food is inseparable from the way we distribute food, which is inseparable from the way we eat food. The original premise, remember, the idea that got Kahn started in 1971, was that the whole industrial food system—and not just chemical agriculture—was in some fundamental way unsustainable. It's impossible to read the papers these days without beginning to wonder if this insight wasn't prophetic. I'm thinking, of course, of mad cow disease, of the 76 million cases of food poisoning every year (a rate higher than in 1948), of StarLink corn contamination, of the 20-year-old farm crisis, of hoof-and-mouth disease and groundwater pollution, not to mention industrial food's dubious "solutions" to these problems: genetic engi-neering and antibiotics and irradiation. Buying food labeled organic pro-tects me from some of these things, but not all; industrial organic may well be necessary to fix this system, but it won't be sufficient.

Many of the values that industrial organic has jettisoned in recent years I find compelling, so I've started to shop with them in mind. I happen to believe, for example, that farms produce more than food; they also produce a kind of landscape, and if I buy my organic milk from halfway across the country, the farms I like to drive by every day will eventually grow nothing but raised ranch houses. So instead of long-haul ultrapasteurized milk from Horizon, I've started buying my milk, unpasteurized, from a dairy right here in town, Local Farm. Debra Tyler is organic, but she doesn't bother mentioning the fact on her label. Why? "My customers can see for themselves what I'm doing here," she says. What she's doing is milking nine pastured Jersey cows whose milk changes taste and hue with the seasons.

"Eat Your View!" is a save-the-farms bumper sticker you see in Europe now. I guess that's part of what I'm trying to do. But I'm also trying to get away from the transcontinental strawberry (5 calories of food energy, I've read, that it takes 435 calories of fossil-fuel energy to deliver to my door) and the organic "home meal replacement" sold in a package that will take 500 years to decompose. (Does that make me a True Natural?) So I've tracked down a local source for grass-fed beef (Chris Hopkins), eggs (Debra Tyler again) and maple syrup (Phil Hart), and on Saturday mornings I buy produce at a farmer's market in a neighboring town. I also have a line on a C.S.A. ("community support-ed agriculture"), or "subscription farm," a new marketing scheme from Europe that seems to be catching on here. You put up a couple of hun-dred dollars every spring and then receive a weekly box of produce through the summer. Not all of the farmers I'm buying from are certi-fied organic. But I talk to them, see what they're up to, learn how they define the term. Sure, it's more trouble than buying organic food at the supermarket, but I'm resolved to do it anyway. Because organic is not the last word, and it's not just lunch.

ABOUT THE TELEVISION SERIES

JULIA CHILD

"How in the world did you ever manage to get on television?" is a question frequently asked me. It was purely by accident. My husband, Paul, had resigned from the diplomatic service in 1961, after almost twenty years. We had settled in our great gray pre-Victorian house in Cambridge with its comfortable kitchen, and *Mastering the Art of French Cooking* had just been published. He was planning to write, paint, and photograph; I was to cook, write, and teach. We had even bought ourselves a budget television set, which was so ugly we hid it in an unused fireplace.

One evening a friend we had known in Paris, Beatrice Braude, who was then working at Boston's educational television station WGBH-TV, suggested it would be a useful push for *Mastering* if I could appear on one of the station's book-review programs. Always happy to do anything for the book, I agreed that it might well be worth thinking about. She persuaded the station and the interview took place with a bit of conversation about food and France, and at one point I beat some egg whites in a large French copper bowl to enliven the talk. The program brought numerous requests for some kind of a cooking program, and WGBH-TV asked me if I would be willing to try three pilots, or experimental half-hour shows, to see whether there might be a real cooking audience out there over the air waves. Paul and I accepted the challenge, although we knew nothing at all about television and had hardly watched a program.

The studio assigned Russell Morash, producer of "Science Reporter," as Producer-Director. Assistant Producer was Ruth Lockwood, who had been working on the Eleanor Roosevelt shows. Because Channel 2's studio had burned almost to the ground a few months before, The Boston Gas Company loaned us its display kitchen. The budget was minute.

Ruth, Paul, and I blocked out a rough sequence of events for three programs: French omelettes, *coq au vin,* and a non-collapsible soufflé, which provided a varied and not-too-complicated sampling of French cooking. After thinking up dozens of titles for the show, we could find nothing better than "The French Chef"; it was short and told a story. Ruth dug around somewhere and came up with the anonymous but spritely musical theme song we are still using. As our own kitchen had enough equipment to furnish a small restaurant, there were no problems in that quarter.

It was out of the question for us to film a live show since we had only two cameras attached by long cables to a mobile bus. Besides, with an absolutely amateur performer, it would have been far too risky. We decided, however, that it would be taped as though it were live. Unless the sky fell in, the cameras failed, or the lights went off, there would be no stops, and no corrections—just a straight thirty minutes from start to finish. This was a good fundamental decision, I think. I hate to stop. I lose that sense of drama and excitement which the uninterrupted thirty-minute limitation imposes. Besides, I would far prefer to have things happen as they naturally do, such as the mousse refusing to leave the mold, the potatoes sticking to the skillet, the apple charlotte slowly collapsing. One of the secrets of cooking is to learn to correct something if you can, and bear with it if you cannot.

The day in June for our first taping, "The French Omelette," Paul and I packed our station wagon with pots, pans, eggs, and trimmings and were off to the Gas Company. Parking was difficult in downtown Boston, so he off-loaded inside the main entrance, and I stood over our mound until he returned. How were the two of us to get everything down to the basement of that imposing office building? There was nobody to help, as we were hours ahead of our WGBH camera crew. Office girls and business-suited executives looked disapprovingly at our household pile as they rushed in and out. A uniformed elevator operator said, "Hey, get that stuff out of this lobby!" Eventually Paul located a janitor with a rolling cart and we clanked down to the basement where we unpacked, setting up our wares according to the master plan we had worked out.

Ruth arrived shortly to arrange a dining room setup for the final scene, and to go over our sequence of events. Then came Russ and our camera crew. After a short rehearsal to check lighting and camera angles, Russ said, "Let's shoot it!" And we did. Within the next week, following the same informal system, we taped the other two shows. I still have my notes. There is the map of the free-standing stove and work counter: "Simmering water in large alum, pan, upper R. burner."

"Wet sponge left top drawer." "6 eggs in nest of 3 alum. plates w. ramekin." Paul, who was acting as invisible helper, had made himself a sheet of instructions: "When J. starts buttering, remove stack molds." "When soufflé is cheesed, take black saucepan."

On July 26, 1962, after we all had eaten a big steak dinner at our house, we pulled the television set out of hiding and turned it on at 8:30. There was this woman tossing French omelettes, splashing eggs about the place, brandishing big knives, panting heavily as she careened around the stove, and WGBH-TV lurched into educational television's first cooking program. Response to the three shows, indicated that there was indeed an audience in New England, Channel 2 suggested we try a series of twenty-six programs, and "The French Chef" was underway. We were to start taping in January, and the first show would be on the air February 11, 1963.

What to pack into each of those thirty minutes? If we showed dishes that were too complicated, we would scare off all but a handful of people. Yet if we remained in the kindergarten, we would soon be a bore. Ruth, Paul, and I decided to start out with a few audience catchers, dishes that were famous, like *boeuf bourguignon,* but easy to make, and then gradually work into the subject. We also wanted to vary the weekly menu and take time to show French techniques, such as how to wield the knife, bone the lamb, clean the leek, whip and fold the egg whites. The idea was to take the bugaboo out of French cooking, to demonstrate that it is not merely good cooking but that it follows definite rules. The simplicity of a *velouté* sauce, for instance, is butter, flour, and seasoned liquid, but the rule is that the flour is cooked in the butter before the liquid is added. Why? (I, myself, will not do anything unless I know why.) "If you don't cook the flour in the butter, your sauce will have the horrid pasty taste of uncooked flour"—I have certainly given tongue to that one a hundred times. Finally we agreed on our program of twenty-six shows, starting with *"Boeuf Bourguignon"* and "French Onion Soup," ending with "Lobster *à l'Américaine*" and *"Crêpes Suzette."*

In January when we started taping four shows a week, WGBH-TV still had no studio. The shows, like the three pilots, would have to be done where the mobile bus could park and string out cables to its two cameras. Fortunately for us, the Cambridge Electric Company offered their display kitchen located in a large loft room, with ample parking space nearby. We could reach it by a front stairway, by a freight elevator from two floors below, or by an outside iron fire escape that descended into the parking lot. Though our lighting arrangements were makeshift and the sound track was likely to mingle with the roar of the freight elevator, the cooking facilities were fine. The ceiling was high enough for us to hang a mirror over the stove that the camera could peer into when it needed the inside view of a pot. Best of all, we had the whole place to ourselves.

Although we were now an actual and official enterprise, our budget remained small. Paul and I did all the shopping and precooking, and he continued to act as porter and unpacker, as well as chief dishwasher, until we got some volunteer cleaneruppers for the taping days. Tuesdays and Thursdays were the long cooking rehearsals for the two shows scheduled the following days. Nobody at WGBH had the slightest idea what we were cooking in our loft until the cameras were lugged up the outside fire escape at 10 o'clock on Wednesdays and Fridays, to begin the tapings. We depended on Paul for advice when we were doubtful, and Russ for great openings and closings as well as all the techniques of camera and direction. Otherwise, Ruth Lockwood and I had complete freedom to work up anything we wished and to present it in any manner we chose.

The general pattern of the first three pilot shows seemed to fit my style, so we continued it, perfecting details as we went along. I found I had no sense of timing whatsoever, 1 minute or 5 minutes meant nothing to me as sadly illustrated by our second show and first try at "Onion Soup." I had to show the proper professional way to slice onions fast, the first cooking to soften them, the second cooking to brown them, the several ways to serve the soup; then there was crouton-making and gratinéing. I rushed through that program like a madwoman but I got everything in, only to find that when I carried the onion soup to the dining room I had gone so fast we still had 8 minutes left. Agony. I had to sit there and talk for all that time. Russ erased the tape back to about the 15-minute point, but after it happened again, Ruth devised the plan of breaking up the recipe into blocks of time. I could go as fast or slow as I wanted in the allotted time block, but I could not go into the next step until I got the signal.

Signals to the performer are written on placards known as "idiot cards." They are handed to the floor manager, who, by earphones, is plugged into one of the television cameras so he can hear and talk to the director who is shut away in the control room. The floor manager holds the idiot card just under the camera lens, and the performer appears to be gazing right into your eyes but is really reading that message: "Turn on burner number three!" In our case, the floor manager has a big looseleaf book, and flips the pages according to a time schedule carefully worked out on a stop watch by Ruth. For the onion soup we were very simple: "The Knife & 1st Cook 5 min," "Browning and Simmering 4 min," "Soup in Bowls 2 min," and so forth. Later we became more elaborate, and put key words onto the idiot cards so I would not forget important points. I remember when we did *brioches,* we opened with a shot of three of them: the great big grandfather *brioche,* the middle-sized mother *brioche,* and the little baby *brioche;* we had obviously fallen into the story of Goldilocks and the Three Brioches. The idiot cards read like an Indian massacre—"This Baby; Remove head," "Punch Grandpa," "Slash Mother," "30 sec. Before Wash Hands." Often I am faced with Ruth's helpful reminders: "Stop gasping," "Wipe face," "Don't gallop."

The nonstop taping we have always continued, and in only a few instances, after the disaster of the first onion soup show, have we had to break off, erase, and pick up again. I can remember only half a dozen occasions, some of which were due to electrical failures, others due to me. Once, doing the "Lobster à *l'Américaine,*" every time I touched the cooktop I got a short-circuit in the microphone against my chest, and kept clutching my breast in a very odd fashion. It felt like a bee sting. We wiped out back to the worst clutch, and were able to continue in midstream. Another time, "The Flaming Soufflé' collapsed in its dish on the way to the dining room; I had forgotten to put in the cornstarch. We merely waited for the standby soufflé to come out of the oven and used that. Otherwise we let the gaffes lie where they fell, and on the whole it is just as well.

About halfway through, at the "Beef Gets Stewed Two Ways" show, WGBH-TV moved into its fine new building and we had a beautiful set with the most modern lighting, sound, and equipment. Wonderful as it is, we miss our old loft. It had an intimate atmosphere. We were a happy and independent family of twenty-four, we could eat up all the food ourselves, and even throw a party on occasion. But we could never have done color television there. In the new series, there are no more gray strawberries, pale and sickly veal, livid lettuce or pallid pickles. Even the tongue is utterly lifelike as it licks the *mousse au chocolat* off the spoon, and "The French Chef" has a new dimension.

MARCELLA HAZAN

THE PRODUCE

I SPEND THE RICHEST HOURS of my life in Venice when I cross the tall bridge at Rialto and reach the stalls on the other side of the Grand Canal where the fruit and vegetable vendors display their wares. It is as difficult for me to pass a single stall by as it would be for a child to ignore any of the windows of a street lined with toy shops.

There may be thousands of courgettes, but every batch looks different, some are slender, some plump, some a deep almost bottle green, some a green so pale it is nearly sallow. When the courgettes are exceptionally fresh, not 24 hours out of the ground, the grower and the vendor may leave their blossoms on. These are the female blossoms, not good to cook, but by their brightness and firmness they are there to show how recently the vegetable has been picked. The male flowers, marvelous when opened up flat and fried with a thin flour and water batter, grow attached not to the courgettes, but to a stem, and are gathered, several in a bunch, to make bold orange yellow posies that outshine anything in the market.

You don't need a calendar to know that spring has come to Rialto. It will have been announced by the appearance of asparagus and young artichoke. The stalls display asparagus of various sizes and colors. There are the spindly stalks of *asparagina,* with more taste than flesh, ideal for omelettes or risotto. There is the fancy white asparagus of Bassano and the brawny, meaty green one of Badoere, both from the Veneto's hinterland. The white is the one many people moon over, and often pay more for, but I much prefer the sweeter, more positive taste of the green. A recent addition is the delicious purple variety of Albenga. originally from the Riviera, but now produced also in Badoere. Late in the spring comes the asparagus grown closest to home, on the islands of the lagoon, whose lean green spears are less remarkable for their appearance than for the unsurpassed intensity of their flavor.

Had Venice nothing else to offer, it would be worth the trip to be here for *castraure* and *canarini*, the first locally grown artichokes to appear in the spring. Before full-grown artichokes begin to sprout from the plant's lateral stems, a tiny bud sprouts at the top, capping it somewhat the way a star does the Christmas tree. It is snipped off to become *castraure*, the product of the plant's 'castration.' A student of mine taking a tour of the market with me dubbed it 'artichoke foreskin.' They are miniatures, so tender there is nothing to trim, each *castraura*, when sautéed in olive oil with garlic and parsley, yielding a concentrated biteful, or two at most, of artichoke essence. *Canarini*, little canaries, are pale golden-green artichokes picked very young from shade-grown plants. They are the tenderest and mildest of their kind, even smaller and more expensive than the already pricey *castraure*.

With one exception, all the artichokes I see, whether full-grown or immature, are the shape of rosebuds, some of them with spiny tips. But, for a few short weeks in the spring, the Roman *mammola*, a large, stout variety similar to the globe artichoke produced in California, appears on some stalls. Like the California globe, it is meatier and blander, less astringent than the rosebud-shaped artichokes. Towards the end of the *mammola's* growing cycle, when its leaves become fibrous and unchewable, it is turned into a Venetian speciality, *fonda di carciofo*. Sitting by their stalls, the artichoke sellers cut off the stems and whittle away all the leaves down to the base, piling the discarded leaves waist-high, dropping the only part that remains, a half-inch thick disc, into a basin of water acidulated with white vinegar or lemon juice to keep the *fondi* from turning black. *Fondi* can be breaded and fried, sautéed in olive oil with garlic and parsley, stewed with potatoes and onions, or used in risotto.

I am fascinated by the number of greens in the market that are called radicchio. Some bear no visible resemblance to each other, but they all belong to the chicory family and share, in varying degrees, the intriguing bitterness that is the family's trait, and that is so agreeable to an Italian palate.

The radicchio best known abroad, the one with a tight, round, cabbage-like head of crisp, white-veined purple leaves, is known as *rosa di Chioggia*. It makes its arrival in the autumn, is best at wintertime, but remains available through the spring. There is a true spring radicchio, with a clump of small, flat, round-tipped leaves, loosely overlapping like a fully opened rose, and gathered at the root end. It can be green or dark red, and when very fresh is splendidly crunchy and nutty in salads. Another salad radicchio, known as radicchietto, appears late in the spring and is abundant all summer and early autumn. It has single small, rounded, dark green leaves, similar to mâche but thinner and more elongated; it is this numerous family's most tender and sweetest offshoot.

The noblest members of the family—*radicchio di Castelfranco, radicchio di Treviso, tardivo di Treviso*—make an eagerly awaited entrance around November. All of them are extravagantly good in salads, but they are bred for loftier uses in the kitchen: in a risotto, in a pasta sauce, braised with a roast, with seafood, or best of all perhaps, just on their own, grilled or baked.

Castelfranco has a large, loosely packed head of soft, dappled leaves, tinged here and there with a lovely pink hue that recalls that of orchids. It once used to exit the scene with the arrival of spring, but now I can find it much later on, although I prefer it in the cold months. Treviso radicchio has the shape of a small cos lettuce, its tapered leaves a deep shade of purple with clear white markings. The greatest of the three and, in my opinion, the most magnificent vegetable grown, is Treviso's dazzling *tardivo* or late-harvest radicchio.

Tardivo's leaves are but a narrow, fiery red ruffle fringing the edges of spear-shaped glossy white ribs that, like overgrown fingernails, curl inwards. They are attached at the base to an elongated root from which, flame-like, they spread out and up. On a misty late autumn day, the displays of *tardivo* in the stalls flare like fireworks against the backdrop of the market's seasonally somber produce

But even without the glamorous presence of radicchio at the end and beginning of the year, I would enjoy the market then no less than at any of its warmer periods. Of course I do look forward to the luscious, ripe taste of summer, to the mounds of red and yellow peppers in the stalls, to six or more kinds of tomatoes, some for salads, some only for sauce, to aubergines with purple, mauve, or white skin. And how could I not be thrilled by those few weeks in autumn when the wild mushrooms arrive? When I come upon a basket of adorably chubby *porcini* that might have been modeled by Disney, their fawn colored stems supporting chocolate dark tops, I am immobilized by desire struggling against indecision. Shall I make risotto, or a sauce for homemade pasta, or shall I do a roast with *porcini trifolati,* the mushrooms sliced very thin and sautéed in olive oil with garlic and parsley? Or are the caps large enough to grill? Or, if I manage surreptitiously to squeeze them while the vendor isn't looking, do they feel so firm that we can eat them raw, with slivers of Parmesan and white truffle?

But many other wonderful things grow only when the approaching chill of winter puts its bite on autumn's tail. There are the blue-green broccoli Venetians call *amorini,* sold with their leaves on, which are so good in soup. There is purple cauliflower, and fist-size white cauliflower, for either one of which there is no preparation so perfect as boiling it, and serving it warm, tossed with wine vinegar and fruity olive oil. And there is red cabbage, with which I make one of my very best chicken fricassées. There is the purple-green cardoon, typical of the Veneto, resembling a celery in appearance, but an artichoke in taste. I braise it or gratinée it with butter and grated Parmesan. There is the dark green, corrugated Savoy cabbage, and *cime di rapa.* The latter is superb for pasta sauces; or I shred and chop the two and sauté them together in olive oil and garlic and serve them over *piadina,* the flat bread of my native Romagna. This is the time of the year for the crispest, sweetest finocchi, not just for salads, but for braising in oil or for breading and frying. And at last, nut gatherers from the hills bring burlap sacks bulging with *marroni,* the fine, shiny, pot-bellied chestnut with which at Christmas time I make my chocolate and chestnut Monte Bianco dessert.

The Fish

The comparatively shallow waters of the northern Adriatic, freshened by cool Alpine streams, are populated by an edible marine life that, for its variety and flavor is unsurpassed, possibly unmatched, elsewhere on the planet. Venice is the queen of the Adriatic and the queen of fish markets is at Rialto. The lofty Gothic arches of the open-sided *pescheria* hall provide covering for some of the fishmongers' stalls, but not for all. There are too many and the others are strung along outside. The abundance of the display would be astonishing even if the market were servicing a metropolis of millions, but Venice has less than 70,000 residents. On any morning from Tuesday to Saturday, between 8 A.M. and 1 P.M., most of those 70,000 seem to coming through with their shopping trolleys. Venetians are mad for seafood. But even if one weren't, it would be impossible to resist the call of the fish market.

These are not just vegetables that have been laid out, they are creatures, as fantastically diverse in expression, shape, size, and color as only creatures of the mysterious deep can be. There are the suave, elegantly tapered blue-backed, white-bellied sea bass, the ferocious monkfish, its tooth-bristling jaws sprung open, the choleric-looking orange-red scorpion fish, so good for a fish soup, there are skate-wings spread out like delicate pink fans, small shark whose skin has been stripped off, exposing the blushing crimson flesh, black and silver sardines evoking thoughts of their dark meat smoking on a charcoal grill, producing the most seductive aroma of the seafood world, their more silvery cousins, the fresh anchovies, born to be floured and fried. There are living shells of all shapes and markings, scallop shells, razor clams, little white sea snails, small conch, sacks of mussels and clams. And there are baskets of desperately clawing crab, trays of pulsating prawns, tubs of sinuous eel ceaselessly doing their snake dance. There is no livelier show in town.

The best known of Adriatic creatures is *scampi* which, notwithstanding having its name misappropriated by that over-garlicked standard of Italian-American menus, shrimp scampi, is not a shrimp at all. It is a small, orange-pink, lobster-like crustacean, whose sweetness and tenderness surpass that of lobster itself. Were I to find freshly caught *scampi* and *porcini* on the same morning I might well grab some of both to make *risotto con scampi e porcini.*

There is seafood in the Rialto market that you rarely find elsewhere, and it is so freshly caught that often it is still alive when you buy it. *Schile,* pronounced 'skee'yeh' is a minute grey shrimp that does not turn red when cooked. The very tiniest ones are fried whole in their shell and popped into the mouth like crisps. Or they are patiently shelled after boiling and served with warm, soft polenta.

There used to be many kinds of crab, including one, *granzoporo,* the flavor of whose claws used to make me think of Florida's stone crab. Overfishing and pollution have nearly extinguished all but two or three varieties. The most striking of the survivors, *granzevola* ('grahnsey'oh-lah') is a large vividly rose-colored crab with long, spidery legs. At home you would boil it, crack it, and spend the next hour picking out the flesh and coral. Restaurants make it very simple for you; after cooking it they scoop clean the beautiful rosy shell and fill it with the picked out body and claw meat. For the pure in palate it is good enough to eat without any seasoning, but waiters usually moisten it with a few drops of olive oil and lemon juice.

Soft-shell crabs (green crabs), about a quarter the size of their American East Coast equivalent, are so local that there is no word for them in Italian: their name, *moleche* ('moeey'keh') is Venetian. Also Venetian are folpeti ('foe pey'tee'), miniature octopus that you boil and serve whole, still warm, drizzled with olive oil and two drops of vinegar, and *garusoli* ('gah-ro-zoh-ee'), very small conch. (If you have been following this, you will have noticed that in Venice people like to drop their l's.)

The cuisine of Venice bears no larger debt than the one it owes to a single product of its waters, the cuttlefish and its ink, *la seppia e il suo nero.* In appearance, cuttlefish vaguely resembles squid, but it has a meatier flesh and more complex flavor. The most significant difference, however, is in the ink, *il nero.* Venetians would never make their superb black risotto or their black pasta with any ink but that of the cuttlefish, a satiny, dense, warm-tasting substance immeasurably richer than the squid's thin and pungent dye. One of the dishes that is most popular with Venetians, both at home and when they go out with the family, is *seppie alla veneziana,* cut-up cuttlefish and their ink stewed with sautéed onions, wine, and tomato purée and served over bricks of grilled polenta. If you were to have it in mid-summer, when baby cuttlefish no larger than a thumbnail are in season, you would have chosen very well indeed. In the vast seafood repertoire of Italy's maritime regions there is not another combination of flavors more savory than this one.

Small size is one of the factors that contribute to the exceptionally fine flavor of Adriatic seafood. The Adriatic sole, the firmest and nuttiest of all soles, is the size of a small hand. I come from a fishing town on the Adriatic where I grew up eating sole and now no other gives me comparable pleasure. When working with fish from American waters, the Atlantic, the Gulf, the Pacific, I have found many whose flavors and textures are adaptable to Italian dishes, but I have never been satisfied with sole or, except for young halibut, with any other flatfish indigenous to those waters.

Our sole are so small that when I fry them for my husband and myself I buy no fewer than ten. Red mullets, fresh sardines, fresh anchovies, are even smaller. Most other fish, such as bream, grey mullet, mackerel, monkfish are just large enough for a single portion, although there are baby monkfish of which you'd need at least a pair. *Branzino,* the very fine Adriatic bass, may be of a size for two persons as may a *rombo,* the native turbot.

Venetians don't buy fillets, they buy whole fish or, occasionally, fish steaks. Except for small Adriatic shark, steak fish is not abundant at the Rialto market. You do see swordfish and tuna, but they are not caught locally.

'Local' is the most powerful selling word in the market and it is never taken in vain. In Italian it is *nostrani* or *nostrane* (depending whether you are using the masculine or feminine form), whose literal meaning is 'ours.' To shoppers, 'ours' means it's better because it has traveled a short distance to the market, hence it's fresher. An underlying, more emotional secondary message is that it will be more satisfying because the taste is the comforting one of home. People pay more, much more for 'ours.' A trayful of baby cuttlefish caught perhaps not a mile from the market and bearing a sign with the magic word, *nostrane,* will bring three or four times the price per kilo of a stupendous salmon, just flown in from Norway. Nor is it only the fishmongers who follow this practice. Fruit and vegetable vendors are even more explicit; they write out signs naming the specific farm island, among those that ring the Venetian lagoon, where the green beans or courgettes or figs may have been grown.

LOOKING, ASKING, SELECTING

A skeptic might see room for deception, but no one who tries to practise deception of this kind would have steady customers for long in Venice. Venetians know their produce and their fish, they know the places they come from, they know their market and its vendors. Nothing is accepted unquestioningly.

To understand how they shop, let us follow a svelte, smartly dressed woman who is going from stall to stall, peering intently only at radicchios and lettuces, and *rucola,* and onions. It is a sultry summer morning and evidently she has decided that all she is going to make for lunch is a salad. To the various greens and sweet onions that she is looking for, she will probably add chunks of very good tuna packed in olive oil, some anchovies that she has bought loose under salt and will clean, fillet, and soak in olive oil herself, and a hard-boiled egg or two. Stay on her heels and eventually you'll see that she settles on what appears to be the most promising of the stalls, where she waits her turn. When it comes she will not order until she has asked the vendor, and received reassuring answers to, such questions as, 'This isn't yesterday's radicchio, is it? Is the *rucola* really wild, not cultivated? Is that S. Erasmo lettuce (one of the farm islands)? Is this truly—*veramente*—Tropea onion (a very sweet red onion from Calabria, in the south)?' Not wanting to lose esteem by showing untoward credulity and shaking her head as if questioning the veracity of the replies, she will finally commit herself: a quarter kilo of that please, and a head of the other, one of those, and a bunch of this. If it seems like a lot of trouble to take over a salad, it is food that she is going to put on the table, isn't it, and what could be more important? There are no decisions she will make, either that morning or in her life, to which she is likely to give more deliberate thought.

KNOWING YOUR MARKET

When I have visitors whom I take to see Rialto, I know in advance that some will remark on how lucky I am and what would I ever do without such a market. I would do as I have always done and as I still continue to do when I am cooking away from Venice. I'd shop carefully, wherever I happen to be.

It has been my practice, however, whenever I am testing a recipe that I hope to publish or cooking for a demonstration either live or on television, to use only products that would be available to most of my readers and my audience, and thus I often rely on selective shopping at the local supermarkets. A genuine farm shop can certainly provide better access to recently picked produce, but if you can't get to one when you need to cook, it would be foolish to wring your hands in discouragement and dismiss a supermarket's resources. They can be quite valuable if you do as my neighbors do at Rialto: get to know the market.

Not all supermarkets are the same. Look for the best one in your area and be willing to travel a little further, if necessary, to get to it. Rely on your eyes rather than on a shopping list. Even in the best produce department, the produce is not of identical freshness and quality every day. Take a long look before you decide.

You have an immense advantage over the shoppers at Rialto, you can touch, feel, and choose. Use it. Bear in mind that moisture is an essential component of freshness and when a vegetable's fiber's begin to lose it, just as our skin does when it ages, it deflates and begins to sag.

If aubergines featured in your plans, make sure their stems are a bright green, their skin lustrous and taut, and that they don't feel too heavy in the hand, which would mean they have too many seeds. Should they be otherwise, change your plans. Green beans should be even and clear in color with no mottling. They should snap sharply. Test an artichoke by bending back one of its leaves. If it is fresh it will offer resistance and remain erect, if long in the tooth it will yield limply. Asparagus tips should be firmly closed. Broccoli florets must be tightly clustered and bright green, with no trace of yellow. A pea pod should be dewy green with no spots. Crack one open, it should do so crisply. Taste a pea, it should be juicy and sweet, not starchy. Peppers should be very firm, their skin tightly stretched, with no bruises, punctures, or soft spots. For Italian cooking, mature peppers, that is red or yellow, are preferable to the green ones, which are unripe. Courgettes ought not to be overgrown. Their flavor is sweetest when they are young, that is, small. Their skin should be glossy, and they must absolutely not droop. Choose them all of a size, so that they will cook uniformly. Garlic heads should be as heavy as possible. They get lighter as they dry out, and as they dry out they become sharper. If you can avoid it, do not buy what you won't be able to cook very soon. There is no point in making the effort to bring home the freshest possible vegetables and then keeping them in a refrigerator for a week.

The Venetian men and women who go to Rialto every day know

their market as though it were their own garden plot. You can get to know your markets and your farm shops with the same thoroughness and soon you will be able to detect what has been trotted out of cold storage for several days running and what, on that day, has come in fresh.

Supermarkets too have people who know. I always try to make the acquaintance of the manager of the produce department, of the butcher, and of the man in charge of the fish. It's in their interest to satisfy a steady and knowledgeable customer. I have found good butchers at many supermarkets who will cut the meat as I want it or, if they don't have it, get it for me, often just in a day. Leave your telephone number with the fishmonger if what you are looking for isn't there and, on the day it comes in, you can be the first to know. The only things I have never been able to find in a supermarket are a really first-rate piece of cheese in good condition and a superior olive oil.

If you are in an area that has speciality food shops, you can apply the same 'look, ask, and select' strategy there. Some shopkeepers are unforthcoming but generally they are grateful to establish a relationship with someone who is as interested as they are in the products they sell. One of the words to which the electronic age has given wide circulation is 'interactive.' I am not quite sure I understand how it works when applied to a computer program, but interactive is exactly what thoughtful food marketing should be, whether you practice it at Rialto or at a suburban supermarket.

GROWING BEANS

CORBY KUMMER

S IPPING A FROTHY CAPPUCCINO or a "regular" with cream and sugar, it can be hard to remember that coffee is the seed of a fruit that grows on trees. Like any fruit, it tastes of where it grew: of the soil, be it volcanic and loamy or crumbly red clay; of the tempestuous summer rains that clear by evening; of the high, hot morning sun and the cool night winds of the dry season.

Connoisseurs will forever argue over just what makes a coffee great. But most people familiar with the art of raising coffee agree that among the best-run coffee plantations in the world is La Minita, in the mountains of Costa Rica. The coffee that bears its name is one of the increasingly available "single-estate" coffees, meaning beans grown on just one farm rather than a blend from many farms and many countries. It is on anyone's short list of the world's finest. The immense care that is taken at La Minita, from enriching the soil to hand-picking the fruits of the coffee tree to processing the beans inside the fruit, illustrates why coffee tastes so different depending not only on where it grows but also on who grows it.

When I paid a January visit to La Minita, toward the end of the bustling, sprawling, cheerful activity of a coffee harvest, I finally found the missing link in my long apprenticeship as an unprofessional coffee taster. I thought I knew a lot about tasting coffee. Going where I had never been, though—to a place where coffee grows—reinspired me. Seeing the passion and work that went into growing the commodity I had encountered only in big burlap sacks or little plastic sample bags made me fall in love with coffee all over again. I also made an idiot of myself in trying to learn to be a coffee picker.

THE GOSPEL OF ARABICA

The list of the world's best coffee almost invariably includes beans from Guatemala and Costa Rica in Central America and, going far back to the origins of cultivated coffee, Ethiopia, Yemen and Kenya. These countries have something in common: an equatorial location and a mountainous subtropical climate, which produces the most fragrant and intensely flavored beans. Fine coffee is *Coffea arabica* (a-*rab*-ica), named for its original popularizers, the Arabs, who brought it from its native East Africa to the Arabian peninsula in the fifteenth century. All the delicate, prized flavors possible in coffee are found in arabica. The new shops that offer freshly roasted beans are putting arabica beans, not robusta, into their machines.

Arabica beans don't do well in very hot and humid weather, flourishing instead in places that offer warm but not fierce days and chilly nights, with temperatures often as low as the fifties but not much lower, and an extended rainy season. Extreme cold is a mortal enemy of any kind of coffee plant. Frosts kill coffee trees, freezing the sap and rupturing their tissues. The greatest disruption to coffee production in this century was a terrible freeze in Brazil in 1975, skyrocketing prices. Disputes over stockpiling among coffee-raising countries further disrupted the market, sending prices so far down that many farmers had to sell their plantations. A frost in 1994 raised prices again, and the market has still not stabilized.

The finickiness of arabica beans and the labor problems of farming at 3,000 to 6,000 feet (think of getting your footing on mountainsides day in and day out) mean it's small wonder that the other commercially important coffee species—robusta, or *Coffea canephora*—caught on fast. Robusta grows very well at sea level, requiring little more than a tropical or semitropical climate.

Native to West rather than East Africa, robusta shares none of the exalted history of arabica. It was first cultivated widely a mere hundred years ago for its low cost and hardiness. It shares none of arabica's exalted taste either. The chief flavor attribute of robusta, which dominates just about any blend you buy in a can, is that of a brown paper bag.

Some longtime coffee observers think that the reason "specialty coffee" has seen such explosive growth in the past few years after a 30-year decline in American coffee consumption is that big commercial coffee companies—the ones that put cans onto supermarket shelves—fell asleep. Colas muscled in on coffee as America's preferred caffeine-delivery system, because coffee packers started putting higher and higher ratios of robusta beans into their blends, driving down both price and quality and sending consumers to the soda aisle. Finally, in the late 1960s, a few people who cared about coffee rediscovered and reintroduced coffee with real flavor—arabica coffee. The gospel spread slowly in the 1970s and finally won large numbers of converts in the late 1980s, setting the stage for the flood of coffee bars of the 1990s. For those interested in watching their caffeine consumption, arabica offers a crucial advantage besides having infinitely greater flavor than robusta: it has about half the caffeine.

A MODEL PLANTATION

La Minita is a showplace of raising and processing coffee because of the passion of its owner, Bill McAlpin. McAlpin is an oversized man in his forties who grew up in a family whose agricultural holdings included a large coffee plantation along the Fila de Bustamonte range of central Costa Rica, a 90-minute drive south of the capital, San José. In 1976, he took over the family coffee farms, and through the early 80s, he sold off land where the wind was too strong or the exposure to the sun less than ideal, all the while improving the heart of the farm.

The road from San José, much of it rocky and rutted, winds up and up the 5,000 feet to La Minita, passing through blue-green mountains as spectacular as the Andes. Along most of them, coffee trees are planted on very steep slopes. It seems incredible that anyone could tend, let alone pick, them. Above 7,000 feet in Costa Rica, coffee won't grow. At those altitudes, visible in the distance, the landscape changes to grass-covered peaks with lines of trees like a checkerboard drawn by a child, denoting property lines for cattle pastures. On either side of the road, hibiscus, bougainvillea, impatiens and other blatantly colored wildflowers grow—an echo of the unchecked growth in the hundreds of square miles of the country's protected rain forests.

The deep green, leafy coffee plants that line the hillsides are kept so short that they look more like bushes than trees. The only recognizable trees are shade trees, either banana or other varieties, planted in a big grid. Shade trees protect coffee by helping to diffuse overzealous sunlight during the day and by keeping the air relatively warm at night. The bushlike height of the coffee trees—rarely more than 5 feet—makes them easier to pick. A few plantations still let their coffee plants grow beyond 8 feet, the usual maximum height for arabica. Unrestricted trees can reach up to 30 feet, but these heights require workers to get up on ladders, meaning a loss of time and possible damage to the trees—workers must bend branches to reach the fruit. Most farms, like La Minita, cut back their trees to maintain a convenient height. The trees on La Minita are young, too—never more than 15 years old, at which point they have lost much of their vigor and are dug up and replaced. It is rare to find productive trees more than 25 years old.

The land at La Minita is covered with fresh, impeccably tended trees of a cultivar called Caturra, which 50 years ago did not even exist. The truism is that old varieties—what farmers call heirlooms—produce coffee with the best, winiest flavor. This is a matter of controversy. Choosing the right variety certainly matters greatly to flavor, but so do soil and climate. A hallowed old variety like Bourbon—the basis of Latin American trade for hundreds of years—is an impractical choice for a farmer today, because its yield is one-third to one-half that of many new arabica varieties. The only place to find an heirloom variety is on an old farm whose owners could not afford to buy new trees or on a modern one whose owners are able to charge a premium for beans from old varieties.

Most experts who have tasted old varieties against new ones bred for production and hardiness report that the flavor of the older ones is more nuanced. It's a comparison few specialty merchants or their customers can make for themselves, because samples sent by brokers are identified by place of origin and date of harvest but rarely by variety. (A broker should immediately say if a sample is arabica or robusta, but sometimes even this is left vague.) Too, for a comparison to be fair, the old and new bean varieties should have been raised in the same soil and the same climate.

A greater threat to the future of high-quality coffee than new varieties of arabica may be breeds incorporating both arabica and robusta. Even if robusta has a dead flavor, it is nonetheless valuable to farmers for its resistance to various blights. Such hybrids are already being raised on a large scale in some South American countries, and breeding experiments are taking place in Kenya, where arabicas that coffee tasters revere grow on hillsides at 5,500 to 7,000 feet. These efforts distress coffee lovers, even if Kenyans understandably want to protect their plants against Coffee Berry Disease—a fungus that is dangerously difficult to control.

Fungicides are relatively gentle: mostly based on copper, they pose a danger neither to the environment nor to the health of the people who apply them. The same is not true of herbicides and pesticides, which do harm workers, although probably not coffee drinkers—they are said not to penetrate to the coffee beans within the fruits of the tree, and certainly not to appear in brewed coffee in any dangerous quantity. The tradeoff facing farmers and connoisseurs the world over is delicate flavor versus disease resistance.

PAINSTAKING HARVEST

La Minita may not have the primeval beauty of Kenyan plantations that spread across plains and follow softly rolling hills on a high, high basin, or the drama of the volcanic cones all around the Guatemalan city of Antigua. But it is stunning nonetheless. Its verdant sugarloafs jut right into the sky—they are cloud-high. I visited La Minita toward the end of the harvest, which takes place between November and January. The plantation is in a region with just one rainy and one dry season, so there is only one harvest. In other climates, including coastal regions of Costa Rica, there can be as many as four or five harvests a year. The longer the ripening time and the cooler the air, the more time the beans will have to develop flavor. The most intensely flavored beans grow at high altitudes in places with a single harvest.

At La Minita, I finally understood why the range of flavors in coffee is described in terms used for fruits. Coffee beans are the seeds of a berry called a "cherry" for the shape and for the deep crimson color of a fully ripe fruit. The even, ovoid shape resembles more a holly berry or plump cranberry.

I arrived at the plantation during the peak of activity, and McAlpin made me enter into it practically without giving me time to drop my bags. He presented me with a rattan basket and a long cord with a pad to attach it to my waist, and set me to picking. None of the terrain is level, and although I had been pointed to one of the flattest areas on the 700 acres, standing in one place was no easy trick. Slung around my waist, the big basket—about 16 inches in diameter and a foot deep—blocked my view of the ground. The crumbly clay soil didn't make things easier.

Neither did the vegetation growing between the trees. Plants between trees prevent soil erosion. Controlling rather than killing weeds—the approach adopted by organic farmers in many parts of the world, and the approach McAlpin takes—costs much more money than the blanket application of herbicides. Three times a year, workers with machetes shaped like scimitars rotate around La Minita cutting back weeds. Shade trees are heavily pruned at the beginning of the rainy season, when the sun must reach the coffee plants to effect photosynthesis; sunlight also discourages fungal diseases. During the dry season, shade trees are instead allowed to luxuriate, because sunlight can burn coffee tree leaves.

The distribution of fruit on a coffee tree varies annoyingly. Twiglike branches splay out from the central trunk, which is usually no more than an inch or two in diameter. Most often, cherries cluster all along them, so a picker can position a basket just beneath and pull off the fruit. But cherries hide, too, in clusters or in ones and twos, often near the top and sometimes under leaves close to the ground.

I became an adept spy, pushing back the lush, curvaceous coffee plant leaves, which look like voluptuous ficus tree leaves. In the closely planted rows, branches brushed against me from all sides, from my toes to my neck, each requiring careful examination. To pick the lower branches, I had to crouch or get down on my knees. All the labor is hands and fingers—no shears or knives, as are used for grapes.

Even more maddening, the cherries along one branch or within the same cluster don't ripen at the same time, and McAlpin insists that pickers pass over the unripe cherries, which in most cases are yellow and olive-green. Yellow cherries dappled with red, called pinion ("painted"), are acceptable. Dark brown or black cherries that have dried on the tree are also picked, to be separated out at the processing mill. It would be much easier just to strip the branches, but wasting so many cherries that could be picked ripe is unthinkable: McAlpin is selling choice beans, and he sends workers back for three and often four pickings over the course of a few days or weeks. If I wasn't careful to leave the green and yellow cherries, I would have to pick them out of my basket before I was paid: McAlpin pays guest workers just like everybody else.

I popped cherries of varying degrees of ripeness into my mouth to see how they tasted. The translucent goop, called *miel* ("honey"), of both red cherries and *pintons* is sweet and somewhat refreshing, with the taste of overripe melon or fresh litchi nuts. The best flavor came from deep vermilion cherries verging on a mahogany color—the color of dead-ripe Bing cherries. McAlpin told me that this color indicates the height of ripeness, and if it were possible, he would pick only these. But after a day or two, cherries so ripe will begin to dry out and lose flavor, and it is risky to assume that enough workers will be free to pick all of them at the right time.

A rival farm of La Minita is using a different method of harvesting, letting all the beans dry and turn brown on the tree. Fazenda Vista Alegre, in the pretty colonial zone of Minas Gerais, in Brazil, irrigates its trees rather than relying on rainfall, and claims that the resulting control of the growing cycle prevents ripe berries from falling off the tree—something that ordinarily happens in the absence of rain. Most processes remove the *mid* from the beans, which are then dried so as not to ferment. At Fazenda Vista Alegre, the mucilage is allowed to harden and dry around the live bean. The farm managers say that sugars from the *miel* are thus transferred to the beans, and that the roasted beans have a sweet flavor reminiscent of tobacco, with notable body. At La Minita, I tasted the hardened *miel* of cherries that had dried on the tree by accident; it tasted like carob.

The beans themselves, which pop out of the cherry with a simple squeeze, are another story. They are a celadon green, rubbery and slimy. The idea of chewing on them the way you would a lozenge or hard candy seems appealing. But Africans do just that, boiling beans from unripe cherries with herbs and then drying them. Certainly the caffeine would provide more energy than the sugar did from the *miel* I chewed on.

Hopelessly slow, I dreamed of mechanical pickers, which are used on huge farms, typically at low altitudes where robusta grows and price is all.

The flatter terrain of these farms allows vibrating machines to pass between rows of trees, shaking the branches until most of the berries fall to the ground. I dreamed even of picking in Kenya, where the trees are higher but are often severely pruned on the side that gets less sun: at least the cherries would be arrayed before me, and I wouldn't have to be a bean scout.

PAYDAY

After an hour, I had a little over a quarter of a basket, which amounted to about a gallon. For my labor, I was solemnly paid 30 cents. Discouraged, I visited several of the pay stations that are set up right along the road, where workers gather at about 3:00, having begun work at sunup. At the height of the harvest, there can be as many as 650 workers, who come from all over the country and live in temporary housing on the plantation. Many Indian families return year after year.

At the station I visited, I saw dozens of teenage boys and girls and a handful of people old enough to be their parents. Many of the boys and men stuffed bandannas into the backs of baseball caps to protect their necks from the sun. Some wore aprons fashioned from cut-up coffee sacks. The footwear was black rubber waders or sneakers or work boots. Dogs who had spent the morning foraging in the ground cover waited for their masters to be paid.

While picking, a worker carries his own lightweight sack, into which he or she empties each strapped-on basket as the hours wear on. At the pay station, the workers empty their sacks onto burlap mats. Others join in to pick out the green cherries, twigs and leaves; the green cherries will be bagged separately and used for Costa Rican consumption.

Everyone watches carefully as the cleaned cherries are poured into *cajuelas,* 20-liter (about 5-gallon) square metal containers, each about the size of a milk crate, painted rust-red. A year-round La Minita worker smooths the top of each container before emptying it into a communal sack, silently keeping track of each picker's number of containers. "Four and a half," he will call out to another worker holding a cash box, or "six and one," meaning six and one-quarter *cajuelas.*

The man at the pay station seemed as stingy in rounding up to the next quarter-container as the man counting my basket had been. It's his job to conserve the plantation's money, of course, but each full container represents a lot of work. At the time of my visit, the rate happened to correspond to about $1.50 per container, although the price is not tied to the dollar. A typical day's wage was $10 to $20, considered a decent day's pay in a country whose cost of living is far lower than America's. McAlpin says that he pays among the highest wages for farm labor in the country, because the work is so hard, and that Costa Rica's standard of living is envied by its neighbors, as is its democratic system of government, the oldest in Central America.

I watched enviously as one picker after another presented cleaned sacks that filled six, seven or nine containers. Once in a great while, the top picker at La Minita fills 50 baskets in a day, equal to about 40 milk-crate *cajuelas*. Clearly, he is material for the annual national picking tournament, with contests for men and for women and rounds of semifinals and finals on various farms. The grand prize is a three- or four-bedroom house of about 1,000 square feet. Whoever wins it really earns it.

Like any sizable plantation, La Minita is a world unto itself, with half the year-round work force of 80 and their families living in new, pleasant housing. McAlpin prides himself on the benefits he provides: high wages, matching contributions to a savings plan, private medical care for serious illnesses, grocery staples at wholesale plus transport, free vegetables from the farm's large garden.

In other countries, however, coffee pickers are frequently not paid fair wages or given anything akin to this range of benefits. Several American-based organizations, such as Coffee Kids and Coffee Exchange, seek contributions that will help workers to be better paid and treated more equitably. Many coffee bars in America ask customers to give their change to one of these groups, collecting it, appropriately enough, in a coffee can.

Even McAlpin, who is faring better than the owners of farms near La Minita, sells coffee from other farms in Costa Rica, Colombia and Guatemala to help support his progressive practices. Most landowners have also had to find some other way to generate income. The 1989 collapse of the International Coffee Agreement, a pact that obliged farmers to hold back supplies in order to keep prices comparatively high, has hurt large and small coffee-producing countries alike. Prices fell to near record lows, because countries no longer sold beans according to prearranged quotas. Efforts to form a new cartel failed. These attempts must continue, though, to ensure the survival of many coffee-producing farms around the world.

Already farms around La Minita are letting jungle overtake some of their coffee trees—a process that can take as little as two years. Farmers who can't afford the costs for labor are offering their land to McAlpin at bargain prices. McAlpin himself is subject to many of their difficulties, though, and can by no means afford to take them up on their offers.

A FINAL SORT

Beans must be liberated from the cherries, and different growers choose different ways—washing them so that water does the work; or sun-drying them, a less expensive or equipment-heavy process that imparts its own flavors, some of them prized and many of them not. All McAlpin's are washed and polished. La Minita coffee, the only one of the half-dozen coffees McAlpin sells that he names for the whole plantation, goes through an extraordinary final step. Perched on stools in front of partitioned wooden work stations, 60 or 70 women hand-sort the beans, separating out those whit adherent silverskin that indicates they are not ripe, and discarding those that are misshapen or discolored. The women work for no more than six hours at a time, with frequent breaks, because the required concentration is so great.The approved beans are double-sewn into big bags.

The sight of a small, brightly lit room full of women poring over green coffee beans one by one seems out of another century. McAlpin admits that light and screen sorters can achieve much of this separation, especially if the beans are fed through slowly and the process is repeated. So far, though, a single machine cannot sort out underripe, discolored and overripe beans at the same time, or make a judgment call on a bean that is only partially flawed. McAlpin says that he's in the business of creating jobs, and this is relatively pleasant: clean and with minimal supervision from a man who goes up and down he aisles to see that the "good" beans really are good. I was assured that when visitors aren't present to look over the women's shoulders, the conversation is nonstop and the music from the radio loud.

The journey from the final sorting room to the hometown specialty-coffee shop is surprisingly short. A bag of coffee from Costa Rica can reach a broker or roaster in a port city in under three weeks and, with land transport, can get from Costa rica to almost any city or town in little over a month. Shipping takes longer from countries that are farther from the United States, but the general method is the same: in bags loaded into containers. The thick metal housing of the container usually ensures that odors from other cargo will not contaminate the beans, but not always. McAlpin has had disasters, like the time the smell of untreated rubber in a neighboring container invaded beans he was shipping—luckily, not La Minita beans. "It was like the inside of new shoes," McAlpin says. "Gross."

Today, synthetic substitutes for burlap are used for he bags; before they came into use, an off-smelling coating could affect the coffee, leading to an old, "baggy" taste.

Compared to the all-important role that soil, climate, careful tending and processing play, though, transport is responsible for few taste defects. This is a lucky thing. A coffee farmer puts his skill and risks his livelihood on each year's crop, and he wants his beans to be at their best when they reach their destination. When they do, they will undergo the inspection that will determine not only their fat but the farmer's as well.

CONFESSIONS OF A
STAND-UP SAUSAGE EATER

CALVIN TRILLIN

I SUPPOSE I WOULD HAVE given up the Feast of San Gennaro years ago if I'd had any choice. San Gennaro has always been the largest Italian festival in the city, and for a long time now Mulberry Street during the Feast has been crowded enough to give the impression that, for reasons lost to history, Manhattan folk customs include an annual outdoor enactment of precisely the conditions present in the IRT uptown express during rush hour. In September, the weather in New York can be authentically Neapolitan—particularly on a street that is jammed with people and sealed on both sides with a line of stands where vendors are boiling oil for *zeppole* or barbecuing *braciole* over charcoal. Occasionally I have become irritated with the Feast even on evenings when I have no intention of attending it, since I have become one of those Manhattan residents who get testy when some event brings even more traffic than usual into the city from the suburbs. Those of us who migrated to New York from the middle of the country may be even less tolerant of incursions by out-of-towners than the natives are. I suppose I might as well admit that, in some particularly frustrating gridlock on some particularly steamy fall day, I may have shouted, "Go back where you came from, you rubes!" in the direction of a lot of former New Yorkers who now live a mile or two into New Jersey—an outburst that would have been even ruder if the objects of my irritation had not been safely encased in soundproof air-conditioned cars.

The traffic congestion caused by San Gennaro is particularly irritating to me because Mulberry Street lies between our house and Chinatown, and the Feast happens to fall at the time of year when I return to the city from a summer in Nova Scotia suffering the anguish of extended

Chinese-food deprivation. For Occidentals, we eat very well in Nova Scotia. Around the middle of August, though, even as I'm plowing through a feast that may include mushroom soup made from wild mushrooms we have gathered in the woods and halibut just off the boat and sugar-snap peas so sweet that even Sarah (whose last recorded expression of enthusiasm for eating anything green came at a street fair that was selling green cotton candy) has been witnessed eating them straight off the vine and freshly baked bread and blueberry pie made from wild blueberries, I become acutely aware of how many miles, nautical and overland, stand between me and Mott Street.

Practically feverish with visions of crabs sloshing around in black-bean sauce, I detour around the Feast in a journey that seems to get longer every year, as the lights of San Gennaro push farther and farther uptown from the heart of Little Italy toward Houston Street, on the edge of the Lower East Side. It would not surprise me, I think, if one of these years commuters from Westchester County pouring out of Grand Central Station some hot September morning walked smack into a line of *calzone* and sausage stands that had crept up in an unbroken line fifty blocks from Grand Street. The vendors, dishing out food as fast as they can, will still have time to complain to the account executives and bank managers they're serving about having been assigned a spot too far from the busiest blocks of the Feast.

I love the elements of San Gennaro that still exist from its origin as a neighborhood festival transplanted practically intact from Naples by Little Italy immigrants—the statue of the saint with dollar bills pinned beneath it, for instance, and the brass band that seems to consist of a half-dozen aging Italians and one young Chinese trumpet player—but the Feast has felt considerably less like a neighborhood celebration in recent years, partly because its size has inevitably brought along some atmosphere of mass production, partly because of the inclusion of such non-Neapolitan specialties as piña coladas and eggrolls and computer portraits, and partly because of the self-consciousness represented by *Kiss Me—I'm Italian* buttons. Also, I find that I can usually catch the brass band during the year around the Chinatown part of Mulberry, below Canal Street; it often works Chinese funerals. The gambling at the Feast does not attract me, and the stuffed animals that are awarded for making a basket or knocking down milk bottles hold no appeal for someone whose family policy on stuffed animals is moving slowly, in the face of some resistance, toward what the Metropolitan Museum of Art used to call deaccessioning.

Still, there I am at San Gennaro every year—admitting to myself that I rather enjoy pushing my way down Mulberry at a time when

Neapolitan music is coming over the loudspeakers and operators of games of chance are making their pitches and food smells from a dozen different booths are competing in the middle of the street. My presence is easily explained: I can't stay away from the sausage sandwiches.

As it happens, we live right around the corner from the South Village, an Italian neighborhood where the sort of sausage sandwiches served at Italian feasts—hot or sweet sausage jammed into a roll with a combination of fried pepper and onions as dressing—can be bought any day of the year in comfortable surroundings, which may even include a stool at the counter. I never buy one. Gradually, it has become clear to me that uncontrolled, year-round eating of sausage sandwiches is not an acceptable option for me. It was instinct more than conscious decision—the sort of instinct that some animals must use to know how many of certain berries to eat in the woods. Alice, who at our house acts as enforcer for the nutrition mob, does not have to speak on the subject of how much devastation a steady diet of Italian sausage could wreak on the human body. The limits are set. I have a sausage sandwich whenever I go to San Gennaro. I have a sausage sandwich at the Feast of St. Anthony, on Sullivan Street, in the spring. If I'm lucky, I might stumble across one of the smaller Italian feasts in Little Italy—I always come back from Chinatown by a circuitous route through there, just on the off-chance—or find a sausage stand that has attached itself to some Village block party. Otherwise, I do without. When I go back for visits to Kansas City, my hometown, and I'm asked by my old high-school friends how I possibly survive in New York, I tell them that the way I survive is simple: I only eat sausage sandwiches standing up.

I am not the only seasonal eater in New York. There is a time in the fall when a lot of people who have spent August in some rural setting—talking a lot of brave talk about how there is nothing better than a simple piece of broiled fish and some absolutely fresh vegetables—come back to the city and head straight for the sort of food that seems to exist only in close proximity to cement. One September I noticed one of them while I was waiting in line at Joe's Dairy on Sullivan Street—right across the street from St. Anthony's, the church that sponsors my spring sausage eating. As it happened, my own mission was seasonal—although one sort of business or another takes me to Joe's all year round. In the early fall, when farmers are still bringing their produce into Manhattan for Saturday morning markets, it is possible to make a stop at the farmer's market in the West Village, pick up some basil and some tomatoes that actually taste like tomatoes rather than Christmas decorations, stop in at Joe's for mozzarella so fresh that it is still oozing milk, and put the tomatoes and mozzarella and basil and some olive oil together to create something that tastes almost too good to be described as salad. The man in front of me at Joe's Dairy was looking around the shelves as if he were a Russian defector getting his first look at Bloomingdale's. He asked for Parmesan cheese. He asked for Romano. He bought some mozzarella. "Jesus Christ! I just had a roast-pork sandwich at Frank's!" he suddenly said. "Boy, am I glad to be back in the city!" Everybody in the store nodded in sympathy.

When I walk down Mulberry Street, just below Canal, during the Feast of San Gennaro, I am strongly affected by what I suppose could be called border tensions: I feel the competing pulls of sausage sandwiches and flounder Fukienese-style. The street just east of Mulberry is Mott, the main drag of Chinatown. There was a time not many years ago when Mott and a few side streets seemed to constitute a small Chinese outpost in the middle of a large Italian neighborhood; those were the days when a Chinese candidate for the New York State Assembly endeared himself to me by telling a reporter from the *Times* that he was running against the Italian incumbent—Louis DeSalvio, the permanent grand marshal of the Feast of San Gennaro—even though he realized that he didn't have a "Chinaman's chance." Over the past ten or fifteen years, though, a surge of Chinese immigration has revitalized Chinatown and pushed out its boundaries—past the Bowery and then East Broadway in one direction, across Mulberry Street in the other. On Mulberry Street below Canal, the *calzone* stands and beer carts of San Gennaro stand in front of Chinese butcher shops and Chinese importing companies and Chinese produce stores. "They left us three blocks," an official of San Gennaro told me while discussing the Chinese expansion. The blocks between Canal and Broome are still dominated by the robust Italian restaurants that represent the tomato sauce side against the forces of Northern Italian cream sauce in what has been called the War of the Red and the White. Even on those blocks of Mulberry, though, some of the windows of second-floor offices have sprouted Chinese writing. There are a lot of Italians left in the tenements of Mulberry Street, but a lot of Italians have moved away—returning only temporarily to shop on Grand Street or sit in one of the coffeehouses or eat sausage sandwiches at the Feast of San Gennaro. The Feast is still run by the grandson of the man who founded the Society of San Gennaro, Napoli e Dintorni, in 1926, but he lives on Staten Island.

Foreign food—non-Italian food, that is—began to creep into San Gennaro and some of the other Italian feasts several years ago, but not from Chinatown. There were some Korean booths and an occasional taco stand and some stands at which Filipinos sold barbecued meat on a stick and fried rice and lo mein and egg rolls and an unusual fritter that was made with vegetables and fried in oil. When I first came across the foreign booths, I decided that the purist belief in restricting Italian festivals to Italian food was narrow-minded and artificial—a decision that was based, I admit, on a certain fondness for the vegetable fritters. These days, any street event in New York—a merchants' fair on Third Avenue, a block party on the West Side—is certain to have at least one Filipino food stand, and a feast the size of San Gennaro will have half a dozen. At the annual One World Festival sponsored by the Armenian diocese—a festival that has always been so aggressively ecumenical that I wouldn't be surprised to discover someday that a few spots had been assigned to food stands run by Turks—the stands selling Armenian *lahmajun* and *boereg* and *yalanchi* and *lule kebab* seem almost outnumbered by stands selling what are sometimes called "Filipino and Polynesian specialties." The man in charge of assigning spots for San Gennaro once told me that if no attempt were made to maintain a balance—and a Feast that is not overwhelmingly Italian would obviously be unbalanced—Mulberry Street would have ten Filipino stands on every block. I have asked Filipino vendors how they accounted for so many of their countrymen being in the street—fair game, but their explanations have never gone much beyond the theory that some people made money at some street fairs in brownstone neighborhoods and other people decided to get in on a good thing. It may remain one of those New York ethnic mysteries that outlanders were not meant to understand. Why are so many fruit-and-vegetable stores that were once run by Italians and so many fruit-and-vegetable stores that previously didn't exist run by Koreans? Why have I never seen a black sanitation man? Why are conversations among vendors of hot dogs at the Central Park Zoo conducted in Greek?

Selecting my sausage sandwich at San Gennaro requires a certain amount of concentration. At San Gennaro, after all, there are always at least thirty stands selling sausage sandwiches. I don't mean that I do nothing else at the Feast. In the spirit of fostering intergroup harmony, I sometimes have a vegetable fritter. I often have a few *zeppole*—holeless doughnuts that are available almost exclusively at Italian feasts. I have a couple of beers, muttering about the price, or some wine with fruit. Mainly, though, I inspect sausage stands—walking slowly the length of the Feast and maybe back again before I make my choice. About halfway through my inspection, I can expect to be told by another member of the party—Abigail and Sarah are ordinarily the other members of the party—that all sausage stands look alike, or maybe even that all sausage sandwiches taste alike. I tell them that they certainly weren't raised to believe that all sausage sandwiches taste alike. I tell them that their expertise in this matter is seriously limited by the refusal of either of them to taste an Italian-sausage sandwich. I remind them that a researcher who is satisfied with a less than adequate sampling risks flawed results. I keep looking.

The stands always look familiar to me. A lot of the food vendors at Italian feasts in Manhattan make a business of going from feast to feast around the New York area from spring to fall. In Little Italy, it is assumed that the food-stand operators spend the rest of the year in Florida, living like kings off the sort of profits that must be accumulated by anyone who sells a tiny plate of ziti with tomato sauce for three dollars cash and doesn't have to furnish so much as a chair or a countertop. Among New Yorkers, it is practically an article of faith that anyone who runs what seems to be a small seasonal business—the ice-cream man in the park, for instance—can be found on any cold day in February casually blowing hundreds off dollars at some Florida dog track. Although I recognize the stands, I can never seem to keep in my mind which one has served me the best sausage sandwich. The last time I went to San Gennaro, the final inspection was carried out on a rainy weekday evening in the company of both Abigail and Sarah. I was convinced that the stand I had patronized at St. Anthony's the previous spring—acquiring a sandwich the memory of which I carried with me through the summer—was called by someone's first name. All the sausage stands at San Gennaro seemed to be called by someone's first name. Had it been Dominic's? The Original Jack's? Rocky & Philly's? Tony's? Angelo's? Smokin' Joe's? Staten Island Frank's? Gizzo's? Lucy's?

There was nothing to do but inspect each stand—Abigail and Sarah tagging along behind me, already full of pasta. I looked for a stand that was frying the sausages on a griddle rather than grilling them over charcoal—and displaying peppers and onions that had been sliced and cooked precisely to my requirements. It was amazing how many sausage stands qualified. My daughters began to remind me that it was a school night. I told them that I would write them notes if they overslept the next morning ("Abigail had to be up late to take advantage of an unusual opportunity to observe the process of pure research"). Under some pressure, I stopped in front of Staten Island Frank's—or maybe it was the Original Jack's; even now the names run together—and said, "This is it." When I started to eat, I was convinced that I had chosen brilliantly—until we passed a stand that I hadn't noticed before. It was serving sausages, with correctly fried peppers and onions, on marvelous-looking rolls that had sesame seeds on top of them.

"Sesame-seed rolls!" I said. "Nobody told me about sesame-seed rolls!"

"Take it easy," Abigail said, giving me a reassuring pat on the arm. "You can have one on a sesame-seed roll next year."

"Not next year," I reminded her as we headed home. "At St. Anthony's in June."

ADAM GOPNIK

M OST PEOPLE WHO LOVE Paris love it because the first time they came they ate something better than they had ever eaten before, and kept coming back to eat it again. My first night in Paris, twenty-five years ago, I ate dinner with my enormous family in a little corner brasserie somewhere down on the unfashionable fringes of the Sixteenth Arrondissement. We were on the cutrate American academic version of the grand tour, and we had been in London for the previous two days, where we had eaten *steamed* hamburgers and fish-and-chips in which the batter seemed to be snubbing the fish inside it as if they had never been properly introduced. On that first night in Paris we arrived late on the train, checked into a cheap hotel, and went to eat (party of eight—no, party of nine, one of my sisters having brought along a boyfriend), without much hope, at the restaurant at the corner, called something like Le Bar-B-Que. The prix-fixe menu was fifteen francs, about three dollars then. I ordered a salad Niçoise, trout baked in foil, and a cassis sorbet. It was so much better than anything I had ever eaten that I nearly wept. (My mother, I am compelled at gunpoint to add, made food like that all the time too, but a mother's cooking is a current of life, not an episode of taste.) My feelings at Le Bar-B-Que were a bit like those of Stendhal, I think it was, the first time be went to a brothel: I knew that it could be done, but I didn't know there was a place on any corner where you could walk in, pay three dollars, and get it.

That first meal in Paris was for a long time one of the few completely reliable pleasures for an American in Europe. "It was the green beans," a hardened New Yorker recalled not long ago, remembering his first meal in Paris, back in the late forties. "The green beans were like nothing I had ever known," he went on. He sat suddenly bolt upright, his eyes alight with memory.

Now, though, for the first time in several hundred years, a lot of people who live in France are worried about French cooking, and so are a lot of people who don't. The French themselves are, or claim to be, worried mostly about the high end—the end that is crowded into the Passard kitchen—and the low end. The word *crise* in connection with cooking appeared in *La Monde* about a year ago, with the news that a restaurant near Lyons, which had earned three Michelin stars, was about to close. Meanwhile, a number of worrying polls have suggested that the old pyramid of French food, in which the base of plain dishes shared by the population pointed upward to the higher reaches of the *grande cuisine,* is collapsing. Thirty-six percent of the French people polled in one survey thought that you make mayonnaise with whole eggs (you use only yolks), 17 percent thought that you put a *travers de porc* in a pot-au-feu (you use beef), and 7 percent believed that Lucas Carton, the Paris restaurant that for a century has been one of the holiest of holies of haute cuisine, is a name for badly cooked meat. More ominously, fully 71 percent of Frenchmen named the banal *steak-frites* as their favorite *plat;* only people past sixty preferred a *blanquette de veau*, or a *gigot d'agneau,* or even a pot-au-feu, all real French cooking. (The French solution to this has been, inevitably, to create a National Council of Culinary Arts, connected to the Ministry of Culture.)

To an outsider, the real *crise* lies in the middle. That Paris first-night experience seems harder to come by. It is the unforced superiority of the cooking in the ordinary corner bistro the *prix-fixe ordinaire*—that seems to be passing. This is partly a tribute to the international power of French cooking and to the great catching up that has been going on in the rest of the world for the past quarter century. The new visitor, trying out the trout baked in foil on his first night in Paris, will probably be comparing it with the trout baked in foil back home at, oh, Le Lac de Feu, in Cleveland—or even back home at Chez Alfie, in Leeds, or Matilda Qui Danse, in Adelaide—and the trout back home may just be better: raised wild or caught on the line. Even the cassis sorbet may not be quite as good as the kind he makes at home with his Sorbet-o-matic.

The fear—first unspoken, then whispered, then cautiously enunciated, and now loudly insisted on by certain competitors—is that the muse of cooking has migrated across the ocean to a spot in Berkeley, with occasional trips to New York and, of all places, Great Britain. People in London will even tell you, flatly, that the cooking there now is the best in the world, and they will publish this thought as though it were a statement of fact and as though the steamed hamburger and the stiff fish had been made long ago in another country. Two of the best chef's in the London cooking renaissance said to a reporter not long ago that London, along with Sydney and San Francisco, is one of the capitals of good food and that the food in Paris—"heavy, lazy, lacking in imagination"—is now among the worst in the world.

All this makes a Francophile eating in Paris feel a little like a turn-of-the-century clergyman who has just read Robert Ingersoll: You try to keep the faith, but Doubts keep creeping in. Even the most ardent Paris lover, who once blessed himself at every dinner for having escaped Schrafft's, may now find himself—as he gazes down one more unvarying menu of *boudin noir* and *saumon unilatéral* and *entrecôte bordelaise* and *poulet rôti*, eats one more bland and buttery dish—feeling a slight pang for that Cuban-Vietnamese-California grill on Amsterdam Avenue or wondering whether he might, just possibly, enjoy the New Sardinian Cooking, as featured that week on the cover of *New York*.

I would still rather eat in Paris than anywhere else in the world. The best places in Paris, like the Brasserie Balzar, on the rue des Écoles, don't just feed you well; they make you happy in a way that no other city's restaurants can. (The Balzar is the place that plays Gallant to the more famous Brasserie Lipp's Goofus.) Even in a mediocre Paris restaurant, you are part of the richest commonplace civilization that has ever been created and that extends back visibly to the previous century. In Paris restaurants can actually go into a kind of hibernation for years and awaken in a new generation: Lapérouse, the famous swanky nineteenth-century spot, has, after a long stretch of being overlooked, just come back to life, and is a good place to eat again. Reading Olivier Todd's biography of Camus, you discover that the places where Camus went to dinner in the forties (Aux Charpentiers, Le Petit St. Benoît, Aux Assassins) are places where you can go to dinner tonight. Some of Liebling's joints are still in business too: the Beaux-Arts, the Pierre à la Place Gaillon, the Closerie des Lilas.

These continuities suggest that a strong allegiance to the past acts as a drag on the present. But, after several months of painstaking, tie-staining research, I think that the real problem lies in the French genius for laying the intellectual foundation for a revolution that takes place somewhere else. With movies (Méliès and the Lumière brothers invented the form and then couldn't build the industry) with airplanes and now even with cooking, France has again and again made the first breakthrough and then got stalled. All the elements of the new cooking, as it exists today in America and in London—the openness to new techniques, the suspicion of the overelaborate, the love of surprising juxtapositions—were invented in Paris long before they emigrated to London and New York and Berkeley. But in France they never coalesced into something entirely new. The Enlightenment took place here, and the Revolution worked out better somewhere else.

The early seventies, when I was first in France, were, I realize now, a kind of Indian summer of French haute cuisine, the last exhalation of a tradition that had been in place for several hundred years. The atmosphere of French cooking was everywhere in Paris then: thick smells and posted purple mimeographed menus; the sounds of cutlery on tables and the jowly look of professional eaters emerging blinking into the light at four o'clock.

The standard, practical account of the superiority of French cooking was that it had been established in the sixteenth century, when Catherine de' Medici brought Italian cooks, then the best in the world, to Paris. It was not until after the French Revolution, though, when the breakup of the great aristocratic houses sent chefs out onto the street looking for someone to feed, that the style of French cooking went public. The most famous and influential figure of this period—the first great chef in European history— was Antonin Carême, who worked, by turns, for Talleyrand, the future George IV, Czar Alexander I, and the Baroness de Rothschild. He invented "presentation." His cooking looked a lot like architecture, with the dishes fitted into vast, beautiful neoclassical structures.

The unique superiority of French cooking for the next hundred years depended on the invention of the cooking associated with the name Auguste Escoffier. Escoffier's formula for food was in essence the same as Jasper John's formula for dada art: Take something; do something to it; then do something else to it. It was cooking that rested, above all, on the idea of the master sauce: A lump of protein was cooked in a pan, and what was left behind in the pan was "deglazed" with wine or stock, ornamented with butter or cream, and then poured back over the lump of protein. Escoffier was largely the creature of courtiers and aristocratic patrons; the great hotelers of Europe, particularly César Ritz, sealed in place the master sauce approach that remains the unchallenged basis of haute cuisine.

It was also an article of faith, dating, perhaps, to Alexandre Dumas père's famous *Grand Dictionnaire de Cuisine,* that the cooking of Carême and Escoffier had evolved from a set of provincial folk techniques. At the heart of French food lay the pot-au-feu, the bouillon pot that every peasant wife was supposed to keep on her hearth, and into which, according to legend, she threw whatever she had, to stew for the day's meal. French classic cooking was French provincial cooking gone to town.

I heard another, more weirdly philosophical account of this history from a professor named Eugenio Donato, who was the most passionately intellectual eater I have ever known. Armenian-Italian, reared in Egypt and educated in France, he spoke five languages, each with a nearly opaque Akim Tamiroff accent. ("It could have been worse," he said to me once, expertly removing one mussel with the shell of another as we ate *moules marinières* somewhere on the place de la Sorbonne. "I had a friend whose parents were ardent Esperantists. He spoke five languages, each with an impenetrable Esperanto accent.") Eugenio was a literary critic whom we would now call a poststructuralist, though he called what he did philosophical criticism.

Most of the time he wandered from one American university to another—the Johnny Appleseed or Typhoid Mary of deconstruction, depending on your point of view. He had a deeply tragic personal life, though, and I think that his happiest hours were spent in Paris, eating and thinking and talking. His favorite subject was French food, and his favorite theory was that "French cooking" was foreign to France, not something that had percolated up from the old pot-au-feu but something that had been invented by fanatics at the top, as a series of powerful metaphors—ideas about France and Frenchness—that had then moved downward to organize the menus and, retrospectively, colonize the past. "The idea of the French chef precedes French cooking" was how he put it. Cooking for him was a form of writing—Carême and Escoffier had earned their reputations by publishing cookbooks—with literature's ability to make something up and then pretend it had been there all along.

The invention of the French restaurant, Eugenio believed, depended largely on what every assistant professor would now call an "essentialized" idea of France. One proof of this was that if the best French restaurants tended to be in Paris, the most "typical" ones tended to be in New York. Yet the more abstract and self-enclosed haute cuisine became, the more inclined its lovers were to pretend that it was a folk art, risen from the French earth unbidden. For Eugenio, the key date in this masquerade was 1855, when the wines of Médoc were classified into the famous five growths in which they remain today. "The form of metropolitan rationalization being extended to the provincial earth, *in the guise of the reflection of an order locked in the earth itself,*" he announced once, bringing his fist down on the tablecloth. He was a big man, who looked uncannily like John Madden, the football coach.

On that occasion we were eating lunch in one of the heavy, dark, smoky Lyons places that were popular in Paris then. (There is always one provincial region singled out for favor in Paris at any moment—*privileged* would have been Eugenio's word. Then it was Burgundy; now it is the southwest. This fact was grist for his thesis that the countryside was made in the city.) The restaurant was, I think, someplace over in the Seventh; it may have been Pantagruel or La Bourgogne. At lunch, in those days, Eugenio would usually begin with twelve escargots in Chablis, then go on to something like a *filet aux moelles*—a filet with bone marrow and Madeira sauce—and end, whenever he could, with a mille-feuille.

The food in those places wasn't so much "rich" as deep, dense. Each *plat* arrived looking mellow and varnished, like an old violin. Each mouthful registered like a fat organ chord in a tall church, hitting you hard and then echoing around the room: There's the bass note (the beef), there's the middle note (the marrow), and there's the treble (the Madeira in the sauce).

It couldn't last. "We have landed in the moment when the metaphors begin to devour themselves, the moment of rhetorical self-annihilation," Eugenio once said cheerfully. This meant that the food had become so rich as to be practically inedible. A recipe from the restaurant Lucas Carton that I found among a collection of menus of the time that Eugenio bequeathed to me suggests the problem. The recipe is for a *timbale des homards.* You take three lobsters, season them with salt and pepper and a little curry, sauté them in a light *mirepoix*—a mixture of chopped onions and carrots—and them simmer them with cognac, port, double cream, and fresh stock for twenty minutes. Then you take out the lobsters and, keeping them warm, reduce the cooking liquid and add two egg yolks and 150 grams of sweet butter. Metaphors like that can kill you.

Something had to give, and it did. The "nouvelle cuisine" that replaced the old style has by now been reduced to a set of clichés and become a licensed subject of satire: the tiny portion on the big oval plate; the raspberry-vinegar infusion; the kiwi. This makes it difficult to remember how fundamental a revolution it worked in the way people cooked. At the same moment in the early seventies, a handful of new chefs—Michel Guérard, Paul Bocuse, Alain Senderens—began to question the do-something-to-it-then-do-something-else-to-it basis of the classic cooking. They emphasized, instead, fresh ingredients, simple treatment, an openness to Oriental techniques and spices, and a general reformist air of lightness and airiness.

The new chefs had little places all around Paris, in the out-lying arrondissements, where, before, no one would have traveled for a first-rate meal. Michel Guérard was at Le Pot-au-Feu, way out in Asnières; Alain Dutournier, a little later, settled his first restaurant, Au Trou Gascon, in the extremely unfashionable Twelfth. In the sad, sedate Seventh Arrondissement, Alain Senderens opened Archestrate, first in a little space on the rue de l'Exposition, in the shadow of the Eiffel Tower, and then on the rue de Varenne.

From the beginning, the new cooking divided into two styles, into what Eugenio identified as "two rhetorics," a rhetoric of *terroirs* and a rhetoric of *épices*—soil and spice. The rhetoric of the *terroirs* emphasized the allegiance of new cooking to French soil; the rhetoric of the *épices* emphasized its openness to the world beyond the hexagon. The soil boys wanted to return French cooking to its roots in the regions; the spice boys wanted to take it forward to the new regions of *outre-mer*. Even as the new cooking tried to look outward, it had to reassure its audience (and itself) that it was really looking inward.

On the surface the beautiful orderly pattern continues. Alain Senderens is now in Michel Comby's place at Lucas Carton amid has replaced the *timbale des homards* cooking with his own style. Senderens's rue de Varenne Archestrate is now occupied by Alain Passard, the Senderens of his generation, while the original Archestrate is occupied by a talented young chef and his wife, just starting out, who have named the restaurant after their little girl, La Maison de Cosima.

But twenty-five years later the great leap forward seems to have stalled. A large part of the *crise* is economic: A hundred-dollar lunch is a splurge; a four-hundred-dollar lunch a moral dubiety. Worse, because of the expense, the cooking at the top places in Paris is no longer a higher extension of a commonplace civilization. It is just three-star cooking, a thing unto itself, like grand opera in the age of the microphone. Like grand opera, it is something that will soon need a subsidy to survive; the kitchen at Arpège depends on regular infusions of range-struck Americans to fill the space left by the French kids who no longer want to work eighteen-hour days for very little money while they train.

And it is like grand opera in this also: You can get too much of it, easily. It is, truth be told, often a challenge to eat—a happy challenge, and sometimes a welcome one, but a challenge nonetheless. It is just too rich, and there is just too much. The new cooking in France has become a version of the old.

At Lucas Carton you begin with, say, a plate of vegetables so young they seem dewy, beautifully done, but so bathed in butter and transformed that they are no longer particularly vegetal, and then you move on to the new lobster dish that has taken the place of the old one. Where the old lobsters were done in a cow-shedful of cream, the new lobsters are done, épicé style, with Madagascar vanilla bean. This is delicious, with the natural sugar of the lobster revealing the vanilla as a spice—although, for an American, the custard-colored sauce, dotted with specks of black vanilla, disconcertingly calls to mind melted lunchroom ice cream. For dessert, you might have a roasted pineapple, which is done on the same principles on which Passard's tomatoes are braised: It ends up encrusted in caramel. This is delicious too, though intensely sweet. Lunch at Lucas these days can fairly be called Napoleonic or Empire; the references to the revolutionary principles are there, but finally it's in thrall to the same old aristocratic values.

Lucas is hardly representative, but even at the lesser, less ambitious places the cooking seems stuck in a rut: a chunk of boned protein, a reduced sauce; maybe a fruit complement, to establish its "inventive" bona fides; and a puree. The style has become formulaic: a disk of meat, a disk of complement, a sauce on top. The new cooking seems to have produced less a new freedom than a revived orthodoxy—a new essentialized form of French cooking, which seems less pleasing, and certainly a lot less "modern," than the cooking that evolved at the same time from the French new cooking in other countries. The hold of the master sauté pan, and the master sauce, and the thing-in-the-middle-of-the-plate is still intact.

Thinking it over, I suspect that Eugenio put his finger on the problem with the new cooking in France when it first appeared. "A revolution can sweep clean," he said, "but a reformation points forward and backward at the same time." The new cooking was, as Eugenio said, a reformation, not a revolution; it worked within the same system of Michelin stars and fifteen-man kitchens and wealthy clients that the old cooking did. It didn't make a new audience; it tried to appropriate the old one.

In America—and in England too, where the only thing you wanted to do with the national culinary tradition was lose it—the division between soil and spice wasn't a problem. You could first create the recipes and then put the ingredients in the earth yourself. The American cooks who have followed in Alice Waters's pathmaking footsteps at Chez Panisse, in Berkeley—the generation whom a lot of people think of as the children of M. F. K. Fisher—created a freewheeling, eclectic cosmopolitan cuisine: a risotto preceding a stir-fry leading to a *sabayon*. Then they went out and persuaded the local farmers to grow the things they needed.

In France the soil boys won easily. Some of what they stood for is positive and even inspiring: The *terroirs* movement has a green, organic, earth-conscious element that is very good news. The *marché biologique* every Sunday morning on the boulevard Raspail has become one of the weekly Parisian wonders, full of ugly, honest fruit and rough, tasty country meat. And it is rare for any restaurant in Paris to succeed now without presenting itself as a "regional" spot—a southwest, or Provençal, or Savoyard place. (Even at the exquisite Grand Véfour, at the Palais Royal, the most beautiful restaurant in the world and a cathedral of the cosmopolitan tradition, it is thought necessary to parade around a plate of the cheeses of the chef's native Savoy.)

Yet the insistence on national, or local, tradition—on truth to *terroirs*—can give even to the best new Paris restaurants a predictability that the good new places in London and New York don't share. The French, who invented the tradition of taking things over and then insisting that they were yours all along, are now shy about doing it. The cooking at a French restaurant must now, for the first time, be French. This tendency came to a head last spring, when a group of important French chiefs actually issued a manifesto protesting the spread of exotic food combinations and alien spices in French cooking and calling for a return to the *terroirs*.

Peter Hoffman, the owner and chief of the influential Savoy, in New York, is one of those American chefs who went to France in the early eighties, were dazzled, and now find that the light has dimmed. He likes to tell about his most recent dinner at the three-star restaurant L'Ambroisie, on the place des Vosges. "We went to L'Ambroisie and had a classic French dish: hare with blood sauce. It was fabulous, everything you want rabbit with blood to be. But then I got talked into ordering one of the chief's specialties, a mille-feuille of langoustines with curry, and it was infuriating. It was a French dish with powder. It was such an insular approach, as though nobody understood that curry isn't a powder that you apply cosmetically. Nobody had read Madhur Jaffrey, or really understood that curry isn't just a spice you shake but a whole technique of cooking you have to understand."

As the writer Catharine Reynolds points out, the new cooking in America and England alike is really Mediterranean cooking, inspired by Italy, Tunisia, and Greece. It suits the fat-allergic modern palate better than the old butter and cream cooking of the north. France, which has a big window south, ought to be open to its influence yet remains resistant. The real national dish of the French right now—the cheap, available food—is couscous. But North African cooking remains segregated in couscous parlors and has not been brought into the main current. A fossilized metropolitan tradition should have been replaced by a modernized metropolitan tradition, yet what took its place was sentimental nationalism.

It was the invasion of American fast food, as much as anything, that made the French turn back to their own tradition and, for the first time, see it as something in need of self-conscious protection. Looking at

America, the French don't see the children of M. F. K. Fisher; they just see the flood tides of McDonald's, which, understandably, strike fear into their hearts. The bistro became an endangered species. To make still one more *blanquette de veau* suddenly became not a habit of commonplace civilization but a form of self-defense.

Waverley Root once divided all Gaul into three fats—lard, olive oil, and butter—and said that they determined the shape of French cooking. That you might be able to cook without putting any fat in the pan at all was an unthinkable notion. The charcoal grill, the brick oven, and all the other nonfat ways of cooking now seen normal everywhere except in France. People who look at cooking more practically than philosophically think that that technical lag is the heart of the problem.

"It's deglaze or die" is how Alexandra Guarnaschelli, an American cook in Paris, puts it. The master sauce approach remains the basis of French cooking, whereas elsewhere it has been overthrown by the grill. The pan and the pot have always been the basic utensils of French cooking—just what was there—in the same way that the grill was the primary element of American vernacular backyard cooking. For Americans, grilled food wasn't new but familiar, and good cooking is made up of familiar things done right. As the excellent American chiefs Chris Schlesinger and John Willoughby have pointed out, grilling forced an entirely new approach to saucemaking: With no residue to deglaze, the cook had to think in terms of savory complements rather than subtle echoes. Grilling demanded chutney, fruit mustards, spice mixes. Although the French tradition included these things, they weren't part of the vernacular.

Alex has seen some of the predicament at first hand. She is twenty-seven; she arrived in France five years ago and, after training in Burgundy, became a *commis* at Guy Savoy's two-star place in the Seventeenth Arrondissement. Within a couple of years she had worked her way up to fish chef, and a little while later Savoy appointed her second-in-command at his bistro, La Butte Chiallot. (This is like a young Frenchman arriving in New York, all enthusiastic about baseball, and ending up five years later as the third baseman of the Yankees.)

The other day, over coffee on the avenue Kléber, Alex, who is from New York (she went to Barnard, Mom's an editor at Scribners, Dad's a professor), said, "I decided I wanted to chop onions, so I tried the CIA—the Culinary Institute of America, the MIT of American cooking—but it was like eighteen thousand a year, *tout compris,* so I decided to go to Burgundy and chop. I started learning the French way, which is half beautiful beyond belief and half 'Please shoot me.' It's by the book. Really, there's a book, and you learn it. There's a system for everything, a way to do it. You can't cut the fish that way, because *ça n'est pas bon*. You can't bone a chicken that way, because *that's* not good. 'We do it the way it's always been done in France.' When I first started at Savoy, there was one old stager who, every time I did something, would just frown and shake his head and say. 'It won't do, it won't do.' Finally, I did *exactly* what he did, and he said, 'Good, now always do it exactly the same way.' So I did. You never get a real attempt to innovate, or to use new flavors. You can change an adjective, but the sentence stays the same.

"Whenever we make a classic sauce, everybody gathers around and *argues* about it. Once we got into a two-hour argument about whether you use chervil as well as tarragon in a true béarnaise. There are certain things these days that I will not do. I will not do mayonnaise or béarnaise. Uh-uh. I don't have time for the postgame analysis.

"Of course, there's that tomato at Passard's place," she went on. "But have you seen the way the poor kid has to work to make it?"

Alex's existence helps to explain why the new cooking went deeper in America than it could in France: In America the cooking revolution was above all a middle-class revolution, even an upper-middle-class revolution. A lot of the people who made the cooking revolution in America were doing it as a second career. At the very least they were doing it after a liberal arts degree. The most mocked of all modern American restaurant manners—the waiter who introduces himself by name—is, on reflection, a sign of something very positive. "I'm Henry, and I'll be your waiter tonight" means, really, "You and I belong to the same social class. Tomorrow night I could be sitting there, and you could be standing here."

The French system of education, unrenovated for a long time, locks people in place. Kids emerge with an impressive respect for learning and erudition, and intimidated by it too. For an American, getting a Ph.D. is a preliminary, before you go someplace else and find your real work, like opening a restaurant. Nobody thinks of changing métiers in France because it's just too hard. In America not only the consumers of the new cooking but, more important, the producers and dealers were college-educated. I once met a pair of American academics who had gone off to live with a flock of goats and make goat cheese. They had named the goats Emily, Virginia, Jessamyn, Willa, and Ursula. It was terrific goat cheese too.

COOKING IN THE NUDE

ISABEL ALLENDE

ONCE HEARD A CELEBRATED designer say, while draping a little semi-transparent, seven-thousand-dollar chiffon over the bones of a bulimic model, that the most flattering thing a woman can wear is a radiant smile. Sometimes that is all that is needed, although, unfortunately, I discovered that rather late, after having spent years of my life standing frothing at the mouth before my closet, and at an age when it is not flattering to go around stark naked.

Everything cooked for a lover is sensual, but it is even more so if both take part in the preparation and seize the opportunity to naughtily shed a garment or two as the onions are peeled or leaves stripped from the artichokes. To my sorrow, my husband is a good cook but not a tease. It would be so entertaining to watch him laboring amidst his pots and pans as articles of clothing go flying through the air. I've told him about the Adamites, an eleventh-century Christian sect whose members went around naked, with the idea that they could recapture the innocence of Adam before the original sin, but he is not a man to pick up on a hint, and until now I've never quite succeeded in getting him out of the greasy blue jeans he wears when exercising his unquestionable authority in the kitchen. There are few virtues a man can possess more erotic than culinary skill. The first thing that attracted me to my husband was his incredible life story—which he was willing to tell me at our first meeting, and which was the inspiration for my fifth book, *The Infinite Plan*—but I actually fell in love with him several hours later as I was watching him prepare dinner for me. The day after we met, he invited me to dinner at his house. At the time, he was living with several monsters I later learned were his children and a collection of detestable pets including neurotic mice that spent their miserable existences in a cage biting one another's tails, a dog that had lost all control of its sphincter, and a tank of agonizing fish. That spectacle would have terrified any normal woman, but I had eyes only for the man moving about so easily among skillets and saucepans. That's an experience very few Latin American women have had; usually the machos of our continent consider any household activity a danger to their perpetually threatened virility. I admit it: while he was cooking, I was mentally taking off his clothes. When my Amphitryon lighted the coals of the grill and with one cruel stroke of his cleaver split a chicken in half, I felt a mixture of vegetarian terror and primitive fascination. Then when he cut fresh herbs from the garden and selected a variety of spices from a kitchen cupboard, I knew that I was in the presence of a potential candidate gifted with excellent raw material, who would, after a few years with me, be polished into a jewel. And when he took a kind of scimitar from the wall and with four samurai passes transformed an insignificant lettuce into a hearty salad, my knees buckled and my head swam with lewd images. That still happens a lot. It has kept our relationship at a constant simmer.

We women are impressed by men who know about food, but that is something that doesn't work in reverse. A man who cooks is sexy, a woman isn't; maybe it's too reminiscent of domestic archetypes. Contrast and surprise are erotic. A girl dressed like a gang member and straddling a motorcycle can be exciting; in contrast, a man in the same posture merely a ridiculous macho. I never admit that I know how to cook; that's fatal. My friend Hannah, who composes that New Age music you hear in beauty spas and dentist's offices, and her last husband are a good example of my thesis. During a brief period as a single woman between her second divorce and her third husband, Hannah answered one of those personal ads in the classified section of the newspaper. Over the phone, the man who was looking for a partner sounded perfect: he earned his living training dogs for the blind and had gone as a volunteer to build schools in Guatemala, where a stray bullet had blown away one ear. My friend, inexperienced in personal ads and not a little desperate, invited him to dinner before she had ever seen him. (Don't even think of it! Blind dates are really dangerous. Most appropriate in such cases is a brief meeting in a neutral place from which either can escape with dignity, never a solitary meal that can turn into an endless martyrdom.) She was expecting a mature version of Che Guevara, but the person who showed up was a replica of Vincent van Gogh. She has nothing against Impressionist painting, even though she prefers astrological motifs for her walls, but that stranger with the carrot-colored hair and crazy eyes was a disappointment. She was sorry the minute she saw him. Oh, well, he was there, and she couldn't shut the door in his face over a matter of an ear, more or less.

My friend was in no position to be fussy about trifles—however, this pipsqueak was worse than anything she had imagined in her solitary nightmares. She had planned candlelight and a few slow sambas from Brazil, but she was afraid to provoke any unwanted moves on her guest part, so she turned on all the lights and put on one of her musical compositions of wind blowing and coyotes howling, which usually produce a hypnotic lethargy. She skipped the preliminary glass of wine and other obligatory courtesies and led the man straight to the kitchen, planning instead to prepare some last-minute spaghetti, feed him in a hurry, and send him on his way before dessert. He followed her tamely, showing no sign of disenchantment, like someone all too accustomed to receiving rather rude treatment.

Once in the kitchen, however, something about him changed; he took a deep breath, puffed out his chest, stiffened his spine, as his rabbity eyes scouted the lay of the land, taking command of the terrain, conquering it. Allow me, he said, and without giving Hannah the opportunity to protest, he gently removed the apron from her hands, tied it around his own waist, and sat her down in a chair to watch. Let's see what we have here, he reflected, and started rescuing from the refrigerator the ingredients she had decided to keep for the next day, as well as some she hadn't thought of. This Van Gogh started wielding pots and skillets as if he had been born within those four walls. With unexpected grace and dexterity, his knives flashed as they danced over vegetables and shellfish he then lightly sautéed in olive oil; he hurled spaghetti into the boiling water and in a thrice had prepared a translucent cilantro-and-lemon sauce, all the while telling my friend about his adventures in Central America. Within a few moments, the pathetic little rabbit was transformed: his clown's mop vibrated with the virile strength of a lion's mane, and his castaway's bearing turned into an air of serene concentration—an irresistible combination for a woman like Hannah.

As aromas billowed from the skillet and water bubbled in the deep pot, my friend was aware of a growing anticipation; her blouse was clammy from the sweat trickling down her backbone, her thighs were steamy, and her mouth was watering—all as she was noticing for the first time, to her utter amazement, the elegant hands and broad shoulders of the man standing before her. His heroic anecdotes about Guatemala and about the dogs for the blind filled her eyes with tears; the lopped-off ear began to take on the cachet of a medal, and an irrepressible desire to caress the scar shook her from head to toes. When Van Gogh set before her a platter with steaming spaghetti *à la pesca-*

tore, which was his name for the dish, she sighed in surrender. From its hiding place, she took the wine she had planned to keep for another, more deserving candidate, turned out the light, lit the candles, and put the slow samba from Brazil on the player. Wait just a minute, she purred, like a kitten, I want to slip into something more comfortable. And returned in her black leather suit and dominatrix's boots.

Gourmets capable of ordering from a French menu and discussing wines with the sommelier inspire respect in women, a respect that can easily be transmuted into a voracious, passionate hunger. We cannot resist men who know how to cook. I'm not talking about those clowns in histrionic caps who dub themselves experts and with great flourishes scorch a hot dog on the patio barbecue. No, I mean epicures who lovingly choose the freshest and most arousing ingredients, prepare them with art, and offer them as a gift to the senses and the soul, men who uncork a bottle with style, breathe in its aroma, and decant the wine into our goblet to taste, as they describe the juices, color, tenderness, aroma, and texture of the filet mignon in the tone we believe they will later use to refer to our own enchantments. It seems to us that all the sensibilities of a man like that must be equally refined, including his sense of humor. Who knows? Maybe he can even laugh at himself! While we watch him clean, spice, and cook the shrimp, we imagine that patience and dexterity applied to an erotic massage. If he delicately tastes a piece of fish to test whether it's done, we tremble, anticipating a similarly knowing nibble on the neck. We suppose that if he can remember how many minutes frog legs can tolerate in the skillet, how much greater reason he will have to remember how many tickles our G spot demands. Of course, that isn't always true; in real life he may be much more interested in the frogs' legs than our own.

Not long ago I got a call from Jason, one of my stepchildren. He was calling from New York to tell me he had met the woman of his life; this would be number seventeen, if I have the count right. He urgently needed instructions for his first date. His salary is as limited as his experience, so it would serve no purpose to suggest a good play, a small Moroccan restaurant, and, to top off the evening, a carriage ride through the park and a jazz session in Harlem. On the other hand, to recommend that he cook for her would be tantamount to a death sentence. Then I remembered my chocolate cake, and it seemed to me that an occasion like this justified a small deceit. It doesn't always pay to be honest; sometimes it's better to he creative. Making a chocolate cake is too complicated for my busy life, and that's why when I'm expecting important visitors, I buy one at a very good pastry shop, remove all the frippery, slide it onto one of our own plates, and then skip around the dining room table a couple of times, until it looks sufficiently languid to have been baked at home. Store-bought cakes, like salon hairstyles, have the undisguisable seal of the professional hand, but with a vigorous shake or two, both are reduced to a state of homemade casualness.

I told Jason to go out and pick up some exotic food, although nothing so exotic that it would be suspicious. Chinese cooking, for example, can't be camouflaged. No one in his right mind would think my stepson capable of preparing wonton or lumpias, but some Arab dish, one of those that looks prechewed, could pass the test, especially if when he invites his date he tells her he'll cook her something with aphrodisiac ingredients. Once out of the disposable container, falafel or shish kebab lose their superiority and quietly adapt to their new surroundings. I told him about Hannah and her new husband and suggested that he set a beautiful table, put on some good music, and, when his date rang the bell, open the door with a pan in one hand and a wooden cooking spoon in the other—the first impression is usually crucial—then ask her to sit down, hand her a glass of chilled wine, and to distract her as he pretends to cook ask her questions about herself. I reminded him to be sure and take off his shoes first, like a California Buddhist, and then unbutton his shirt to show off his pecs. He should get some good out of all that weight lifting.

Unlike men, who think only of the objective, we women are inclined toward rituals and processes. I should have explained to Jason that the ceremony I have just described, although an illusionist's act, would surely be as exciting for the girl as the subsequent erotic acrobatics. Don't rush her, I begged him; savor with her the perfume of the candles, the delicacy of the flowers, each sip of wine and each mouthful of food. Talk very little yourself, and pretend to pay attention to everything she says. No woman is truly interested in what a man says, only what he murmurs. Dance with her—that way you can put your arms around her without resembling a gorilla in rut, and when you think that the moment has come to take her to a more comfortable place, wait. And then wait a good while longer. You can't hurry the perfecting of a good stew. Joke with her, I told Jason, knowing that laughter is an excellent aphrodisiac, something this boy with literary aspirations tends to forget in his immoderate enthusiasm for tragedy. And if there's a second date, remember that the shared preparation of food is a good preamble to love. It doesn't matter too much whether or not the recipes are actually aphrodisiac—from the scientific point of view, I mean—just that the nibbles and nuzzling in the kitchen are. Make a game of bed and a game of food.

Great authors, from Henry Miller in his tropics to Pablo Neruda in his infinite poetic metaphors, have turned food into sexual inspiration. Think of the aged dictator in Gabriel García Márquez's novel *The Autumn of the Patriarch*, I told him, how he attracted schoolgirls to the gardens of his palace to rub their erogenous zones with salad ingredients and then . . . Hey, read the book, Jason, for God's sake! I had heard an exclamation of disgust over the line. Jason is too young for such subtleties. So I referred him to one of the forgotten texts lying around in some corner of my house, G. Legman's *Oragenitalism,* in which he suggests something similar with strawberries and bananas, as well as serving sweet wine in the same location, but evidently that author never thought about itching. This kind of thing should be tested by the person who proposes it. Gallants of long ago drank champagne from courtesan's high-top slippers, and we can always place the best mouthfuls in the valleys, mountains, and clefts of our lover's anatomy. (Be careful about the rug and sheets, Jason, it's hard to get the stains out.) All of this I tried to summarize in a long-distance phone call, but my stepson answered that nowadays girls wear combat boots, not slippers laced up to the ankle, and that the radiant smile my designer had suggested would look stupid on a young person.

I don't want to give the impression, however, that I'm one of those grandmothers who's capable of swathing herself in an odalisque's veils to chop onions, or of serving dinner in curly-toed Turkish babouches while rippling her navel like an exotic dancer, because that would be a dangerous lie. It could induce in other women a depression similar to the one that flattens me when I compare myself to those homemakers in magazines who use the leftover guacamole for facial masks and paint flowers on the toilet paper. If I ever did that—the belly dance, I mean—it was in my youth, maybe at the beginning of a passionate affair that I thought was transcendental at the time and today can scarcely remember, but I don't have the same desire I had to look ridiculous, and as my mother always says, if I waste my energies in costumes, who's going to watch the soufflé?

FROM OUR KITCHEN
TO YOUR TABLE

ANTHONY BOURDAIN

I SAW A SIGN THE other day outside one of those Chinese-Japanese hybrids that are beginning to pop up around town, advertising "Discount Sushi." I can't imagine a better example of Things to Be Wary Of in the food department than bargain sushi. Yet the place had customers. I wonder, had the sign said "Cheap Sushi" or "Old Sushi," if they'd still have eaten there.

Good food and good eating are about risk. Every once in a while an oyster, for instance, will make you sick to your stomach. Does this mean you should stop eating oysters? No way. The more exotic the food, the more adventurous the serious eater, the higher the likelihood of later discomfort. I'm not going to deny myself the pleasures of morcilla sausage, or sashimi or even ropa vieja at the local Cuban joint just because sometimes I feel bad a few hours after I've eaten them.

But there are some general principles I adhere to, things I've seen over the years that remain in my mind and have altered my eating habits. I may be perfectly willing to try the grilled lobster at an open-air barbecue shack in the Caribbean, where the refrigeration is dubious and I can see with my own eyes the flies buzzing around the grill (I mean, how often am I in the Caribbean? I want to make the most of it!), but on home turf, with the daily business of eating in restaurants, there are some definite dos and don'ts I've chosen to live by.

I never order fish on Monday, unless I'm eating at Le Bernardin—a four-star restaurant where I *know* they are buying their fish directly from the source. I know how old most seafood is on Monday—about four to five days old!

You walk into a nice two-star place in Tribeca on a sleepy Monday evening and you see they're running a delicious-sounding special of Yellowfin Tuna, Braised Fennel, Confit Tomatoes and a Saffron Sauce. Why not go for it? Here are the two words that should leap out at you when you navigate the menu: "Monday" and "Special."

Here's how it works: The chef of this fine restaurant orders his fish on Thursday for delivery Friday morning. He's ordering a pretty good amount of it, too, as he's not getting another delivery until Monday morning. All right, *some* seafood purveyors make Saturday deliveries, but the market is closed Friday night. *It's the same fish from Thursday!* The chef is hoping to sell the bulk of that fish—your tuna—on Friday and Saturday nights, when he assumes it will be busy. He's assuming also that if he has a little left on Sunday, he can unload the rest of it then, as seafood salad for brunch, or as a special. Monday? It's merchandizing night, when whatever is left over from the weekend is used up, and hopefully sold for money. Terrible, you say? Why doesn't he throw the leftover tuna out? The guy can get deliveries on *Monday*, right? Sure, he can . . . but what is preventing his seafood purveyor from thinking exactly the same way? The seafood vendor is emptying out *his* refrigerator, too! But the Fulton Street fish market is *open* on Monday morning, you say!! He can get *fresh!* I've been to the Fulton Street market at three o'clock on Monday morning, friends, and believe me, it does *not* inspire confidence. Chances are good that that tuna you're thinking of ordering on Monday night has been kicking around in the restaurant's reach-ins, already cut and held with the mise-en-place on line, commingling with the chicken and the salmon and the lamb chops for four days, the reach-in doors swinging open every few seconds as the line cooks plunge their fists in, blindly feeling around for what they need. These are not optimum refrigeration conditions.

This is why you don't see a lot of codfish or other perishable items as a Sunday or Monday night special—they're not sturdy enough. The chef *knows*. He anticipates the likelihood that he might still have some fish lying around on Monday morning—and he'd like to get money for it without poisoning his customers.

Seafood is a tricky business. Red snapper may cost a chef only $4.95 a pound, but that price includes the bones, the head, the scales and all the stuff that gets cut and thrown away. By the time it's cut, the actual cost of each piece of cleaned fillet costs the chef more than *twice* that amount, and he'd greatly prefer to sell it than toss it in the garbage. If it still smells okay on Monday night—you're eating it.

I don't eat mussels in restaurants unless I know the chef personally, or have seen, with my own eyes, how they store and hold their mussels for service. I love mussels. But in my experience, most cooks are less than scrupulous in their handling of them. More often than not, mussels are allowed to wallow in their own foul-smelling piss in the bottom of a reach-in. *Some* restaurants, I'm sure, have special containers, with convenient slotted bins, which allow the mussels to drain while being held—and maybe, just maybe, the cooks at these places pick carefully through every order, mussel by mussel, making sure that *every* one is healthy and alive before throwing them into a pot. I haven't worked in too many places like that. Mussels are too easy. Line cooks consider mussels a gift; they take two minutes to cook, a few seconds to dump in a bowl, and *ba-da-bing,* one more customer taken care of—now they can concentrate on slicing the damn duck breast. I have had, at a very good Paris brasserie, the misfortune to eat a single bad mussel, one treacherous little guy hidden among an otherwise impeccable group. It slammed me shut like a book, sent me crawling to the bathroom shitting like a mink, clutching my stomach and projectile vomiting. I prayed that night. For many hours. And, as you might assume, I'm the worst kind of atheist. Fortunately, the French have liberal policies on doctor's house calls and affordable health care. But I do not care to repeat that experience. No thank you on the mussels. If I'm hungry for mussels, I'll pick the good-looking ones out of *your* order.

How about seafood on Sunday? Well . . . sometimes, but never if it's an obvious attempt to offload aging stuff, like seafood salad vinaigrette or seafood frittata, on a brunch menu. Brunch menus are an open invitation to the cost-conscious chef, a dumping ground for the odd bits left over from Friday and Saturday nights or for the scraps generated in the normal course of business. You see a fish that would be much better served by quick grilling with a slice of lemon, suddenly all dressed up with vinaigrette? For *en vinaigrette* on the menu, read "preserved" or "disguised."

While we're on brunch, how about hollandaise sauce? Not for me. Bacteria *love* hollandaise. And hollandaise, that delicate emulsion of egg yolks and clarified butter, *must* be held at a temperature not too hot nor too cold, lest it break when spooned over your poached eggs. Unfortunately, this lukewarm holding temperature is also the favorite environment for bacteria to copulate and reproduce in. Nobody I know has *ever* made hollandaise to order. Most likely, the stuff on your eggs was made hours ago and held on station. Equally disturbing is the likelihood that the butter used in the hollandaise is melted table butter, heated, clarified and strained to get out all the bread crumbs and cigarette butts. Butter is expensive, you know. Hollandaise is a veritable petri dish of biohazards. And how long has that Canadian bacon been aging in the walk-in anyway? Remember, brunch is served only once a week—on the weekends. Buzzword here, "Brunch Menu." Translation? "Old, nasty odds and ends, and twelve dollars for two eggs with a free Bloody Mary." One other point about brunch. Cooks hate brunch. A wise chef will deploy his *best* line cooks on Friday and Saturday nights; he'll be reluctant to schedule those same cooks early Sunday morning, especially since they probably went out after work Saturday and got hammered until the wee hours. Worse, brunch is demoralizing to the serious line cook. Nothing makes an aspiring Escoffier feel more like an army commissary cook, or Mel from Mel's Diner, than having to slop out eggs over easy with bacon and eggs Benedict for the Sunday brunch crowd. Brunch is punishment block for the "B" Team cooks, or where the farm team of recent dishwashers learn their chops. Most chefs are off on Sundays, too, so supervision is at a minimum. Consider that before ordering the seafood frittata.

I *will* eat bread in restaurants. Even if I *know* it's probably been recycled off someone else's table. The reuse of bread is an industry-wide practice. I saw a recent news expose, hidden camera and all, where the anchor was *shocked . . . shocked* to see unused bread returned to the kitchen and then sent right back onto the floor. Bullshit. I'm sure that some restaurants explicitly instruct their Bengali busboys to throw out all that unused bread—which amounts to about 50 percent—and maybe some places actually do it. But when it's busy, and the busboy is crumbing tables, emptying ashtrays, refilling water glasses, making espresso and cappuccino, hustling dirty dishes to the dishwasher, and he sees a basket full of untouched bread, most times he's going to use it. This is a fact of life. This doesn't bother me and shouldn't surprise you. Okay, maybe once in a while some tubercular hillbilly has been coughing and spraying in the general direction of that bread basket, or some tourist who's just returned from a walking tour of the wetlands of West Africa sneezes—you might find that prospect upsetting. But you might just as well avoid air travel, or subways, equally dodgy environments for airborne transmission of disease. Eat the bread.

I *won't* eat in a restaurant with filthy bathrooms. This isn't a hard call. They let you *see* the bathrooms. If the restaurant can't be bothered to replace the puck in the urinal or keep the toilets and floors clean, then just imagine what their refrigeration and work spaces look like. Bathrooms are relatively easy to clean. Kitchens are not. In fact, if you see the chef sitting unshaven at the bar, with a dirty apron on, one finger halfway up his nose, you can assume he's not handling your food any better behind closed doors. Your waiter looks like he just woke up under a bridge? If management allows him to wander out on the floor looking like that, God knows what they're doing to your shrimp!

"Beef Parmentier"? "Shepherd's pie"? "Chili special"? Sounds like leftovers to me. How about swordfish? I like it fine. But my seafood purveyor, when he goes out to dinner, won't eat it. He's seen too many of those three-foot-long parasitic worms that riddle the fish's flesh. You see a few of these babies—and we all do—and you won't be tucking into swordfish anytime soon.

Chilean sea bass? Trendy. Expensive. More than likely frozen. This came as a surprise to me when I visited the market recently. Apparently the great majority of the stuff arrives frozen solid, still on the bone. In fact, as I said earlier, the whole Fulton Street market is not an inspiring sight. Fish is left to sit, un-iced, in leaking crates, in the middle of August, right out in the open. What isn't bought early is sold for cheap later. At 7:00 A.M. the Korean and Chinese buyers, who've been sitting in local bars *waiting* for the market to be near closing, swoop down on the overextended fishmonger and buy up what's left at rock-bottom prices. The next folks to arrive will be the cat-food people. Think about that when you see the "Discount Sushi" sign.

"Saving for well-done" is a time-honored tradition dating back to cuisine's earliest days: meat and fish cost money. Every piece of cut, fabricated food must, ideally, be sold for three or even four times its cost in order for the chef to make his "food cost percent." So what happens when the chef finds a tough, slightly skanky end-cut of sirloin that's been pushed repeatedly to the back of the pile? He can throw it out, but that's a total loss, representing a three-fold loss of what it cost him per pound. He can feed it to the family, which is the same as throwing it out. Or he can "save for well-done"—serve it to some rube who *prefers* to eat his meat or fish incinerated into a flavorless, leathery hunk of carbon, who won't be able to tell if what he's eating is food or flotsam. Ordinarily, a proud chef would hate this customer, hold him in contempt for destroying his fine food. But not in this case. The dumb bastard is *praying for the privilege of eating his garbage!* What's not to like?

Vegetarians, and their Hezbollah-like splinter faction, the vegans, are a persistent irritant to any chef worth a damn. To me, life without veal stock, pork fat, sausage, organ meat, demi-glace or even stinky cheese is a life not worth living. Vegetarians are the enemy of everything good and decent in the human spirit, an affront to all I stand for, the pure enjoyment of food. The body, these waterheads imagine, is a temple that should not be polluted by animal protein. It's healthier, they insist, though every vegetarian waiter I've worked with is brought down by any *rumor* of a cold. Oh, I'll accommodate them, I'll rummage around for *something* to feed them, for a "vegetarian plate," if called on to do so. Fourteen dollars for a few slices of grilled eggplant and zucchini suits my food cost fine. But let me tell you a story.

A few years back, at a swinging singles joint on Columbus Avenue, we had the misfortune to employ a sensitive young man as a waiter who, in addition to a wide and varied social life involving numerous unsafe sexual practices, was something of a jailhouse lawyer. After he was fired for incompetence, he took it on himself to sue the restaurant, claiming that a gastrointestinal problem, caused apparently by amoebas, was a result of his work there. Management took this litigation seriously enough to engage the services of an epidemiologist, who obtained stool samples from *every* employee. The results—which I was privy to—were enlightening to say the least. The waiter's strain of amoebas, it was concluded, was common to persons of his lifestyle, and to many others. What was interesting were the results of our Mexican and South American prep cooks. These guys were *teeming* with numerous varieties of critters, none of which, in their cases, caused illness or discomfort. It was explained that the results in our restaurant were no different from the results at any other restaurant and that, particularly among my recently arrived Latino brethren, this sort of thing is normal—that their systems are used to it, and it causes them no difficulties at all. Amoebas, however, are transferred most easily through the handling of raw, uncooked vegetables, particularly during the washing of salad greens and leafy produce. So think about that next time you want to exchange deep tongue kisses with a vegetarian.

I'm not even going to talk about blood. Let's just say we cut ourselves a lot in the kitchen and leave it at that.

Pigs are filthy animals, say some, when explaining why they deny themselves the delights of pork. Maybe they should visit a chicken ranch. America's favorite menu item is also the most likely to make you ill. Commercially available chickens, for the most part (we're not talking about kosher and expensive free-range birds), are loaded with salmonella. Chickens are dirty. They eat their own feces, are kept packed close together like in a rush-hour subway and when handled in a restaurant situation are most likely to infect other foods or cross-contaminate them. And chicken is boring. Chefs see it as a menu item for people who don't know what they want to eat.

Shrimp? All right, if it looks fresh, smells fresh and the restaurant is busy, guaranteeing turnover of product on a regular basis. But shrimp toast? I'll pass. I walk into a restaurant with a mostly empty dining room, and an unhappy-looking owner staring out the window? I'm not ordering shrimp.

This principle applies to anything on a menu, actually, especially something esoteric and adventurous like, say, bouillabaisse. If a restaurant is known for steak, and doesn't seem to be doing much business, how long do you think those few orders of clams and mussels and lobster and fish have been sitting in the refrigerator, waiting for someone like you to order them? The key is rotation. If the restaurant is busy, and you see bouillabaisse flying out the kitchen doors every few minutes, then it's probably a good bet. But a big and varied menu in a slow, half-empty place? Those less popular items like broiled mackerel and calf liver are kept moldering in a dark corner of the reach-in because they look good on the menu. You might not actually want to eat them. Look at your waiter's face. He knows. It's another reason to be polite to your waiter: he could save your life with a raised eyebrow or a sigh. If he likes you, maybe he'll stop you from ordering a piece of fish he knows is going to hurt you. On the other hand, maybe the chef has ordered him, under pain of death, to move that codfish before it begins to *really* reek. Observe the body language and take note.

Watchwords for fine dining? Tuesday through Saturday. Busy. Turnover. Rotation. Tuesdays and Thursdays are the best nights to order fish in New York. The food that comes in Tuesday is fresh, the station prep is new, and the chef is well rested after a Sunday or a Monday off. It's the real start of the new week, when you've got the goodwill of the kitchen on your side. Fridays and Saturdays, the food is fresh, but it's busy, so the chef and cooks can't pay as much attention to your food as they—and you—might like. And weekend diners are universally viewed with suspicion, even contempt, by both cooks and waiters alike; they're the slackjaws, the rubes, the out-of-towners, the well-done-eating, undertipping, bridge-and-tunnel pretheater hordes, in to see *Cats* or *Les Miz* and never to return. Weekday diners, on the other hand, are the home team—potential regulars, whom all concerned want to make happy. Rested and ready after a day off, the chef is going to put his best foot forward on Tuesday; he's got his best-quality product coming in and he's had a day or two to think of creative things to do with it. He *wants* you to be happy on Tuesday night. On Saturday, he's thinking more about turning over tables and getting through the rush.

If the restaurant is clean, the cooks and waiters well groomed, the dining room busy, everyone seems to actually *care* about what they're doing—not just trying to pick up a few extra bucks between head shots and auditions for *Days of Our Lives*—chances are you're in for a decent meal. The owner, chef and a bored-looking waiter sitting at a front table chatting about soccer scores? Plumber walking through the dining room with a toilet snake? Bad signs. Watch the trucks pull up outside the restaurant delivery entrance in the morning if you're in the neighborhood. Reputable vendors of seafood, meat and produce? Good sign.

If you see sinister, unmarked step-vans offloading all three at once, or the big tractor trailers from one of the national outfits—you know the ones, "Servicing Restaurants and Institutions for Fifty Years"—remember what institutions they're talking about: cafeterias, schools, prisons. Unless you *like* frozen, portion-controlled "convenience food."

Do all these horrifying assertions frighten you? Should you stop eating out? Wipe yourself down with antiseptic towelettes every time you pass a restaurant? No way. Like I said before, your body is *not* a temple, it's an amusement park. Enjoy the ride. Sure, it's a "play you pay" sort of an adventure, but you knew that already, every time you ever ordered a taco or a dirty-water hot dog. If you're willing to risk some slight lower GI distress for one of those Italian sweet sausages at the street fair, or for a slice of pizza you just *know* has been sitting on the board for an hour or two, why not take a chance on the good stuff? All the great developments of classical cuisine, the first guys to eat sweetbreads, to try unpasteurized Stilton, to discover that snails actually taste *good* with enough garlic butter, these were daredevils, innovators and desperados. I don't know who figured out that if you crammed rich food into a goose long enough for its liver to balloon up to more than its normal body weight you'd get something as good as foie gras—I believe it was those kooky Romans—but I'm very grateful for their efforts. Popping raw fish into your face, especially in prerefrigeration days, might have seemed like sheer madness to some, but it turned out to be a pretty good idea. They say that Rasputin used to eat a little arsenic with breakfast every day, building up resistance for the day that an enemy might poison him, and that sounds like good sense to me. Judging from accounts of his death, the Mad Monk wasn't fazed at all by the stuff; it took repeated beatings, a couple of bullets and a long fall off a bridge into a frozen river to finish the job. Perhaps we, as serious diners, should emulate his example. We are, after all, citizens of the world—a world filled with bacteria, some friendly, some not so friendly. Do we really want to travel in hermetically sealed pope-mobiles through the rural provinces of France, Mexico and the Far East, eating only in Hard Rock Cafes and McDonald's? Or do we want to eat without fear, tearing into the local stew, the humble taqueria's mystery meat, the sincerely offered gift of a lightly grilled fish head? I know what I want. I want it all. I want to try everything once. I'll give you the benefit of the doubt, Señor Tamale Stand Owner, Sushi-chef-san, Monsieur Bucket-head. What's that feathered game bird hanging on the porch, getting riper by the day, the body nearly ready to drop off? I want some.

I have no wish to die, nor do I have some unhealthy fondness for dysentery. If I *know* you're storing your squid at room temperature next to a cat box, I'll get my squid down the street, thank you very much. I will continue to do my seafood eating on Tuesdays, Wednesdays and Thursdays, because I know better, because I can wait. But if I have one chance at a full-blown dinner of blowfish gizzard—even if I have not been properly introduced to the chef—and I'm in a strange, Far Eastern city and my plane leaves tomorrow? I'm going for it. You only go around once.

ST. JOSEPH'S BREAD

MARY TAYLOR SIMETI

*I*F HUNGER IS ONE—and possibly the best—reason for looking upon bread as the staff of life, the Sicilian peasant was also heir to a centuries-old iconography of bread, an awe and veneration for this basic foodstuff that is lost to contemporary America. Even today the Sicilian feels closer to the ancients in this regard than he would to the diet-conscious U.S. housewife who "tries not to keep bread in the house."

For the Greeks, in fact, the cultivation of grain and the baking of bread were the distinctive marks of civilized man: "men who eat bread" is the conventional formula with which Homer distinguishes the Greeks and their likes from giants and lotus eaters and other exotic and barbaric races. All activities involving the production and processing of wheat were circumscribed by an intricate net of invocations, taboos, rituals, and festivities, many of which have survived to the present century, albeit in a more or less Christianized version. The first ears of ripened wheat, which are still offered to the Madonna in many towns of the Sicilian interior, were once placed on the altars of Demeter, and it is hard to tell just where on the religious continuum one should place the eighteenth-century harvest festival witnessed by Houel:

In the countryside surrounding this town [Catania], the peasants celebrate the wheat harvest with a sort of orgy, a popular festival of thanksgiving for the good harvest they have gathered. Young people dancing in a circle open the procession; they are followed by a man riding on an ass and beating a drum; five or six men similarly mounted parade after him carrying long poles decorated from top to bottom

with sheaves of wheat; in their midst another man, also mounted, carries a large banner which floats majestically in the breeze. A young
woman, dressed in white and seated on an ass, comes next; she is surrounded by men on foot who carry bunches of wheat on their heads
and in their arms, and who seem to be paying her homage. An entire
crowd of country people follow this procession, playing on different
musical instruments.

The most educated people in Catania have assured me that this
is a very old custom, of which the origins are unknown; but they do
not doubt that it is a remnant of the ancient festivals dedicated to
Ceres, and that the young woman represents this goddess, to whom
the harvests thought to have been obtained through her good will are
offered.

—JEAN HOUEL, *Voyage pittoresque,* 1785

The Greeks were not the only people in the ancient world to vener-
ate bread. Ever since the Egyptians first stumbled upon the mystery of
leavening, some four millennia before the birth of Christ, bread has
played an important part in the religious traditions of the Near East,
and this liturgy of bread was easily absorbed by the followers of Moses,
of Christ, and of Mohammed. Documents in the Palermo archives
speak of Muslim Sicilians who take oaths *tacto pane ad legem
Mukumet*—touching bread according to Mohammedan law. And bread
was, of course, central to the celebration of the Jewish Passover and the
Christian Eucharist.

In Sicily the symbolic value of bread was not confined to the
churches. At home, the women who kneaded and baked bread paused
at each step to recite special prayers and invocations, such as this one
from southeastern Sicily, to be uttered just as the last loaf is placed in
the oven.

Pattri, Figghiu e Spirdussantu	Father, Son, and Holy Ghost
pozza crìsciri: n' àuttru tantu;	may the bread double in size;
Santa Rrosulia,	Santa Rosalia,
iancu e rrussu comu a-ttia;	white and red just like you;
nné—gghiàriu nné-passatu	neither acid nor grown stale,
comu Mmaria senza piccatu;	just like Mary without sin;
crisci pani ô furnu	may the bread grow in the oven,
comu Ggesuzzu crisciù nta lu munnu.	just as little Jesus grew in this world.

—ANTONINO UCCELLO, *Pani e dolci di Sicilia,* 1976

Once baked, bread must be treated with the greatest respect: in the past the task of slicing the bread was the prerogative of the head of the household, who would trace the sign of the cross over the loaf before touching the knife to it, and would take care never to place it upside down on the table. Probably few Sicilians still believe that if they let a breadcrumb fall on the floor they will be punished in the hereafter by having to gather it up with their eyelashes. And few families today would do as my husband's family did when he was small: kiss a piece of bread that had fallen on the floor before throwing it away (not into the garbage, of course, but to the chickens). Nonetheless to waste bread is still considered very, very wrong.

This pious frugality no doubt helps to explain the importance of breadcrumbs in Sicilian cooking. Breadcrumbs were commonly used to thicken sauces in both Roman and Renaissance recipes, and this may be where the Sicilian habit of sprinkling them over pasta originated, but elsewhere their function is economical. An addition of breadcrumbs serves to stretch out more expensive ingredients such as meat or eggs: when our tenant farmer's wife prepares meatballs for the harvest crew, she mixes the ground meat with almost twice its quantity in breadcrumbs. Another harvest favorite is *frittatine,* eggs beaten up with breadcrumbs, parsley, and cheese, fried in little omelets about two inches in diameter, and then simmered like meatballs in tomato sauce. The memory of such economy remains in the different kinds of *involtini* that are to be found on almost every restaurant menu in Sicily, in which slices of meat or fish or even eggplant are wrapped around a breadcrumb stuffing.

Piety can be expressed not only in the use of bread but also in its shaping. The forms of *pane rimacinato*—the rings and braids and curves into which Sicilian bakers, be they housewives or professionals, fashion the dough—are legion. Most perpetuate ancient traditions, like the flower-shaped *rosetta* or the braided *mafalda* or the ring-shaped *cucciddatu,* which an English traveler to nineteenth-century Catania found "hanging in bunches upon forked sticks on the outside of almost every cottage door." All these can be traced back through the centuries in the descriptions of Theocritus, in the ashes of Pompeii, and in the carvings on the Adelphia sarcophagus in the Archeological Museum at Syracuse.

Bread dough is also fashioned for the amusement of children into dolls and animals: roosters or birds or fish for the fun of it, and spectacles for Saint Lucy (the patron of eyesight), grasshoppers for Saint Biagio, and twin children for the feast of Saints Cosimus and Damian. And, to celebrate pure creative verve, into the intricate Nativity scenes, scaly crocodiles, or three-foot motorcycles complete in every detail that are displayed by the Palermo Bakers' Confraternity at their annual exhibit.

Of all the various saints, Catholic, pagan, or postmodern, to whom these edible votive offerings are dedicated, the most important is Saint Joseph. He is celebrated on March 19 with a ritual banquet known as the *altare di San Giuseppe*. Like the bread around which it revolves, the shape and the liturgy of this ritual vary greatly from town to town. In some places it is a votive offering from the whole community, but more frequently the banquet is offered by a single family whose prayers the saint has answered—a thanksgiving for an illness cured or a disaster averted.

In the mountain towns east of Palermo, the banquet is a fairly simple meal prepared in enormous quantity and served to all and anyone, friend or stranger, who passes by. At the one I attended in Làscari we ate in four shifts of at least sixty people each, including all the members of the town band. Elsewhere it is traditional to prepare a very elaborate meal for the benefit of three poverty-stricken townspeople dressed up for the occasion as the Holy Family. In Alcamo, for example, a professional Saint Joseph, an old man known as a *San Giusepparo,* who knows the rites and prayers, chooses a young girl and a little boy of his family or acquaintance to play Mary and the Christ Child. Costumed and crowned with flowers, the "saints" wander up and down the street, knocking on doors from which they are turned away, until they arrive at the house of the family that has prepared the altar. This door is flung wide and with cheers and music the saints are welcomed in.

There is also considerable variation in the dishes that are served at Saint Joseph's altar, but these always include legumes and bread. The former may appear, as at Làscari, in the simple guise of *pasta con fagioli.* Or they may go almost unremarked amidst the ten or fifteen different first courses of a banquet at Alcamo or Salemi. Elsewhere legumes play a protagonist's role: in the interior and to the south the main dish of the day is often a special soup, made of all different kinds of legumes mixed together, the leavings of the past year's harvest. These soups are reminiscent of the Roman *tisanum* and like *cuccìa* and other ritual dishes bear witness to the conservative power of religious tradition.

I have never managed to stray far enough from home on Saint Joseph's Day to taste any of these soups in their proper setting, and my expectations as I approached the recipes in the Sicilian cookbooks were anthropological rather than gastronomic. The rest of the family shared my skepticism when I brought one to the table, but we were very pleasantly surprised. This is a soul-satisfying soup, and to a hungry wanderer on a raw March day it would indeed seem like a gift from heaven. The ingredients would change, of course, from place to place and from year to year, depending on what the fields and the cupboard had to offer, so don't feel that you can't try the soup because you lack one or two ingredients from the list.

MACCU DI SAN GIUSEPPE
(Saint Joseph's Soup)

Serves 6 to 8

½	pound dried shelled fava beans	1	onion, sliced
¼	pound dried Borlotti or kidney beans	1	teaspoon fennel seeds
¼	pound dried chickpeas	3	ribs celery
½	pound dried chestnuts or ¾ pound fresh, shelled	3	sprigs fresh wild fennel
		1	large bunch fresh borage shoots
¼	pound dried split peas	½	pound fresh spinach or Swiss chard
¼	pound dried lentils		Salt and freshly ground black pepper
2	dried tomatoes cut into small pieces	¼	cup olive oil

Soak the fava beans, Borlotti or kidney beans, chickpeas, and chestnuts overnight in abundant water (if using fresh chestnuts, you don't need to soak them). Add the split peas and the lentils for the last hour or two of soaking.

Drain and place in a large earthenware pot with 9 to 10 cups of water. Bring to a boil and simmer for about 3 hours or until all the legumes are tender.

After the first hour and a half, add the tomatoes, onion, and fennel seeds. Chop the celery and other greens into fairly small pieces, and add them to the soup. Salt to taste. About 5 minutes before removing from the heat, correct the salt and add pepper and olive oil.

NOTE: Pino Correnti suggests accompanying the soup with croutons fried in olive oil, and although these are not an orthodox presence at the altar of San Giuseppe, they are a good idea.

Legumes also appeared most unexpectedly at the end of the banquet in Làscari, when baskets of fried turnovers called *cassateddi* were passed about, and turned out to be filled not with the usual sweet ricotta but with chickpeas, boiled and mashed with sugar and spices.

CASSATEDDI DI CECI
(Sweet Chickpea Turnovers)

Makes about 3 dozen

PASTRY

3¾ cups flour	½ cup white wine
⅓ cup sugar	(approximately)
Pinch of salt	½ cup lard

FILLING

2 cups puréed boiled chickpeas (cooked without salt)	¼ cup almonds, toasted and chopped
¼ cup honey	1 teaspoon ground cinnamon
¼ cup sugar	¼ cup semisweet chocolate bits
¼ cup pine nuts, toasted and chopped	¼ cup diced zuccata or candied citron

Vegetable oil for frying   Sugar
Cinnamon

Sift together the flour, sugar, and salt onto a marble or wooden surface. Make a well, and add the wine slowly, using just as much as it takes to keep the dough together. Cut the lard into small pieces and knead it piece by piece into the dough. Knead for at least 15 minutes, working the dough out into a long strip and then folding it back on itself so as to incorporate as much air as possible, until you have a very smooth and elastic dough that is shiny but not greasy to the touch. Cover the dough and let it stand for at least 1 hour.

Mix together all the ingredients for the filling, and blend well.

Roll out the dough to a very thin sheet, and cut out 3-inch disks. On each disk place a scant tablespoon of filling. Fold the disk over into a half-moon and, moistening the edges with a little water, seal them carefully.

Fry the turnovers in abundant and very hot (about 375°F.) vegetable oil (at least 3 inches deep) until they are delicately browned. Drain on absorbent paper and serve while still warm, sprinkled with ground cinnamon and superfine sugar, or granulated sugar that has been ground to a fine texture in a mortar.

NOTE: Some people prefer to make *cassateddi* dough using ⅓ cup white wine and ⅓ cup *vino cotto,* and eliminating the sugar.

At Làscari we were given bread with our meal as well as legumes; it was special bread only in that, as ritual required, it had been baked at home. At the altars over which San Giuseppe presides "in person," bread assumes much greater significance. One of the more common loaves is the ring-shaped *cucciddatu.* In the past the *cucciddati* that were baked for San Giuseppe were enormous, weighing as much as twenty-five pounds and requiring that some of the bricks around the oven door be removed before they could be put in to bake. The saints would carry the *cucciddati* home at the end of the ceremony, slung over their shoulders like coils of rope. But today the poor are no longer so poor as to welcome twenty-five pounds of stale bread, and the *cucciddati* have shrunken noticeably.

In the towns west of Palermo the altars themselves, spectacularly decorated with intricate forms of bread, become the center of attention: the women of these towns work together for weeks to prepare the altars, in a marathon of collective creativity in which they obviously and rightfully take great pride. In Salemi, a small town in the Belice Valley, the altar is placed within a most extraordinary bower, constructed of poles covered with myrtle branches, decorated with oranges and lemons, and hung with hundreds of little breads, each one lovingly fashioned into a flower, a beast, a saint; roses, daisies, and fava beans in their pods; butterflies, birds, and fish; even Saint Joseph himself, the bread of his monk's habit colored dark brown by cocoa added to the dough.

The amount of bread baked varies according to the possibilities of the family: a modest altar would require 350 to 400 pounds of durum-wheat flour, and more than a week's work on the part of eight or ten women, but a really fancy altar could employ as much as 900 pounds of flour.

The bread dough is prepared with a *criscenti,* the same way as normal bread, except that the amount of water is slightly reduced. The dough must be kneaded, with the help of one's feet when the quantities are big enough, just as *Dio comanda,* so that it has a very fine grain and no large bubbles, which would distort the shapes. It is then shaped into the basic forms and "put to bed" under tablecloths and woolen blankets.

After this single rising, the details—the flower petals and tiny birds, the decorative cuts and curlicues—are added, the surface is brushed with egg beaten up with a few drops of lemon juice, and the bread is ready to be put in the oven to bake.

Once they have finished with the bread, the women set to cooking the banquet. One family told me with understandable pride that they had prepared sixty-two different dishes. Of each of these the children representing the Holy Family would eat barely a mouthful, and they would distribute the rest to the people who came to see the altar.

Unlike in Salemi, in Alcamo there is no bread on the canopy itself, which in older and simpler times was contrived out of the best fringed silk bedspread. Nowadays it is possible to rent an entire stage set with receding arches, angels clinging to rococo columns, and a banner reading, "Long Live Jesus, Mary, and Joseph!"

Here the bread is fashioned into about twenty large forms, each with precise symbolic significance, and into a series of smaller, merely decorative pieces, all of which are displayed on a seven-tiered reredos behind the altar. At the top is the monstrance with the Host, an angel bearing a candlestick on either side. On the second step stands the "Name of Mary," an elaborate M decorated with flowers and angels, which is flanked by branches heavy with fruit and flowers. The third level belongs to the eagle, insignia of Alcamo, a noble beast sitting at Mary's feet. Below him there is a bower of roses through which Saint Joseph leads the Christ Child, and then the *Calata degli angeli* (the "Descent of the Angels"), a tower of roses surmounted by a cross, with three angels descending on each side. (The preparations and the symbolism were explained to me by an elderly woman in Alcamo who had been a great specialist in the preparation of Saint Joseph's bread. Inspecting with critical eye the photographs I had brought with me, she remarked that she herself used to get *eight* angels onto *her calata.*)

The tradition of preparing the Saint Joseph's altar appears to enjoy great vitality and an encouraging ability to incorporate modern elements. The fresh pineapples decorating the altars, the Coca-Cola served to the saints along with the wine, and the pop hits that alternate with Sicilian tarantellas on the record player or the hired accordion are innovations that may be anathema to the purists, but to the ethnologically open-minded they spell good health.

The tenacity of this tradition in the face of all the distractions offered by the advent of consumerism in Sicily bears witness to how profoundly significant it is to the people here, significant in ways of which they are only dimly aware, but which speak of centuries of bitter experience. The altar of Saint Joseph is most commonly read as a rite in propitiation of the saint for the new harvest, and the banquet as an orgy in which the last remnants of the old harvest are consumed just before the new crop of fava beans ripens and the new wheat quickens into seed, an overabundance of eating to invoke a commensurate generosity on the part of the saint.

Yet the banquet of Saint Joseph is also a ritualization of famine relief. It comes during Lent, a period of liturgical fasting that coincides with and gives religious significance to the fasting imposed by nature, the period when the provisions of the summer are exhausted, and when, in years past,

> crowds of poor people, hungry and undernourished, who wandered through the countryside in search of food, gave a disquieting and threatening air to the agrarian and to the human landscape. . . . Saint Joseph's Day, which falls in the middle of Lent, was the festivity in which the search for and the offering of food could take place in a ritualized, controlled and regulated form.
>
> —V. TETI, "Carni e maccaruni assai," 1985

I belong to that very small percentage of humanity that has the great good fortune never to have known real hunger. Had I continued to live in America, I might still consider bread as one more element in the category of foods that are delicious yet potentially dangerous and not really necessary, like chocolate or jam or gravy. Sicily has taught me otherwise.

> He never asked, it's true, but I gave him a loaf of bread which I had taken out of the oven not an hour before, and I put oil and salt and oregano on it, and he sniffed the air and the smell of the bread, and said, "Bless the Lord!"
>
> —ELIO VITTORINI, *Conversazioni in Sicilia*, 1941

A WINTER FEAST

PAUL SCHMIDT

And now it's dark. He gets into a sleigh.
Behind him trails the coachman's cry: "Away!"
The frost with sparkling silver dusts
The beaver collar of his winter coat.
He drives to Talon's restaurant; he is sure
Kavérin will be waiting for him there.
He enters, corks go pop, they pour champagne
(1811, the year the comet came).
Before them, a roast-beef ensanguine;
Truffles, that extravagance of youth
And finest flower of the French cuisine;
Strasbourg's immortal dish, *foie gras en croûte;*
Soft, ripening Limburger cheese
And golden pineapples from overseas.

(*Eugene Onegin,* Chapter One, Canto XVI)

P USHKIN'S HERO EUGENE ONEGIN drives off in a swirl of snow to a dinner that celebrates the birth of the nineteenth century. The celebration is late; 1819 is not the turn of the century; those twenty years would make an adolescent, at least, of anyone. This is a special moment, though, in a special age. The nineteenth century was perhaps the youngest of centuries when it was young; the eighteenth century, for instance, was born old and died older. But the nineteenth century in Europe was born in a thunderclap; it sprang to life in a fit of revolution, of turmoil, of fire and excitement; it was the work of the young. A group of very young people, all of them stimulated to a frenzy by the military exploits, the daring, the very existence of Napoleon. Napoleon, that very young man, whose height kept him a perpetual symbol of adolescence. He was the image that soared over those first decades, as he looms today over Paris on his column in the Place Vendome. He was a supreme symbol of prodigality, an emperor who distributed crowns and kingdoms to his family and friends as if they were Christmas gift baskets. But he was not alone; it was an age of prodigious adolescents:

George IV, Pushkin, Shelley, Keats, Byron, Beau Brummel, Chopin, Bellini, Rossini, Mme. de Stael, Mme. Récamier. They strewed their talents lavishly in every direction, all of them spurred on to imitate the acts of the emperor himself. They were prodigious eaters and drinkers, prodigious dressers, *bon vivants*—they lived the good life. Dinner for them, like dress, was a symbol of luxury, of triumph; it was a sign that they had conquered. If they could not conquer like the emperor, they could at least eat like him. They assembled feasts that were fantasies: imagined feasts, literary feasts, feasts thought up as much as anything else for the description, simply for the report of the thing. Like the ideal military dispatch, what was important was the image evoked by the words, not the facts of the case.

But the facts of the case were stunning enough. Look at the dinner awaiting Onegin: champagne, roast beef, truffles, a Strasbourg *foie gras,* Limburger cheese, fresh pineapple. None of this is homegrown, especially in a Russian January. Everything is imported, taken by force from the places it comes from. The feast itself was a metaphor of conquest. Cooking and eating came to reflect the incessant heaving to and fro across frontiers and continents that marked the Napoleonic era, and the triumphant movers of that cooking, like the emperor's armies, were French. The mark of France remains upon cooking still; the terminology of the kitchen resists translation. French cooks fed the world, and they fed it in French. Here is Louis-Eustache Udé a French cook of the period who wrote for an English audience: "Military tactics, fortifications, music, dancing, and millinery, etc., being of foreign extraction . . . it must not be wondered at if in this work I have made use of original, or native expressions."

Food was a metaphor for the age, and the age was a military one. Udé is right: military tactics and food reflected one another. It was all an enormous attempt at the table to live for a while like Napoleon, to conquer as many lands as he had by bringing their produce to the table, to be devoured there like a great living map. We forget, in our simplified age, the visual splendor of those tables. The last vestige of it we see today only in wedding cakes: those white towers are all that a middle-class era preserves—for marriage, that most important of middle-class occasions—of an imaginary architecture. Remember the great dream palaces we see in early nineteenth-century Beaux Arts building projects? None of them were ever built—except by pastry cooks, who covered dinner tables with edible architecture. It was the custom then to lay all the courses on the table at once, so that the table itself looked like a tiny city, an entire state, an empire in miniature, and it was surrounded by the diners the way an attacking army surrounds its target.

The table was besieged—the very word means to sit down around something. The more glorious the city, the greater the triumph, and those table-cities were each more glorious than the last. Carême, the greatest cook of the era, has left us a book to describe his obelisks and monuments, his triumphal arches, his hanging gardens, all built of icing and spun sugar. Cakes shaped like castles and obelisks of paté rose over teeming neighborhoods of pastry crusts packed with populations of small birds and lesser beings; platters curved like the shoreline of a port town, the silver scallops and gadroons of their edges winking like the frill of an evening wave, with creamy billows full of fish and crustaceans waiting behind it to tumble in turn upon that silver shore. Long trays lined with glazed domes and molded pinnacles made broad formal avenues that led off to more relaxed suburban sections planted with flower-garden salads; there, cool groves of greenery shaded fountains of champagne. Animals and fruits from all over the world were crammed into this city-table; its treasure was an imperial prize. This was the *ancien régime,* the elegant older civilization, worth the storm of revolution, worth the effort of destruction, worth devouring. And night after night such cities were besieged and sacked by battalions of brilliant, clamoring young men and women. The military dash of such a dinner, the jingling hussars' uniforms, the noise, the flames of a hundred constantly burning candles—it was all a vast piece of poetry, a metaphor. Every banquet a campaign, as every imperial campaign, until the end, had been a banquet.

Our banquets to this day recall those campaigns—some of the great classic dishes of French cooking commemorate Napoleonic victories. Chicken Marengo from the Italian campaign, Chicken Albuféra from the Iberian campaign. Defeats, of course, are not recorded. There is no Cooked Goose Waterloo. There is only that one strange dish where all the main ingredients of Pushkin's menu are combined: Roast beef is covered with *foie gras,* enclosed in a pastry, and served with truffle sauce: Beef Wellington, a case of winner-take-all. (The dish is *not* a French invention.)

Pushkin's dinner, though, is a Russian dinner, and Napoleon never conquered Russia; Moscow burned, true, but the imperial capital St. Petersburg, that distant, frozen city, remained untouched. Untouched? No need of conquest; it had belonged to Europe from the start. The city was the creation of foreigners, of European imaginations. This is a foreign dinner, after all: not only are the ingredients imported, but the restaurant itself is French: Talon's, at no. 15 Nevsky Prospect. Talon, "the well-known restaurant owner," Pushkin calls him; Talon, the Frenchman who had come to Petersburg in the wave of imported artists that swept through the city and created its sensual environment: Didelot the French ballet master, Rastrelli the Italian architect, Cameron the Scottish architect, John Field the Irish pianist, Fabergé the Huguenot jeweller. These were the people who provided the texture of the city, its tastes and styles, the web of sights and sounds and shapes and smells against which Pushkin moved and his verses sounded.

It was a poet, after all, who created this menu, and the menu is perfect Petersburg poetry: As the dishes were imported, so were the words used to describe them. The stanza is full of foreign words as the menu is full of foreign dishes. Roast beef *(rost-bif* in the original: an anglicism), Strasbourg, Limburger, truffles, pineapple *(ananas* in the original: a gallicism)—are these dishes or words? Consider the power of words to make us salivate, to awaken sensation, memory, or even an image of something we've never experienced. This menu is a poem first of all, and so began with words: Pushkin imported it from all over. The English *rost-bif* he found in a French poem by Parny; it replaced a dish he considered for an earlier draft, a *bécasse,* a French woodcock that he'd found in an English poem by Byron. And the *bécasse* was there in the first place not because he liked woodcock but because *bécasse* rhymes with *ananas.* So this stanza is as much an imported delicacy as the menu it describes, for poetry breaks down more frontiers than Napoleon could.

And yet what richness Pushkin offers us, what sensuality, what an imperial meal! Champagne, roast beef, truffles, Strasbourg *foie gras,* Limburger cheese, fresh pineapple. All the senses are put to work in this description: the ear, in the pop and spurt of a newly-opened bottle of iced champagne; the eye, in the crimson of roast beef, the velvet blackness of truffles, the gold of a pineapple; the nose, supremely, in the Limburger, the tactile sense in various textures and temperatures—the icy chill of a glass, the tearing of hot, succulent flesh from a rib bone, the sweet wetness of a piece of pineapple. And the taste-buds, each of them subjected to an elaborate succession of triumphant, conquering experiences. This is poetry not so much about food as about the effects of food on heightened senses, on the finely-tuned palate and the riotous sensual imagination. Words are paramount, but this is a poetry of the flesh—one that borders, perhaps, on pornography. Pushkin knew that. He knew that conquest was not only a military matter, but a sexual one, and that food was ammunition in that crucial war. As his chapter progresses, his hero Onegin becomes gradually disenchanted with the sensual excitements of the life he leads, and Pushkin lumps them all together:

> . . . Was he in vain amid these feasts
> Hale, and hearty, and without a care?
> Yes. His emotions cooled early.
> Society began to weary him.
> Beautiful women were no longer all
> His occupation: betrayals took their toll;
> Friends and friendship got to be a bore.
> Clearly he could not constantly wash down
> Paté and beef with bottles of champagne,
> Nor scatter wit and bright remarks about
> When he was hung over. And even though
> He was a hothead, and a touchy one,
> He grew at last definitively bored
> With duelling pistols, lead, and sword.

The youth of the era was at an end; the disorder of so much violence and richness in the blood was clear. Europe felt bilious and gouty, and turned to plainer local dishes: simple national stews instead of foreign delicacies. The great dinner party was over. It came to an end, like the empire, in a giant crash, as if some firm maternal hand had pulled the tablecloth from the table and everything hit the floor—crystal, dishes, flowers, food, and wine—in a teeth-shattering crash and a clatter of silverware. It all went, all of it, the luxury, the extravagance, the opulence, everything: Sèvres basins broke and dissolved their assemblies of strawberries, bottles of Médoc cracked their necks and rolled into corners, slapping spurts of bloody fluid and drowning the painted flowers of the porcelain plates. The golden candelabra toppled and fell from their sphinx-ridden bases, while the whole debacle was reflected for a moment in the wild eye and wacky grin of an ormolu cupid, astride one sphinx with his arm thrown out, urging the mess on as if he were leading a cavalry charge to the floor. Then he slid face-first into a platter of whipped cream, and over him toppled the spun-sugar temples, the icing Arches of Triumph, the sticky garlands and the carved ice swans, all of it tumbling and smashing, bouncing and skidding across the parquet floor, a torrent of rubbish finally, full of the squish of smeared sauces and congealed grease, a great rolling, rotting mess.

It all vanished. There was nothing left on the polished wooden surface of the table but a plain white Biedemeier coffee pot, two cups of coffee, a plate of bread and butter. And a long domestic silence, broken only by the tick of a clock and a cat's occasional purr.

Foie Gras en Croûte

Truffles

Roast Beef

Limburger

Pineapple

Champagne D'ay, 1811

FOIE GRAS

There is a dark side to food—the inside. Most of what we consider edible is the inside of something, and to get at it we have to open something up: cut it open, crack it open, rip it open, pull it out. The first step in cooking is to get things out in the open.

Of all the inside parts we eat, the richest and rarest is *foie gras,* fat goose liver; the effort and expense of obtaining it are legendary. It is a pleasure we pay dearly for. And yet, a curious thing—once we get the *foie gras,* we almost always serve it covered up again: in a pastry crust as here in Pushkin's menu, in a terrine, or in a block of aspic. Aspic is the most revealing of these coverings, for its transparence emphasizes the innerness of the thing, encased almost in shining crystal. And only by destroying the outside can we get at the inside, ever. To serve the dish we must perform again the act by which we got the liver in the first place—cutting open the goose.

To eat *foie gras en croûte* we must attack it; it is a military operation. It is Brillat-Savarin who says so; he describes a party once where the diners were served "an enormous *foie gras* in pastry from Strasbourg, in the shape of a bastion . . . a real Gibraltar." The image is compelling, and the diners proceeded to conquer the *foie gras* as the British had conquered Gibraltar and taken it from Napoleon not many years before. But in Brillat-Savarin's description that conquest is as much sexual as military. "In effect," he continues, "all conversation ceased as if hearts were too full to go on; all attention was riveted on the skill of the carvers; and when the serving platters had been passed, I saw spread out in succession on every face the fire of desire, the ecstacy of enjoyment, and then the perfect peace of satisfaction."

Perfection, satisfaction—it's true, we strive for satisfaction in love, for perfection in food: That is what every serious dinner for two is all about. But can *foie gras* content us? Can perfection satisfy? That liver, after all, is a triumph of our desire for perfection in food. We do strange and unnatural things to plants and animals in our attempts to perfect them for food. Those geese in Strasbourg, for instance. The facts are known. The geese are kept in stalls, immobilized from goslinghood, and force-fed. They are hourly crammed with corn until their livers, from coping with cholesterol, are swollen many times their normal size. That "fat liver" is a work of art, and its creation begins long before it even reaches the kitchen, long before it even leaves the goose. Delectable monstrosity! Delicious perversion!

We do that to the geese; do we do it to ourselves? We manipulate our bodies this way and that toward perfection, toward fat or thin mostly, back and forth, constantly. Fat yearns toward Thin, Thin strives for Fat; rarely are we content with our casings. The beautiful woman sweating off a last invisible pound in some perfumed retreat, a Greenhouse not for growing but for diminishing, or Arnold Schwarzenegger straining a last metaphysical inch onto a bicep in some clanking gym—what's the difference? Two discontented people, we think, and in a kind of Piranesi prison of their own imaginations: the steel cage and winking windows of the Greenhouse, the steel bars and mirrors of the gym—two views of the same edifice. But suppose we rethink the matter: Is it discontent that moves them to such effort? Or are they rather Platonic philosophers striving toward a perfection of pure form? Both have firmly fixed in mind an image of perfection, and both strive hungrily toward it; that it is a perfection of the flesh doesn't negate the seriousness of their search. The search seems endless, because the flesh is endlessly imperfect, but the very impossibility of the task conveys a certain nobility upon it; we admire that, the way we admire mountain climbers. For these two, though, there is never any fixed summit waiting frozen in the sunshine. The flesh is always unstable; what we see and are pleased with in the evening's mirror we cannot even face in the morning's reflection. But what we see in the morning can give us a goal for the day— at least if we take the matter at all seriously, which Arnold Schwarzenegger and the lady in the Greenhouse do. For both of them the striving and the yearning go on forever, while the image of a beautiful body glows in the air above their heads, always a few inches, just a few inches out of reach.

But who knows what risks they take? Can we manipulate one part and not another? Perhaps Arnold Schwarzenegger himself has a *foie gras,* an enormous glistening liver to accompany the matchless gleaming outside. Perhaps the beautiful lady's insides diminish as she thins her thighs: Perhaps she is left with a skinny, shrivelled heart. There's the real problem, and the real question: Do we prize the inside more than the outside, or the outside more than the inside? Is the beauty of the body somehow within, like a Platonic private part, and are Arnold Schwarzenegger and the beautiful lady both striving to set free something they feel within them, to dig out their *foie gras,* to make an inner perfection visible to the outside world?

Well, we may manipulate inside to make it reflect *out,* or outside to make it reflect *in,* but sooner or later we must come to understand that the one is incomplete without the other: An outside with no inside is empty, and an inside with no outside is helpless. And so we surround *foie gras* with pastry crust, and stuff the goose it came from.

But once surrounded, once inside, the stuff becomes an object of desire. We rush to conquer the bastion, and to conquer we must cut. There's an excitement to the act of opening up—Brillat-Savarin's diners waiting with anticipation the way we all do when something is exposed, the way children wait for a birthday present, or the way we watch a new lover undress for the first time. Conquest, we call it, and the opening can be violent. How often do children rip fiercely at the wrapping, how often do we tear passionately at a new lover's clothes!

Yet that violence bothers me, somehow; I have the feeling it must somehow be paid for, and it may be in a way we little expect. Consider the whole perverse procedure by which we get *foie gras:* Is it really possible to manipulate one part and not affect the whole? If we make the goose livers grow, what about the geese? Mightn't they grow, too? And may there not be, somewhere in the woods back of Strasbourg, great hordes of hulking geese, twelve feet high, honking like fire engines? The goddamn birds by now may even have turned into some sort of strange mutants: Their intelligence may have grown with their livers, as if they had taken a cram course in the awful ways of the world, and they may even now be mobilizing to march upon Paris, out to destroy every three-star restaurant in their path. Revenge! Revenge for perverting Platonic philosophy! Revenge for generations of livers sent to feed the fat-mouthed middle class! There may be hissing firebrands among them, revolutionary geese hoping to bring bourgeois civilization and all its philosophies to its knees. Who knows? We have only the word of a few smiling Alsatian farm ladies that the geese die regularly and gracefully, at normal size.

Perhaps the real expense of *foie gras,* like the price we pay for conquest or for love, is anxiety—the nervous fear of what may be lurking in the dark woods out back. Perfection may be within us, but satisfaction requires something from without, and must somehow be paid.

TRUFFLES

A truffle is a rarity, the way things that require discovery are always rare. It must be discovered quite literally: disclosed, uncovered, dug up. It shares with oysters the quality of being *rock-like:* of lying in silent, undisturbed darkness beneath a surface, and of having to be found out, dragged into the light, like a secret, or like meaning out of a complex event. I think it is this as much as anything that makes truffles attractive to us; anything that must be uncovered—discovered—will yield up more than itself, because we seek in it, as compensation for our search, some meaning beyond the brute fact of its being. So we read a truffle as if it were a text; it means more to us than just another mushroom. It enters our existence more importantly, and lingers longer. Its scarcity, its price, its seldomness, keep it in a metaphoric part of our minds. We say truffle, we write truffle, we imagine truffle, as often as—more often than, perhaps, for most of us—we ever eat truffle. We confront, indeed, in truffle-eating, a dark and hidden behavior. Darkness, after all, is its fundamental quality, its very image, and this may be for us the dark suggestion of an old idea, dragged up from our unconscious as the truffle is dragged up to light. When it is set before us, our imaginations confront a fact: This plaything for grown-ups at their most grown-up may yet bring us in a blink to a buried part of childhood. Are we about to eat *that?* Is a truffle not, perhaps, earth's excrement?

It is certainly something more than itself: The very complication of its provenance assures us of that. A truffle is snuffled out, snorted from the earth, passed from pig to peasant, from village to town, from earth to water; it is washed and polished and cooked and glazed, and sent ceremoniously to a candle-lit table. There it ends its passage from darkness to light, as a great dark eye opens slowly from primordial sleep, and finds reflected in its shiny surface the glance of a lady in satin and diamonds—a glance intended for the gentleman two places down the table from her. And that glance is checked, perhaps, by the sweep of a napkin, and a white wave winks for an instant in the truffle's surface, but as the napkin drops slowly lower and lower, the lady's diamonds are revealed, reflected in the truffle's glaze. Then in both truffle and diamond some kinship is revealed, a cousinage of underground darkness, two lumps of stuff dug out of the earth, brought to light, cleaned and polished and taken finally to the same table, there to reflect each other: perfect darkness and perfect light. In those reflecting surfaces, what secrets may pass! And yet they pass through the diamond, refract, dissolve, and disappear: Diamonds hold nothing. But in the truffle those secrets remain. As darkness embraces all, reveals nothing, so does a truffle. It yields up only an ancient aroma, a black taste, and recalls us to the deepest parts of ourselves. Our latter-day frivolities are judged in that stern earthen eye, the feast darkens, and all the glitter of the diamond is denied. The candles on this table will soon gutter and go out, the truffle tells us, and so will we.

ROAST BEEF

Roast beef is a different phenomenon in different times and in different places, but it is the intractable item in any menu, and the dominant one. All over the world it is called by its English name—it is always roast beef (or roastbeef or rostbif or rosbif or rozbif). Why? Because the English invented it, we say; but the fact is, there was nothing to invent. Roast beef has nothing to do with recipes. It was originally not a matter for the kitchen at all. It is roast meat, grilled meat, a barbecue, something done out-of-doors and done since time immemorial. In a sophisticated age it is the last vestige of our aboriginal past, and to see a slice of roast beef on a Sèvres plate on a candle-lit table is to see an extraordinary combination of things—the gilt and painted flowers of the porcelain glittering in the candle flame, beneath the almost raw hunk of what was once, very obviously, except for its exposure to flame, live meat.

Roast beef is a dish that comes to the table with less human meditation than anything except oysters on the half shell. And except for oysters, which we try to eat live, rare beef is the closest thing to living flesh we eat. We have eaten roast meat in European culture longer than we have eaten anything else. Boiled beef is modern compared to roast beef, and the product of a subtle technology. It takes less art to boil beef than to roast it, but the results are more certain; like most technological innovations, boiled beef is surer than roast beef, but duller. A piece of roast beef is no triumph of the kitchen. It barely belongs in the dining room. It is, rather, the triumph of the principle of conservation, of the idea of habit. Roasting was the first physical meditation of humanity upon the things we eat—again, except for opening oysters. But there it lies, still faintly bleeding, a shocking anachronism. Look closely sometime at a slice of rare roast beef—who brought *that* into the house, we wonder; it shrieks of savagery and the out-of-doors.

The closer the meat seems to the bleeding animal that fell beneath the arrow, the better. Grilled meat is the primal luxury: It means you have been a successful hunter and can afford to offer fresh meat to your friends. And it must be fresh, too; other forms of cookery can disguise tainted meat, but grilling is simple: only flesh and fire. The process is always kept visible, as the fire is always visible, always a focus, always social. All cultures keep grilled meat as a separate item, and most cultures keep some kind of outdoor barbecue for special occasions. A restaurant with a grill almost always displays it. And when we ask the neighbors over, how often is it to the backyard and for grilled meat? An Indian with his slice of bleeding buffalo, an Eskimo with his hunk of bloody seal, a caveman with his messy piece of mammoth, are all cousins to the man in the yard next door with his pile of hamburgers, his grill, and his silly apron. He never went on a hamburger hunt, but that nevertheless is the premise he celebrates.

Outdoor cooking is man's work, too, not woman's. In the primal division of labor, men hunted animals and women gathered plants, and that distinction holds clearly when we think of grilled meat. Not much is ever done to roast beef. It is served without sauces, basted only in its own fat, and its traditional accompaniment is only the complementary food, vegetables. What had been hunted by men is eaten with what had been gathered by women. With the rare, the raw. Salad. Vegetables raw, or only cooked enough, as the meat is ideally, to make them attractive to eat. And as the meat is always basted in its own fat, so a salad is always dressed with vegetable liquids: olive oil and vinegar. There is an immense human satisfaction in this combination of opposites: roast beef and salad, when the masculine activity and the feminine come to rest, side by side, on the same plate. And there we can combine the sexes however we want. As Escoffier notes: ". . . many gourmets like to sop their salad in the meat juice."

LIMBURGER CHEESE

Finding food is an animal problem; preserving it is a human one. To set about preserving food, one must first be aware of time—not merely the fact of it: distinguish day from night, and you can tell time—but rather the effect of time on the world. Time will transform what we eat without touching it; astonishingly, before our very eyes and under our very noses, what used to be food stops being food. At some point it dawned on a caveman, downwind from some stinking mound of mammoth, that the carcass he had been dining off for a week had gone beyond the point of dinner.

But long before that, at some odd, early moment, some thoughtful creature made a curious discovery. She stands-perhaps alone, perhaps with a creature beside her—beneath a tree whose branches are heavy with apples. She eats one. The fruit of the tree tastes "good." But then there is a rustling in the leaves, a cloud for a moment obscures the sun, and the creature near her begins to move away; touched by a certain fear, she starts to follow him—and on an impulse she grabs four or five apples and carries them away with her. Perhaps she offers one of them to the creature near her. Perhaps she eats one of them herself as she goes. Perhaps she decides to keep the others until "later"—and it dawns on her, as she eats another one later, that it tastes "better." Eventually, "much later," she discovers that the last one tastes "bad." Awful, in fact. She has attained a certain knowledge: things ripen and then they rot, and that is a measure of time. Ripeness tastes good but rot tastes bad, and the time of the tasting makes all the difference. And from that moment of perception beneath that tree, down an endless chain of grandmothers, comes that knowledge: The idea of preserving food, or trying to make the taste of the apple last forever.

But preserving food is a complex affair: containers must be invented and proper techniques discovered. Through centuries of trial and error, attempts were made to preserve everything, and apples are an easy matter compared, let's say, to milk. But once we learned to herd cattle and make bowls and baskets, the problem of preserving milk inevitably arose. And so we come to cheese.

To make cheese is to preserve milk. But with cheese the idea of preservation takes a strange turn: The process reverses itself. Time, that we struggle against to preserve food, becomes suddenly beneficial, and the process of ripening is extended to extremes—aging, we call it, and like it. The desirable end of cheese-making is not to preserve youth but to encourage age, not to keep freshness but to lose it, not to safeguard innocence but to ensure an enjoyable corruption. Clearly at some point in the process of corruption, or rot, we draw a line and say: That's it, no further; nobody could eat *that*. But at what point? An attractive gaminess is an acquired taste—acquired with age, at that, and it may simply be that age is drawn to age, decay to decay. What we puke up at six we will gorge on at sixteen; what seems gross at sixteen may be a delicacy at sixty. What sort of progression is this?

The truest understanding of cheese is that it concerns, precisely, milk. Do we ever lose a taste for our first food? The change from mother's milk to other foods is an awful drama of wailing and dribbling and drooling, and it may even be that the messy pain of weaning continues forever. Perhaps it involves more than the lost breast; perhaps it colors the entire world always. Milk sours, as affection sours; do we mark with cheese our disenchantment with the world? Do cheeses provide us with attractive lumps of disappointment?

More than that, I think. Our progress from milk to cheese, and from cheese to stronger cheese, is a change of sexuality. A baby takes only milk, and at some point is noisily and painfully weaned away from the breast; is cheese-eating then a metaphor for the way we relate to our mother's body? Do we attempt to retrieve some other part of what was so forcibly taken from us? As we move from the taste and smell of fresh milk to the taste and smell of aged cheese, do we move from one sexuality to another, from the breast to other parts? The gamey taste and smell of ripened cheese is sexual, and provocative; the smell is maternal still, but now it is the smell of cyclical time. Time is measured constantly and inexorably in the swelling and emptying of maternal organs, and its trace is recalled, surely, in the change of milk to Limburger.

For Limburger is the ultimate palatable state of pure milk. We first drink milk in all innocence; it is the taste of childhood. When we are older and wiser we eat Limburger, and that is the taste of age and decay. One is the odor of life, the other the odor of death, and in the transformation of one to the other, and in the change in our taste for one to the other, we record our body's encounter with time. An interesting encounter, after all. All things are subject to corruption, true; but that's no matter for despair, rather for acceptance, and even for delectation.

Ripeness is indeed all, in cheese as in ourselves, and that's surely the reason we love Limburger.

PINEAPPLES

Pushkin's meal ends with the pineapple, as his poem began with it, for *ananas* was the first rhyme word in Pushkin's stanza. Pineapple poetry? Why not? The pineapple has always been a sign of the high life, of good living, in Russia, all over Europe, and here in America as well: Witness the carved pineapple that crowns eighteenth-century doors, carved mirrors, and furniture.

But it has a deeper meaning, and an older one. When the *ananas* arrived in England, it was called pine-apple because it resembled the pinecone, and the pinecone has an ancient history. The Greeks and Romans associated the pinecone with Bacchus the wine god and the fertility rites of Dionysios, and that association persisted. Beyond luxurious living, the pineapple is a sign of license and sexuality.

Like most tropical fruits, the pineapple provides an astonishing distinction between exterior and interior—the outside never quite prepares us for the inside, which sometimes comes as a shock. That was what fascinated Europe with the tropical fruits brought back from the distant discoveries of the sixteenth, seventeenth, and eighteenth centuries. European fruits were obvious. Cherries and grapes are thin-skinned, or barely skinned at all. Whatever is inside shows through an almost transparent exterior, and colors it. In Europe the only things rough and forbidding-looking but still edible were nuts, but the inside of a nut was also hard, and small. Here suddenly were new fruits, enormous ones; they were scaly, rough, and hurtful on the outside, and yet within they were all softness, paleness, and juice.

Symbol indeed of the deepest hospitality, the pineapple is an androgynous fruit. It does not deny either sex, or equivocate about sexuality, but affords an image of masculinity and femininity totally, one within the other. Think of the whole pineapple: the phallic thrust of the thing displayed erect, as it so often is, over doorways and at the tops of lavish heaps of lesser fruit; and then cut one down the middle: the yonic pattern of the thing, with its pulpy fascicules radiating from a central ovoid cone, and its sticky juice and rich, musty smell. Brought from conquered islands to European tables, and there cut up and eaten, its rough thrust reduced to a yielding wetness, the pineapple is both an image of sexual conquest and as great a military metaphor as any of the columns and arches of Carême's imperial banquets.

But the great masters of the table, if they could, wanted it both ways. Udés recipe reduces his pineapple to a heap of feminine slices, and then carefully reconstructs it as a phallic pile, in a transparent tower of jelly. And in this form he makes of it, perhaps, the truest phallic symbol of all: That proud, glistening height, as we know all too well, has too often a very shaky foundation. Depending on the temperature of the occasion and the lay of the land, all that shining phallic promise can dissolve, begin to wobble, and at last topple weeping into a puddle.

CHAMPAGNE

They pour champagne? The perfect wine for Russia; only blizzards and snowstorms can ever chill it properly. *1811, the year the comet came?* We need no year to qualify champagne, for every year is comet year: Champagne is just a comet in a bottle. The cork goes pop, it spurts a shower of stars; the foamy moment glitters with wild excitement, the ahs and sighs of satisfaction afterward, always, as it subsides into a bed of bubbles. Bravo! Open a bottle of champagne: The comet always comes.

SUSAN SONTAG

1. Dancers on a Plane

I don't see them.

There. The dancers are there, invisible—an analogue to racing thoughts.

Framed by the utensils of eating.

A meal to be eaten?

An invisible meal.

Two meals: one light, one dark. One sprightly, one stained with sexual dread.

Dancers on a plate?

No. They need more space than that.

2. Eating and Dancing

Recombinant arts.

A domain of pleasure. A domain of courtesy.

Rule-bound. Who sets the rules? Behavior with standards.

An idea of order. First one thing, then another. Then one is full. Then it is finished—the belly sated, the limbs heavy. After a decent interval: then again. All over again. All over, again.

They remind us we live in the body-house.

Living "in" the body. But where else could we live?

Dancing as the realm of freedom, that's less than half the story.

Eating as the realm of necessity. Not necessarily. What about eating idyllically (as in Paris)?

Everyone eats, everyone can dance. Not every one dances (alas).

I watch dance, with pleasure. I don't watch eating. If I watch someone eating when hungry, I wish it were I eating. A meal watched by a hungry person is always savory. If I watch someone eating when full, I may turn away.

You can dance for me. (You do the dancing in my place, I'll just watch.) You can't eat for me. Not much pleasure there. . . .

You can dance to please: Salome. You can eat to please, too: as a child might eat to please its mother or a nurse. (As Suzanne Farrell is said to have said that she danced for God and for Mr. Balanchine.) But except to doting parents eating is a poor spectator sport. Mildly disgusting unless you're doing it as well.

To eat is to put metal in one's mouth. Delicately. It's not supposed to hurt. The eater fills the hole.

A dancer eats space.

Space eats time.

Sounds eat silence.

3. THE KNIFE

It cuts. Don't be afraid. This is not a weapon. It's just a tool to help you eat. See. Passing it to you—you asked for it—I proffer it by the handle, keeping the blade pointed at myself. The blade is pointing at me.

One should not move the point of the knife toward someone as in an attack.

You can lay it down two ways. Blade in, blade out.

Don't be timorous. It isn't sharp. It's just a plain, ordinary . . . knife. Straight. Two-sided.

In the fairy tale, a mermaid who has fallen in love with a prince begs to be allowed to assume human form so she can leave the water and make her way to the court. Yes. She will have legs, she will walk. But with each step she takes it will feel as if she were walking on knives.

You can dance with a knife. (Between the teeth? Between the shoulder blades? Hard to imagine dancing with a fork. Or with a spoon.

The knife seems like the master utensil, the one from which all others depend. (Swiss Army Knife.) You could spear food with your knife, eliminating the fork. (As everyone knows, you can eat the peas with your knife. You're just not supposed to.) As for the spoon—well, we could do without that, too. Just lift up the bowl dish cup, and drink it.

Only the knife is really necessary. And it is the knife, more than any other eating utensil, whose use is most restricted. The evolution of table manners is mainly about what to do with knives. Use the knife more and more unobtrusively, elegantly. With your fingerends. Don't grasp it against your palm, like a stick.

"There is a tendency that slowly permeates civilized society, from the top to the bottom, to restrict the use of the knife (within the framework of existing eating techniques) and wherever possible not to use the instrument at all" (Norbert Elias). For instance, to eliminate or at least limit the contact of the knife with round or egg-shaped objects. Not all restrictions are successful. The prohibition on eating fish with a knife, once fairly strict, was circumvented by the introduction of a special fish knife.

That oxymoron: the butter knife.

To eat is to put metal in one's mouth. But not knives. The mere sight of someone putting her knife in her mouth produces an uneasy feeling.

4. THE SPOON

The spoon seems to belong in the mouth.

The spoon is not quite grown-up in the way the knife and fork are. It doesn't menace. It isn't a tamed weapon.

The spoon is the utensil of childhood, the friendliest utensil. The spoon is a child—or child-like—forever. Yum yum. Scoop me up, pour me in. Like a cradle, a shovel, a hand cupped. Doesn't cut or pierce or impale. It accepts. Round, curved. Can't stick you. Don't trust your child with a knife or a fork, but how can a spoon harm? The spoon is itself a child.

The world is full of pleasures. One has only to be where one is. Here. Now.

Give me my spoon, my big spoon, and I'll eat the world. A metal spoon is an afterthought. While a wooden knife is less of a knife, a wooden spoon isn't less of a spoon. It's just fine.

"Spooning": embracing, kissing, petting. Lovers in bed fit together, in sleep, like spoons.

To bring about a music "that will be part of the noises of the environment will take them into consideration. I think of it as melodious, softening the noises of the knives and forks, not dominating them, not imposing itself," wrote John Cage, quoting Erik Satie.

What happened to the spoons? Don't spoons make noises, too?

Softer noises.

And music. Music is made with two spoons (not with two forks, two knives).

Spoon music.

5. THE FORK

There's a hesitation about the fork. You hold down the food with the fork in your left hand while you cut it with the knife held in your right. Then—if you're not only right handed but also American—you put down the knife, then transfer the fork to your right hand and send the speared morsel up to your mouth.

Grown-ups throw knives. Children throw spoons. Nobody (I think) would throw a fork. It may be four-thirds of a toy trident, but it can't be thrown as one. It wouldn't arrive, spear-like, tines first.

The weight is in the handle.

The fork as emblem—emblem of the real. Jasper Johns, explaining something about "my general development so far," said: "That is to say, I find it more interesting to use a real fork as a painting than it is to use painting as a real fork."

What would a fork that wasn't real look like?

The fork is the youngest of the three great eating utensils. The Last Supper was set with knives and spoons only. No forks either at the wedding feast in Cana.

It made its appearance when the knife and spoon were well established. Invented in Italy, thought a foppish pretension when it arrived in England in the early 17th century: a set of gold "Italian forkes" presented to Elizabeth I by the Venetian ambassador were put on display at Westminster; she never used them.

The principle of fastidiousness. Embodied in objects that now could hardly seem more everyday, plain.

The introduction of that vital implement, the fork (for a long time despised as effete), enabled people to distance themselves from the eating process by avoiding manual contact with the food.

New forms of distance, new forms of delicacy.

New rules of finicky behavior at table proliferated. People were expected to manipulate an increasingly complicated battery of utensils.

It seemed hard, setting up and keeping this distance.

Now we take forks for granted.

6. Knife, Spoon, Fork

A secular trinity—knife, spoon, fork.

No hierarchy. The list can only be varied, systematically. As in knife, fork, spoon. As in fork, knife, spoon. As in fork, spoon, knife. As in spoon, fork, knife. As in spoon, knife, fork.

Seemingly immutable (after all that history).

They lie there, flat. On a plain (plane) surface. Perpendicular to the edge of the table.

A trialogue.

A stately relationship. Not all on the same side of the plate. Three divides into two and one. Fork on the left side. Knife and spoon on the right.

The knife is scary by itself. But as part of a setting, something else. Lying beside the spoon, the knife becomes quite . . . domestic. Knife and spoon: the odd couple. They don't go together, you don't use them together. But they *are* together.

The fork is solitary. Always is. Even in an ampler setting, all you could have next to it is another (smaller, larger) fork.

That's how they're arranged at the start of the meal, one step down from the plate. Escorting the plate on either side.

No excuse now to eat with your hands. Civil eating (versus gluttony).

After finishing eating you arrange them neatly on the plate.

Not alphabetically. Not in order of importance, if there were one.

A trinity but quite contingent.

They seem to complement each other.

We have learned to use all three. But they can be taken separately, of course.

7. DANCERS ON A PLAIN

On a plane? An airplane?

On a plain. As open (borderless) as feasible.

Low, level. Don't try for any of those old heights. Depths.

What is essential about a surface that makes it different from another surface? How do we experience smoothness in a surface, a movement, a sound, an experience?

Smoothness?

Yes. Something continues, plausibly.

Pleasurably. With parts.

What does it mean to say of something that it is one part of something (a surface, a movement, a sound, an experience)?

The old heights. Mirroring. Look down. These are my genitals.

Be more modest. (Elegant.)

Sometimes light, sometimes heavy—it's all right to be heavy sometimes.

Make it new. Yes. And make it plain.

8. SYMMETRIES

Dancers on a plane. No center. Always off-side. Any place is the center.

We seem symmetrical. Two eyes, two ears, two arms, two legs; two ovaries—or two hairy testicles. But we're not. Something is always dominating.

A mirror image: a fantasy of symmetry. The right the reverse of the left, or vice versa.

We *seem* symmetrical. But we are not.

They cross-refer (knife, spoon, fork). As in the brain. Right-handedness means the left side of the brain is dominant. Left-handedness means the brain's right side dominates.

How to find out which side of your brain is dominant. Close your eyes, think of a question, then slowly think of an answer to the question. If while you're doing this you turn your head slightly to the right, that means the left side dominates.

And vice versa.

The question-master.

An art that asks questions.

How do we understand how one part of a surface, a movement, a sound, an experience relates to another? Note: you have a choice of questions. But if *that's* the question you choose to ask, you can be sure the answer will include a bias toward asymmetry.

"The non-relationship of the movement," Cunningham has declared, "is extended into a relationship with music. It is essentially a non-relationship."

The dancer must be light. Food makes you heavy.

You eat with your hands, dance on your legs. Eating can be right-handed or left-handed. Is dancing left-legged or right-legged?

Any place is the center.

A real symmetry: chopsticks.

9. SILENCES

Lots of prattle. That, too, is a kind of silence. (Since there is no silence.) The deaf hear their deafness. The blind see their blindness.

Controlling through silence. Whoever speaks less is the stronger.

Is there a warm silence?

The noise of ideas.

Take it to language.

No, take it to babble. Cut up the words in strips, like raw vegetables. Make meals out of words. A culinary relation to words.

Suppose Knife, Spoon, and Fork are three people. And they get together on a plane (plain). What would they have to say to each other?

I know. "Who brought the marshmallows?"

Mushrooms, surely you mean mushrooms.

As I said, marshmallows.

That's not what I had in mind. Then what?

Then they get very particular about how the marshmallows are to be cooked.

All three of them know a lot about food. (About eating. Preceded by gathering, preparing, cooking. . . .

But these are just marshmallows. American junk.

You can be fastidious about anything. And marshmallows can be botched, too; can disappoint. It's a question of (yes, once again) the relation of inside to outside. The inside has to be cooked very well, while not letting the outside catch fire. Ideally the outside will get crusty but not burnt, while the inside melts. Then, right before it falls off the stick, you pluck it off with your fingers and pop it whole into your mouth.

Stick? What happened to the fork? Don't you toast marshmallows with a fork?

All right, the fork. But this is better as a gooey experience than as a refined one.

"Everywhere and at all times," Lévi-Strauss has observed, "the European code of politeness rules out the possibility of eating noisily."

And you don't always have to be polite.

10. In Memory of Our Feelings

In the first—buoyant, allegro vivace—painting, this is real flatware that has been painted white. In the second, heavy painting, the artist has cast the utensils in bronze.

Repeating as a means of varying. Accepting as a way of discriminating. Indifference as a form of emotional vitality.

Use me as you will.

Savoring non-relatedness. Put the emphasis on savoring. "I am more interested in the *facts* of moving rather than in my feelings about them" (Merce Cunningham).

Would you like to play chess? Chess seriously.

We were younger then. Who would have thought then—when we were younger; then—that it would be like this?

We meet. This could be at a dinner party (forks, knives, spoons, etc.). We say things like, How lovely to see you. I've been busy. I think so. I don't know. That must have been very interesting. (Everything is interesting. But some things are more interesting than others.) Probably not. I've heard. In Frankfurt, in Illinois, in London. Next year. What a pity. He's gone away. He'll be back soon. They're organizing something. You'll get an invitation.

We smile. We nod. We are indefatigable. I think I'm free next week. We say we wish we saw more of each other.

We eat, we savor.

Meanwhile, each harbors a secret idea of ascending, of descending. We go on. The plane's edge beckons.

Want

OUR DAILY BREAD: ON THE TRIUMPH OF AMERICAN GASTROSOPHY

FREDERICK KAUFMAN

> *For a man to follow nature, to live according to physiological laws, or to obey God, is one and the same thing.*
> —THOMAS L. NICHOLS,
> *Esoteric Anthropology,* 1853

> *Nutrition, like religion, is extremely visceral.*
> —BARRY SEARS, *Enter the Zone,* 1995

I RECENTLY ASKED A FRIENDLY sales clerk at my local Borders bookstore for a printout of all his current diet books. About an hour later emerged twelve single-spaced pages, heralding, in small type, the existence of a collection of more than 700 titles. The clerk handed me the list and shook his head, perhaps wondering whether ever in the history of bookstore databases there had been such a textual purge.

A steady emesis of diet books, I wanted to tell him, has long been symptomatic of this century's publishing practices, at least since the days when Emerson, Thoreau, and company were furiously scribbling curricular content for the next century's Am. Lit. courses. Those who shudder at the sight of Barry Sears's *Mastering the Zone* and Suzanne Somers's *Get Skinny on Fabulous Food* on today's bestseller lists should keep in mind that neither *Walden* nor *Moby-Dick* could boast sales anywhere near Sylvester Graham's *Discourses on a Sober and Temperate Life* or Marx Edgeworth Lazarus's *Passional Hygiene and Natural Medicine: Embracing the Harmonies of Man with His Planet.*

A raft of academics have expended their careers variously accounting for the sudden bloom of American Transcendentalism, the strange, homegrown spiritual product that proclaims every individual's ability to absorb and secrete omnipotent power. But who has paid proper attention to the far more popular and, arguably, more influential diet books of 150 years ago? Transcendentalists have long been enshrined in the cultural pantheon while their cohorts, these early American prophets of the stomach, have been unfairly neglected, even ghettoized.

Who were these newfangled figures of cultural dominion who identified themselves as founders of a social movement rooted deep within that sacrosanct area neither polities nor economics could touch—the digestive tract?

Such proto-paranoiacs of processed white flour were known at the time as gastrosophists, and to this new brand of sage the stomach was nothing less than the "central organ and sovereign of life." "The science of gastrosophy," Marx Edgeworth Lazarus asserted in 1852,

> will place epicurism in strict alliance with honor and the love of glory.
>
> Of all our enjoyments, eating being the first, the last, and the most frequent pleasure of man, it ought to be the principal agent of wisdom in the future harmony.
>
> A skillful gastrosophist, also expert in the functions of culture and medical hygiene, will be revered as an oracle of supreme wisdom.

In the midst of our present-day political chaos, economic excitements, and slickly marketed mineral waters, Lazarus's prophecy has finally come true: after years of gradual cultural accession, gastrosophists now stand as America's reigning "oracle[s] of supreme wisdom." The food we choose to ear or nor to eat, and the precise ways in which we either do or don't eat it, has now become the authoritative measure not only of our physical selves but of our emotional and spiritual well-being.

This is not to say that all our present day gastrosophical geniuses can agree on what it is we should be ingesting. They do hold certain truths to be self-evident, however, first among them the dictum that the mandates of human physiology are divine entities, "one and the same thing" as obeying God. Although European gastronomers have remained perfectly satisfied with Anthelme Brillat-Savarin's brilliant reduction of what we are to what we eat, American gastrosophists must ceaselessly revisit, revise, and appease our dietary deities.

The origins of this phenomenon are as old as our country. The climax of the second part of Benjamin Franklin's *Autobiography* centers on the particulars of his "bold and arduous project of arriving at moral perfection." Franklin's "thirteen names of virtues" prescribe justice, duty, industry, sincerity, cleanliness, chastity, and humility—and even a casual reader cannot help but be reminded of his strongest literary antecedent, the Ten Commandments. Of course, the First Commandment for the ancient Hebrew was, "Thou shalt have no other gods before me," whereas Franklin's first "virtue" is

TEMPERANCE.
eat not to dullness
drink not to elevation.

Now, the observant Jew must submit to numerous dietary laws, but none of these laws dislocates Yaweh from His preeminent place in the hierarchy of belief. But Benjamin Franklin places diet above every other "Commandment" given to his new nation.

Franklin was a scientist forging a new American religion within his ample gut. Today, even our most scientific gastrosophists have their Pentecostal moments, railing against sinners in the hands of an angry stomach, "stuck in carbohydrate hell," and declaring that "when patients lose excess body fat, it's as if the hand of God touched them." To these exhortations, Dr. Barry Sears adds that the stories he retells "are nor unlike the typical testimonials that you'd expect to hear at a faith-healing revival meeting." Dr. Robert Atkins actually identifies himself as "an evangelist." And Victoria Moran's first sacred "affirmation" is "I eat in love, nor in guilt."

In order for oral consumption—or the lack thereof—to become our God, nutriment itself must reach a transcendent status. So here's the latest gastrosophical gospel: Food is no longer food. Food is a drug. Such an identity is perfect for our post-psychedelic, better-living-through-chemicals, human-genome-obsessed world. And, as Barry Sears has noted, for this widely variegated neuropharmacological spirit of life and death (that is, food), there is one single most efficient "oral drug-delivery system": eating.

Dr. Sears, architect of the wildly successful "Zone" diet, in which grandma's injunction to eat balanced meals has transmogrified into science, had originally hoped to "become a pharmaceutical tycoon." When he discovered what to this day he believes is the key to "health and illness," nothing less than "a molecular definition of 'wellness,'" he got his wish. The much-hyped Zone refers nor just to a mundane set of rules governing the intake of foods; it does no less than define a place where physical, mental, and spiritual perfection meet. "Fleeting but all-powerful," the Zone redefines the Transcendental dreams Americans have held for themselves since the time of Emerson, the threshold of "that mysterious but very real state in which your body and your mind work together at their ultimate best." Of course, fasting works just as well.

The secret to entering this entering utopia turns out to be a kind of hormone called an eicosanoid. And since an eicosanoid is not a food group but a molecule, it is just as easily obtained from Burger King and Jack in the Box as it is from oatmeal and sardines. Best of all, these eicosanoids are nor only the panacea for obesity but for cancer, heart disease, diabetes, arthritis, HIV, PMS, eczema and jet lag, depression and alcoholism—indeed, for "virtually every disease state."

This kind of medical monomania has a long history and a fancy name. Single-etiology was Enlightenment shorthand for the proposition that there must be one single cause for all sickness. Driven out of ortho- dox science at the end of the eighteenth century, single-etiology is still in vogue among modern diet mavens. In *Eat Right 4 Your Type*, Peter J. D'Adamo asserts that your blood type is the key that unlocks the door to the mysteries of health, disease, longevity, physical vitality, and emotional strength." Robert Atkins, whose *New Diet Revolution* remained number 1 on the *New York Times* "Advice, How-to and Miscellaneous" paperback bestseller list for 161 weeks, and who loves to italicize, declares, in an earlier book, *Diet Revolution,* that "*only one thing matters for the rest of your life. Does what you are about to put in your mouth contain carbohydrate?*"

Right in line with this great tradition of gut-centric theories of the everything, Atkins proposes that the way we eat is to blame not only for how overweight Americans are but for a host of disorders familiar to readers of pharmaceutical-side-effect warnings:

> irritability, nervousness, dizziness, headaches, faintness, cold sweats, cold hands and feet, weak spells, drowsiness, forgetfulness, insomnia, worrying, confusion, anxiety, palpitations of the heart, muscle pains, hostility, belligerence, antisocial behavior, indecisiveness, crying spells, lack of concentration, twitching of muscles, gasping for breath . . .

Atkins's patients "have gained energy, cheerfulness, self-confidence. They're new people." Of course, Robert Pritikin preaches a diametrical- ly opposed program that claims to have the same benefits: people "expe- rience a significant improvement in weight, vitality, and clarity of mind. Many feel more optimistic and positive about themselves and the future."

One hundred and seventy-three-years ago, James Johnson outlined these same claims in his popular "Essay on Indigestion." He was, he noted,

> convinced that many strange antipathies, disgusts, caprices of temper, and eccentricities, which are considered solely as obliquities of the *intellect,* have their source in corporeal disorder.

And Johnson was only confirming the decade-old wisdom of Thomas Trotter:

> The human stomach is an organ endued by nature, with the most complex properties of any in the body; and forming a centre of sympathy between our corporeal and mental parts, of more exquisite qualifications than even the brain itself.

Thus, from the days when Federalists ruled the earth, there has been no mind-body problem in this country. In fact, technically speaking, there *is* no American mind, only an American body—that is, an American stomach. Mental health depends upon gastric health. Every ailment stems from improper aliment. All this explains why Americans, more ardently religious than ever before, don't bother with church attendance. In the age of biotech miracles, salvation resides in our molecules. And just in case your spiritual (that is, intestinal) software malfunctions, Sears provides "Technical Support" in one of his appendices, replete with an 800 number. And so the gastrosophist has transumed the most dreaded and worshiped sobriquet of our day: he has become a techie.

Moreover, to the American, generally lacking pedigree, nothing could be more satisfying than to discover our deepest roots enveloped within our bodies. So, like each religion, each diet comes with its own creation myth, its own ambition to exist on a par with the most ancient forms of life on the planet. Sears's eicosanoids "have been around for more than five hundred million years," while Atkins insists that his D-Zerta, Baken-ets, and pork-rind regimen most closely aligns with the primal eldest diet:

> As cavemen, we humans evolved mainly on a diet of meat. And that's what our bodies were and are built to handle. For fifty million years our bodies had to deal with only minute amounts of carbohydrates. . . .

Robert Pritikin profoundly intones:

> Let me take you back through the long tunnel of time to a point in human evolution when the modern humans, the first Adam and Eve, were born into the original garden.

Pritikin subsequently ensures the veracity of his assertion that our collective grandparents were eating grilled vegetables from that "original garden" by minute analyses of "copralite," the petrified feces of early humans.

D'Adamo plumbs the depths of our antiquated guts even more deeply than Pritikin's disinterment of ancient shitting grounds when he announces that the science of "paleoserology" has shown that "blood types are as fundamental as creation itself. . . . They are the signature of our ancient ancestors on the indestructible parchment of history." It should come as no surprise to anyone that St. Martin's Press recently released the ultimate gastrosophical how-to for achieving sveltitude the sexy caveman way: *NeanderTHIN,* by Ray Audette with Troy Gilchrist.

There is some sense in going backward. As innumerable statistics from these contemporary tomes illustrate, the more we as a culture have dieted, the fatter we have become. Thus, the single most important feature all these diets must possess is their insistence that they are not diets. Everyone, it seems, has had it with diets.

> We have been nearly bored to death for the last fifteen years, with prosy moralities about health, and the dragchain of duty has been hitched on to the simplest offices of life, until what shall we eat, and what shall we drink, and wherewithal shall we be clothed, have come to be the all-absorbing meditations and discussions of a large class of cabbage-headed philosophers.

The "fifteen years" Marx Edgeworth Lazarus here alludes to are 1837–1852. If it was bad then, it's worse now. No diet book presently on the market would dare advertise itself as such. The Zone is not a diet but a "dietary technology" that simply employs "Successful Eicosanoid Modulation." As for Atkins, his mantra is "WHEN IN DOUBT— EAT!" Americans must not "put up with feeling deprived."

Behind this anti-diet veil lurks the 1833 gospel of Sylvester Graham, the man Emerson dubbed our "prophet of bran bread and pumpkins," whose modern-day eponymous cracker might well have turned his stomach. Graham viewed hunger as a dangerous erection of the digestive apparatus. He lectured on sexual hygiene as often as on diet reform and warned against the frightful dangers of onanism. For a Grahamite the ultimate goal was social—a strictly hygienic community of hard-working, God-fearing, gluten-munching, anesthetized celibates:

> "Whatever pleases the palate, must agree with the stomach and nourish the body!" This lying proverb is older than the Christian Religion, and has sent millions of human beings thro' years of misery to an early grave. . . . But let it ever be remembered that the palate may be educated to any thing . . .

Therefore,

Treat your stomach like a well governed child; carefully find out what is best for it, as the digestive organ of your body, and then teach it to conform to your regimen.

Such a total peristaltic reprogramming amounts to a voluntary creation of entirely new fields of involuntary desire: I *want* tepid gruel for breakfast, lunch, and dinner; ergo, this is not a diet. (Repeat ten times.)

Thus does Robert Pritikin (whose father, Nathan, was known to ingest his fair share of gruel) uncover our dread "instinct" for Graham's evil twins, the palate-pleasing fleshpots of fat and sugar. He then unveils the carnal "couch potato . . . in our genes." Such inherited biological drives are, like any satanic emanation worth its salt, temptations that must be conquered. Like all faithful Graham acolytes, Pritikin announces that

we can no longer live by instinct alone. Patterns of behavior that long ago were unconscious, and imposed upon us by the environment must now be practiced consciously if we are to achieve optimal health.

In other words, we do not diet. By reprogramming our instincts, we raise our consciousness.

The ultimate Grahamite discipline-your-instincts anti-diet diet can be found in the ever-capitalized, ever-trademarked, ever-exclamation-pointed *SUGAR BUSTERS!*™ In this *New York Times* bestseller, H. Leighton Steward (a Fortune 500 CEO) and a team of doctors express dietary perfection to be the gospel of corporate America. As CEOs of our bodies, we can regulate our metabolism as a capitalist exercise in balancing fungibles. Like money within the economic system, food within the digestive tract follows iron laws of consolidation and dispersal as "units" that may or may nor move into or out of the system at optimal "rates." Blood cholesterol levels become a matter of "the manufacture" and "distribut[ion]" of glucose, while fat and excess calories can be completely excised through a "constant restructuring" of corporate gullet.

Again, we're not dieting. We're exercising our God-given American right to maximize profitability.

At the other end of the diet-denial spectrum lies Victoria Moran's *Love Yourself Thin: The Revolutionary Spiritual Approach to Weight Loss.* This is not a book that proposes molecular layoffs so much as a "Love-powered release of weight." Only "Love can revolutionize your relationship with food," only love can regulate "your Love-powered cholesterol level."

What emerges here is a synthesis of our most dreaded national literary archetypes: one part mystico-spiritual 12-step recovery lingo, one part vacuous self-help pep talk, and the rest a miscellany of nutritional cliché: "Because you're worth the best, your way of eating will reflect the low-far, high-fiber, and high-carbohydrate recommendations of the surgeon general's report. . . ."

Whereas Atkins prescribes megadoses of vitamins to make up for all those vegetables you're not eating, Moran insists that "the most important nutritional element is vitamin YOU," which can only be "activated by contact with a Higher Power." In the killer corporate world of *SUGAR BUSTERS!*™ we feast on antelope and alligator. *Love Yourself Thin* is strictly vegan. "Spirituality is the inner side; gentle, natural food choices the outer."

Such a harmony between outer "food choices" and "inner nourishment" is essential to American gastrosophy. If all this sounds like a hokey rip-off of the sublime harmonic convergences of American Transcendentalism, that's because it is. "Your primary obligation," Moran flatly stares, is to neither family nor country but "to your own unfolding." Based on what you choose to put in your stomach, "you can establish your own unique connection with universal Love." And so it is that the dietary koans these best-selling authors are chanting align them with our great heritage of self-reliance. In the distant future Emerson and Thoreau will be known only as the shadowy precursors of Sears and Somers.

Yes, after centuries of airy theories promoting this country's ideal of privatized perfectionism, it is Suzanne Somers who descends from the clouds to that televised Promised Land, the Home Shopping Network. Our greatest indication that "the future harmony" is upon us is the presence of this bona fide prophetess, our luminous spirit in the electronic flesh.

Somers's Transcendental Zone is a misty never-never land of personal, economic, and domestic bliss meticulously documented on every over-produced page of her cloyingly warm and fuzzy modern gastrosophical masterpiece, *Get Skinny on Fabulous Food* (which reached number 1 on the *New York Times* list). Every square pica of the book is peppered with casual snapshots of Somers posing with "beautiful stuffed zucchini flowers" or her "darling granddaughter Daisy." "I can't give my home phone number to everyone," she laments, and we almost believe her.

Even without that phone number we can achieve intimacy through the act of "Somersizing." By this latest miracle in a long line of edible

American eucharists, we can becomne one with her perfect flesh. And there are tremendous dividends to such digestive election: once Somerizing is achieved, "any questions you have will be answered by your own body."

Any questions?

Like Walt Whitman, Suzanne Somers contains multitudes. Her dietary Vegas act parades everybody's routines. She co-opts Sears's technical language of insulin secretions into the bloodstream and outright steals his assertion that "cholesterol and far are essential to health." In the great tradition of Graham, she abhors "white flour," asserts a doctrine of "control" over diet, and insists that we must "reprogram our metabolism. Like Atkins, she blabs that "I eat whenever I am hungry. . . . I eat until I am full, and I never skip meals." She swallows whole and then regurgitates Steward's doctrine: *"sugar is the body's greatest enemy!"* Like Moran, she declares herself "a recovering sugar addict" and knowingly adds that we eat "to fill some emotional void." Like D'Adamo, she gushes that when her "cells thrive" she can "feel empowered."

And so Somers posits *Get Skinny on Fabulous Food* as the voice heard in the howling gastric wilderness, her own Ur-body as the redemptive core of all digestive effluvia.

For the litmus test of who we are is no longer our race, our gender, our creed, or even what we buy and sell. What we eat has become the ultimate form of identity politics. For the American grounds his agony and ecstasy, his desire and his insight, his most annoying neurotic obsessions along with his most sublime receptions of universal truth, within the organic mysterium of his maw, the ceaseless dilations and graspings of his intestines.

So now, as this bloated and intemperate millennium lurches toward its dyspeptic denouement, the cause of that lingering nausea, which churns from the esophagus to the cloaca of our collective gut, can finally be revealed. Transcendentalism has come and gone. American gastrosophy, its pimple-faced, oversize cousin, will endure.

FRANK J. PRIAL

E ACH DAY OF HIS THREE years' captivity in Lebanon, Jean-Paul Kauffmann recited to himself the names of the sixty-one chateaus in the 1855 clas-sification of the wines of Bordeaux. "I'd try to write them down on empty packets from Cedars, the revolting Lebanese cigarettes they gave us," said the French former hostage, "but I lost my list each time we were moved." Mr. Kauffmann's captors moved him eighteen times and eventually took away his pen.

"By the end of 1986," he said, "I began to forget some of the Fourth Growths, invariably Châteaux Pouget and Marquis-de-Terme." As time went on, he began to forget some of the Fifth Growths as well. (The 1855 classification organized the sixty-one chateaus into five groups, by quality and price.)

"Not to know the famous classification by heart was devastating:' Mr. Kauffmann recalled. "Was I losing all touch with civilization, becoming some kind of barbarian?"

When Moslem fanatics kidnapped Mr. Kauffmann near the Beirut airport on May 22, 1985, he had just arrived in Lebanon as a corre-spondent for the French newsmagazine *L'Évènement du Jeudi*. But Jean-Paul Kauffmann was also editor in chief of a small but influential wine magazine, *L'Amateur de Bordeaux,* which is published in Paris four times a year. In the most recent issue, published after his release last May, he recounts his long ordeal in a moving article.

"Could anything be more ridiculous," he wrote, "than the editor of *L'Amateur de Bordeaux* being kidnapped by fanatics of the Koran for whom the very word for wine, *nabid,* is an abomination. . . . I, who had loved the friendly, elegant world of Bordeaux, suddenly found myself in this brutal, elementary world.

"I who had loved the subtle shadows of the *chais*, redolent of the vanilla aroma of new oak barrels, was going to spend three years in a labyrinth of dark cells, a subterranean world of pain and suffering, a universe out of the drawings of Piranesi.

"During the entire three years," Mr. Kauffmann wrote, "I never forgot the taste of wine, even though it was no more than a memory, a fleeting sensation. I was Proust without a madeleine; my madeleine was my memory.

He compared his memory to the armoire of a dedicated wine collector. Each night, while his captors murmured prayers in the next room, he dreamed of Bordeaux. "How often I walked the roads of the Médoc," he wrote. "Fastened to my chain though I was, I never ceased to wander through the lovely hills of the Entre-Deux-Mers. I saw in my mind the rows of plane trees leading to Château Margaux, the Tuscan-style gardens of Yquem, the towers of Cos d'Estournel, the flowers at Giscours."

Through the long hours, he introduced his fellow prisoner, the sociologist Michel Seurat, to the mysteries of wine. "He taught me Kant and Hegel," Mr. Kauffmann said. "I talked of literature and the world of Bordeaux." Later, Mr. Kauffmann was to watch helplessly as his friend wasted away and died of cancer. At one point, the guards admitted another prisoner, the Jewish Lebanese physician Elie Hallak, to the cell to treat Mr. Seurat. Dr. Hallak had read about Jean-Paul Kauffmann and said, with a smile, "After we get out of here, you must teach me about wine." Later, the guards told Mr. Kauffmann that Dr. Hallak had been shot.

Before he became ill, Mr. Seurat received some books: a Bible, the collected novels of Jean-Paul Sartre, and Tolstoy's *War and Peace*. Over and over, the two prisoners discussed a passage in one of the Sartre novels, *Le Sursis*.

Two characters dine at Juan-les-Pins, on the Côte d'Azur, in 1938, drinking Château Margaux. In stirring words, one of the two, a painter, renounces his art and resolves to go off to Spain to join the Loyalists. Chained in their sweltering cell in Beirut, the two prisoners wondered which vintage of Margaux would have been served. Sartre didn't mention one. Eventually they settled on 1934.

"We decided that only a superb vintage could have inspired such rhetoric," Mr. Kauffmann wrote.

Several times, Mr. Kauffmann was moved to another prison in a metal coffin. Once, in 1987, after spending twelve hours in the box, he was sure his jailers had abandoned him. "If I get out of this nightmare alive," he promised God, "I will never again drink alcohol. But then, it occurred to me that life wouldn't be worth much without good Bordeaux, so I compromised on three months."

Even in the depths of his despair, Mr. Kauffmann noted later, he never completely gave up hope. His offer must have been acceptable because he was released from the coffin shortly thereafter. (True to his word, for the first three months after his release, he drank no alcohol.)

Two other hostages, Marcel Fontaine and Marcel Carton, both officers at the French embassy in Beirut, turned up later in 1985, to join what Mr. Kauffmann called "our fraternity of misery." Mr. Kauffmann undertook to teach his two new pupils about wine. Mr. Seurat was soon too ill to join in. "I don't feel like talking," he told the others, "but I enjoy listening to you."

Mr. Fontaine enjoyed Champagne, so Mr. Kauffmann composed a crossword puzzle for him that included the word "Ay." Ay is a famous Champagne village, the home of Deutz & Geldermann and Bollinger; it is also, for obvious reasons, a popular word in French crossword puzzles.

Mr. Carton knew and loved the town of Langon, not far from Sauternes, at the southern end of the Bordeaux region, and had occasionally bought wine from Pierre Coste, a prominent Langon wine shipper. Mr. Carton liked to recall one of his favorites: Château L'Étoile, an attractive white Graves.

"We knew hunger, cold, heat, fear," Mr. Kauffmann wrote, "but we never stopped talking about wine. It was our last connection with the world of the living."

WHAT BENGALI WIDOWS
CANNOT EAT

CHITRITA BANERJI

M Y FATHER DIED AT THE beginning of a particularly radiant and colorful spring. Spring in Bengal is teasing and elusive, secret yet palpable, waiting to be discovered. The crimson and scarlet of *palash* and *shimul* flowers post the season's banners on high trees. Compared to the scented flowers of the summer and monsoon—jasmine, *beli, chameli, kamini,* gardenias, all of which are white—these scentless spring flowers are utterly assertive with the one asset they have: color. My father, who was a retiring, unassuming man, took great pleasure in their flaunting, shameless reds. When I arrived in Calcutta for his funeral, I was comforted by the sight of the flowers in full bloom along the road from the airport.

That first evening back home, my mother and I sat out on our roof, talking. As darkness obscured all colors, the breeze became gusty, laden with unsettling scents from out-of-season potted flowers on neighboring roofs.

My mother had always been dynamic, forceful, efficient: the family's principal breadwinner for nearly thirty years, she had risen above personal anxiety and ignored social disapproval to allow me, alone, young and unmarried, to pursue my studies in the United States. Yet overnight, she had been transformed into the archetypal Bengali widow—meek, faltering, hollow-cheeked, sunken-eyed, the woman in white from whose life all color and pleasure must evaporate.

During the thirteen days of mourning that precede the Hindu rituals of *shraddha* (last rites) and the subsequent *niyambhanga* (literally, the breaking of rules), all members of the bereaved family live ascetically on one main meal a day of rice and vegetables cooked together in an earthen pot with no spices except sea salt, and no oil, only a touch of ghee. The sanction against oil embraces its cosmetic use too, and for me, the roughness of my mother's parched skin and hair made her colorless appearance excruciating. But what disturbed me most was the eagerness with which she seemed to be embracing the trappings of bereavement. Under the curious, observant and critical eyes of female relatives, neighbors and visitors, she appeared to be mortifying her flesh almost joyfully, as if those thirteen days were a preparation for the future. As if it is utterly logical for a woman to lose her self and plunge into a life of ritual suffering once her husband is dead.

Hindu tradition in Bengal holds that the widow must strive for purity through deprivation. In contrast with the bride, who is dressed in red and, if her family's means permit, decked out in gold jewellery, the widow, regardless of her wealth and status, is drained of color. Immediately after her husband's death, other women wash the *sindur,* a vermilion powder announcing married status, from the parting in the widow's hair. All jewellery is removed, and she exchanges her colored or patterned sari for the permanent, unvarying uniform of the *thaan,* borderless yards of blank white cotton. Thus transformed, she remains, for the rest of her life, the pallid symbol of misfortune, the ghostly twin of the western bride, dressed in virginal white, drifting down the aisle towards happiness.

As recently as fifty years ago, widows were also forced to shave their heads as part of a socially prescribed move towards androgyny. Both of my grandfather's sisters were widowed in their twenties: my childhood memories of them are of two nearly identical creatures wrapped in shroud-like white who emerged from their village a couple of times a year and came to visit us in the city. Whenever the *thaan* covering their heads slipped, I would be overcome with an urge to rub my hands over their prickly scalps that resembled the spherical, yellow, white-bristled flowers of the *kadam* tree in our garden.

Until the Hindu Widow Remarriage Act was passed in 1856, widows were forbidden to marry for a second time. But for more than a hundred years after the act became law, it did not translate into any kind of widespread social reality (unlike the 1829 edict abolishing the burning of widows on the same pyre as their dead husbands—the infamous practice of suttee). Rural Bengali households were full of widows who were no more than children, because barely pubescent girls often found themselves married to men old enough to be their fathers.

It was not until the morning before the actual *shraddha* ceremony that I was forced to confront the cruelest of the rules imposed on the widow by the Sanskrit *shastras,* the body of rules and rituals of Hindu life to which have been added innumerable folk beliefs. One of my aunts took me aside and asked if my mother had made up her mind to give up eating fish and meat—*amish,* non-vegetarian food, forbidden for widows. With a sinking heart, I realized that the image of the widow had taken such a hold of my mother that she was only too likely to embrace a vegetarian diet—all the more so because she had always loved fish and had been renowned for the way she cooked it. If I said nothing, she would never again touch those wonders of the Bengali kitchen—*shorshe-ilish, maacher jhol, galda chingrir malaikari, lau-chingri, doi-maach, maacher kalia.* It was an unbearable thought.

The vegetarian stricture is not considered a hardship in most regions of India where the majority, particularly the Brahmins and some of the upper castes, have always been vegetarians. But Bengal is blessed with innumerable rivers criss-crossing a fertile delta, and it is famed for its rice and its fish. Even Brahmins have lapsed in Bengal by giving in to the regional taste for fish, which plays a central part in both the diet and the culinary imagination of the country. Fish, in its ubiquity, symbolism and variety, becomes, for the Bengali widow, the finest instrument of torture.

Several other items are forbidden to widows simply because of their associations with *amish. Puishak,* for instance, a spinach-like leafy green often cooked with small shrimps or the fried head of a *hilsa* fish, is disallowed. So are onion and garlic, which were eschewed by most Hindus until the last century because of their association with meat-loving Muslims. They are further supposed to have lust-inducing properties, making them doubly unsuitable for widows. Lentils, a good source of protein in the absence of meat, are also taboo—a stricture which might stem from the widespread practice of spicing them with chopped onion.

Social historians have speculated that these dietary restrictions served a more sinister and worldly function than simply that of moving a widow towards a state of purity: they would also lead to malnutrition, thus reducing her lifespan. A widow often has property, and her death would inevitably benefit *someone*—her sons, her siblings, her husband's family. And in the case of a young widow, the sooner she could be dispatched to the next world, the less the risk of any moral transgression and ensuing scandal.

My grandmother lived the last twenty-seven of her eighty-two years as a widow, obeying every stricture imposed by rules and custom. The memory of her bleak, pinched, white-robed widowhood intensified my determination to prevent my mother from embracing a similar fate. I particularly remember a scene from my early teens. I was the only child living with an extended family of parents, uncles and aunts—and my grandmother. It had been a punishingly hot and dry summer. During the day, the asphalt on the streets would melt, holding on to my sandals as I walked. Night brought sweat-drenched sleeplessness and the absorbing itchiness of prickly heat. Relief would come only with the eagerly awaited monsoon.

The rains came early one morning—dark, violent, lightning-streaked, fragrant and beautiful. The cook rushed to the market and came back with a big *hilsa* fish which was cut up and fried, the crispy, flavorful pieces served at lunchtime with *khichuri,* rice and dhal cooked together. This is the traditional way to celebrate the arrival of the monsoon. Though I knew my grandmother did not eat fish, I was amazed on this occasion to see that she did nor touch either the *khichuri* or the battered slices of aubergine or the fried potatoes. These were vegetarian items, and I had seen her eat them before on other wet and chilly days. This time, she ate, in her usual solitary spot, *luchis,* a kind of fried bread, that looked stale, along with some equally unappetizing cold cookcd vegetables.

Why? I asked in outrage. And my mother explained that this was because of a rare coincidence: the rains had arrived on the first day of Ambubachi, the three-day period in the Bengali month of Asharh that, according to the almanac, marks the beginning of the rainy season. The ancients visualized this as the period of the earth's receptive fertility, when the summer sun vanishes, the skies open and mingle with the parched land to produce a red or brown fluid flow of earth and water, nature's manifestation of menstruating femininity. How right then for widows to suffer more than usual at such a time. They were not allowed to cook during the three-day period, and, although they were allowed to eat some foods that had been prepared in advance, boiled rice was absolutely forbidden. Since nature rarely conforms to the calculations of the almanac, I had never noticed these Ambubachi strictures being observed on the long-awaited rainy day.

The almanac was an absolute necessity for conforming to the standards of ritual purity, and my grandmother consulted it assiduously. On the day before Ambubachi started, she would prepare enough *luchis* and vegetables for three midday meals. Sweet yogurt and fruit, mixed with *chira*—dried, flattened rice—were also permissible. That first night of monsoon, newly aware of the sanctions of Ambubachi, I went to look for my grandmother around dinner time. All she ate was a small portion of *kheer,* milk that had been boiled down to nearly solid proportions, and some pieces of mango. I had hoped she would at least be permitted one of her favorite evening meals—warm milk mixed with crushed mango pulp. But no. Milk cannot be heated, for the widow's food must not receive the touch of fire during Ambubachi. The *kheer,* a traditional way of preserving milk, had been prepared for her the day before.

It is true that despite deprivations, household drudgery and the imposition of many fasts, widows sometimes live to a great age, and the gifted cooks among them have contributed greatly to the range, originality and subtlety of Hindu vegetarian cooking in Bengal. A nineteenth-century food writer once said that it was impossible to taste the full glory of vegetarian food unless your own wife became a widow. And Bengali literature is full of references to elderly widows whose magic touch can transform the most mundane or bitter of vegetables to nectar, whose subtlety with spices cannot be reproduced by other hands.

But however glorious these concoctions, no married woman envies the widow's fate. And until recently, most widows remained imprisoned within the austere bounds of their imposed diets. Even if they were consumed with temptation or resentment, fear of discovery and public censure were enough to inhibit them.

I knew the power of public opinion as I watched my mother during the day of the *shraddha.* My aunt, who had been widowed when fairly young, had been bold enough, with the encouragement of her three daughters, to continue eating fish. But I knew that my mother and many of her cronies would find it far less acceptable for a woman in her seventies not to give up *amish* in her widowhood. As one who lived abroad, in America, I also knew that my opinion was unlikely to carry much weight. But I was determined that she should not be deprived of fish, and with the support of my aunt and cousins I prepared to fight.

The crucial day of the *niyambhanga,* the third day after the *shraddha,* came. On this day, members of the bereaved family invite all their relatives to lunch, and an elaborate meal is served, representing the transition between the austerity of mourning and normal life—for everyone except the widow. Since we wanted to invite many people who were not relatives, we arranged to have two catered meals, lunch and dinner, the latter for friends and neighbors. My mother seemed to recover some of her former energy that day, supervising everything with efficiency, attending to all the guests. But she hardly touched any food. After the last guest had left, and the caterers had packed up their equipment, leaving enough food to last us for two or three days, I asked her to sit down and eat dinner with me. For the first time since my father's death, the two of us were absolutely alone in the house. I told her I would serve the food; I would be the grown-up now.

She smiled and sat down at the table. I helped her to rice and dhal, then to two of the vegetable dishes. She held up her hand then. No more. I was not to go on to the fish. Silently, we ate. She asked for a little more rice and vegetables. I complied, then lifted a piece of *rui* fish and held it over her plate. Utter panic filled her eyes, and she shot anxious glances around the room. She told me, vehemently, to eat the fish myself.

It was that panic-stricken look around her own house, where she was alone with me, her daughter, that filled me with rage. I was determined to vanquish the oppressive force of ancient belief, reinforced by whatever model of virtue she had inherited from my grandmother. We argued for what seemed like hours, my voice rising, she asking me to be quiet for fear of the neighbors, until finally I declared that I would never touch any *amish* myself as long as she refused to eat fish. The mother who could not bear the thought of her child's deprivation eventually prevailed, though the woman still quaked with fear of sin and retribution.

I have won a small victory, but I have lost the bigger battle. My mother's enjoyment of food, particularly of fish, as well as her joyful exuberance in the kitchen where her labors produced such memorable creations, have vanished. Sometimes, as I sit and look at her, I see a procession of silent women in white going back through the centuries. They live as household drudges, slaves in the kitchen and the field; they are ostracized even in their own homes during weddings or other happy ceremonies—their very presence considered an invitation to misfortune.

In the dim corners they inhabit, they try to contain their hunger. Several times a year, they fast and pray and prepare spreads for priests and Brahmins, all in the hope of escaping widowhood in the next life. On the eleventh day of each moon, they deny themselves food and water and shed tears over their blameful fate, while women with husbands make a joyous ritual out of eating rice and fish. Their anguish and anger secreted in the resinous chamber of fear, these white-clad women make their wasteful progress towards death.

CARA DE SILVA

I

No matter how many times Anny told the story, its power to affect her and her listeners never diminished. She was not a person who cried easily; yet even before she began to speak, her lively brown eyes would be brimful of tears.

"I remember so well the day the call came," she would say as she brushed the dampness from her timeworn cheeks, "because, in a way, it was my past at the other end of the line. 'Is this Anny Stern?' the woman on the phone asked me, and when I answered yes, she said, 'Then I have a package for you from your mother.'"

With those words, a quarter-century-long journey from the Czechoslovakian ghetto/concentration camp of Terezín (also known as Theresienstadt) to an apartment building on Manhattan's East Side came to an end.

Inside the package was a picture taken in 1939 of Anny's mother, Mina Pächter, and Anny's son, Peter (now called David). His arms are around her neck, her beautiful gray hair is swept back, and they are both smiling—but dark circles ring Mina's eyes.

There were letters, too—"Every evening I kiss your picture . . . please, Petrichku, don't forget me," Mina had written to her grandson. But it was a fragile, hand-sewn copy book that made up the bulk of the package, its cracked and crumbling pages covered with recipes in a variety of faltering scripts.

A cookbook born out of the abyss, it is a document most of us can comprehend only at the farthest reaches of our minds. Did setting down recipes bring comfort amid chaos and brutality? Did it bring hope for a future in which someone might prepare a meal from them again? We can not know. But certainly the creation of the cookbook was an act of psychological resistance, poignant testimony to the power of food to sustain us, not just physically but spiritually.

Food is who we are in the deepest sense, and not because it becomes blood and bone. Our personal gastronomic traditions—what we eat, the foods and foodways we associate with the rituals of childhood, marriage, and parenthood, moments around the table, celebrations—are critical components of our identity. To recall them in desperate circumstances is to reinforce a sense of self and to assist us in doing battle to preserve it. "My mother was already in her seventies at this time," said Anny, "yet this book shows that even in adversity her spirit fought on."

Among the weapons with which Mina and her co-authors fought were *Heu und Stroh*, fried noodles topped with raisins, cinnamon and vanilla cream; *Leber Knödel*, liver dumplings with a touch of ginger; *Kletzenbrot*, a rich fruit bread; and *Zenichovy Dort* or Groom's Cake. There were also *Erdäpfel Dalken* or Potato Doughnuts, and *Badener Caramell Bonbons*, Caramels from Baden—about eighty recipes in all. Some were hallmarks of Central European cookery. A few, like *Billige Echte Jüdische Bobe*, Cheap Real Jewish Coffee Cake, were specifically Jewish. And one, written down by Mina, is particularly poignant. For *Gefüllte Eier*, stuffed eggs with a variety of garnishes, the recipe is followed by the words, "Let fantasy run free."

"When first I opened the copybook and saw the handwriting of my mother, I had to close it," said Anny, describing the day she received the package. "I put it away and only much later did I have the courage to look. My husband and I we were afraid of it. It was something holy. After all those years, it was like her hand was reaching out to me from long ago."

In a way, it was. Just before Mina died in Theresienstadt she entrusted the package to a friend, Arthur Buxbaum, an antiques dealer, and asked him to get it to her daughter in Palestine. But there was a problem. Because most of Anny's letters hadn't reached Mina during the war, she couldn't provide him with an address.

Unable to honor his friend's deathbed request, Buxbaum simply kept the package. Then, one day in 1960, his cousin, Irma Buxbaum, told him she was leaving for Israel and, still mindful of his promise, he asked her to take the manuscript with her. However, by the time Irma got news of Anny and her husband, George Stern, they had moved to the United States to be near their son. No one knows exactly what happened after that, and Anny's account has uncertainties in it that can no longer be resolved. But a letter found in the package, and written in 1960, indicates that just as it had been entrusted to Irma to take to

Israel, Irma entrusted it to someone else to carry to New York. According to Anny, however, it didn't arrive until almost a decade later when a stranger from Ohio brought the package to a Manhattan gathering of Czechs and asked if anyone there knew the Sterns. "Yes, I think I do," responded one woman. A moment later she had become the parcel's final custodian. At last, Mina's deathbed gift to her daughter, her startling *kochbuch*, was to be delivered.

Its contents, written in the eliptical style characteristic of European cookery books, are evidence of the fact that the inmates of Terezín thought constantly about eating. "Food, memories of it, missing it, craving it, dreaming of it, in short, the obsession with food colors all the Theresienstadt memoirs," writes Ruth Schwertfeger, in *Women of Theresienstandt, Voices from a Concentration Camp.*

Bianca Steiner Brown, the translator of the recipes in this book, and herself a former inmate of Terezín, explains it this way: "In order to survive, you had to have an imagination. Fantasies about food were like a fantasy that you have about how the outside is if you are inside. You imagine it not only the way it really is but much stronger than it really is. I was, for instance, a baby nurse, and I worked at night and I looked out at night—Terezín was a town surrounded by walls, a garrison town—so I looked out at all the beds where the children were and, out of that window, I could look into freedom. And you were imagining things, like how it would be to run around in the grass outside. You knew how it was, but you imagined it even better than it was, and that's how it was with food, also. Talking about it helped you."

Most of us can grasp that concept. Far more disquieting is the idea that people who were undernourished, even starving, not only reminisced about favorite foods, but also had discussions, even arguments, about the correct way to prepare dishes they might never be able to taste again.

In fact, such behavior was frequent. Brown remembers women sharing recipes in their bunks late at night. "They would say, 'Do you know such and such a cake?'" she recounts. "'I did it in such and such a way.'"

"The hunger was so enormous that one constantly 'cooked' something that was an unattainable ideal and maybe somehow it was a certain help to survive it all," wrote Jaroslav Budlowsky, on a death march from Schwarzheide to Terezín in 1943. (The Budlowsky manuscript is at Beit Theresienstadt, the cultural center, library, and archive at Israel's Kibbutz Givat Chaim Ichud, founded by survivors of the ghetto/camp.)

And Susan Cernyak-Spatz, a professor at the University of North Carolina who was in Terezín and Auschwitz, describes people in both places as speaking of food so much that there was a camp expression for it. "We called it 'cooking with the mouth,' she says. "Everybody did it. And people got very upset if they thought you made a dish the wrong way or had the wrong recipe for it."

It is not far from there to setting down those recipes and Mina and her friends weren't the only ones to do it.

Two smaller manuscripts (one written entirely and one written partially in Theresienstadt) are in the possession of Beit Theresienstadt. And there are a number of other recipe collections known now, too, and almost certainly more at Israel's Yad Vashem, and elsewhere.

Of course, paper was a rare and highly desirable commodity in such stark circumstances ("If we had had paper at Auschwitz," said Israeli Sabina Margulies, "we would have written recipes down even there"), and, as a consequence, instructions on how to make a dish were inscribed on any kind of scrap available. Take, for example, the four-part manuscript in Yad Vashem. Authored by Malka Zimmet in Lenzing work camp in Austria (Lenzing was a sub-camp of Mauthausen), one section is written on multiple copies of a propaganda leaflet telling inmates that those who surround them "Hold the Reich against death and destruction, / stand and fight, a strong stock. / Our promise: Loyalty to the Führer. / Our slogan: Now more so." There are even recipes scrawled across the photograph of Hitler used to illustrate the leaflet.

Unlike Mina's cookbook, which seems to be an accretion of whatever individual contributors felt like setting down, Zimmet's has a classic cookbook format with specific kinds of dishes assigned to each of the four volumes. Writing in Czech and German, she gives recipes for appetizers, desserts, preserves and jams, puddings and fish, meats, vegetables, and specifically Jewish fare. Among the dishes are Karlsbad goulash with sour cream and sauerkraut; a Mikado torte made with caramelized sugar; a dish of carp and potatoes from Serbia; amd a matzo brei made with wine and prunes.

Of the other manuscripts, there are Arnotka Klein's and Jaroslav Budlovsky's, both in Beit Theresienstadt.

Klein writes of sacher torte and a Londoner Schnitten made with marmalade, grated almonds, flour, butter, sugar, eggs, and lemon rind.

Budlovsky, the engineer who began his notes on the death march, wrote recipes down alongside the terse record he kept of the places he and fellow prisoners were forced to walk and of what happened there. "Teichstadt, disappearance of the sick" is the notation for April 23rd, 1944.

He continued his notes after arriving in the ghetto. "This diary was brought to Theresienstadt and is therefore 100% from the time of the camp," he wrote, before he was transported to Auschwitz in December of the same year. Among the dishes he gives recipes for are fladen, small cakes made with goose fat or beef tallow and filled with cheese, ground figs, or chocolate.

While it was primarily women who recorded recipes during the war—just as it was primarily women who cooked at home—there were other cookbooks created by men. *A Wartime Log*, by Art and Lee Beltrone, an account of prisoner-of- war diaries kept during the Second World War, mentions the constant talk of food, the night dreams and daydreams caused by hunger, and the use of log books to write down recipes." Among these manuscripts was one created by American prisoners of war in a Japanese camp in the Philippines, and ultimately published in 1946 as *Recipes out of Bilibid*.

"Their thoughts were inevitably and ceaselessly focused on food," wrote Dorothy Wagner, in the book's foreword. "Discussion of its preparation and the heated arguments concerning the superiority of one method over another served as more than an anodyne for their tortured nerves. It strengthened their resolution to survive, if only because it made more vivid, not what they sought to escape from, but what they were resolved to return to."

The same was true for those in Terezín, of course, because for many the hope of a return to a normal existence was constant."My life right now is not easy but I suffer everything willingly in the hope of seeing you again," wrote Mina to Anny. But the Terezín cookbook also provided something else.

To a degree that may be unfathomable to Americans at the end of the twentieth century, cooking, both doing it and talking about it, was central to the societies from which many of the women of Terezín, and most European women of the period, came. It was also among the chief activities that defined them as wives and mothers.

Some cooked even in the ghetto, albeit in a limited way. "Theresienstadt really happened after May '42, when all civilians were out and we could move freely and women would try to make some kind of meal while putting rations together," says Cernyak-Spatz. (It was only after the Czechoslovak townspeople, who had occupied Terezin before its complete conversion, were gone that the Jews "could move freely.")

But a cookbook, even if only imaginatively, offered possibilities for "preparing" foods that were more culturally and psychologically meaningful. While written recipes might not feed the hungers of the body, they might temporarily quell the hungers of the soul.

Marion Kaplan in her article "Jewish Women in Nazi Germany: Daily Life, Daily Struggles, 1933-1939," supports this idea when she says that among the many actions of the League of Jewish Women to help its middle-class constituency through the hardships of daily life, and the readjustments required by a constantly deteriorating standard of living, was the production of a cookbook. "The league," she writes, "knew that people whose social and economic conditions had declined so rapidly needed psychological and material support. One creative way to resist demoralization was to publish a cookbook."

As for manuscript cookbooks, not only their contents, but even their familiar form may have brought a small amount of solace to those creating them. "It used to be the custom in Europe to make your own handwritten cookbooks," says Brown. "Probably if I had stayed in Prague and lived the life I left, I would also have started a manuscript cookbook exactly like this one." And the Czech Wilma Iggers, a retired professor of German literature who now focuses on Jewish social history, says, "I have a lot of handwritten cookbooks from my relatives, from my own Bohemian Jewish background. It was common."

Perhaps the authors of the Terezin cookbook were attempting to preserve this tradition. Perhaps getting the copybook to Anny was important to Mina because it resembled a family manuscript that she might once have given her herself.

But whatever its explicit or implicit functions, Mina's cookbook—and the others—make it clear that half a century after the Holocaust, when we thought we were familiar with all the ways in which human beings expressed themselves during the long years of horror, at least one small creative genre, the making of cookbooks, has gone largely unnoticed.

In the case of Mina's manuscript—a product of Terezin where cultural ferment was constant—such a demonstration of the domestic arts must also be seen as part of a larger artistic whole.

This surrealistic camp, positioned by the Nazis as a model ghetto, evidence of the Reich's benevolence toward the Jews, was the ultimate publicity ploy. Designed to distract the world from the final solution and all that preceded it, it was in fact a way station to the killing centers of the East and itself a place where many died.

The most dramatic example of this artifice was the "embellishment" undertaken for the inspection visit of the International Red Cross, when a portion of the population of Terezin was sent to their deaths in order to reduce the appearance of overcrowding. In addition, buildings were painted; flowers were planted; a carousel installed; and devious means used to create the impression that everyone had enough to eat. "There were four months of beautification before the Red Cross delegation came," says George Brown, interned in the ghetto at the time, and a lot of it was pretending there was food."

Paradoxically, Terezin was also a crucible of creativity. Among the multitude of Central Europeans whom the Reich sent to this "Paradise Ghetto" were painters, writers, musicians, intellectuals, composers, designers, and others who were too well known for their removal to less-deceptive places to go unremarked. Many contrived ways to continue their work, and because cultural activities fostered the illusion of a model camp, the Nazis generally turned a blind eye to such endeavors. As a consequence, there flourished in this bizarre environment an artistic and intellectual life so fierce, so determined, so vibrant, so fertile as to be almost unimaginable. Despite overcrowding that created pestilent conditions and in defiance of raging infections, a high death toll, and hunger—all as constant a presence as fear of the transports— here the flower of Central European Jewry participated in what those at Beit Theresienstadt have called "a revolt of the spirit."

They gave well-attended lectures; put on opera performances; composed music; performed cabaret; drew; painted; compiled a sixty-thousand-volume library; and attended to the education of the young with a fervor born of determination to keep Jewish life alive (and, for some, of determination to ready the young for a future they hoped they still might have in Palestine). "It was heroic, superhuman, the care given the children," says Cernyak-Spatz. "In the face of death, with the SS looking on, these people tried to persist intellectually and artistically."

The resulting juxtapositions overwhelm the mind—"Today, the milk froze in the pot," wrote Gonda Redlich, who kept a diary throughout his stay in Theresienstadt. "The cold is very dangerous. The children don't undress, and so there are a lot of lice in their quarters. Today, there was a premier performance of *The Bartered Bride*. It was the finest I had ever seen in the ghetto. (*The Terezin Diary of Gonda Redlich*, entry for November 25, 1942.)

This was what some have described as "the special reality" of Terezín, and Mina's *kochbuch*, a testament to a lost world and its flavors, was part of it.

Like most of the cuisines of the Austro-Hungarian empire, the Czechoslovakian kitchen, in which the majority of the writers appear to have been raised, placed great emphasis on the pleasures of the table. Robust, with sophisticated overtones, it was well-known for its soups; its roast birds and smoked meats; its love of savory sausages and wild mushrooms; its moderate use of spices (caraway and poppy seeds were popular); its goulash and weiner schnitzel; its large variety of dumplings (eaten from soup to dessert); cheeses such as hoop cheese (similar to a dry pot cheese); yeasted pastries (part of a great baking tradition); palachinky, sweet crepe-like pancakes; and, of course, its beer.

Food traditions overlapped with those of Hungary and especially Austria, but also with a number of other countries, the result of proximity and cultural exchange when they were all part of the Habsburg Empire. Some say it was the Czechoslovakians who benefitted the most, others that it was the other way around. "Bohemian cooks were held in high regard in Austria. They were always valued for their skill. The Viennese learned from us," says the Bohemian Iggers. Of course, Moravian cooks, too, have their fans.

Regardless of who influenced whom, Czechoslovakian cuisine was beloved, both beyond its natural geographic boundaries and within them, and eating, at least for the middle class, was a major pastime.

Listen to Joseph Wechsberg, the author of *Blue Trout & Black Truffles*, writing on Prague. "It was customary to have five meals a day. Breakfast was at half past seven in the morning. At ten o'clock, children had their *déjeuner à la fourchette*, sandwiches, sausages, hard-boiled eggs, fruit. Many men would go for half an hour to a beer house for a goulash or a dish of carved lungs and a glass of beer. Between ten and ten thirty little work was done in offices and shops; everybody was out eating. Two hours later, people were having lunch—at home, since eating lunch in a restaurant was unknown—and afterward they had a nap. Then to the coffee house for a demitasse and a game of whist or bridge, and back to the salt mines for an hour's work." Wechsberg also describes the custom of "A genuine, Central-European *jause*, several large cups of coffee topped with whipped cream, bread and butter, Torte or Guglhopf . . . and assorted pattiserie." In the countryside or in smaller cities, of course, customs would have been different, but no less enthusiastic.

What a contrast to the food on which contributors to the cookbook survived as they wrote their recipes. Provisions and the means of getting them varied somewhat over the time of Theresienstadt's existence, but some things appeared to have remained more-or-less constant. Ask a survivor about the fare and you are likely to be told of queuing outdoors for food—some say for as long as four or five hours even in inclement weather; of the daily ration of soup, variously described as tasteless to disgusting; of the sauce that some days might have a tiny bit of meat in it; of the loaf of bread that had to last three days; of the margarine; the barley; the turnips; and for those fortunate enough to get them, of the food packages from Gentile friends or Jewish organizations on the outside or, earlier on, from family or friends who were still free.

In his memoirs, published as *Theresienstadt, Hitler's Gift to the Jews*, Norbert Troller, one of the camp's most famous artists, speaks of salads made from weeds, and, in general, no fruits or vegetables were supplied to the population of Theresienstadt. In his diary entry for May 5, 1943, Gonda Redlich mentions a young girl who is sent to prison for five weeks for stealing a head of lettuce.

Cakes were also clever improvisations. Inge Auerbacher, who was a child during her time in the camp, writes in *I am a Star, Child of the Holocaust*, about having a palm-sized birthday cake made of mashed potato and a small amount of sugar. And Troller describes a "ghetto torte," saying it was particularly well made by a Mrs. Windholz whose version "tasted almost exactly like the famous Sachertorte. "The recipe was secret," he writes, "its ingredients . . . bread, coffee, saccharine, a trace of margarine, lots of good wishes, and an electric plate. Very impressive and irresistible."

Though food was sparse and often barely edible, and diseases caused by vitamin deficiencies were a constant problem, to some who went on to Auschwitz, such as Chernyak-Spatz or Mina's step-grand-daughter, Liesl Laufer, conditions in Terezin seemed not so bad. The camp's cultural life, described by Laufer as marvelous, also compensated for a great deal.

Others experienced the camp differently. "Like everyone else," Troller wrote, "I suffered greatly from hunger, so that I was plagued all through the day with thoughts of the kind of food I had been used to, as compared to the food we received. Until that time I had hardly ever suffered the pangs of hunger—I could fast for one day during Yom Kippur—but here, without any transition, our rations were shortened to such an extent (approximately one-third of the customary calories in their most unappetizing form) that hunger weakened and absorbed (one's) every thought."

But while almost all were hungry, some were more hungry than others. In the early days of Theresienstadt (May 1942), it had become clear to the Council of Jewish Elders, the group forced by the Nazis to run the internal affairs of the camp, that the limited food supplies could not be divided equally. They determined that those who labored at the hardest jobs had to be allotted more to eat than those whose work was less arduous and that children, the hope of the future, also had to be fed more than others.

They decided, too, that the fewest calories—and usually the worst accommodations—would have to go to those least likely to survive the ordeal of Terezín, namely, the elderly like Mina Pächter, who had been born in Southern Bohemia in 1872 . Such people were sacrificed so that others might live. "For younger people, Theresienstadt was bearable," says Liesl Laufer. "For older people, it was hell."

One must suppose that Mina passed many sorrowful nights remembering that, despite her daughter's entreaties, she had refused to accompany her when she left for Palestine late in 1939.

After almost a year spent expediting the emigration of Jews at the Prague branch of the Palestine Office under Adolf Eichmann and his staff, it had became increasingly clear to Anny that she and her son now had to leave themselves (her husband was already in Palestine). She pleaded with her mother to come, too, but Mina replied, "You don't move an old tree. Besides, who will do anything to old people?"

She was shortly and tragically to find out who.

How one fared in Theresienstadt depended, to a certain extent, on how well one could negotiate the system. Norbert Troller, for instance, traded portraits of the cooks and bakers to their subjects for extra food; others schemed to get jobs that permitted them greater access to provisions. But the elderly, "unlike the young workers," writes Zdenek Lederer in *Ghetto Theresienstadt*, "had no access to the food stores of the Ghetto, while their debility prevented them from making clandestine contacts with a view to acquiring some food.

"Starving elderly men and woman begged for watery soup made from synthetic lentil or pea powder, and dug for food in the garbage heaps rotting in the courtyard of the barracks," he writes. ". . . . In the morning, at noon, and before nightfall they patiently queued up for their food clutching saucepans, mugs or tins. They were glad to get a few gulps of hot coffee substitute and greedily ate their scanty meals. Then they continued their aimless pilgrimage, dragging along their emaciated bodies, their hands trembling and their clothes soiled."

"The decision [to reduce their rations] transformed many of the elderly into scavengers and beggars," writes George Berkley in *The Story of Theresienstadt*. "They would . . . pounce on any morsel of food such as a pile of potato skins, food considered fit only for pigs." (The scene was so common that it is frequently depicted by Terezín artists.) As a result of eating the raw peelings, many of the elderly developed severe enteritis and diarrhea, a chronic camp condition, but one especially common, and especially serious, among the aged.

No one knows for certain to what degree this describes Mina's life in Theresienstadt but we do know it was extremely hard. (Her family believes she escaped transportation only because during the First World War she had been given an order of merit from the German Red Cross for her aid to German soldiers passing through Czechoslovakia.)

By the time she was found, in the fall of 1943, by Liesl Laufer, who had been sent to Terezín earlier that year, Mina was suffering from protein deficiency, a condition that Liesl refers to as hunger edema. "An acquaintance of my parents told me where she was and she was in living quarters that were very bad," says Laufer, now a resident of Israel. "When I came, she was really in a poor state. She was suffering very badly from malnutrition. And I saw that she couldn't take care of herself anymore."

Because she was a nurse, Liesl was able to get Mina into the hospital, where she could take slightly better care of her. Hospitalization also meant that Liesl's husband, Ernest Reich, a doctor, could include Mina in his study of the effects of protein deficiency. Along with other patients, she was allotted two spoonfuls of white cheese a day (all that was available) to see what effect that small addition to her regular diet would have on her health. It was of little use.

Mina's fear, expressed in one of her poems, that no good would come to her in Terezín, proved true. She never got to kiss her grandson again. On Yom Kippur 1944, she died in the ghetto hospital.

II

Though written in recipes, the collective memoir that Mina and her friends left behind is, in some ways, as revealing as prose.

The contents, for example, reflect the fact that it was war time. One recipe is actually entitled *Kriegs Mehlspeise* or War Dessert; one, *Tobosch Torte*, calls for imitation honey, several others for coffee substitute, and many for margarine, which almost certainly would have been butter in peace time, when it was less scarce. Eggs were rationed and often appear in parentheses indicating that one should be used if you have it, but that such use is optional.

Actual shortages were probably much more acute. "Even before deportations began," writes Karel Lagus in *Terezín*, "the Jews were already being systematically starved under wartime rationing. Their ration books were stamped "J." On such rations books no white bread, meat, eggs, were issued. Jews were not allowed to receive any pulse, fruit, jam and marmalade, stewed fruit, cheese, and other dairy products, sweets, fish and fish products, poultry and game, yeast, sauerkraut, onions and garlic, honey, alcoholic drinks including beer, etc."

We can also tell from looking at the recipes, a number of which aren't Kosher, that, for the most part, they were likely to have been written by Jews from Bohemia and Moravia. Although Czechoslovakia certainly had Orthodox and observant Jews—"The religious split in town ran straight through the populace's Sunday menu: the Jews had Weiner Schnitzel, the Gentiles had roast pork with sauerkraut and dumplings," wrote Joseph Wechsberg of Prague—Bohemian Jews in general were among the most assimilated in Europe. For many, this meant that Jewishness was maintained through tradition and, perhaps, holiday *shul*-going rather than through observance of the Kosher laws.

Moreover, though the manuscript doesn't impart biographical details, if we didn't already know the condition its authors were in and the circumstances under which their cookbook had been created, we could still discern their distress from the recipes. Although, occasionally, as you turn the pages you hear the precious sound of the authors' voices rising above the pit. "Sehr gut," "Very good," writes one contributor of her cake. "Let fantasy run free," says Mina in her *Gefüllte Eier*. It is far more common to hear them in its depths.

Whether out of starvation-induced illness or weakness, an unsettling interruption, or the discovery that a contributor's name was on a transport list, a number of the recipes are muddled or incomplete. In some, an ingredient is left out (the bean torte, for instance, usually requires an egg; the cream strudel has no dough); in others a process is omitted (dumplings are made and sauced without ever being cooked). Steps are inverted and punctuation, too, is nonexistent or perplexing.

These are recipes that bear witness.

"The farther it is away, the worse it gets, this enormous thing that happened to the Jews," said Anny late one afternoon as she clutched the cookbook in her elegant hands. "When you look in the cauldron, you can't believe what was in it. Yet here is the story of how the inmates of the camp, living on bread and watery soup and dreaming of the cooking habits of the past, found some consolation in the hope that they might be able to use them again in the future. By sharing these recipes, I am honoring the thoughts of my mother and the others that there must be, somewhere and somehow, a better world to live in."

A PLEA FOR CULINARY MODERNISM: WHY WE SHOULD LOVE MODERN, FAST, PROCESSED FOOD

RACHEL LAUDAN

MODERN, FAST, PROCESSED FOOD is a disaster. That, at least, is the message, conveyed by newspapers and magazines, on television cooking programs and in prizewinning cookbooks. It is a mark of sophistication to bemoan the steel roller mill and supermarket bread, yearning for stone ground flour and brick ovens; to seek out heirloom apples and pumpkins, while despising modern tomatoes and hybrid corn; to be hostile to agronomists who develop high yielding modern crops, and to home economists who invent new recipes for General Mills. We hover between ridicule and shame when we remember how our mothers and grandmothers enthusiastically embraced canned and frozen foods. We nod in agreement when the waiter proclaims that the restaurant showcases the freshest local produce. We shun Wonder Bread and Coca-Cola. Above all, we loathe the great culminating symbol of Culinary Modernism, McDonald's— modern, fast, homogenous, and international.

Like so many of my generation, my culinary style was created by those who scorned industrialized food; Culinary Luddites, we may call them, after the English hand workers of the nineteenth century who abhorred the machines that were destroying their traditional way of life. I learned to cook from the books of Elizabeth David who urged us to sweep our store cupboards "clean forever of the cluttering debris of commercial sauce bottles and all synthetic flavorings." I progressed to the Time-Life *Good Cook* series and to *Simple French Cooking* in which Richard Olney hoped against hope that "the reins of stubborn habit are strong enough to frustrate the famous industrial revolution for some time to come." I turned to Paula Wolfert to learn more about

Mediterranean cooking and was assured that I wouldn't "find a dishonest dish in this book . . . The food here is real food, . . . the real food of real people." Today I rush to the newsstand to pick up *Saveur* with its promise to teach me to "Savor a world of authentic cuisine."

Culinary Luddism involves more than just taste. Since the days of the counterculture, it has also presented itself as a moral and political crusade. Now in Boston, the Oldways Preservation and Exchange Trust works to provide "a scientific basis for the preservation and revitalization of traditional diets." Meanwhile Slow Food, founded in 1989 to protest the opening of a McDonald's in Rome, is a self-described Green Peace for Food; its manifesto begins "we are enslaved by speed and have all succumbed to the same insidious virus: Fast Life, which disrupts our habits, pervades the privacy of our homes and forces us to eat Fast Foods . . . Slow Food is now the only truly progressive answer." As one of its spokesmen was reported as saying in the *New York Times*, "Our real enemy is the obtuse consumer."

At this point I begin to back off. I want to cry "Enough!" But why? Why would I, who learnt to cook from Culinary Luddites, who grew up in a family that, in Elizabeth David's words, produced their "own home-cured bacon, ham and sausages . . . churned their own butter, fed their chickens and geese, cherished their fruit trees, skinned and cleaned their own hares" (well, to be honest, not the geese and sausages) not rejoice at the growth of Culinary Luddism? Why would I (or anyone else) want to be thought an "an obtuse consumer"? Or admit to preferring unreal food for unreal people? Or to savoring inauthentic cuisine?

The answer is not far to seek: because I am a historian. As a historian I cannot accept the account of the past implied by Culinary Luddism, a past sharply divided between good and bad, between the sunny rural days of yore and the gray industrial present. My enthusiasm for Luddite kitchen wisdom does not carry over to their history, any more than my response to a stirring political speech inclines me to accept the orator as scholar. The Luddites' fable of disaster, of a fall from grace smacks more of wishful thinking than of digging through archives. It gains credence not from scholarship but from evocative dichotomies: fresh and natural versus processed and preserved, local versus global, slow versus fast, artisanal and traditional instead of urban and industrial, healthful versus contaminated and fatty. History shows, I believe, that the Luddites have things back to front.

That food should be fresh and natural has become an article of faith. It comes as something of a shock to realize that this is a latter-day creed. For our ancestors, natural was something quite nasty. Natural often tasted bad. Fresh meat was rank and tough, fresh milk was warm and unmistakably a bodily excretion, fresh fruits (dates and grapes being rare exceptions outside the tropics) were inedibly sour, fresh vegetables were bitter. Even today, natural can be a shock when we actually encounter it. When the well-known chef, Jacques Pepin, offered free-range chickens to friends, they found "the flesh tough and the flavor too strong" prompting him to wonder whether they would really like things the way the naturally used to be.

Natural was unreliable. Fresh fish began to stink, fresh milk soured, eggs went rotten. Everywhere seasons of plenty were followed by seasons of hunger when the days were short, the weather turned cold, or the rain did not fall. Hens stopped laying eggs, cows went dry, fruits and vegetables were not to be found, fish could not be caught in the stormy seas. Natural was usually indigestible. Grains, which supplied from fifty to ninety per cent of the calories in most societies, have to be threshed, ground and cooked to make them edible. Other plants, including the roots and tubers that were the life support of the societies that did not eat grains, are often downright poisonous. Without careful processing, green potatoes, stinging taro, cassava bitter with prussic acid are not just indigestible, but toxic.

Nor did our ancestors' physiological theories dispose them to the natural. Until about two hundred years ago, from China to Europe, and in Mesoamerica too, everyone believed that the fires in the belly cooked foodstuffs and turned them into nutrients. That was what digesting was. Cooking foods in effect pre-digested them and made them easier to assimilate. Given a choice, no one would burden the stomach with raw, unprocessed foods.

So to make food tasty, safe, digestible and healthy, our forebears bred, ground, soaked, leached, curdled, fermented, and cooked naturally occurring plants and animals until they were literally beaten into submission. To lower toxin levels, they cooked plants, they treated them with clay (the Kaopectate effect), they leached them with water, acid fruits and vinegars, and alkaline lye. They intensively bred maize to the point that it could not reproduce without human help. They created sweet oranges, juicy apples, and non-bitter legumes, happily abandoning their more natural but less tasty ancestors. They built granaries for their grain, dried their meat and their fruit, salted and smoked their fish, curdled and fermented their dairy products, and cheerfully used whatever additives and preservatives they could-sugar, salt, oil, vinegar, lye—to make edible foodstuffs. In the twelfth century, the Chinese sage Wu Tzu-mu listed the six foodstuffs essential to life: rice, salt, vinegar, soy sauce, oil, and tea. Four had been unrecognizably transformed from their naturally occurring state. Who could have imagined vinegar as rice that had been fermented to ale and then soured? Or soy sauce as cooked and fermented beans? Or oil as the extract of crushed cabbage seeds? Or bricks of tea as leaves that had been killed by heat, powdered and compressed? Only salt and rice had any claim to fresh or natural and even then the latter had been stored for months or years, threshed, and husked.

Processed and preserved foods kept well, were easier to digest, and were delicious: raised white bread instead of chewy wheat porridge; thick, nutritious, heady beer instead of prickly grains of barley; unctuous olive oil instead of a tiny, bitter fruit; soy milk, sauce and tofu instead of dreary, flatulent soy beans; flexible, fragrant tortillas instead of dry, chewy maize; not to mention red wine, blue cheese, sauerkraut, hundred-year-old eggs, Smithfield hams, smoked salmon, yogurt, sugar, chocolate, and fish sauce.

Eating fresh, natural food was regarded with suspicion verging on horror, something to which only the uncivilized, the poor and the starving resorted. When the compiler of the Confucian classic, the *Book of Rites* (ca. 200 B.C.), distinguished the first humans—people who had no alternative to wild, uncooked foods—from civilized peoples who took "advantage of the benefits of fire . . . [who] toasted, grilled, boiled, and roasted," he was only repeating a commonplace. When the ancient Greeks took it as a sign of bad times if people were driven to eat greens and root vegetables, they too were rehearsing common wisdom. Happiness was not a verdant Garden of Eden abounding in fresh fruits but a securely locked storehouse jammed with preserved, processed foods.

Local food was greeted with about as much enthusiasm as fresh and natural. Local foods were the lot of the poor who could not escape the tyranny of local climate and biology, nor the monotonous, often precarious, diet it afforded. Meanwhile the rich, in search of a more varied diet, bought, stole, wheedled, robbed, taxed, and ran off with appealing plants and animals, foodstuffs, and culinary techniques from wherever they could find them.

By the fifth century B.C., Celtic princes in the region of France now known as Burgundy were enjoying a glass or two of Greek wine, drunk from silver copies of Greek drinking vessels. The Greeks themselves looked to the Persians, acclimatizing their peaches and apricots and citrons, and emulating their rich sauces, while in turn the Romans hired Greek cooks. From around the time of the birth of Christ, the wealthy in China, India and the Roman Empire paid vast sums for spices brought from the distant and mysterious Spice Islands. From the seventh century A.D., Islamic caliphs and sultans transplanted sugar, rice, citrus and a host of other Indian and Southeast Asian plants to Persia and the Mediterranean, transforming the diets of West Asia and the shores of the Mediterranean. In the thirteenth century, the Japanese had naturalized the tea plant of China and were importing sugar from Southeast Asia. In the seventeenth century, the European rich drank sweetened coffee, tea and cocoa in Chinese porcelain, imported or imitation, proffered by servants in Turkish or other foreign dress. To ensure their own supply, the French, the Dutch and the English embarked on imperial ventures and moved millions of Africans and Asians around the globe. The Swedes, who had no empire, had a hard time getting these exotic foodstuffs, so the eighteenth-century botanist Linnaeus set afoot plans to naturalize the tea plant in Sweden.

We may laugh at the climatic hopelessness of his proposal. Yet it was no more ridiculous than other, more successful, proposals to naturalize Southeast Asian sugarcane throughout the tropics, apples in Australia, grapes in Chile, Hereford cattle in Colorado and Argentina, and Caucasian wheat on the Canadian prairie. Without our aggressively global ancestors, we would all still be subject to the tyranny of the local.

As for slow food, it is easy to wax nostalgic about a time when families and friends met to relax over delicious food and to forget that, far from being an invention of the late-twentieth century, fast food has been a mainstay of every society. Hunters tracking their prey, fishermen at sea, shepherds tending their flocks, soldiers on campaign, and farmers rushing to get in the harvest all needed food that could be eaten quickly and away from home. The Greeks roasted barley and ground it into a meal to eat straight or mixed with water, milk or butter (as the Tibetans still do), while the Aztecs ground roasted maize and mixed it with water to make an instant beverage (as the Mexicans still do).

City dwellers, above all, relied on fast food. When fuel cost as much as the food itself, when huddled dwellings lacked cooking facilities, and when cooking fires might easily conflagrate entire neighborhoods, it made sense to purchase your bread or noodles, and a little meat or fish to liven them up. Before the birth of Christ, Romans were picking up honey cakes and sausages in the Forum. In twelfth-century Hangchow, the Chinese downed noodles, stuffed buns, bowls of soup, and deep-fried confections. In Baghdad of the same period, the townspeople bought ready-cooked meats, salt fish, bread, and a broth of dried chickpeas. In the sixteenth century, when the Spanish arrived in Mexico, Mexicans had been enjoying tacos from the market for generations. In the eighteenth century, the French purchased cocoa, apple turnovers, and wine in the boulevards of Paris, while the Japanese savored tea, noodles and stewed fish in the streets of Edo.

Deep-fried foods, expensive and dangerous to prepare at home, have always had their place on the street: donuts in Europe, churros in Mexico, andagi in Okinawa, and sev in India. Bread, also expensive to bake at home, was one of the oldest convenience foods. For many people in west Asia and Europe, a loaf fresh from the baker was the only warm food of the day. To these venerable traditions of fast food, Americans have simply added the electric deep fryer, the heavy iron griddle of the Low Countries, and the franchise. The McDonald's in Rome was, in fact, just one more in a long tradition of fast food joints reaching back to the days of the Caesars.

What about the idea that the best food was country food, handmade by artisans? That food came from the country goes without saying. The presumed corollary—that country people ate better than city dwellers—does not. Few who worked the land were independent peasants baking their own bread, brewing their own wine or beer, and salting down their own pig. Most were burdened with heavy taxes and rents, paid in kind (that is, food), or worse, they were indentured, serfs, or slaves. Barely part of the cash economy, they subsisted on what was left over. "The city dwellers," remarked the great Roman doctor Galen in the second century A.D., "collected and stored enough grain for all the coming year immediately after the harvest. They carried off all the wheat, the barley, the beans and the lentils and left what remained to the countryfolk."

What remained was pitiful. All too often, those who worked the land got by on thin gruels and gritty flat breads. North of the Alps, French peasants prayed that chestnuts would be sufficient to sustain them from the time when their grain ran out to the harvest still three months away. South of the Alps, Italian peasants suffered skin eruptions, went mad, and in the worst cases died of pellagra brought on by a diet of maize polenta and water. The dishes we call ethnic and assume to be of peasant origin were invented for the urban, or at least urbane, aristocrats who collected the surplus. This is as true of the lasagne of northern Italy, as it is of the chicken korma of the Mughal Delhi, the moo shu pork of imperial China, the pilafs, stuffed vegetables, and baklava of the great Ottoman palace in Istanbul, or the mee krob of the nineteenth-century Bangkok. Cities have always enjoyed the best food and have invariably been the focal points of culinary innovation.

Nor are most "traditional foods" very old. For every prized dish that goes back two thousand years, a dozen have been invented in the last two hundred. The French baguette? A twentieth-century phenomenon, adopted nationwide only after World War II. English fish and chips? Dates from the late-nineteenth century, when the working class took up the fried fish of Sephardic Jewish immigrants in East London. Fish and chips, though, will soon be a thing of the past. It's a Balti and lager now, Balti being a kind of stir-fried curry dreamed up by Pakistanis living in Birmingham. Greek moussaka? Created in the early-twentieth century in an attempt to Frenchify Greek food. The bubbling Russian samovar? Late-eighteenth century. The Indonesian rijstafel? Dutch colonial food. Indonesian padang food? Invented for the tourist market in the past fifty years. Tequila? Promoted as the national drink of Mexico during the 1930s by the Mexican film industry. Indian tandoori chicken? The brainwave of Hindu Punjabis who survived by selling chicken cooked in a Muslim-style tandoor oven when they fled Pakistan for Delhi during the Partition of India. The soy sauce, steamed white rice, sushi and tempura of Japan? Commonly eaten only after the middle of the nineteenth century. The lomilomi salmon, salted salmon rubbed with chopped tomatoes and spring onions, which is a fixture in every Hawaiian luau? Not a salmon is to be found within two thousand miles of the islands and onions and tomatoes were unknown in Hawaii until the nineteenth century. These are indisputable facts of history though if you point them out you will be met with stares of disbelief.

Not only were many 'traditional' foods created after industrialization and urbanization; a lot of them were dependent on it. The Swedish smorgasbord came into its own at the beginning of the twentieth century when canned out-of-season fish, roe, and liver paste made it possible to set out a lavish table. Hungarian goulash was unknown before the nineteenth century, not widely accepted until after the invention of a paprika-grinding mill in 1859.

When lands were conquered, peoples migrated, populations converted to different religions or accepted new dietary theories, whole cuisines were forgotten and new ones invented. Where now is the cuisine of Renaissance Spain and Italy, or of the Indian Raj, or of Tsarist Russia, or of medieval Japan? Instead we have Nonya food in Singapore, Cape Malay food in South Africa, Creole food in the Mississippi Delta and Local Food in Hawaii. How long does it take to create a cuisine? Not long: less than fifty years, judging by past experience.

Were old foods more healthful than ours? Inherent in this vague notion are several different claims, among them that foods were less dangerous, that diets were better balanced. Yet while we fret about pesticides on apples, mercury in tuna, and mad cow disease, we should remember that ingesting foods is, and has always been, inherently dangerous. Many plants contain both toxins and carcinogens, often at levels much higher than any pesticide residues. Grilling and frying add more. Some historians argue that bread made from moldy, verminous flour, or adulterated with mash, leaves or bark to make it go further, or contaminated with hemp or poppy seeds to drown out sorrows meant that European poor of five hundred years ago staggered around in a drugged haze subject to hallucinations. Certainly many of our forebears were drunk much of the time, given that they preferred beer or wine to polluted water. In the cities, unhygienic water supplies brought intestinal diseases in their wake. In France, for example, no piped water was available until the 1860s. Bread was likely to be stretched with chalk, pepper adulterated with the sweepings of warehouse floors, and sausage stuffed with all the horrors famously exposed by Upton Sinclair in *The Jungle*. Even the most reputable cookbooks recommended using concentrated sulfuric acid to intensify the color of jams. Milk, suspected of spreading scarlet fever, typhoid, and diphtheria as well as tuberculosis, was sensibly avoided well into the twentieth century when the United States and many parts of Europe introduced stringent regulations. My mother sifted weevils from the flour bin; my aunt reckoned that if the maggots could eat her home-cured ham and survive, so could the family.

As to dietary balance, once again we have to distinguish rich and poor. The rich, whose bountiful tables and ample girths were visible evidence of their station in life, suffered many of the diseases of excess. In the seventeenth century, the Mughal Emperor, Jahangir, died of overindulgence in food, opium and alcohol. In Georgian England, George Cheyne, the leading doctor, had to be wedged in and out of his carriage by his servants when he soared to four hundred pounds while a little later Erasmus Darwin, grandfather of Charles and another important physician, had a semicircle cut out of his dining table to accommodate his paunch. In the nineteenth century, the fourteenth shogun of Japan died at age twenty-one, probably of beriberi induced by eating the white rice available only to the privileged. In the Islamic countries, India and Europe the well-to-do took sugar as a medicine, in India they used butter; in much of the world they avoided fresh vegetables, all on medical advice.

Whether the peasants really starved, and if so how often, particularly outside Europe, is the subject of ongoing research. What is clear is that the food supply was always precarious: if the weather was bad or war broke out, there might not be enough to go around. The end of winter or the dry season saw everyone suffering from the lack of fresh fruits and vegetables, scurvy occurring on land as well as at sea. By our standards, the diet was scanty for people who were engaged in heavy physical toil. Estimates suggest that in France on the eve of the Revolution one in three adult men got by on no more than 1,800 calories a day, while a century later in Japan daily intake was perhaps 1,850 calories. Historians believe that in times of scarcity peasants essentially hibernated during the winter. It is not surprising, therefore, that in France the proudest of boasts was "there is always bread in the house," while the Japanese adage advised that "all that matters is a full stomach."

By the standard measures of health and nutrition—life expectancy and height—our ancestors were far worse off than we are. Much of the blame was due to the diet, exacerbated by living conditions and infections that affect the body's ability to use the food that is ingested. No amount of nostalgia for the pastoral foods of the distant past can wish away the fact that our ancestors lived mean, short lives, constantly afflicted with diseases, many of which can be directly attributed to what they did and didn't eat.

Historical myths, though, can mislead as much by what they don't say as by what they do. Culinary Luddites typically gloss over the moral problems intrinsic to the labor of producing and preparing food. In 1800, ninety-five percent of the Russian population and eighty percent of the French lived in the country; in other words, they spent their days getting food on the table for themselves and other people. A century later, eighty-eight percent of Russians, eighty-five percent of Greeks, and over fifty percent of the French were still on the land. Traditional societies were aristocratic, made up of the many who toiled to produce, process, preserve, and prepare food, and the few who, supported by the limited surplus, could do other things.

In the great kitchens of the few—royalty, aristocracy and rich merchants—cooks created elaborate cuisines. The cuisines drove home the power of the mighty few with the symbol that everyone understood: ostentatious shows of more food than the powerful could possibly consume. Feasts were public occasions for the display of power, not private occasions for celebration, for enjoying food for food's sake. The poor were invited to watch, groveling as the rich gorged themselves. Louis XIV was exploiting a tradition going back to the Roman Empire when he encouraged spectators at his feasts. Sometimes, to hammer home the point while amusing the court, the spectators were let loose on the leftovers. "The destruction of so handsome an arrangement served to give another agreeable entertainment to the court," observed a commentator, "by the alacrity and disorder of those who demolished these castles of marzipan, and these mountains of preserved fruit."

Meanwhile most men were born to a life of labor in the fields, most women to a life of grinding, chopping, and cooking. "Servitude," said my mother as she prepared home-cooked breakfast, dinner and tea for eight to ten people three hundred and sixty five days a year. She was right. Churning butter and skinning and cleaning hares, without the option of picking up the phone for a pizza if something goes wrong, is unremitting, unforgiving toil. Perhaps, though, my mother did not realize how much worse her lot might have been. She could at least buy our bread from the bakery. In Mexico, at the same time, women without servants could expect to spend five hours a day—one third of their waking hours—kneeling at the grindstone preparing the dough for the family's tortillas. Not until the 1950s did the invention of the tortilla machine release them from the drudgery.

In the eighteenth and early-nineteenth centuries, it looked as if the distinction between gorgers and grovelers would worsen. Between 1575 and 1825 world population had doubled from 500 million to a billion, and it was to double again by 1925. Malthus sounded his dire predictions. The poor, driven by necessity or government mandate, resorted to basic foods that produced bountifully even if they were disliked: maize and sweet potatoes in China and Japan, maize in Italy, Spain and Romania, potatoes in northern Europe. They eked out an existence on on porridges or polentas of maize or oats, on coarse breads of rye or barley bulked out with chaff, or even clay and ground bark, and on boiled potatoes; they saw meat only on rare occasions. The privation continued. In Europe, 1840 was a year of hunger, best remembered now as the time of the devastating potato famine of Ireland. Meanwhile the rich continued to indulge, feasting on white bread, meats, rich fatty sauces, sweet desserts, exotic hothouse-grown pineapples, wine, and tea, coffee and chocolate sipped from fine china. In 1845, shortly after revolutions had rocked Europe, the British prime minister, Benjamin Disraeli described "two nations, between whom there is no intercourse and no sympathy . . . who are formed by a different breeding, are fed by a different food, are ordered by different manners, and are not governed by the same laws . . . THE RICH AND THE POOR."

In the nick of time, in the 1880s, the industrialization of food got under way long after the industrialization of the other common items of consumption, textiles and clothing. Farmers brought new land into production, utilized reapers and later tractors and combines, spread more fertilizer, and by the 1930s began growing hybrid maize. Steamships and trains brought fresh and canned meats, fruits, vegetables and milk to the growing towns. Instead of starving, the poor of the industrialized world survived and thrived. In Britain the retail price of food in a typical workman's budget fell by a third between 1877 and 1887 (though he would still spend seventy-one percent of his income on food and drink). In 1898 in the United States a dollar bought forty-two percent more milk, fifty-one percent more coffee, a third more beef, twice as much sugar and twice as much flour as in 1872. By the beginning of the twentieth century, the British working class were eating white bread spread with jam and margarine, canned meats, sugary tea drunk from china teacups, canned pineapple, and an orange from the Christmas stocking.

To us, the cheap jam, the margarine, the starchy diet look pathetic. Yet white bread did not cause the "weakness, indigestion, or nausea" that coarse whole wheat bread did when it supplied most of the calories (not a problem for us since we never consume it in such quantities). Besides it was easier to detect stretchers such as sawdust in white bread. Margarine and jam made the bread more attractive and easier to swallow. Sugar tasted good and hot tea in an unheated house in mid-winter provided cheer. For those for whom fruit had been available, if at all, only from June to October, canned pineapple and a Christmas orange were treats to be relished. For the diners, therefore, the meals were a dream come true, a first step away from a coarse, monotonous diet and the constant threat of hunger, even starvation.

Nor should we just think it was only the British, not famed for their cuisine, who were delighted with industrialized foods. Everyone was, whether American, Asian, African or European. In the first half of the twentieth century, Italians embraced factory-made pasta and canned tomatoes. In the second half of the century, Japanese women welcomed factory-made bread because they could sleep in a little longer instead of having to get up to make rice. Mexican women seized on bread as good food to have on hand when there was no time to make tortillas. Working women in India are happy to serve commercially-made pita bread during the week, saving the time-consuming business of making chapatis for the weekend. As supermarkets appeared in East Europe and in Russia, housewives rejoiced at the choice and convenience of ready-made foods. For all, Culinary Modernism had provided what was wanted: food that was processed, preservable, industrial, novel, and fast, the food of the elite at a price everyone could afford. Where modern food became available, populations grew taller, stronger, had fewer diseases, and lived longer. Men had choices other than hard agricultural labor, women other than kneeling at the metate five hours a day.

So the sunlit past of the Culinary Luddites never existed. So their ethos is based not on history but on a fairy tale. So what? Perhaps we now need this culinary philosophy. Certainly no one would deny an industrialized food supply has its own problems, problems we hear about every day. Perhaps we should eat more fresh, natural, local, artisanal, slow food. Why not create a historical myth to further that end? The past is over and gone. Does it matter if the history is not quite right?

It matters quite a bit, I believe. If we do not understand that most people had no choice but to devote their lives to growing and cooking food, we are incapable of comprehending that the foods of Culinary Modernism—egalitarian, available more or less equally to all, without demanding the disproportionate amount of the resources, either in terms of time or money that traditional foodstuffs did—allow us unparalleled choices not just of diet but of what to do with our lives. If we urge the Mexican to stay at her metate, the farmer to stay at his olive press, the housewife to stay at her stove instead of going to McDonald's, all so that we may eat handmade tortillas, traditionally pressed olive oil, and home-cooked meals, we are assuming the mantle of the aristocrats of old. We are reducing the options of others as we attempt to impose our elite culinary preferences on the rest of the population.

If we fail to understand how scant and how monotonous most traditional diets were, we can misunderstand the "ethnic foods" we encounter in cookbooks, restaurants, or on our travels. We let our eyes glide over the occasional references to servants, to travel and education abroad in so-called ethnic cookbooks, references that otherwise would clue us in to the fact that the recipes are those of monied Italians, Indians or Chinese with maids to do the donkey work of preparing elaborate dishes. We may mistake the meals of today's European, Asian or Mexican middle class (many of them benefiting from industrialization and contemporary tourism) for peasant food or for the daily fare of our ancestors. We can represent the peoples of the Mediterranean, Southeast Asia, India or Mexico as pawns at the mercy of multinational corporations bent on selling trashy modern products—failing to appreciate that, like us, they enjoy a choice of products in the market, foreign restaurants to eat at, and new recipes to try. A Mexican friend, suffering from one too many foreign visitors who chided her because she offered Italian, not Mexican food, complained "Why can't we eat spaghetti too?"

If we unthinkingly assume that good food maps neatly on to old or slow or homemade food (even though we've all had lousy traditional cooking), we miss the fact that lots of industrial foodstuffs are better. Certainly no one with a grindstone will ever produce chocolate as suave as that produced by conching in a machine for seventy-two hours. Nor is the housewife likely to turn out fine soy sauce or miso. And let us not forget that the current popularity of Italian food owes much to the availability of two convenience foods that even purists love, high-quality factory pasta and canned tomatoes. Far from fleeing them, we should be clamoring for more high-quality industrial foods.

If we romanticize the past, we may miss the fact that it is the modern, global, industrial economy (not the local resources of the wintry country around New York, Boston or Chicago) that allows us to savor traditional, peasant, fresh and natural foods. Virgin olive oil, Thai fish sauce, and udon noodles come to us thanks to international marketing. Fresh and natural loom so large because we can take for granted the preserved and processed staples-salt, flour, sugar, chocolate, oils, coffee, tea-produced by agribusiness and food corporations. Asparagus and strawberries in winter come to us on trucks trundling up from Mexico and planes flying in from Chile. Visits to charming little restaurants and colorful markets in Morocco or Vietnam would be impossible without international tourism. The ethnic foods we seek out when we travel are being preserved, indeed often created, by a hotel and restaurant industry determined to cater to our dream of India or Indonesia, Turkey, Hawaii or Mexico. Culinary Luddism, far from escaping the modern global food economy, is parasitic upon it.

Culinary Luddites are right, though, about two important things. We need to know how to prepare good food and we need a culinary ethos. As far as good food goes, they've done us all a service by teaching us how to use the bounty delivered to us (ironically) by the global economy. Their culinary ethos, though, is another matter. Were we able to turn back the clock, as they urge, most of us would be toiling all day in the fields or the kitchen, many of us would be starving. Nostalgia is not what we need. What we need is an ethos that comes to terms with contemporary, industrialized food, not one that dismisses it, an ethos that opens choices for everyone, not one that closes them for many so that a few may enjoy their labor, and an ethos that does not prejudge, but decides case-by-case when natural is preferable to processed, fresh to preserved, old to new, slow to fast, artisanal to industrial. What we need, in a word, is culinary modernism.

VEGGING OUT

JEFFREY STEINGARTEN

MY FIRST LOVE AFFAIR with vegetarianism ended on a dark and chilly night in 1975 on the corner of Eighth Street in Greenwich Village with a hot dog from Nathan's Famous. For four years, I had been a lacto-ovo vegetarian, meaning that I allowed myself eggs and dairy products but no fish or shellfish, no chicken or other feathered things, no meat either red or pink. The question of insects never arose because, like most Americans (though unlike members of many other cultures), I have always reacted with revulsion to the idea of eating insects, despite their high nutritive value, crunchy texture, and wide availability. My bible was *Diet for a Small Planet,* by Frances Moore Lappé, published in 1971. The message of this utopian, spiral-bound volume was that consuming meat is tantamount to consuming the environment. My other motivation was the conviction that meat is murder.

Eighteen omnivorous, Lucullan years later, I am a vegetarian again, much stricter this time, a full-fledged vegan, which is pronounced "VEE-g'n" and means that I avoid animal products entirely, including milk and eggs, butter and cheese. My first act as a vegan was to eat a carrot, and my second act was to make a list of sixty vegetarian and natural-food restaurants within a taxi ride from my house. Then I ordered some Archer Daniels Midland Harvest Burgers, the kind you see advertised on television. I've always wondered if they taste as good as they are made to look.

Everybody tells me that vegetarianism is a happening thing. Last year, *Vegetarian Times* magazine, to which I now subscribe, commissioned a study by Yankelovich Clancy Shulman. About 6.7 percent of the adults they telephoned told the pollsters that they are vegetarians, way up from 3.7 percent in 1985. This works out to 12.4 million vegetarians nationwide, an apparent jump of 80 percent. Two-thirds of vegetarians are women. At this rate, I calculate, everybody will be a vegetarian by the year 2024, or at least everybody will say they're a vegetarian by the year 2024. But then how can over half of them possibly be women? Maybe something is wrong with my calculations.

The problem with the Yankelovich survey is that many people who say they're vegetarian have an extremely eccentric idea of what a vegetarian is. Forty percent of them report that they eat fish or poultry or both every week. Maybe I'm using the wrong dictionary, but it seems to me that somebody who eats chicken at least once a week and claims to be a vegetarian is the very definition of an impostor, a charlatan, a pretender or a mountebank. The survey also discovered a hitherto-unrecognized category—the 10 percent of vegetarians who eat red meat at least once a week. I cannot decide whether to call them bovo-vegetarians or psycho-vegetarians.

The survey's results are broadly consistent with recent trends in food consumption. From 1976 to 1990, the average American's consumption of beef dropped from 94.5 pounds a year to 68, but an increase in poultry and fish more than made up for it. So the teal trend is the rise of chicken, turkey, and cod, and of people who would like to think of themselves as vegetarians. Because vegetarianism is a happening thing.

Amazingly, only 4 percent of today's vegetarians avoid animal products entirely, an inconsequential quarter of a percent of the total American adult population, or a mere five hundred thousand people from coast to coast. This is the group I joined a month ago, we few, we happy few, we band of brothers.

Most Americans go vegetarian for their health, giving "not sure" as their runner-up reason, distantly followed by the environment and animal rights. Vegetarians do have fewer heart attacks, lower blood pressure, and trimmer figures than meat eaters. But as vegetarians tend to lead healthier lives in general, and exercise more than average, a vegetarian diet in itself may not have much advantage over an omnivorous diet low in saturated fat, full of fruits and vegetables, and moderate though not phobic when it comes to meat. As a lacto-ovo vegetarian in the 1970s, I more than made up for the presumed health advantages of a vegetarian diet by cooking with generous quantities of butter and cream, consuming cheese to my heart's content, and keeping the ice-cream churn perpetually spinning. That is why I am a vegan this time around.

The day before becoming a vegan, I had my cholesterol tested, and yesterday I had my blood taken again. I expect the results tomorrow. Then I will know whether strict vegetarianism does me any good.

People vary widely in how closely their serum cholesterol reacts to changes in their diet. If I am very diet-sensitive, my cholesterol should have dropped by about 15 percent—half the maximum benefit one can hope for after staying on a diet extremely low in saturated fat for several months. But the problem is this: If my cholesterol has fallen by as much as 15 percent, how can I justify eating meat ever again for the rest of my life? I can't decide which way to root.

The food press has recently been full of statements like "Eating low on the food chain has tended to be pretty disastrous from the gastronomic point of view—but not any longer!" The evidence presented is always a photo of an exquisite and sumptuous vegetable feast created by one of the country's top young chefs. I happily sample several of these every year, and the problem with them is usually the same. They may be lovely to look at, artfully cooked, and sometimes delicious, but you would not survive very long on meals like these, because they rarely contain any protein. For that you must consume large platefuls of unglamorous legumes and grains.

Strict vegetarians need to be careful in making their nutritional ends meet. Most would suffer deficiencies of vitamin B12, vitamin D, and iron if they did not take vitamin pills or eat fortified foods such as Total and Special K cereals. These three common deficiencies are the subject of intense controversy, but pregnant or lactating women, children, and the elderly should be particularly watchful. Early signs that your body is starved for B_{12} can be dangerously masked (even until irreversible nerve damage occurs) by the plentiful folic acid in vegan diets.

Back in the palmy days of *Diet for a Small Planet,* protein was seen as the main thing to worry about. The average American diet serves up double the amount of protein we actually need (usually given as 0.36 grams for every pound of your weight, at least for adults, or about two ounces a day for a 180-pound man), but getting enough protein as a strict vegetarian does take a bit of planning. You won't find much protein in a plate of delicate emerald greens dressed with balsamic vinegar or in a jewel-like mosaic of asparagus and beets. Lappé's solution was to build complete proteins out of the partial proteins found in plants, either by supplementing them with dairy products and eggs (not an option for vegans) or by obsessively pairing plants rich in a few of the nine essential amino acids (protein building blocks that our bodies cannot produce) with those rich in the others. Nowadays, matching complementary proteins is easier than in 1971 because, the experts tell us, essential amino acids can be matched up over the course of an entire day rather than at every meal. A few even claim that we needn't worry about complementarity at all. But the simplest solution is to make dishes, like many of the best recipes in *Diet for a Small Planet,* that draw on the familiar third-world combinations of cornmeal and beans, pasta and beans, rice and soy, rice and lentils, and so forth—all somehow discovered long ago by cultures that depend on plants for much of their protein, and all quite delicious.

Most vegetarian, whole-food, health-food, and organic restaurants pay much greater attention to their ideology than to their cooking. Their dishes are typically artless, often drawing (promiscuously and sloppily) on real or imagined foreign dishes. American vegetarians eat vegetables because they hate meat. Europeans eat vegetables because they love vegetables. Nearly all the voluntary vegetarians in the world (those not vegetarians from poverty or religious belief) live in America and England. Neither group is known for its skills in the kitchen.

The first thing you notice about a restaurant's menu is how high up the food chain the chef has dared to climb and which foods on the lower rungs he or she has chosen to exclude. All pollo-vegetarian restaurants seem to allow fish (though some pesco-vegetarians avoid shellfish on the grounds that these are scavengers and bottom dwellers), but some oddly eliminate the ovos from which the pollos came, not to mention the milk that flows like kindness from the pollos' barnyard neighbors. It is common to find ovos where lactos are excluded and vice versa.

Not even every plant food is welcome. Many restaurants do not offer alcohol, whether fermented from barley or hops or grapes. Some do not even let you bring your own. Others eschew the dark, aromatic liquor of the roasted coffee bean, and most banish the purest, whitest forms of sugar and flour. Restaurants following strict Buddhist rules also eliminate onions, scallions, and garlic, which are thought to inflame the passions, while most macrobiotic restaurants flee from members of the nightshade family, such as eggplants and tomatoes. One man's poison is another man's essential amino acid.

China, Japan, and India—unlike the United States and the countries of northern Europe—have strict native vegetarian cuisines of long standing and great sophistication. The exquisite Japanese *shojin ryori,* or Buddhist temple cooking, does not seem to have immigrated to this country; its principal protein combination is rice paired with the myriad forms of soybean curd. Unlike *shojin ryori,* Chinese Buddhist cooking specializes in what you might call facsimile food, astounding imitations of traditional meat and poultry dishes in which wheat gluten, tofu, textured soybean protein, arrowroot, and chopped yams simulate animal flesh; bean curd and potatoes stand in for fish, fresh walnuts for crab, cabbage for chicken. Versions ranging from crude to creative (with or without onions and garlic) can be found in at least seven New York

City restaurants. As 80 percent of the population of India is vegetarian (according to estimates I have read), its cuisine is rich in plant protein combinations, especially if one is willing to supplement the rice-lentils-wheat-chickpea quartet with a teeny bit of *raita,* made with yogurt. I was unable to find a truly admirable vegetarian Indian restaurant in any of the five boroughs.

And so my month of dining at two-thirds of New York City's vegetarian restaurants was, on the whole, excruciating. The intricate vegetarian cuisines of Japan, China, and India should make it obvious that when you eliminate most of the possibilities that nature offers—all animal flesh, plus eggs and milk and nearly everything else that is white, including onions and garlic—you must show greater artistry in the kitchen rather than less. The more foods you avoid, the more imagination and skill you need to keep your life palatable, not to mention scrumptious.

Today's supermarkets and health-food stores are full of imitation meat, usually lower in fat and calories than the real thing (but often higher in salt, to make up for the savory taste of animal protein). In addition to an endless variety of burgers made from grains, nuts, or soybeans, you can find faux hot dogs that at least look right (one cleverly called a Not Dog), simulated breakfast sausage, and phony bacon complete with stripes.

Though the Archer Daniels Midland Harvest Burger is not quite as good as it looks, I managed with a little imagination to extract several satisfying meals from the product. You can apparently buy frozen pre-formed patties at some health-food stores, but I ordered a variety of its dry mixes direct from the company by dialing (800) 8-FLAVOR—Burger 'n Loaf (original or Italian), Chili Fixin's, Sloppy Joe Fixin's, and Taco Filling 'n Dip. All contain little granules of concentrated soy protein with various flavorings and lots of preservatives.

To make a Harvest Burger you empty a foil bag labeled "Burger 'n Loaf" into a bowl, add a cup and a quarter of water, wait fifteen minutes, and form the thick tan-and-gray mixture into patties (fewer patties than the label calls for if you want a mock hamburger that exceeds 3.2 ounces). I tried panfrying, microwaving, baking, and broiling. All the results resembled overdone hamburgers, edible, even tasty, but not juicy; the broiled version was best because it had a charred flavor reminiscent of grilled beef. In a hamburger bun with lots of ketchup and a pile of natural-flavor Wise potato chips washed down with a tall glass of diet Coke, the broiled Harvest Burger was good enough to eat. Harvest Burgers contain no cholesterol and very little saturated fat, but as with raw soybeans, nearly 30 percent of their calories come from fat.

All the other Archer Daniels Midland imitation-beef creations are fun to mix and eat. You add tomato sauce to the sloppy joe mix and tomato sauce and beans (canned) to the chili package; then you cook them for fifteen minutes. Despite the dried and artificial flavors evident in both products, the results were savory and quick and, because of the heavy spicing, quite like the ground-meat originals.

And then suddenly I thought, in a flash of blinding insight: Wait just one minute! Is this what I have been reduced to? What in the world am I doing, standing in my own kitchen, mixing up packets of micro-wavable, artificial Tex-Mex convenience food? Is this what being a strict vegetarian boils down to? And in large part, I'm afraid the answer is yes. Only as a vegan would I have been able to stomach more than 30 percent of what I have eaten over the past month. It was then that I decided to let my cholesterol test determine whether I would remain a vegetarian for another month.

I have come to the conclusion that Mother Nature never wanted us to become strict and unyielding vegetarians. There is nothing natural about it at all. Visit any vegan, and you will find his cabinet of vitamin supplements at least as well stocked as his larder. The truth is that humans were designed to be omnivores, complete with all-purpose den-tition and digestive systems. Vegetarianism is not our natural diet. Anthropologists know that for most of the past million years of our evolution, humans have eaten meat, especially fish and low-fat wild game. The only source of plant protein that does not require cooking to become digestible is, I think, nuts. But cooking was invented only fifty thousand years ago, long after most of our physiology and genetic structure had evolved. I cannot think of a traditional, nonindustrial cul-ture (we used to call them primitive cultures) that practices vegetarian-ism if it can help it. Vegetarianism is always the product of scarcity, of religion, or of ideology, including nutritional fads and fashions.

The environmental arguments against meat are strong, but they apply mainly to factory farming—vast numbers of animals kept in close confinement, fed with grain and water hauled from long distances and producing more waste than we can possibly use as fertilizer or fuel. I have read that more than half of America's water consumption goes to raising beef and that twenty pure vegetarians like me can be fed on the same amount of land needed to feed one meat eater. Meat has been called a petroleum by-product: you can grow forty pounds of soybeans with the amount of oil consumed in producing a pound of beef.

But unless you insist that we must all eat in the most economical manner possible—though few of us dress in the cheapest way or live in the smallest possible space—these are arguments not for avoiding all meat but for eating less meat and raising it in a sustainable way.

Universal vegetarianism would not be an unmixed blessing for the environment. Ecological nutritionist Joan Gussow explained to me that for millennia livestock has been indispensable for its magical ability to convert agricultural waste, failed crops, and the vegetation on unfarmable land into high-quality protein. And without grazing animals, it would be difficult to practice environmentally sound crop rotation. Cutting your meat consumption by 50 or 75 percent makes more environmental sense than becoming a vegan like me.

As you can see, I was furiously preparing myself for the switch back to meat. Everything depended on the cholesterol test. And then my doctor called with the results. I don't know whether to be happy or sad, but my serum cholesterol is, if anything, slightly higher than when I started. Even with a near-zero intake of saturated fat, my cholesterol has not budged. For better or worse, my ultimate fate does not seem to depend on my diet. Tonight I will eat a lobster.

Savoring Life

THE REPORTER'S KITCHEN:
A RECIPE FOR WRITING

JANE KRAMER

THE KITCHEN WHERE I'M MAKING dinner is a New York kitchen. Nice light, way too small, nowhere to put anything unless the stove goes. My stove is huge, but it will never go. My stove is where my head clears, my impressions settle, my reporter's life gets folded into *my* life, and whatever I've just learned, or think I've learned—whatever it was, out there in the world, that had seemed so different and surprising—bubbles away in the very small pot of what I think I know and, if I'm lucky, produces something like perspective. A few years ago, I had a chance to interview Brenda Milner, the neuropsychologist who helped trace the process by which the brain turns information into memory, and memory into the particular consciousness called a life, or, you could say, into the signature of the person. Professor Milner was nearly eighty when I met her, in Montreal, at the neurological institute at McGill, where she'd worked for close to fifty years, and one of the things we talked about was how some people, even at her great age, persist in "seeing" memory the way children do—as a cupboard or a drawer or a box of treasures underneath the bed, a box that gets fill and has to be cleaned out every now and then to make room for new treasures they collect. Professor Milner wasn't one of those people, but I am. The memory I "see" is a kind of kitchen, where the thoughts and characters I bring home go straight into a stockpot on my big stove, reducing old flavors, distilling new ones, making a soup that never tastes the same as it did the day before, and feeds the voice that, for better or worse, is *me* writing, and not some woman from another kitchen.

I knew nothing about stockpots as a child. My mother was an awful cook, or, more accurately, she didn't cook, since in her day it was fashionable not to go anywhere near a kitchen if you didn't have to. Her one creation, apart from a fluffy spinach soufflé that for some reason always appeared with the overcooked turkey when she made Thanksgiving dinner (a task she undertook mainly to avoid sitting in the cold with the rest of us at the Brown Thanksgiving Day home football game), would probably count today as haute-fusion family cooking: matzo-meal-and-Rhode-Island-johnnycake-mix pancakes, topped with thick bacon, sour cream, and maple syrup. Not even our housekeeper and occasional cook could cook—beyond a tepid, sherried stew that was always presented at parties, grandly, as lobster thermidor, and a passable apple filling that you could spoon out, undetected, through the large steam holes of an otherwise tasteless pie. I don't think I ever saw my father cook anything, unless you can call sprinkling sugar on a grapefruit, or boiling syringes in an enamel pan, the way doctors did in those days, cooking. (I use the pan now for roasting chickens.) The only man in my family with a recipe of his own was my brother Bobby, who had mastered a pretty dessert called pumpkin chiffon while courting an Amish girl who liked pumpkins. My own experience in the kitchen was pretty much limited to reheating the Sunday-night Chinese takeout early on Monday mornings, before anyone else was awake to eat it first.

I started cooking when I started writing. My first dish was tuna curry (a can of Bumble Bee, a can of Campbell's cream-of-mushroom soup, a big spoonful of Durkee's curry powder, and a cup of instant Carolina rice), and the recipe, such as it was, came from my friend Mary Clay, who claimed to have got it directly from the cook at her family's Kentucky farm. It counted for me as triply exotic, being at once the product of a New York supermarket chain, the bluegrass South, and India. And never mind that the stove I cooked on then was tiny, or that "dining" meant a couple of plates and a candle on my old toy chest, transformed into the coffee table of a graduate-school rental, near Columbia; the feeling was high sixties, meaning that a nice girl from Providence could look forward to enjoying literature, sex, and cooking in the space of a single day. I don't remember whom I was making the curry for, though I must have liked him, because I raced home from Frederick Dupee's famous lecture on symbolism in *Light in August* to make it. What I do remember is how comforting it was to be standing at that tiny stove, pinched into a Merry Widow and stirring yellow powder into Campbell's soup, when I might have been pacing the stacks at Butler Library, trying to resolve the very serious question of whether, after Dupee on Faulkner, there, was anything left to say about literature, and, more precisely, the question of whether *I'd* find anything to say in a review—one of my first assignments in the real world—of a book of poems written by Norman Mailer on the occasion of having stabbed his second wife. I remember this because, as I stood there, stirring powder and a soupçon of Acapulco Gold into my tuna curry, I began to accept that, while whatever I did say wasn't going to be the last word on the poetics of domestic violence, it would be *my* word, a lot of Rhode Island still in it, a little New York, and, to my real surprise, a couple of certainties: I was angry at Norman Mailer; I was twenty-one and didn't think that you should stab your wife. Mailer, on the other hand had produced some very good lines of poetry. He must have been happy (or startled) to be taken for a poet at all, because a few weeks after my review ran—in a neighborhood paper you could pick up free in apartment-house lobbies—his friend Dan Wolf, the editor of what was then a twelve-page downtown alternative weekly called the *Village Voice*, phoned to offer me a job.

I bought a madeleine mold, at a kitchen I shop near the old *Voice* offices, on Sheridan Square. It was my first purchase as a reporter who cooked—a long, narrow pan of shallow, ridged shells, waiting to produce a Proust—but though I liked madeleines, they didn't collect my world in a mouthful, the way the taste of warm apples, licked from the cool tingle of a silver spoon, still does, or, for that matter, the way the terrible chicken curry at the old brasserie La Coupole, in Paris, always reminded me of Norman Mailer's wife. The mold sat in my various kitchens for ten years before I moved to the kitchen I cook in now, and tried madeleines again, and discovered that, for me, they were just another cookie—which is to say, not the kind of cookie that belonged in the ritual that for years has kept me commuting between my study and my stove, stirring or beating or chopping or sifting my way through false starts and strained transitions and sticky sentences.

The cookies I like to make when I'm writing are called "dream cookies." I made my first batch in my friend John Tillinger's kitchen, in Roxbury, Connecticut, at one in the morning, in a mood perhaps best described by the fact that I'd just been awakened by the weight of a large cat settling on my head. The cookies were a kind of sand tart. They had a dry, gritty, burned-butter taste, and I must have associated them with the taste of deliverance from sweet, smooth, treacherous things like purring cats. I say this because a few years later I found myself making them again, in North Africa, in the middle of reporting a story about a tribal feud that involved a Berber wedding and was encrypted—at least, for me—in platters of syrupy honeyed pastries, sugared couscous, and sweet mint tea.

At the time, my kitchen was in the Moroccan city of Meknès, where my husband was doing ethnographic research, but my story took me to a village a couple of hours up into the foothills of the Middle Atlas Mountains. It was a wild, unpleasant place. Even today, some thirty years, a couple of wars and revolutions, and an assortment of arguably more unpleasant places later, I would call it scary. The wedding in question, a three-day, her-house-to-his-house travelling celebration, was about to begin in the bride's village—which had every reason to celebrate, having already provided the groom's village with a large number of pretty virgins and, in the process, profited considerably from the bride-prices those virgins had commanded: goats, chickens, silver necklaces, brass plates, and simple, practical, hard cash, some of it in negotiable European currencies. The problem was that none of the young men in the bride's village were at all interested in the virgins available in the groom's village, whose own supply of goats, chickens, necklaces, plates, and money was consequently quite depleted. All that village had was an abundance of homely daughters—or, you could say, the bad end of the balance of trade in brides. As a result, the men in the groom's village were getting ready to fight the men in the bride's village, a situation that left the women in both villages cooking day and night, in a frantic effort to turn their enemies into guests.

By then, I was close to being an enemy myself, having already broken one serious taboo: I had asked the name of somebody's aunt in a conversation where the naming of paternal aunts in the company of certain female relatives was tantamount to calling catastrophe down on the entire family, and the women had had to abandon their cooking in order to purge the premises, which they did by circling the village, ululating loudly, while I sat there in the blazing sun, under strict orders to keep the flies off a platter of dripping honey cakes. It hadn't helped any that, in a spirit of apology (or perhaps it was malice), I then invited the villagers to Meknès and served them my special Julia Child's *boeuf bourguignon,* which made them all quite ill. A few days later, I went to the medina and bought some almonds for dream cookies. I don't know why I did it. Maybe I was homesick. Certainly, I was being spoiled, knowing that Malika, the young Arab woman who worked for me and became my friend, would grind those almonds into a sandy paste as quickly as she had just peeled peaches for my breakfast—which is to say, in less time than it took me to check for scorpions underneath the two cushions and copper tray that were then my dining room. But I think now that I was mainly trying to find my voice in a country where some women couldn't mention an aunt to a relative—where the voices of most women, in fact, were confined to their ululations. Once, I heard that same shrill, flutey cry coming from my own kitchen and rushed in to find Malika shaking with pain and bleeding; she was sixteen, and had taken something or done something to herself to end a pregnancy that I had never even suspected. After that, I would sometimes hear the cry again, and find her huddled in a corner of the room, struck with a terror she could not describe. No one had ever asked her to describe it, not even the man she'd married when, by her own reckoning, she was twelve years old.

I never finished the story about the Berber bride. I was a bride myself, and this posed something of a problem for my erstwhile village friends, who had wanted to find me a husband from the tribe and thus assure themselves of the continued use of, if not actually the title to, my new Volkswagen. In the event, one night, after we'd been trading recipes, the women sent me home with a complicated (and fairly revolting) "love recipe" to try out on the husband I already had, and it turned out—at least, according to the neighbors who warned me not to make it—to be a bit of black magic whose purpose was, to put it discreetly, less amorous than incapacitating. I took this as a sign that it was time to come down from the mountains. I wrote a book about an Arab wedding instead, and I waited until I was back in my study in New York to finish it. The lesson for me, as a writer, was that I had to burrow back into my own life before I could even start thinking clearly about someone else's or come to terms with the kinds of violence that are part of any reporter's working life, or with the tangles of outrage that women reporters, almost inevitably, carry home with their notes.

In New York, I cook a lot of Moroccan food. I keep a *couscousière* on the shelf that used to hold the madeleine mold, and then the Swedish pancake skillet and the French crêpe pan and the Swiss fondue set and the electric wok that my husband's secretary sent for Christmas during a year when I was stir-frying everything in sesame oil—something I gave up because stir-frying was always over in a few fraught seconds and did nothing at all for my writing. The cooking that helps my writing is slow cooking, the kind of cooking where you take control of your ingredients so that whatever it is you're making doesn't run away with you, the way words can run away with you in a muddled or unruly sentence. Cooking like that—nudging my disordered thoughts into the stately measure of, say, a good risotto simmering slowly in a homemade broth—gives me confidence and at least the illusion of clarity. And I find that for clarity, the kind that actually lasts until I'm back at my desk, poised over a sentence with my red marker, there is nothing to equal a couscous steaming in its colander pot, with the smell of cumin and coriander rising with the steam. That's when the words I was sure

I'd lost come slipping into my head, one by one, and with them even the courage to dip my fingers in and separate the grains.

Some of the food I learned to cook in Morocco didn't translate to New York. I have yet to find a hen in New York with fertilized eggs still inside it—a delicacy that the Meknasi would produce for their guests in moments of truly serious hospitality—not at the halal markets on Atlantic Avenue or even at International Poultry, on Fifty-fourth Street, poulterer to the Orthodox carriage trade. I cannot imagine slaughtering a goat on Central Park West and then skinning it on the sidewalk, if for no reason other than that I'm an ocean away from the old *f'qui* who could take that skin before it stiffened and stretch it into a nearly transparent head for a clay drum with a personal prayer baked into it. I have never again squatted on my heels, knees apart and back straight, for the hours it takes to sift wheat through a wooden sieve and then slap water into it for a flat-bread dough, though in the course of various assignments I have made chapati with Ugandan Asian immigrants in London, stirred mealie-mealie with Bushmen in Botswana, and rolled *pâte feuilletée* with Slovenian autoworkers in the projects of Södertälje, Sweden. And I am still waiting for permission to dig a charcoal pit in Central Park for the baby lamb that I will then smother in mint and cumin, cover with earth, and bake to such tenderness that you could scoop it our and eat it with your fingers.

But when I'm starting a piece about politics, especially French politics, I will often begin by preserving the lemons for a chicken *tagine,* perhaps because a forkful of good *tagine* inevitably takes me back to the home of the French-speaking sheikh whose wives taught me how to make it (to the sound of Tom Jones singing "Delilah" on a shortwave radio), and from there to the small restaurant in Paris where I ate my first *tagine* outside Morocco, and from *there* to the flat of a surly French politician named Jean-Pierre Chevènement, who lived near the restaurant, and who unnerved me entirely during our one interview by balancing cups of espresso on the breasts of a hideous brass coffee table that appeared to be cast as a woman's torso, while barking at me about French nuclear policy. Similarly, I make *choucroute* whenever I'm starting a piece that has to do with music, because my first proper *choucroute*—the kind where you put fresh sauerkraut through five changes of cold water, squeeze it dry, strand by strand, and then braise it in gin and homemade stock, with a ham hock and smoked pork and sausages buried inside it—was a labor of love for the eightieth birthday of the composer George Perle; and since then the smell of sausage, gin, and sauerkraut mingling in my oven has always reminded me of the impossible art of composition, and set my standards at the level of his luminous woodwind suites.

On the other hand, when I write about art I like to cook a rabbit. My first rabbit was also, unhappily, my daughter's pet rabbit, and I cooked it with understandable misgiving, one summer in the Vaucluse, after an old peasant sorcerer who used to come over during the fill moon to do the ironing took it from its hutch and presented it to her, freshly slaughtered and stuffed with rosemary, on the morning of her first birthday, saying that once she ate it she would have her friend with her "forever." We had named the rabbit Julien Nibble, in honor of our summer neighbor Julien Levy, a man otherwise known as the dealer who had introduced Ernst and Gorky and most of the great Surrealists to New York, and my daughter, who is thirty-one now, has refused to eat rabbit since we told her the story, when she was six or seven. But I have kept on cooking rabbit, changing recipes as the art world changes, and always asking myself what Julien would have made of those changes and, of course, whether he would have liked the dinner. There was the saddle of rabbit in a cognac-cream sauce that smoothed out my clotted thoughts about a middle-aged Italian painter with what I'd called "an unrequited sense of history." There was the *lapin niçoise,* with olives, garlic, and tomatoes, that saw me through the first paragraphs of a story about the politics of public sculpture in the South Bronx. There was the rich, bitter rabbit ragout—a recipe from the Croatian grandmother of the Berlin artist Renata Stih—that got me started after a couple of earthquakes hit Assisi, shattering the frescoes on the ceiling of San Francesco into a million pieces. Dishes like these become invocations, little rituals you invent for yourself, in the hope that your life and your work will eventually taste the same.

Good cooking is much easier to master than good writing. But great cooking is something different, and during the years that I've stood at my stove, stirring and sprinkling and tasting, waiting for a sauce to thicken and a drab sentence to settle—if not precisely into echoing, Wordsworthian chords, at least into a turn of phrase that will tell you something you didn't already know about Gerhard Schröder, say, or Silvio Berlusconi—my cooking has leaped ahead by several stars, leaving my writing in the shade. Some dishes have disappeared from my repertoire; tuna curry, for example, has been replaced by the crab-and-spun-coconut-cream curry I first tasted in Hong Kong in 1990 and have been working on ever since, and never mind that the crab in Hong Kong turned out to be doctored tofu, while mine arrives from a Broadway fishmonger with its claws scissoring through the paper bag. Some dishes I've sampled in the course (and cause) of duty are memorable mainly because I've tried so hard to forget them. For one, the crudités I managed to get down at Jean-Marie Le Pen's gaudy and heavily guarded Saint-Cloud villa, with M. Le Pen spinning an outsize plastic globe that held a barely concealed tape recorder, and a couple of Dobermans sniffing at my plate. For another, the rat stew I was served in the Guyana jungle by a visibly unstable interior minister, who had accompanied me there (en route to a "model farm" hacked out of the clearing that had once been Jonestown) in a battered Britten-Norman Islander with no radar or landing lights and a thirteen-year-old Air Force colonel for a pilot. Some dishes I've repressed, like the cauliflower soup that was ladled into my plate in the dining room of a Belfast hotel just as a terrorist's bomb went off and a wing of the building crumbled, leaving me, the friend whose couch I'd been using for the past week, and a couple of other diners perched in the middle of the sky—"like saints on poles," a man at the next table said, returning to his smoked salmon. Some dishes I've loved but would not risk trying myself, like the pork roast with crackling that Pat Hume, the wife of the politician and soon-to-be Nobel peace laureate John Hume, was in the process of carving, one Sunday lunch in Derry, when a stray bullet shattered the window and lodged in the wall behind her; she didn't stop carving, or even pause in her conversation, which, as I remember, had to do with whether the New York subways were so dangerous as to preclude her visiting with the children while John was in Washington, advising Teddy Kennedy on how to get through a family crisis.

Some dishes I've left in better hands. It's clear to me that I'm no match for the sausage vender at the Frankfurt Bahnhof when it comes to grilling a bratwurst to precisely that stage where the skin is charred and just greasy enough to hold the mustard, and then stuffing the bratwurst into just enough roll to get a grip on, but not *so* much roll that you miss the sport of trying to eat it with anything fewer than four paper napkins and the business section of the *Frankfurter Allgemeine Zeitung*. In the same way, I know that I will never equal my friend Duke, a Herero tribesman known from the Kalahari Desert to the Okavango Delta by his "Dukes of Hazzard" T-shirt, in the art of thickening a sauce for a guinea fowl or a spur-winged goose in the absence of anything resembling flour. Duke was the cook at my fly camp when I was out in the delta researching a piece about "bush housekeeping," and he thickened his sauces there by grating roots he called desert potatoes into boiling fat. But the secret was how many potatoes and, indeed, how to distinguish those potatoes from all the other roots that looked like potatoes but were something you'd rather not ingest. I never found out, because the day we'd planned to fly to the desert to dig some up a tourist camping on a nearby game preserve was eaten by a lion, and my pilot volunteered to collect the bones. Food like that is, as they say in the art world, site-specific.

Take the dish I have called *Canard sauvage rue du Cherche Midi*. I cooked my first wild duck in a kitchen on Cherche Midi in 1982, and during the sixteen years that I lived between Paris and New York I tuned the recipe to what my friends assured me was perfection. But it has never produced the same frisson at my New York dinner table that it did at the picnic table in my Paris garden, if for no reason other than that my neighbors across the court in New York do not punctuate my dinner parties with well-aimed rotten eggs, accompanied by shouts of "Savages!," the way one of my Paris neighbors—a local crank by the name of Jude—always did, and that consequently my New York guests know nothing of the pleasure that comes from pausing between bites of a perfect duck in order to turn a hose full blast on the open window of someone who dislikes them.

Some dishes just don't travel no matter how obvious or easy they seem. I know this because I tried for a year to duplicate the magical fried chicken known to aficionados as Fernand Point's Poulet Américain—a recipe so simple in itself that no one since that legendary Vienne chef has ever dared to put it on a menu. I have never even attempted to duplicate the spicy chicken stew that the actor Michael Goldman heats up on a Sterno stove in his damp, smelly Paris *cave,* surrounded by the moldy bottles of Lafite and Yquem and Grands Echezeaux that you know he's planning to open as the night wears on. Nor have I attempted the Indonesian rijsttafel—which is basically just a platter of rice with little bowls of condiments and sauces—that my late friend George Hoff, a Dutch kendo master and night-club bouncer, tossed off one night, in London, after a long and strenuous demonstration that involved raising a long pole and slamming it down to within a centimetre of my husband's head. Or the fish grilled by a group of young Portuguese commandos in the early summer of 1974—I was covering their revolution; they were taking a break from it—over a campfire on a deserted Cabo de São Vicente beach. Or, for that matter, the S'mores my favorite counsellor roasted over a campfire at Camp Fernwood, in Poland, Maine (and never mind that I hated Camp Fernwood). Or even popcorn at the movies.

But most things do travel, if you know the secret. A lot of cooks don't share their secrets, or more often lie, the way my mother-in-law lied about the proportion of flour to chocolate in her famous "yum-yum cake," thereby ending whatever relationship we had. *My* best secret dates from a dinner party at Gracie Mansion when Ed Koch was the mayor of New York. I had known Koch from his Village Independent Democrat days, when he pretty much starved unless his mother fed him. But now that he was Hizzoner the Mayor of New York City he could, as he repeatedly told his guests, order anything he wanted to eat, no matter what the hour or the season or inconvenience to a staff best trained in trimming the crusts off tea sandwiches. The dinner in question got off to an awkward start—"You're Puerto Rican? You don't *look* Puerto Rican" is how, if I remember correctly, he greeted the beautiful curator of the Museo del Barrio—and it was frequently interrupted by phone calls from his relatives, who seemed to be having some sort of business crisis. But everybody agreed that the food was delicious. It wasn't elaborate food, or even much different from what you'd cook for yourself on a rainy night at home: pasta in a tomato sauce, good steaks, and hot-chocolate sundaes for dessert. But the meal itself was so oddly remarkable that I went back to the kitchen afterward and asked the cook how he'd made it, and he told me, "Whatever Ed likes, whatever he says he never got as a kid, I double the quantity. I doubled the Parmesan on the pasta. I *tripled* the hot-chocolate sauce on the ice cream." Ed's principle was "More is more."

It's not a principle I would apply to writing, but it's definitely the one I cook by now, on my way from excess in the kitchen to a manuscript where less is more. If my couscous is now the best couscous on the Upper West Side, it's because, with a nod to Ed, I take my favorite ingredients from every couscous I've ever eaten—the chickpeas and raisins and turnips and carrots and almonds and prunes—double the quantity, toss them into the broth, and then go back to my desk and cut some adverbs. I put too many eggs in my matzo balls, too much basil in my pesto, too much saffron in my paella. I have no patience with the kind of recipe that says "¼ teaspoon thyme" or "2 ounces chopped pancetta." I drown my carrots in chervil, because I like the way chervil sweetens carrots. I even drown my halibut in chervil, because I like what it does to the reduction of wine and cream in a white fish sauce— though, now that I think of it, when I'm on a bandwagon, when I'm really mad at the world I'm writing about and the people in it, I will usually switch to sorrel.

The first time I cooked halibut on a bed of sorrel, I was in New York, laboring over a long piece about liberation theology in South America and, in particular, about a young priest whose parish was in a favela with the unlikely name of Campos Elísios, about an hour north of Rio de Janeiro. I wasn't mad at my Brazilian priest—I loved the priest. I was mad at the Bishop of Rio, who was on the priest's back for ignoring orders to keep his parishioners out of politics. At first, I thought I could solve the problem by taking the afternoon off to make *moqueca,* which was not only my favorite Brazilian dish but, in my experience, an immensely soothing one—a gratin of rice, shrimp, lime, and coconut cream, served with (and this is essential, if you're serious) a sprinkling of toasted manioc flour—which provides the comforts of a *brandade* without the terrible nursery taste of cod and potatoes mushed together. I made *moqueca* a lot in Rio, because I was angry a lot in Rio. Angry at the poverty, at the politics, at the easy brutality of people in power and the desperate brutality of people without it. But it's hard to make my *moqueca* in New York unless you have a source of manioc flour, and the closest I came to that was the seven-foot-long flexible straw funnel leaning against a beam in my living room—an object devised by the Amerindians, centuries ago, to squeeze the poison out of manioc so that they wouldn't die eating it. I had wasted the better part of the afternoon on Amsterdam Avenue, searching for manioc flour, when I happened to pass a greengrocer with a special on sorrel. I bought him out, and a couple of hours later I discovered that the patient preparation of sorrel—the blanching and chopping and purée-ing and braising in butter—had taken the diatribe in my head and turned it into a story I could tell.

There are, of course, moments in writing when even the most devoted cook stops cooking. Those are the moments that, in sex, are called "transporting" but in journalism are known as an empty fridge, an irritable family, and the beginnings of a first-name friendship with the woman who answers the phone at Empire Szechuan. When I am lost in one of those moments, I subsist on takeout and jasmine tea, or if takeout is truly beyond me—the doorbell, the change, the tip, the mismatched chopsticks, the arguments when I won't share—on chili-lime tortilla chips and Diet Coke. If the hour is decent, I'll mix a Bloody Mary or a *caipirinha* like the ones that the priest and I used to sneak in the kitchen of the parish house of Campos Elísios on evenings when the Seventh-Day Adventists would arrive at the favela in force, pitch a tent in a field, and call the poor to salvation through amps rented by the hour from a Copacabana beach band. But moments like those are rare.

My normal state when beginning a piece is panic, and by now my friends and family are able to gauge that panic by the food I feed them. This past spring, in the course of a few weeks of serious fretting over the lead of a story about an Afghan refugee, I cooked a small Thanksgiving turkey, two Christmas rib roasts, and an Easter lamb. I cooked them with all the fixings, from the corn-bread-and-sausage stuffing to the Yorkshire pudding and horseradish cream—though I stopped short of the Greek Easter cheesecake that three cookbooks assured me had to be made in a clean flowerpot. My excuse was that I'd worked through Thanksgiving and been snowbound in Berlin through Christmas, and, of course, it *was* nearly Easter when I began my holiday cooking. Easter, actually, went well. No one mentioned the fact that we were celebrating it on a Saturday night, or, for that matter, that at noon on Sunday we were due, as always, for our annual Easter lunch at the home of some old friends. But Thanksgiving in April brought strained smiles all around, especially since my next-door neighbor had already cooked a lovely Thanksgiving dinner for me in February. And while my first Christmas was a big success—one of the guests brought presents and a box of chocolate mushrooms left over from a *bûche de Noël*— my second Christmas, a few days later, ended badly, when my daughter suggested that I "see someone" to discuss my block, my husband announced to a room full of people that I was "poisoning" him with saturated fats, and my son-in-law accused me of neglecting the dog. But I did end up with a paragraph. In fact, I thought it was a pretty good paragraph. And I finished the piece the way I usually finish pieces, with notes and cookbooks piled on the floor, working for a few hours, sorting the Post-its on my desk into meaningless, neat stacks, and then heading for my big stove to do more cooking—in this case, to add the tomatoes to a Bolognese sauce, because my last paragraph was too tricky to handle without a slow, comfortable Italian sauce, and I'd been using Bolognese for tricky characters since I first tackled the subject of François Mitterrand, in a story on his inauguration, in 1981.

It seems to me that there is something very sensible about keeping your memories in the kitchen, with the pots and the spices, especially in New York. They take up no space; they do not crash with your computer; and they collect the voice that you can't quite hear—in tastes and smells and small gestures that, with any luck, will eventually start to sound like you. I'm not in New York right now. The dinner I was cooking twenty-five pages ago—the clam-and-pork stew with plenty of garlic and *piri-piri* that I first ate in a Portuguese fishermen's tavern near Salem, the day I tacked wrong and sailed my boyfriend's sixteen-footer into a very big ketch and broke his mast and, with it, whatever interest he had in me—is not the dinner I am cooking today, at a farmhouse in Umbria. My stove is smaller here (though my pots are bigger). I do not write easily about myself. I am not as tasty or exotic as the characters I usually choose. My first attempt at anything like autobiography was a thinly disguised short story, and it was returned with the gentle suggestion that I replace myself with someone "a little less like the kind of person we know everything about already." But twenty years later I did manage to produce a reminiscence of sorts. It was about my mother and my daughter and about being a feminist, and it ended where I am writing now, in Umbria, looking across a pond to a field of wheat and watching a family of pheasants cross my garden. It occurred to me, worrying over *this* ending—not quite a panic but enough of a problem to have already produced a Sardinian saffron-and-sausage pasta, a cold pepper soup with garlic croutons, nightly platters of chicken-liver-and-anchovy *bruschetta,* pressed through my grandmother's hand mill, and twenty jars of brandied apricot jam—that I might possibly solve the problem by cooking the same dinner that I'd cooked then. It turns out to be one meal I can't remember.

tone
themes,
lit. devices

MAXINE KUMIN

JANUARY 25. Three days of this hard freeze; 10 below at dawn and a sullen 2 above by midday. After the morning barn chores, I start hauling quart containers of wild blackberries up from the basement freezer. I am a little reluctant to begin.

Last August, when the berries were at their most succulent, I did manage to cook up a sizable batch into jam. But everything peaks at once in a New England garden, and I turned to the importunate broccolis and cauliflowers and the second crop of bush beans, all of which wanted blanching and freezing straightaway. Also, late summer rains had roused the cucumber vines to new efforts. There was a sudden spurt of yellow squash as well.

Victor went on picking blackberries. Most mornings he scouted the slash pile along upturned boulders, residue from when we cleared the last four acres of forage pasture. We've never had to fence this final field, for the brush forms an impenetrable thicket on two sides and deep woods encircle the rest.

We've always had blackberries growing wild here and there on the property, good-sized ones, too. But never such largess, such abundance. I wondered what this bumper crop signified, after a drought-filled summer. Were the Tribulation and the Rapture at hand?

Long ago I wrote in a poem, "God does not want / His perfect fruit to rot," but that was before I had an addicted picker on my hands—whose enthusiasm became my labor. It is the habit of the deeply married to exchange vantage points.

Even the horses took up blackberries as a snack. Like toddlers loose in a popcorn shop, they sidled down the brambly row, cautiously curling their lips back so as to pluck a drooping cluster free without being stabbed in the muzzle by truly savage thorns. It was a wonderful sight.

Making jam—even though I complain how long it takes, how messy it is with its inevitable spatters and spills, how the lids and the jars somehow never match up at the end of the procedure—is rich with gratifications. I get a lot of thinking done. I puff up with feelings of providence. Pretty soon I am flooded with memories.

My mother used to visit every summer during our pickling, canning, freezing, and jamming frenzy. She had a deep reservoir of patience, developed in another era, for repetitive tasks; she would mash the blender-buzzed, cooked berries through a strainer until her arms were as weary as a weightlifter's at the end of a grueling workout. She prided herself on extracting every bit of pulp from the purple mass.

I find myself talking to her as I work. I am not nearly as diligent, I tell her, thumping the upended strainer into the kitchen scraps pile, destined for compost. I miss her serious attention to detail.

Scullery work used to make my mother loquacious. I liked hearing about her childhood in the southwestern hilly corner of Virginia at the turn of the century, how the cooking from May to October was done in the summer kitchen, a structure loosely attached to the back of the house, much as many New England sheds and barns connect to the farmhouses they supplement. I liked hearing about my grandfather's matched pair of driving horses—Saddlebreds, I gather, from the one surviving snapshot that shows my mother's three youngest brothers lined up on one compliant horse's back. My mother talked about the family pony that had a white harness for Sundays. I wonder aloud what a white harness was made of in the 1890s. Perhaps she had imagined this item, but fabricated it lovingly so long ago that it had become real.

One spectacular late summer day we took my mother down North Road along Stevens Brook in search of elderberries. We hiked up and down the sandy edge of the water in several locations before coming upon an enormous stand of the berries, ripe to bursting, branches bent double with the weight of them. After filling the five-gallon pail we had brought with us, greedily we started stuffing whole racemes of berries into a spare grain bag.

I had not thought much about dealing with the booty until we had lugged it triumphantly home. Mother sat at the kitchen table well past midnight, stripping the berries from their slender finger filaments into my biggest cooking pot. Even so, the great elderberry caper took two more days to complete. We prevailed, eventually boiling the berries with some green apples from our own trees so that the released pectin would permit the mass to jell. I don't believe in additives and scorn commercial pectin, but I will lean on home-grown apples or rhubarb in order to thicken the berry soup.

It was amazing what those elderberries had reawakened in my mother; she was transported. There was the cold cellar, there stood the jars of pickled beets, the Damson plum conserve larded with hazelnuts; there, too, the waist-high barrel of dill pickles weighted down with three flatirons atop a washtub lid. Potatoes and sweet potatoes, carrots, onions, and apples were stored in areas appropriate to their needs—apples in the dark far corner which was the driest (and spookiest), and so on. There was the springhouse, where milk from the family cow cooled unpasteurized in a metal can set down in a cavity of rocks, and a butter churn which took hours of push-pulling the paddle to turn the cream into a finished product.

It was never an idyll Mother described. She remembered sharply and wryly the labor, the peonage of childhood, when the most menial and least absorbing tasks were invariably assigned to the smallest children, especially the girls. She could not escape the chores of housekeeping for the imagined dramas of field and barn. But interestingly, chickens seemed always to have been relegated to the care of females.

Mother loathed the chickens that pecked her feet when she went into the coop to scatter their scratch. She detested egg gathering, having to shoo brood hens off their nests and then be quick about plucking the eggs into the basket; eggs from which fluff, feathers, and bits of crusty manure had to be removed. I never saw my mother eat an egg, boiled soft or hard, poached, or sunny-side up. They were a bit too close to nature for her taste.

Another kitchen thing I hear my mother say as I work, this cold January noon: "Warm the plates!" she croons to me from the Great Beyond. She abhorred the common practice of serving hot food on cold china. *Common* is the epithet she would have applied to it, a word that carried powerful connotations of contempt.

This wintry day, then, I reduce five gallons of blackberries to serviceable pulp, measure out three cups of sugar to every four of berry mash, and set it boiling. We will have successive batches on the stove the rest of this day. I have already rummaged for suitable jars from the cellar shelves and these I will boil for fifteen minutes on a back burner. Toward the end I will grow more inventive about jars, for there are never enough of the good, straight-sided variety.

But for now, the jam puts up lacy bubbles, rolling around the top third of my giant cooking pot at a full boil. Despite candy thermometers, the only way I trust to gauge when the jam is ready is dip and drip. From a decent height, off a slotted spoon, I perform this test until the royal stuff begins to form a tiny waterfall. This is known as sheeting; all the cookbooks describe it, but it's a delicate decision to arrive at.

Stop too soon and you have a lovely blackberry sauce to serve over ice cream, sponge cake, or applesauce. Continue too long and you have a fatally overcooked mess of berry leather.

There is no quality control in my method. Every batch is a kind of revisionism. It makes its own laws. But the result is pure, deeply colored, uncomplicated, and unadulterated blackberry jam, veritably seedless, suitable for every occasion. After it has cooled, I pour melted paraffin on top of it, tilting the glass to get an airproof seal. Modern science frowns on so casual an approach to shutting out microbes, but I don't apologize. If the wax shows a spot of mold growing on top after a few months on the shelf, I can always remove it, wipe the sides clean, and pour a new layer of wax over all.

My mother would go home from her summer visits with a package of pickles and jams for her later delectation. When she died, there were several unopened jars in her cupboard. I took them back with me after the funeral. We ate them in her stead, as she would have wanted us to. Enough jam for a lifetime, she would say with evident satisfaction after a day of scullery duty. It was; it is.

THE FARM-RESTAURANT CONNECTION

ALICE WATERS

I HAVE ALWAYS BELIEVED that a restaurant can be no better than the ingredients it has to work with. As much as by any other factor, Chez Panisse has been defined by the search for ingredients. That search and what we have found along the way have shaped what we cook and ultimately who we are. The search has made us become part of a community—a community that has grown from markets, gardens, and suppliers and has gradually come to include farmers, ranchers, and fishermen. It has also made us realize that, as a restaurant, we are utterly dependent on the health of the land, the sea, and the planet as a whole, and that this search for good ingredients is pointless without a healthy agriculture and a healthy environment.

We served our first meal at Chez Panisse on August 28, 1971. The menu was pâté en croûte, duck with olives, salad, and fresh fruit, and the meal was cooked by Victoria Wise, who, together with Leslie Land and Paul Aratow, was one of the three original cooks at the restaurant. The ducks came from Chinatown in San Francisco and the other ingredients mostly from two local supermarkets: the Japanese produce concession at U-Save on Grove Street and the Co-op across the street. We sifted through every leaf of romaine, using perhaps 20 percent of each head and discarding the rest. We argued about which olives we ought to use with the duck and settled without much enthusiasm on green ones whose source I don't recall, agreeing after the fact that we could have done better. To this day we have yet to find a source of locally produced olives that really satisfies us.

We don't shop at supermarkets anymore, but in most respects the same processes and problems apply. Leslie Land recalls, "We were home cooks—we didn't know there were specialized restaurant suppliers. We thought everybody bought their food the way we did." I think that ignorance was an important, if unwitting, factor in allowing Chez Panisse to become what it is. Often, we simply couldn't cook what we wanted to cook because we couldn't find the level of quality we needed in the required ingredients, or we couldn't find the ingredients at all. Our set menus, which we've always published in advance so customers can choose when they want to come, featured the phrase "if available" with regularity during the first seven or eight years. Since we've always felt that freshness and purity were synonymous with quality, there were few guarantees that what we needed would appear in the form and condition we wanted when we wanted it.

If, as I believe, restaurants are communities—each with its own culture—then Chez Panisse began as a hunter-gatherer culture and, to a lesser extent, still is. Not only did we prowl the supermarkets, the stores and stalls of Chinatown, and such specialty shops as Berkeley then possessed (some of which, like the Cheese Board and Monterey Market, predated us and continue to develop from strength to strength) but we also literally foraged. We gathered watercress from streams, picked nasturtiums and fennel from roadsides, and gathered blackberries from the Santa Fe tracks in Berkeley. We also took herbs like oregano and thyme from the gardens of friends. One of these friends, Wendy Ruebman, asked if we'd like sorrel from her garden, setting in motion an informal but regular system of obtaining produce from her and other local gardeners. We also relied on friends with rural connections: Mary Isaak, the mother of one of our cooks, planted fraises des bois for us in Petaluma, and Lindsey Shere, one of my partners and our head pastry cook to this day, got her father to grow fruit for us near his place in Healdsburg.

Although most of our sources in the restaurant's early days were of necessity unpredictable, produce was the main problem area, and we focused our efforts again and again on resolving it. Perhaps more than any other kind of foodstuff, produce in general and its flavor in particular have suffered under postwar American agriculture. Although we've been able to have as much cosmetically perfect, out-of-season fruit and vegetables as anyone could possibly want, the flavor, freshness, variety, and wholesomeness of produce have been terribly diminished. With the notable exception of Chinese and Japanese markets that even in the early seventies emphasized flavor and quality, we really had nowhere to turn but to sympathetic gardeners who either already grew what we needed or would undertake to grow it for us.

Our emphasis—and, today, our insistence—on organically grown produce developed less out of any ideological commitment than out of the fact that this was the way almost everyone we knew gardened. We have never been interested in being a health or natural foods restaurant; rather, organic and naturally raised ingredients happen to be consistent with both what we want for our kitchen and what we want for our community and our larger environment. Such ingredients have never been an end in themselves, but they are a part of the way of life that inspired the restaurant and that we want the restaurant to inspire. Most of us have become so inured to the dogmas and self-justifications of agribusiness that we forget that, until 1940, most produce was, for all intents and purposes, organic, and, until the advent of the refrigerated boxcar, it was also of necessity fresh, seasonal, and local. There's nothing radical about organic produce: It's a return to traditional values of the most fundamental kind.

It had always seemed to us that the best way to solve our supply problems was either to deal directly with producers or, better still, to raise our own. By 1975, we'd made some progress with the first approach, regularly receiving, for example, fresh and smoked trout from Garrapata in Big Sur. One of my partners, Jerry Budrick, had also set up a connection with the Dal Porto Ranch in Amador County in the foothills of the Sierra Nevada, which provided us with lambs and with zinfandel grapes for the house wine Walter Schug made for us at the Joseph Phelps Winery. Jerry also acquired some land of his own in Amador, and it seemed an obvious solution to our produce needs for us to farm it. In 1977 we tried this, but we knew even less about farming than we thought we did, and the experiment proved a failure.

Fortunately, during the late 1970s some of our urban gardens were producing quite successfully, notably one cultivated by the French gardener and cook at Chez Panisse, Jean-Pierre Moullé on land in the Berkeley hills owned by Duke McGillis, our house doctor, and his wife, Joyce. In addition, Lindsey Shere returned from a trip to Italy laden with seeds, which her father planted in Healdsburg, thereby introducing us to rocket and other greens still exotic at that time. Meanwhile, we were also learning how to use conventional sources as best we could. Mark Miller, then a cook with us, made the rounds of the Oakland Produce Market each dawn, and we discovered useful sources at other wholesale and commercial markets in San Francisco. Closer to home, we bought regularly—as we still do—from Bill Fujimoto, who had taken over Monterey Market from his parents and had begun to build its reputation for quality and variety.

It's difficult now to remember the kind of attitude to flavor and quality that still prevailed in the mid- and late-1970s. When Jeremiah Tower, who was our main cook at Chez Panisse from 1973 to 1977, once sent back some meat he felt wasn't up to scratch, the supplier was apoplectic: No one had ever done that before. And Jerry Rosenfield, a friend and physician who has worked on many of our supply problems over the years, caused an uproar one morning when he was substituting for Mark Miller at the Oakland Produce Market: Jerry insisted on *tasting* some strawberries before buying them. Jerry was also a key figure in securing our sources for fish, probably the first of our supply problems that we were able to solve successfully. During the restaurant's first few years, we served very little fish at all, such was the quality available—despite our being across the bay from a city renowned for its seafood. But, in 1975, Jerry brought us some California sea mussels he'd gathered near his home, and they were a revelation. We asked him to bring us more, and in late 1976 he became our fish dealer, buying from wholesalers and fishermen ranging up the coast from Monterey to Fort Bragg. Along the way he began to be assisted by Paul Johnson, a cook from another Berkeley restaurant called In Season, who took over from Jerry in 1979 and who today sells what is arguably the best fish on the West Coast.

Our produce problem, however, remained unsolved, and we decided to have another try at farming. John Hudspeth, a disciple of James Beard who later started Bridge Creek restaurant just up the street from us, owned some land near Sacramento that he was willing to make available to us in 1980 and 1981. In some respects, this farm was a success—producing good onions and potatoes and wonderful little white peaches from a tree John had planted—but we weren't equipped to deal with the valley heat or the land's penchant for flooding. While the farm did produce, it produced unreliably, and we had to continue to obtain supplies from elsewhere. It also finally disabused us of any illusion that we were farmers. We realized that there seemed to be only two solutions available: extending and formalizing the system of urban gardeners we already had in place, and establishing direct connections with sympathetic farmers who could grow what we needed—that is, farmers who, since we didn't know enough farming to do it ourselves, would farm on our behalf.

In the early 1980s, two members of the restaurant staff, Andrea Crawford and Sibella Kraus, and Lindsey Shere's daughter Thérèse established several salad gardens in Berkeley, one of which was in my backyard. These eventually met most of our needs for salad greens, but for other kinds of produce we remained dependent on a hodge-podge of often-unreliable sources. Two things happened in 1982, however, that turned out to be tremendously important. First, Jean-Pierre Gorin, a friend and filmmaker teaching in La Jolla, introduced us to the produce grown near there by the Chino family. And, second, Sibella Kraus became the forager for the restaurant and eventually started the Farm-Restaurant Project. Jean-Pierre happened by the Chinos' roadside stand, tasted a green bean, and arranged to have two boxes sent to us immediately. The beans were exquisite, and I flew down to find out who had grown them. We became good friends, and to this day we receive nine boxes of produce from the Chinos each week.

Meanwhile, as Sibella had become more and more involved with our salad gardens, she decided that she would like to work with produce full-time and proposed that she become the restaurant's first full-time forager, an idea we agreed to with enthusiasm. Sibella spent her time on the road locating farmers, tasting their produce, and, if we liked it, arranging for a schedule of deliveries to Chez Panisse. In 1983, we funded the Farm-Restaurant Project under Sibella's direction, which set up a produce network among a number of Bay Area restaurants and local farmers and culminated in the first Tasting of Summer Produce, now an annual event at which dozens of small, quality-conscious farmers show their produce to the food community and the general public. Sibella left us to work for Greenleaf Produce (from whom we still regularly buy) and has become an important figure in the sustainable-agriculture movement. She was succeeded as forager by Catherine Brandel, who has since become one of the head cooks in our upstairs café. During this period, Green Gulch, run by the San Francisco Zen Center, became an important supplier, as did Warren Weber, whom we continue to work with today. We were also fortunate to have Thérèse Shere and Eric Monrad producing tomatoes, peppers, beans, lettuce, and lamb for us at Coulee Ranch near Healdsburg.

During her tenure as forager, Catherine continued to develop the network Sibella had created, finding, for example, a regular source of eggs for us at New Life Farms. But she was frustrated, as we all were, by the seeming impossibility of finding meat that was both flavorful and raised in a humane and wholesome way. Since the beginning of Chez Panisse, we had been forced to rely on conventional suppliers, a continuing disappointment given how much progress we had made with other kinds of materials. But, in late 1986, Jerry Rosenfield took over as forager from Catherine, and over the next two years he made enormous strides in finding meat sources for us. Jerry had been living in the Pacific Northwest and had discovered a number of ranchers and farmers there who were attempting to raise beef, veal, and lamb without hormones and under humane conditions. In particular, the Willamette Valley between Portland and Eugene, Oregon, became a source for rabbits, lambs, goats, and beef, although Jerry also located producers closer to home, including ones for game and for that most elusive bird—a decently flavored, naturally raised chicken. We still have a way to go, but today, for the first time in our history, we are able to serve meat that really pleases us.

We have made progress on other fronts, too. In 1983, for example, we helped Steve Sullivan launch Acme Bakery, which bakes for us and for many other local restaurants. And, recently, we've realized a close approximation of our dream of having a farm. In 1985, my father, Pat Waters, began looking for a farmer who would be willing to make a long-term agreement to grow most of our produce for us according to our specifications. With help from the University of California at Davis and local organic food organizations, Dad came up with a list of eighteen potential farmers, which he narrowed down to a list of four on the basis of interviews, tastings, and visits. We settled on Bob Cannard, who farms on twenty-five acres in the Sonoma Valley.

Bob is very special, not only because he grows wonderful fruits and vegetables for us—potatoes, onions, salad greens, tomatoes, beans, berries, peaches, apricots, and avocados, to name a few—but also because he is as interested in us as we are in him. He likes to visit the restaurant kitchen and pitch in, and we send our cooks up to him to help pick. He takes all the restaurant's compostable garbage each day, which he then uses to grow more food. He is also a teacher at his local college and a major force in his local farmer's market. He sees that his farm and our restaurant are part of something larger and that, whether we acknowledge it or not, they have a responsibility to the health of the communities in which they exist and of the land on which they depend.

The search for materials continues, and I imagine it always will. We are still looking for good sources for butter, olives, oil, and prosciutto, to name a few. But, even when we find them, the foraging will continue. Ingredients will appear that we'll want to try, and we in turn will have new requirements that we'll want someone to fulfill for us. Whatever happens, we realize that, as restaurateurs, we are now involved in agriculture and its vagaries—the weather, the soil, and the economics of farming and rural communities. Bob Cannard reminds us frequently that farming isn't manufacturing: It is a continuing relationship with nature that has to be complete on both sides to work. People claim to know that plants are living things, but the system of food production, distribution, and consumption we have known in this country for the last forty years has attempted to deny that they are. If our food has lacked flavor—if, in aesthetic terms, it has been dead—that may be because it was treated as dead even while it was being grown. And perhaps we have tolerated such food—and the way its production has affected our society and environment—because our senses, our hearts, and our minds have been in some sense deadened, too.

I've always felt it was part of my job as a cook and restaurateur to try to wake people up to these things, to challenge them really to taste the food and to experience the kind of community that can happen in the kitchen and at the table. Those of us who work with food suffer from an image of being involved in an elite, frivolous pastime that has little relation to anything important or meaningful. But in fact we are in a position to cause people to make important connections between what they are eating and a host of crucial environmental, social, and health issues. Food is at the center of these issues.

This isn't a matter of idealism or altruism but rather one of self-interest and survival. Restaurateurs have a very real stake in the health of the planet, in the source of the foodstuffs we depend on, and in the future of farmers, fishermen, and other producers. Hydroponic vegetables or fish raised in pens will never be a real substitute for the flavor and quality of the ingredients that are in increasing jeopardy today. Professionally and personally, both our livelihoods and our lives depend on the preservation of what we have and the restoration of what we have lost. The fate of farmers—and with them the fate of the earth itself—is not somebody else's problem: It is our fate, too.

There is clearly so much more to do. But ultimately it comes down to realizing the necessity of the land to what we do and our connection to it. Few restaurants are going to be able to create the kind of relationship we have with Bob Cannard, but there are other routes to the same goal. I'm convinced that farmer's markets are an important step in this direction; they also contribute to the local economy, promote more variety and quality in the marketplace, and create community. As restaurateurs and ordinary consumers meet the people who grow their food, they acquire an interest in the future of farms, of rural communities, and of the environment. This interest, when it helps to ensure the continuing provision of open space near cities and the diversity of food produced on it, is to everyone's benefit. Country and city can once again become a mutual support system, a web of interdependent communities. That's why fresh, locally grown, seasonal foodstuffs are more than an attractive fashion or a quaint, romantic notion: They are a fundamental part of a sustainable economy and agriculture—and they taste better, too. Of course, people respond, "That's easy for you to say: In California you can have whatever you want all year round." I tell them that's true, but I also tell them that most of it tastes terrible. And, while there's no reason to forgo all non-locally-produced ingredients— I wouldn't want to give up our weekly shipment from the Chinos— local materials must become the basis of our cooking and our food; this is true for every region of the planet that has produced a flavorful, healthy cuisine.

What sometimes seem to be limitations are often opportunities. Earlier this year, in the lee between the early spring vegetables and those of mid-summer, we had an abundance of fava beans, which we explored in the kitchen for six weeks, served in soups, in purées, as a garnish, and, of course, by themselves—and we discovered that we had only *begun* to tap the possibilities. There was a stew of beans with savory and cream, a fava-bean-and-potato gratin, fava bean pizza with lots of garlic, a pasta fagioli using favas, a rough puree of favas with garlic and sage, and a vinaigrette salad, to name a few. The point is that what constitutes an exciting, exotic ingredient is very much in the eye of the beholder and that few things can be as compelling as fresh, locally grown materials that you know have been raised in a responsible way.

When I was first thinking about opening what would become Chez Panisse, my friend Tom Luddy took me to see a Marcel Pagnol retrospective at the old Surf Theater in San Francisco. We went every night and saw about half the movies Pagnol made during his long career, including *The Baker's Wife* and his Marseilles trilogy—*Marius, Fanny,* and *César.* Every one of these movies about life in the south of France fifty years ago radiated wit, love for people, and respect for the earth. Every movie made me cry.

My partners and I decided to name our new restaurant after the widower Panisse, a compassionate, placid, and slightly ridiculous marine outfitter in the Marseilles trilogy, so as to evoke the sunny good feelings of another world that contained so much that was incomplete or missing in our own—the simple wholesome good food of Provence, the atmosphere of tolerant camaraderie and great lifelong friendships, and a respect both for the old folks and their pleasures and for the young and their passions. Four years later, when our partnership incorporated itself, we immodestly took the name Pagnol et Cie., Inc., to reaffirm our desire to recreate a reality where life and work were inseparable and the daily pace left time for the afternoon anisette or the restorative game of *pétanque,* and where eating together nourished the spirit as well as the body—since the food was raised, harvested, hunted, fished, and gathered by people sustaining and sustained by each other and by the earth itself. In this respect, as in so many others, the producers and farmers we have come to know not only have provided us with good food but have also been essential in helping us to realize our dreams.

SOUPS

JANE GRIGSON

*T*HE BEST ENGLISH SOUPS are unrivaled, but one might wish there were more of them. Soup is a primitive dish. Such soups as mulligatawny and oxtail and mutton broth—or the Welsh cawl—are continuing good versions of very old ways of cooking meat, at least as old as the first making of metal pots. All the same, soups are capable of great refinement and delicacy, particularly the fish and vegetable soups. They have the advantage of being easy to make, and variable within quite wide limits. A soup can be a meal, or it can be the introduction to a meal. It can be a comfort in itself, or an appetizer. And in these late days praise for a good home-made soup is out of all proportion to the effort involved—and it doesn't cost much.

Soup, or pottage as it was called, was eaten by everyone in the earlier centuries of our history. If you were poor it consisted of water thickened with oatmeal, rye flour or bread, and flavored with such vegetables and pulses as fields and gardens might provide. Bones or a scrap of bacon, milk, cream and butter all helped to give extra interest, as did parsley and other herbs. Root vegetables were known as potherbs, even as late as the thirties, when I was a child: you could go to the shop and get a cheap collection of roots for flavoring soups and stews. I notice that this practice has been taken up by supermarkets, though the name has been dropped. Alas the bargain is not such a good one, as the various vegetables have all been washed, prepared and packed in plastic which deprives them of flavor.

The pottage of the rich in pre-Renaissance times, though made in a similar way in great pots, was more varied and finer in its grace notes. Rice that came from the Arabs on boats that brought us spices, almonds and raisins, was used as thickener as were eggs and a powdered wheat

starch known as amidon. Spices flavored the soups and soup-stews—
the borderline between the two was a tenuous one—as did wine.
Thicker soups might be colored by streaking in ripples of saffron and
saunders (sandalwood) which gave a red tint against saffron's glowing
yellow. By using the white part of leeks and other pale vegetables, with
rice and almond milk, cooks produced an elegant white soup which was
still being made centuries later for parties and special dinners in the
time of Jane Austen and Eliza Acton.

Cooks to the medieval grand family played with sweet-sour effects
in a way that seems decidedly exotic today. Lenten and fastday soups
might consist of puréed apples and white wine, thickened with rice
flour, embellished with currants, chopped dates and slivered almonds:
there would be a flavoring of mace, cloves, pepper, cinnamon and ginger, a marbling of saffron and saunders, and finally a decorative scatter
of poached, shredded pears. The French may sneer at our taste for
sweet and savory together, but many such recipes came from the French
court in the first place, as did some notable soup-stews such as the civet
which we still make in both countries: the name comes from the char-
acterizing addition of onion in some form, *cive* in Old French, which is
still used for chives, along with *civette* and *ciboulette*. We think of it as
a hare dish: in the grand kitchens of fifteenth century cooks it was made
with other game, too, or with fish. Tench, an easily caught freshwater
fish, was popular for a civet: it was simmered and roasted (in that
order), mixed with pepper, saffron, bread and ale, and finally flavored
with onions fried in oil.

It seems to me that cooks in those days were resourceful at many
levels of society. A greater variety of herbs and potherbs was grown in
gardens than is normal now. In the middle of the sixteenth century, one
much travelled writer, Andrew Boorde, complimented them when he
remarked that "Pottage is not so much used in all Christendom as it is
used in England."

Food writers have remarked that we seemed to have lost our taste
for vegetables in some mysterious way in the sixteenth century.
Certainly the variety grown seems to have declined, but in quantity vegetables played an important part in people's diets especially if they were
poor, especially in the years of wheat famine. I suspect, too, that our
ways of cooking them lack finesse. Foreign visitors commented on the
many little heaps of vegetables swimming in too much butter.

What happened, I think, was that the style of eating changed, at
least for the upper and increasingly powerful middle classes, who were
affected by some of the new ideas about eating abroad in mainland
Europe of the Renaissance (though not affected enough according to

one Italian visitor, Giacomo Castelvetro, writing in 1614. Instead of being the main item of the meal, soups and soup-stews drew further apart, with the stews becoming less liquid and more elegant. Soups were relegated to the opening stage. If you look at a plan for the first course of a dinner party in an eighteenth century cookery book, say Mrs. Raffald's *Experienced English Housekeeper,* you will see that the meal was organized very differently from our dinner parties today. For each course the table was covered with a large number of different dishes of varying sizes according to the position they occupied (this is known as the French service). At each end there was a large tureen of soup, one thick and one thin. When the guests had drunk a polite bowlful, the tureens were removed and their place was filled with splendid roasts, beef or venison, and a large fish: these were carved and cut up by the host and hostess. To all the other dishes, people helped their neighbors and themselves.

Sitting down to such a spread of food, much of it cooling rapidly, people came to regard soup as little more than an appetizer. And when this old buffet style was superseded by the Russian service in the middle of the nineteenth century, with one dish being served at a course and everybody eating the same thing at the same time—the way we eat today—this status was confirmed. Simplicity and high quality became the standards of a good dinner.

In families, something of the old style remained, with stews and thick soups becoming standard winter fare. Not until the last forty years, with the popularity of Elizabeth David's books, have we dared to serve *civets* and *daubes* and *potées* and *garbures* and *cassoulets* at dinner parties. With the popularity of *nouvelle cuisine* cookery, such dishes went out for a while in the seventies, in favor of delicate soups rather in the Japanese style followed by decorative plates of beautifully cut meat or fish and a few vegetables. This very tricky and last-minute cookery began to readmit the family soup-stews in a refined form and now a return to *cuisine grandmère,* much easier to control and therefore more economic, is in full swing.

A great relief all round. Nothing is more difficult than trying to give visitors at home a *nouvelle cuisine* dinner with plate-service. Everything gets cold, for a start, and the waits between courses become nerve-wracking. After one attempt, most of us gave it up. All the same it was a comfort to me to read James Beard's introduction to his new cookery book in 1981; the section headed *Feel Free.* He talked of the old tyranny of the Russian service, dinner Escoffier style: "In my youth, a 'proper' dinner had to have something light at each end, like consommé to begin and fruit to finish—you could call the menu diamond-shaped, with a big bulge at the main course. . . . Usually it was a roast, with something starchy and several vegetables." In the next paragraph comes liberation with his blessing . . . "the main course is whatever you want to star— the nicest thing, perhaps, that you are offering at that meal. For some cooks, it may well be dessert, though not for me . . . This year for my annual celebration of the first shad roe, we had a luscious pair of sautéed roes apiece—with parsley—then very small paillards of veal with a little cucumber salad . . . and wound up with just a taste of fresh strawberry sorbet. A wedge-shaped dinner, then. And why not? It tasted wonderful, and taste is the only rule a cook need acknowledge, in this happy time of freshness and freedom."

An English cook has to be quite brave to treat a soup or soup-stew as the main course of a meal. Scotch cooks can do it with their cockie-leekie or the Welsh with their cawl. Perhaps we have been put off by the tradition of Dickens and the workhouse, and little boys' bones in the cauldron, and manor house ladies with their charitable soups. Nearly every Victorian cookery book has a recipe for beneficent or charitable soup, to be trotted round the parish by mother and unmarried daughters to the deserving poor. The French chef of the Reform Club, the great Alexis Soyer, caused a sensation by nobly going over to Ireland in the potato famine to save Irish souls with his soup (like most other benevolent soups of the time, it was not very nutritious). But soups are a good thing all the same. We have no need to blush for our Palestine soup, pea soup, smoked haddock soup, proper mulligatawny. And English eel soup and oyster soup are superb, so is the old white soup made from almonds—a masterpiece of delicacy.

Meat or poultry stock is not essential for vegetable soups—indeed it can spoil the flavor when you are using particularly good fresh vegetables. However I can recommend making a simple stock from the peelings and detritus of the vegetables you are using, with such additions of onion, herbs and spices as seem appropriate. Fish stock is no trouble to anyone, as it can be produced in half an hour from a couple of pounds of sole, turbot, whiting, cod or salmon bones, head and skin which most fishmongers will give you for nothing or for a few pence (note that fish bones should not be cooked for any longer than 30 minutes—unless you like your fish soup flavored with glue).

Which leaves us with meat, poultry and game stock. This is simple for microwave or Aga and other solid fuel stove owners: without trouble they can produce excellent stocks and store them in the freezer. If you put meat on the bone into the pot—bone being essential to many good soups—you do not need to prepare a preliminary stock. Most hearty English, indeed most British soups, are of this type—boiling fowl, boiling beef, boiling mutton or lamb cooked gently for hours in water with a few potherbs. A stock pot is a bad idea outside a professional kitchen, where it can be properly looked after, skimmed, reboiled and used quickly (this is not to say that liquor left over from boiling chicken, beef or fish is not a good idea if you happen to have it, but store it in the freezer and never keep it hanging around). A few years ago it was quite the fashion for cookery books to suggest that you keep a stock pot on the go, adding bits and pieces to it day by day, topping it up with water as you removed the contents for soups. This is a sure route to food poisoning and nasty flavors. When you make a stock, strain the liquor from the debris, cool it fast and freeze it in convenient sized containers as rapidly as possible. It is quite a good idea to reduce the strained stock to a strong flavor and freeze it in an ice-cube tray: the cubes can be stored in a plastic bag, ready for use. This is much more satisfactory than recourse to stock cubes.

Stock or soup cubes are, incidentally, nothing new to the English. Before the days of canning, meat was simmered, and the resulting liquid boiled down to a gluey sediment or glaze, which was cut into small lumps and known as portable soup. Explorers, sailors, anyone on the move would carry a little bagful, then heat up a few lumps with water to make an instant soup, that could be improved with any ingredients to hand (a splash of vinegar, for instance, which is a great brightener of flavor). Today's cubes with their monosodium glutamate give a second-rate flavor and sameness, which is to be avoided.

Some of the pleasure of soups consist in such final additions and embellishments as fried cubes of bread, crumbs of crisp bacon, chopped green herbs, an egg custard *royale* cut into little diamonds. Brandy and port make a wonderful difference to meat and game soups, just as a little dry white wine makes all the difference to several of the fish soups. This has been much more of an English practice than you would suppose, going back at least to the court cookery of Chaucer's time. Cream, chopped parsley, egg yolks, grated Parmesan, a knob of butter are all good enrichments for vegetable soups. The Welsh—and Scots—chop leeks and add them to meat soups before they are served. The leek softens slightly in the heat without cooking properly, and so retains an agreeable crispness and a light overtone of onion which is not in the least aggressive.

NIGEL SLATER

I CANNOT EVEN BEGIN to tell you how much I love eating. Hot, rustling chips with slightly too much salt on them, a piece of crisp-skinned duck or a round of thick white toast dripping with butter. Sometimes I just have to stop what I am doing and make a bacon sandwich or walk down the road to get a piece of cake. And although I prefer to eat something with a perfect provenance and made with the very best ingredients, I am not half as fussy as I could or should be. The way I look at it is this: a slice of commercially made chocolate cake might not be as good as a home-baked one, but it's better than no chocolate cake at all.

Being skinny, I have never had to worry about the side effects of such a gargantuan appetite. I have never had to question whether the second or even third helping of pie might not be a good idea. Fat was other people's problem. Then, one night about 18 months ago, just as I was climbing into bed, I caught a glimpse of something in the mirror that shocked me. Around my middle was a thick layer of fat. I shook myself and it wobbled like a blancmange at a child's birthday party. I squeezed it, prodded it, pummelled it, and kneaded it like bread dough. I lay on the bed and grasped it with both hands. I got down on all fours and watched it hang underneath me. At one point I contorted into a pretty accurate impression of a . . . no, you really don't want to know.

Now I have never had, or especially wanted, a washboard-flat stomach—I am about the world's least vain person and it shows—but neither did I want a sack of jelly strapped to my gut. So I decided to have my fat measured, professionally, and while I was about it everything else, too, from blood pressure to cholesterol. Because I am so rarely ill (I haven't even got a doctor, let alone recently visited one) I booked a private health check. While most things were as good as I could wish for (apparently due to the fact that I have never smoked and tend to walk rather than use a car) my body fat was very firmly in the "caution" zone. While being a good eight percent away from being officially obese, I was, for the first time in my life well on the wrong side of the line.

Like millions before me I have discovered there are more ways to lose weight that you can shake a hosepipe at. But it wasn't weight I wanted to lose. I have pin thin arms and legs and am apparently the perfect weight for my height. What I wanted to lose was fat. Some of the diets I checked out were, to say the least, intriguing. Others were frankly bonkers. Friends talked ecstatically of losing pounds by not eating carbohydrates, or only eating meat. Deciding on a diet is only marginally more difficult than choosing a chocolate from a box of Black Magic. It didn't inspire me with confidence when one dietician I spoke to actually said that one of the more high-profile weight-loss gurus should be taken out and shot.

But you know what? Virtually none of the diets I came across were even remotely compatible with good eating. Most of the people peddling their half-assed lose-pounds-in-a-fortnight diets seem to have no idea of what makes something worth eating. I'm not sure they even like food. What, please tell me, is the point of eating a steak without the bearnaise sauce and fries, or the point of pasta without the Parmesan? I needed a way of getting rid of this millstone of fat, while being able to continue to eat for pleasure.

I will tell you what I did, and how over 12 months I cut my body fat from 22 per cent to 13. Which, incidentally, is described by much of the medical profession as "ideal." It didn't force me to rethink my entire life, it didn't make me drastically change what I eat and it didn't cause me any pain or discomfort. To be frank, this was a diet based as much on common sense as anything else. But it is easy to stick to, and that, to most dieters, is half the battle.

For the entire 12 months I kept a record of everything I put in my mouth. I religiously noted every slice of smoked salmon, every sausage sandwich and each and every olive, strawberry and chocolate digestive. Until you write down your daily food consumption you will never really know what you eat. Believe me, having to admit, in your own handwriting to three walnut whips, two bacon butties and an entire tub of chocolate ice cream in one day beats any low carb, low protein, low fat, wacko diet hands down. I also discovered one or two helpful things. The first was the question of whether I was actually hungry or just thirsty. Now, I like to think I'm a fairly bright guy, but I have to admit to getting these two confused. So often, when I thought I was hungry, my body was just telling me it was dehydrated. This, more than any other single thing, is what has helped me to lose fat. In other words, next time you think you need a Mars bar, a pile of Pringles or a slice of cheesecake in between meals, try a glass of water or juice first. You might be as surprised as I was. To give you a clue, I downed over 600 litres of Evian in 2002. I also found that eating less helps. The main reason most of us are overweight is because we eat too much. I know that was true in my case. So I simply cut down the amount of food I put into my mouth. I won't pretend it was easy, especially when you work within six feet of your kitchen cupboards, but it is perfectly possible, with practice, to put the lid on a tub of Ben and Jerry's and put it back for tomorrow. "Serves four" can sometimes mean just that. And then I took up a moderate amount of exercise. By "moderate" I mean that I took the stairs not the lift (this isn't always possible, just try and find the staircase in Harvey Nichols) and I walked for about 30-40 minutes a day. I also swam for two to three hours a week. None of this took up much time and I was only "tweaking" my normal lifestyle. I know if I had taken up serious exercise I would have lasted no more than five minutes. Slightly accelerating my normal routine was easy and I stuck to it. It also helped to identify the comfort foods I turn to when I am stressed, bored or angry and substitute something healthy for some of them. For the record, mine are ice cream, pies (of any sort, it's the pastry I'm after) and chocolate bars. I simply swapped most of them for fruit. So, instead of eating a roll of Munchies I would scoff a handful of blueberries. Grapes, raspberries, strawberries and tangerines were the easiest; no matter how carefully you peel them, oranges tend to cover everything on your desk in fine sticky spray. Bananas leave you with the skin to get rid of. In really desperate moments I did not even attempt to deny my true needs. Sometimes only a slice of cheesecake will do. The other thing I discovered was water. There was never a day when I drank less than 1.5 litres of Evian, sometimes as many as three. The downside is that I pee like a horse. Here is exactly what I ate last year . . .

I ate 72 kilos of fish (not counting 40 fish fingers and 472 pieces of sushi) which is only slightly less than the average polar bear. In fact it actually comes in at just over 200g a day. I should explain, quickly, that fish, rather than meat or poultry is my protein of choice. I love its silky texture and the fact that it is light on the gut. Gram for gram I ate more smoked salmon than almost anything else (9.7kg, I know it's hideously expensive, but I don't smoke or drive a car, so give me a break), hotly followed by rollmop herrings at 7.3kg. The reason for this is my habit of having a little of each as I'm preparing dinner. Light as they are, they soon add up. I also managed to swallow 12kg of mackerel, most of which I grilled so that the skin was all black and toasty, 4kg of halibut (and rather a lot of Hollandaise sauce), 2.5kg of cod, 16 dressed crabs, 17 whole plaice, 13 sea bass, 3.5kg of smoked mackerel and 194 oysters. I saw off 10 squid, 5 grilled sole, 1.2kg of skate and 500g of salt cod. What I didn't eat much of were scallops (a measly 2) and tuna (of which I am honestly not fond). I did manage 472 pieces of sushi, 7 bowls of moules marinière (2 of which came up again), and 3.7kg of salmon (which didn't). The best fishy thing I ate all year was a crab salad at Nahm in the Halkin Hotel, though it was difficult to beat the piece of halibut I cooked at home with bearnaise sauce and green beans from the garden.

MEAT

I love meat, especially any part of the pig, yet somehow I consumed a pathetic 97g a week last year. That's about the weight of the average sausage. At only 13g per day I know vegetarians who eat more meat than I do. But that doesn't include the cured meats, all those satin-textured slices of Italian ham such as the 1.5kg of Parma I got through or any of the fat-speckled salamis. I think this low score is because of the way I eat meat as an occasional pig-out, say, a piece of organic roast pork or a plate of bloody steak and chips, rather than as a regular weekday thing. I ate only two portions of lamb, both roast, the entire year but managed 20 or more bacon or sausage sandwiches, 6 pork pies, a black pudding, a Big Mac (I was drunk), rather a lot of Chinese pork dishes and several portions of delectably fatty rillettes. I'll never stop eating meat, especially the crackling off roast pork and blood-oozing rump steaks but I admit I haven't made much of a hole in Europe's beef mountain.

GAME AND POULTRY

Again this seems low at only 100g a week but what I did eat was sensational. A vast pot of stewed goose with butterbeans and broth, cold roast duck in Chinatown and several crispy ones with pancakes too, 500g of fluffy bunny, 800g of chicken livers and nearly a kilo of coq au vin. The best thing I ate was one of several pieces of grilled chicken with herbes de Provence cooked over the grill at home. The worst was an undercooked, overpriced partridge at a fashionable West End restaurant. They should have shot the chef rather than the poor partridge.

FRUIT

I'm just showing off now: 175 apples, 33 apricots, 179 bananas, 1730g blackcurrants, 5.625g blackberries, 10 kilos of blueberries (yes, 10), 7 kilos of cherries, 64 clementines, 4kg of damsons, 1.25kg dates, only 8 figs, 10.55kg of black grapes and 1.8 of green, 1kg of poached gooseberries, 40 kiwis (I must be quite, quite mad), 250g loganberries, 1kg lychees, 67 mangoes and 38 papaya, 194 oranges not counting those squidged up for juice, 42 passion fruit, 66 peaches, 148 pears, 11 pineapples, 3 persimmons, 100 plums (I am so regular they could set Big Ben by me), 430 strawberries, 3 pomegranates, 120 portions of raspberries, 2kg redcurrants, three portions of whitecurrants from the garden and 9 melons. That's about 191 kilos a year, which works out at 525g a day.

VEGETABLES

About 110kg, that's about 2kg a week or 300g per day, which I reckon is low enough to get me a black star, but add that to the fruit and I reckon it looks much more rosy. My bowels certainly think so. I ate 198 portions of greens which I think isn't bad. If I add green salads onto that, we are up to 394 which makes me sound like a hero.

Most of the 198 were some form of Chinese greens, purple sprouting or that beautiful, ruffled Cavolo Nero. Somehow I also pushed down 31 portions of green beans, 110 raw carrots, 10 chicory salads, 10 corn on the cobs, 36 courgettes, 2 punnets of cress, a plate of courgette fritters, and then another, 4 cucumbers, 6 portions of curly kale, a marrow, about a kilo of mushrooms, several portions of mushrooms on toast, and 14 parsnips. I can't believe I only ate 14 parsnips but that's not counting mash. I ate 4 pumpkins, 2 portions of samphire, 31 portions of spinach, some of which was chopped and mixed with cream in the French style, some simply steamed, 30 raw tomatoes and 218 roast ones, a grilled radiccio, 9 bunches of watercress and 8 portions of peas. I ate 2 cooked carrots under duress. I cut back on the potatoes and ate only 16 portions of mash, 9 boiled, 5 portions of French fries, 5 of roast and 2 of dauphinoise. I ate slices of potato hash, 4 portions of Jerseys and 10 sweet potatoes. For someone who loves their spuds this is pathetic. Some of the fault lies with the restaurants who think it's naff to serve them at all and some with me for being too lazy to peel them. Which reminds me. I got through 26 baked ones.

PASTA, PULSES, NOODLES
AND STUFF

1kg butterbeans, 500g chickpea curry, 300g chickpea mash, 450g flageolet beans, 1,600g baked beans, 1,100g lentils, 8 portions of dhal, 6 portions tabbouleh, 150g white haricot beans, 2,250g brown basmati rice, 250g white rice and 8 risotto. There were falafels too, about 12 of them, 12 portions of couscous, and 6 Italian rice balls. Quite how I chomped my way through 27 kilos of organic muesli I will never know.

I wolfed down 1.5kg soba noodles, 1kg macha noodles, 400g gnoccetti, 2 portions of cannelloni, 250g of inedible pasta salad which I only forced down because I was tired and hungry and trapped on the Virgin Birmingham to London train, 1 rigatoni with chili sauce, 13 portions of penne, 2kg of stuffed tortelloni, 250g ravioli stuffed with potato and cheese which sounds divine but I can't remember where I ate it, 2 portions of Kathy Burke's gorgeous spaghettini with spinach, 4 portions of wholewheat pasta.

I am not sure how to measure the 20 portions of dim sum and 28 portions of mezze, the 48 sandwiches and 6 pizzas, or the 22 bagels, but I ate them too. And 48 loaves of bread, 70 rounds of which were made into toast or bruschetta. Did I mention the 390 oatcakes?

DAIRY

I am not sure life is worth living without cheese. My total consumption was 21kg, most of which was goats' and sheep's cheese. It sounds a lot less if you say it as 60g a day. I got through rather a lot of goats' yogurt too, a cool kilo a week. Oh, and 3kg of sheep's.

CAKE

I could kill for cake. Here's the list: 1 carrot cake, 2 cheesecakes, 3 chocolate cakes, 3 slices of fruit bread, 9 slices of fruit cake, 2 slices of birthday cake, 2 slices of Pret a Manger pecan pie, 5 slices lemon cake, 1 apricot tart, half a ricotta tart, 5 fairy cakes (once you start you can't stop), 2 battenburg and a slice of walnut pie. Not bad, until you add it to the 32 biscotti, 8 flapjacks, 4 Jaffa cakes, 500g pan forte, 2 madeleines, 14 double choc chip cookies, 4 meringues, 12 amaretti and a fortune cookie, which I promptly spat out.

PUDDINGS

I have separated puddings and cake for obvious reasons (put them together and I sound like Billy Bunter). Anyway: three chocolate banana fritters (which I didn't want but Ruth Watson made me eat), half a pannacotta with passion fruit, 2 mouthfuls of zabaglione, 1 apple crumble and custard, 4 plum crumbles and custard, 1 blueberry tart, 1 apricot tart, 1 raspberry tart, 1 lemon tart, 1 fig tart, 1 gooseberry tart, 6 mince pies, 1 prune tart, 1 plum pie, 1 prune tart, 5 portions of trifle and a summer pudding. On the ice cream front I managed to get by with only 2 tubs of vanilla ice, 2 of orange sorbet, 1 portion of rose, 2 of pear, and 500ml of mango. Oh, and I almost forgot, 2kg of chocolate ice cream.

CHOCOLATE

1460 chocolates, 20 chocolate digestives, 6 brownies, 12 pralines, 20 chocolate almonds, 22 bars of hazelnut chocolate, 2 chocolate sesame bars, 2 chocolate truffles, a bar of Fry's Turkish delight, 2 Ferrero Rocher, 2 Easter eggs and a portion of chocolate mousse.

A few other things I should mention include 142 pots of green tea, 17 mint, 150 beers and 124 lemon verbena tea. There were a couple of mango lassi, 140 cubes of Turkish Delight, 12 pots of jasmine tea, 14 travelling cappuccino and 48 bowls of soup. As you might expect from a guy who has just written a juice book, I managed to down 358 juices, some of which were made at home and some of which were juices picked up on my way back from swimming. Of the 292 bottles of wine 4 were Australian, 3 New Zealand, 6 Californian and the rest were Italian and French.

All of which kept me at 72 kilos and reduced my body fat to a smug 13 percent. None of this involved eating weird diets of low fat foods, cutting out carbohydrates or eating masses of meat and no veg. Neither did it involve any pills or potions and, unlike the famous cabbage soup diet, it didn't make me fart for England. At least no more than usual anyway. This was a diet that allowed me to eat everything I would normally—the cheese, the toast and the cakes—just a little less of it. Okay, I won't make a million out of my diet, but why should anyone make money out of what is so glaringly obvious. The best way to lose fat is to throw the diet books out of the window, eat a bit less and always, always take the stairs. It works, and I've proved it.

FEEDING YOUR CRITTER

LAURIE COLWIN

A T ANY GIVEN MOMENT, there is someone in the world—usually a woman—trying to coax a small child to eat something he or she does not feel like eating.

There is nothing trickier than trying to write about what to feed children. Everyone has notions about this. Naturally, they think theirs are better than yours. Actually, mine are better than theirs.

I am what not-so-nice persons might call a food crank. I believe in all those good things food cranks believe in: breast-feeding, homemade baby food, the baby-food grinder. As a bona fide food crank I make the assumption that unless I make it or buy it from a local source or am convinced of its purity, it probably isn't pure. This is an extreme stance, and naturally I am not consistent. I buy tomato paste from Italy that comes in a tube as well as all kinds of Italian pasta. I don't know what is in them, but I buy them anyway. I don't know where the milk in the Parmesan cheese comes from. My theory is: Provision as much pure and organic food as you can and let the rest go by.

When my daughter reached toddlerhood, I ordered quantities of organic apple juice by mail. I was scared of Alar and other, less well-publicized pesticides. I did not want to lie in bed all night worrying about them. Our children are ingesting pesticides and additives that did not exist when we were children, and we have no idea what their long-range effect will be.

I am, of course, a moving target. I work at home; therefore, if I go to the greenmarket in the morning to buy organic eggs and milk, no one is going to dock my pay. Tell a working mother that she ought to find organic food for her child, and that mother's face will show you what desolation really means. There is simply no time and often not enough money.

Most parents also have to cope with television, which does almost nothing but beam into the extremely trusting brains of children what they ought to eat. We do not have television, but my daughter has a bash at one every now and again. She once came to me, her face awash with concern, and said, "Mom, I don't want you to make soup anymore." I asked her why she felt that way. She said, "Because it says on the television that Campbell's is better than homemade." This, I felt, was a dire indication of what's really out there in television land. The underlying reality here is that for all our food processors and fancy food stores, our connection with food is really very tenuous. We eat breakfast on the run. Our children's lunch boxes are filled with instant pudding, instant soup, peanut butter and jelly on packaged bread. Very often our evening meal comes from a package.

Although I do believe that people should sit down together at dinnertime, I realize that for people who work this is a struggle and a hardship. This is not an argument for begging women to stay at home. On this subject I feel people most often do what they have to do but also should do what they want. Somewhere along the line we as parents have got to reclaim some of the things that make life worth living.

I do not believe that delicious food is a frill.

In my years as a parent, I have made a nonacademic, hands-on study of this matter. I have come to two realizations. The first is that food to children is not what it is to adults. Their taste buds are developing in a way we can't imagine and science can't deduce. A plate of ratatouille may be very attractive to a toddler, especially if it is *your* plate and you are trying to finish your lunch. But offer him or her a plate of it for lunch and you will be met with a look of sheer outrage. This child may eat all the chick-peas out of a blazing-hot Pakistani curry dinner one night and shun spicy food the next.

Chinese food, for city dwellers, is one of the staffs of life (providing your city has a Chinese population). There are non-Chinese children in New York City who will eat almost nothing else. I once watched in perfect awe when, at a Chinese meal, the worst eater in my daughter's kindergarten class, whose mother claimed he was living on hot dogs and his baby sister's puréed pears, chowed down a large quantity of moo shoo pork, which contains, among other things, tree ear (quite a gelatinous fungus), bamboo shoots, baby corn, and egg—things he would never have eaten at home. Home is full of prejudices and rules, but a restaurant is not. It is, in fact, amazing what children will eat if they are given the chance.

Children, in my experience, do not like mixtures. To their pure, unadulterated palates, foods taste more intense. So they like things one at a time, in separate portions (the exception here is soup). Because they are young, they are happy to experiment. I will never forget the look of rapture that crossed my daughter's face at her first taste of steamed zucchini. I myself hadn't eaten an unadorned vegetable in years. I tried some and discovered the joys of vegetables that you leave alone. This is one of the many things you can learn from children.

My second observation is that mealtime means nothing to small children if they happen not to be hungry. Mealtime is a perfectly justifiable management technique. Family life would be impossible without some order. Furthermore, we must see that our small children are fed; and we are responsible for feeding them. And yet we expect of children what we do not expect of ourselves as grown-ups: to eat at mandated times, to eat what is given, to eat what we want them to eat *when* we want them to eat. Unlike Mary Poppins, we do not remember what life was like for us when we were small, so the deck is stacked against us.

Children eat what they are used to, and once they leave the stage of puréed food and graduate to mashed-up editions of grown-up food, they eat what *we* eat, unless we decide on what we feel children should eat and feed them that. Just as we make constant, unconscious gender distinctions for them *(Girls don't do that! Be a big boy!),* so do we make food distinctions. Oh, we say, he won't like lobster ravioli, or sautéed mushrooms, and thereby we cheat our children out of things they might very well adore.

Just as there are house styles governing the grammar rules for magazines and books, so there are house styles in families, and children pick them right up. They can hear even the remotest bat squeak from parents concerning the Big Issues, one of which is food. Like love and money, food can be encrusted with all manner of other things.

For instance, I have a friend for whom the family dinner is a sacred obligation. She comes home from work and prepares an old-fashioned dinner. This ritual makes her *feel* a certain way, but it does not make her child feel a certain way. The more the mother wants a confirming reaction from her child, the less her child is inclined to eat. The child's reluctance is seen as a power play by a mother yearning for what she considers an appropriate response from her child.

I have another friend who is in fact a marvelous cook, but the burden of cooking, shopping, and planning is a chore (every cooking mother in the world has felt this way) and a bore and a dreaded obligation. Her own attitudes about food are complicated at best; she herself often forgets to eat. Her child, who is fearless in most other ways, is a reluctant eater.

When you think about what messages you are sending your child, you must always remember the messages that were sent to you. We have all been brainwashed into thinking that a proper diet consists of one starch or grain, some protein, and some vegetables. Almost any Asian above a certain income level would look at our tables in astonishment at how impoverished our diet is. Any Indian, Korean, Japanese, or Chinese meal contains a number of dishes of vegetables and meat or fish, plus noodles, rice, and something pickled. Our tables still feature the large piece of meat, the potato, and some vegetables that are very much an afterthought. What would happen if the vegetables were the first thought?

Because I am a crank, and because I was brought up by a family that found food interesting, entertaining, and valuable as well as necessary and sustaining, I took my child to the greenmarket with me when I shopped. There we encountered such things as zucchini blossoms, which, when fried in batter, were a great success. We discovered something called minaret broccoli or broccoli *romanesco,* also a hit. We bought quail eggs (very successful) and infinite varieties of apple (Arkansas black twig and mutsus are the two favorites).

What I was doing with my daughter was what was done with me. I was taken into the world of food—to the poultry lady who sold chickens and guinea hens, to the fish market, out crabbing for blue crabs. I have passed on to my daughter what was given to me: a sense of pleasure and delight in the bounty of the table.

My daughter grew up on bread that was either made by me or bought at a greenmarket from an organic bakery. At the age of two and a half she was offered a little carton of goat yogurt. She ate three cartons in a row and has never looked back.

At the age of three, my child uttered the following sentence: "Mom, go to Balducci's and get me some goat yogurt and some garlic sourdough bread." This is the sort of thing that makes the mothers of noneating children hate me. I would hate me, too, but I am the parent of an omnivore. She is the daughter of two people who like to eat, who take pleasure in food.

Although it is perfectly true that perfectly healthy adults may start their lives as children who eat nothing but peanut butter for weeks at a time, it seems to me more interesting, more fun and more life-affirming, if children eat lots of things in the spirit of good health, culinary pleasure, cultural exchange, and happiness in the world. The rule in our house, like the rule I grew up with as a child, is: "You don't have to like it, but you have to try it. If you don't like it you can spit it out." This is an attractive proposition to a child of spitting age. In the process of enforcing this rather benign rule, you may find your child liking things you never dreamed of.

Of course, there are children who eat almost nothing at all. My upstairs neighbor's oldest child lived on oatmeal for three years. I don't have one of these children, but the trick seems to be to wait it out. We cannot know what is going on inside them, and oatmeal is a perfectly reasonable food. What we don't want to do, it seems to me, is to train children to want processed food, loaded with unnecessary sugar and fat. I myself have nothing against sugar and fat, but they seem to be addictive to children whose palates are tainted by them. I would much rather have children who ate nothing but oatmeal than one who only ate food from a can.

We are now living in a time of severe economic crunch. Everyone works. There is no one at home to cook. Our children are being fed, as Ralph Nader says, by large corporations who do not have their best interests at heart. The stress of modern life has taken away our leisure, our relaxations, our hobbies, and our family time. It has robbed people who like caregiving of the opportunity to give care. And it has abased our sense of pleasure at the table, one of life's greatest pleasures.

As parents we need to find ways to bring some of this back so that our children can have childhood memories of home-cooked food and a family meal. We have to start pressuring our supermarkets for organic food. We must lean on our government to protect us from agribusiness. We have to pressure our local governments to sponsor greenmarkets so our children can learn that vegetables do not come out of plastic bags. We have to get our sons into the kitchen so our daughters will not end up marrying fellows who don't know their way around a stove. We have to feed our child everything and anything—what *we* like—and eventually they will find things we never tasted before and bring them home to educate us.

But first we must realize that food is not only fuel, not only health-giving: It is pleasure, instruction, delight. It is consoling, transporting, and a comfort. As far as children and food go, everything else follows.

Encourage your child to try everything. Make one family meal a week. If you are a single parent, invite some friends and tell them to bring something. Or invite yourself and your family to the home of someone who works at home and makes Friday-night supper *(you* bring something). Take your child to the farm stand, the greenmarket, the produce section of the supermarket. Get your child into the kitchen with you if you cook. If you don't, acquire a nice, user-friendly cookbook (the *Joy of Cooking* is everyone's friend) and learn to cook with your child. Try some appealing new thing as often as possible. Don't obsess about health. Ask your child's opinion and solicit his or her advice.

If you want a happy eater, run a happy kitchen. These things take time, but so do all good things. Rejoice in what you have, be it rice and beans or baked Alaska. Be charmed by vegetables and your child will be charmed, too. If it is delicious, there is a good chance children will eat it.

We want our children to be independent thinkers, happy sweethearts, and cheerful parents, and it is not too much to ask that they be cheerful cooks and eaters, too.

FRESH HERBS

ELIZABETH DAVID

T HE USE OF HERBS in cooking is so much a matter of tradition, almost
of superstition, that the fact that it is also a question of personal taste
is overlooked, and experiments are seldom tried; in fact the restriction
of this herb to that dish is usually quite arbitrary, and because somebody long ago discovered that basil works some sort of spell with tomatoes, fennel with fish, and rosemary with pork, it occurs to few people
to reverse the traditional usage; to take an example, fennel is an excellent complement to pork, adding the sharpness which is supplied in
English cookery by apple sauce, while basil enhances almost anything
with which it is cooked; for ideas one has only to look to the cooking
of other countries to see how much the use of herbs as a flavoring can be
varied. In England mint is considered to have an affinity for lamb, new
potatoes, and green peas; the French regard the use of mint as a flavoring as yet another sign of English barbarism, and scarcely ever employ it,
while all over the Middle East, where the cooking is far from uncivilized,
mint is one of the most commonly used of herbs; it goes into soups,
sauces, omelettes, salads, purées of dried vegetables and into the sweet
cooling mint tea drunk by the Persians and Arabs. In Spain, where the
cooking has been much influenced by the Arabs, it is also used in stews
and soups; it is usually one of the ingredients of the sweet sour sauces
which the Italians like, and which are a legacy from the Romans, and in
modern Roman cooking wild mint gives a characteristic flavor to stewed
mushrooms and to vegetable soups. The Indians make a fresh chutney
from pounded mint, mangoes, onion and chillies, which is an excellent
accompaniment to fish and cold meat as well as to curries. Mint is one of
the cleanest tasting of herbs and will give a lively tang to many vegetables, carrots, tomatoes, mushrooms, lentils; a little finely chopped mint is

good in fish soups and stews, and with braised duck; a cold roast duck served on a bed of freshly picked mint makes a lovely, fresh-smelling summer dish; a few leaves can be added to the orange salad to serve with it. Dried mint is one of the most useful of herbs for the winter, for it greatly enlivens purées and soups of dried peas, haricot beans and lentils. Finely powdered dried mint is a characteristic flavoring of Turkish, Egyptian and Lebanese cooking. It is particularly good in mixtures of tomatoes and aubergines, and with rice dishes cooked in olive oil.

In England basil is one of the traditional herbs for turtle soup, and it is well known that it brings out the flavor of tomato salads and sauces; although it was common at one time in English kitchen gardens it is now extremely hard to lay hands on fresh basil, a state of affairs which should be remedied as fast as possible, for, with its highly aromatic scent, it is one of the most delicious of all herbs. In Provence, in Italy, in Greece, basil grows and is used in great quantities. The Genoese could scarcely exist without their *pesto,* a thick compound of pounded basil, pine nuts, garlic, cheese and olive oil which is used as a sauce for every kind of pasta, for fish, particularly red mullet, and as a flavorng for soups and minestrones. The Niçois have their own version of this sauce called *pistou* which has given its name to the Soupe au Pistou made of french beans, potatoes and macaroni, flavored with the *pistou* sauce. To the Greeks basil has a special significance, for the legend goes that basil was found growing on the site of the Crucifixion by the Empress Helena, who brought it back from Jerusalem to Greece, since when the plant has flourished all over the Greek world; scarcely a house in Greece is to be seen without its pot of basil in the window. Once you have become a basil addict it is hard to do without it; Mediterranean vegetables such as pimentos and aubergines, garlicky soups and wine-flavored dishes of beef, salads dressed with the fruity olive oil of Provence or Liguria and all the dishes with tomato sauces need basil as a fish needs water, and there is no substitute.

Of that very English herb sage I have little to say except that, and this is where the question of personal taste comes in, it seems to me to be altogether too blatant, and used far too much; its all pervading presence in stuffings and sausages is perhaps responsible for the distaste for herbs which many English people feel. The Italians are also very fond of sage, and use it a great deal with veal and with liver; it seems to give a musty rather than a fresh flavor, and I would always substitute mint or basil for sage in any recipe. The same applies to rosemary, which when fresh gives out a powerful oil which penetrates anything cooked with it; in southern France it is used to flavor roast lamb, pork and veal, but should be removed from the dish before it is served, as it is disagreeable to find those spiky little leaves in one's mouth; in Italy rosemary is stuffed in formidable quantities into roast sucking pig, and in the butchers' shops you see joints of pork tied up ready for roasting wreathed round and threaded with rosemary; it looks entrancing, but if you want to taste the meat, use only the smallest quantity, and never put it into stock destined for a consommé or for a sauce.

Thyme, marjoram and wild marjoram are all good and strong flavored herbs which can be used separately or together for robust stews of beef in red wine, for those aromatic country soups in which there are onions, garlic, bacon, wine, cabbage; the *garbures* of southwestern France and the minestrones of northern Italy; one or other of these herbs should go into stuffings for chicken, goose and turkey, for pimentos and aubergines, into meat croquettes (accompanied by grated lemon peel), terrines of game, and stews of hare and rabbit; either thyme or marjoram is almost essential to strew in small quantities on mutton, pork and lamb chops and liver to be fried or grilled; wild marjoram is called *origano* in Italy and Spain and is used for any and every dish of veal and pork, for fish and fish soups, and is an essential ingredient of the Neapolitan pizza, that colorful, filling, peasant dish of bread dough baked with tomatoes, anchovies and cheese. The marjoram which grows wild in Greece and Cyprus called *rígani* is a variety which has a more powerful scent; the flowers as well as the leaves are dried and no kebab of mutton, lamb or kid is thinkable without it. Lemon thyme is at its best fresh rather than cooked and is particularly good in a buttery potato purée, and in salads; there are dozens of varieties of thyme each with its particular scent, the best for cooking being perhaps the common thyme which grows wild on the downs. A curious thyme which has a scent of caraway seeds is good with roast pork.

Fennel, both the leaves and stalks of the variety which grows rather too easily in English gardens, and the root-bulb of the Florentine fennel which is imported from France and Italy, has many uses besides the sauce for mackerel which is found in all old English cookery books. For the famous Provençal *grillade au fenouil* the sun-dried, brittle stalks of the fennel are used as a bed on which to grill sea-bass *(loup de mer)* or red mullet; there is a Tuscan chicken dish in which the bird is stuffed with thick strips of ham and pieces of fennel bulb and pot-roasted; in Perugia they stuff their sucking pig and pork with fennel leaves and garlic instead of the rosemary prevalent elsewhere in Italy; one of the best of Italian sausages is *finocchiona,* a Florentine pork *salame* flavored with fennel seeds; if you like the aniseed taste of fennel use it chopped up raw in soups, particularly iced soups, and in vinaigrette sauces, in rice salads to give the crisp element so necessary to soft foods, in mixed vegetable salads, in fish mayonnaises, in the court-bouillon in which fish is to be poached, in stuffings for baked fish, in chicken salads, and mixed with parsley and juniper berries for a marinade for pork chops which are to be grilled. The leaves of dill are not unlike those of fennel, but the aniseed flavor is less pronounced; it is a herb much used in Scandinavian and Russian cooking, particularly to flavor pickled cucumber and for soups.

Tarragon is essentially a herb of French cookery; *poulet à l'estragon* and *oeufs en gelée à l'estragon* are classics of the French kitchen; without tarragon there is no true Sauce Béarnaise; with chives and chervil (which also goes well with carrots, potatoes, and in salads) or parsley it is one of the *fines herbes* for omelettes, sauces, butters, and many dishes of grilled meat and fish. It is a herb to be used with care for its charm lies in its very distinct and odd flavor and too much of it spoils the effect, but a few leaves will give character to many dishes and particularly to smooth foods such as sole cooked in cream, eggs *en cocotte*, cream soups, bisques of shell fish, stewed scallops, potato purées and also to tomato salads. In Italy, tarragon is to be found only in and around Siena, where it is used in the stuffing for globe artichokes, and to flavor green salads. When buying tarragon plants be sure to insist on the true French tarragon. Common tarragon, sometimes called Russian tarragon, has a rank taste and no scent at all.

The routine *bouquet garni* of French cookery consists of a sprig of thyme, parsley and a bay leaf (which besides its well-known use in soups and stews and marinades gives a good flavor to béchamel sauce if put in the milk while it is heated, and then removed). Chives, with their delicate onion flavor and brilliant green coloring, are one of the best of summer garnishes for eggs, vegetables, salads and soups. Borage is used by the Genoese to mix with the stuffing for ravioli, and to make fritters; the finely chopped leaves give a delicate cucumber taste to cream cheese, and its use in wine cups is traditional. The Sardinians flavor roast pork with myrtle, the French consider savory *(sarriette)* indispensable as a flavoring for broad beans; lovage, a member of the *Umbelliferae* family, has a peppery leaf with a faint hint of celery and gives an interesting taste to a salad of haricot beans and to fish soups. Among its thousands of uses in the kitchen, parsley is the perfect foil for garlic; the fresh leaves of angelica can be used in salads, while the translucent green stalks have a very strong fresh scent, which when candied give such a delicious flavor and elegant appearance to sweet creams and cream cheese puddings; the leaf of the sweet-scented geranium gives a lovely scent to a lemon water ice and an incomparable flavor when cooked with blackberries for jelly. The fresh leaves of coriander are much used in Oriental, Middle Eastern and Mexican cookery, while the dried seeds are one of the essential ingredients of nearly all curries and Oriental cooking; with their slightly burnt orange peel taste they are also good to flavor pork, mutton and venison, and in sauces for coarse fish; they can also be used to flavor milk and cream puddings and junkets. All these herbs and many others, tansy, violets, balm, marigold petals, nasturtium flowers and leaves, penny-royal, yarrow, costmary, burnet, rocket, sorrel and rue, were familiar ingredients of country cookery all over Europe until the twentieth century brought such a battery of chemical flavorings and synthetic essences that the uses and virtues of fresh plants have been almost forgotten. But when you are accustomed to their presence in food they are as necessary as salt; during the summer months while their flavors are fresh and their leaves green they add enormously to the appearance as well as to the flavor of food.

The quantity in which any given herb is to be used is a matter of taste rather than of rule. Cookery books are full of exhortations to discretion in this matter, but much depends on the herb with which you happen to be dealing, what food it is to flavor, whether the dish in question is to be a long simmered one in which it is the sauce which will be ultimately red with the herbs, or whether the herbs are to go into a stuffing for a bird or meat to be roasted, in which case the aromas will be more concentrated, or again whether the herbs will be cooked only a minute or two as in egg dishes, or not cooked at all, as when they are used to flavor a salad or a herb butter. Whether the herbs are fresh or dried is an important point. The oils in some herbs (rosemary, wild marjoram, sage) are very strong, and when these dry out the flavor is very much less powerful. But in the drying process nearly all herbs (mint is an exception) acquire a certain mustiness, so that although in theory one should be able to use dried herbs more freely than fresh ones, the opposite is in fact generally the case.

Some fresh herbs disperse their aromatic scent very quickly when in contact with heat; a few leaves of fresh tarragon steeped in a hot consommé for 20 minutes will give it a strong flavor, whereas if the tarragon is to flavor a salad considerably more will be necessary. Lemon thyme and marjoram are at their best raw, or only slightly cooked, as in an omelette; the flavor of fennel stalks is brought out by slow cooking; basil has a particular affinity with all dishes in which olive oil is an ingredient, whether cooked or in salads. Knowledge of the right quantities, and of interesting combinations of herbs, can be acquired by using egg dishes, salads and soups as a background. Even if the herbs have been dispensed with a less cautious hand than is usually advised the result will not be a disaster, as it can be when some musty dried herb has completely permeated a roast bird or an expensive piece of meat. You may, on the contrary, have discovered some delicious new combination of tastes, and certainly the use of fresh herbs will be a startling revelation to all those people who know herbs only as something bought in a packet called 'mixed dried herbs' and for which you might just as well substitute sawdust.

It is particularly to the dishes in which fresh herbs are an essential rather than an incidental flavoring that I would like to call attention, for it is this aspect of cookery which is passed over by those writers who enjoin so much caution in the use of herbs. Sometimes it is a good thing to forget that basil, parsley, mint, tarragon, fennel, are all bunched together under the collective word "herbs" and to remember that the difference between leaf vegetables (sorrel, spinach, lettuce) and herbs is very small, and indeed at one time all these plants were known collectively as "salad herbs." Nobody tells you to "use spinach with caution," and neither can you be 'discreet with the basil' when you are making a *pesto* sauce, because the basil is the essential flavoring (so for that matter is mint in mint sauce).

In a slightly different way, a plain consommé or potato soup can be used as a background for a flavoring of herbs, tarragon being a particularly good one for this purpose. An *omelette aux fines herbes* needs tarragon as well as parsley and chervil. So do many sauces; the delicious *sauce verte* and *sauce ravigote* are two of them; the wonderful Sauce Messine is another.

For the dispensing of fresh herbs into salads and soups it is advisable to keep a pair of kitchen scissors handy, and for chopping larger quantities a two-handled, crescent-shaped chopper such as may now be obtained in the larger kitchen equipment stores. Small sturdy wooden bowls complete with a little axe-shaped chopper are also now obtainable in some stores and are invaluable in any kitchen where fresh herbs are frequently in use.

OLIVE HEAVEN

MORT ROSENBLUM

> *These trees so fresh, so full, so beautiful; when they display their fruit, green, golden, and black, it is among the most agreeable sights one might ever see.*
>
> —MIGUEL CERVANTES

> *Because of butter and dairy products* which *are much used in Flanders and Germany, lepers abound in these countries.*
>
> —CARDINAL OF ARAGON, reporting home to olive country in *1517*

IN THE HEART OF ANDALUSIA, Paco and Andrés Núñez de Prado offer elaborate apologies for everything in their pressing process that has changed since the Philistine presses at Ekron. There is not much to excuse. Instead of hand-powered stone rolling pins, their cone-shaped granite crushers are driven by some late Iron Age machinery. The tower of mats is squeezed not by stones hung on a wooden lever but rather by a 1936 hydraulic motor that works so slowly you know it is operating only by its wheezing cough.

The brothers' oil bears the treasured shield of Baena, one of four Denominación de Origen (DO) labels recognized in Spain. Their fanatical purism is not the reason. Large local cooperatives also qualify, and they use high-speed centrifugal continuous systems with computerized digital display control panels that look like the dashboard of the starship *Enterprise*. It is simply that the Núñez de Prado brothers are passionately, desperately in love with olives and everything about them.

I made a pilgrimage to Baena in November, just as the olives were turning black and the lovely fall colors faded into a stark beauty. Andalusia, Spain's largest and most populous region, stretches from the Mediterranean and the Atlantic Ocean to the steppes of Don Quixote's La Mancha. Phoenicians settled it a thousand years before Christ. The Romans took it from Carthage and made it their rich province of Baetica. The Moors came in 711, leaving behind exotic, crenelated forts after Castillians drove them off nearly eight centuries later.

I saw Baena long before I reached it, a small white town with a cut-stone skyline perched upon a hilltop. The Núñez de Prado brothers I found by a cheery olive-wood fire in the brick hearth of their mahogany paneled office. Their family coat of arms hung on a wall among *objets* dating back to Isabela la Católica. There was a monster iron safe. A gigantic carved table, littered with fountain pens and gold-stamped ledgers, stood by overstuffed, cracked leather armchairs. The lovingly maintained Smith Premier typewriter was so old it used two keyboards: one for lower-case letters and another for capitals. Only a muttering fax machine suggested the 1990s.

Paco had studied diplomacy and spent three months in the Spanish Foreign Service in Vienna before coming home again. He wears baggy English tweeds and Italian silk ties. Andrés, an agronomy engineer, never took his eyes off the trees. He wears baggy English tweeds and an ascot.

Andrés, the shy one, looks after the technical end. Paco, with slicked-back hair and the slightly crazed gleam of a likable zealot, handles packaging and public relations; he is also the philosopher. At one point, midway through two days of oleic minutiae, he seized me by the arm. "It is simple," he said. "Making good oil is a series of small steps. If you mess up any one of them, your oil is bad, and nothing you do later can change that. The truth is in the nuances."

In Spain, where everyone else beats their trees with sticks, the Núñez de Prados insist on delicacy. Each season skilled crews from Seville finish picking table olives near home and hurry, some for the twenty-fifth year, to the family's four groves around Baena, in Córdoba province. The olives are picual and picuda, similar tart high-country Andalusian varieties which produce a flavorful oil that stays fresh for years.

Planning strategically, they pick only trees with olives that have just slipped from deep purple to black. The fruit is ripe and firm but not yet soft. Plenty of pressable olives lie freshly fallen under the trees, but they are left on the ground.

Six good harvesters can whack a tree clean in a few minutes. Hand-pickers take twenty minutes, if they work at lightning speed. Skilled fingers slide down a branch, detaching olives with a gentle milking motion. This protects the olives from bruises, which trigger acidity, and it protects the trees.

At the end of each morning and afternoon picking, the olives are trucked to the mill and pressed immediately. Most producers take pride in turning olives into oil within a few days, before fermentation begins. The obsessive brothers start to worry after two hours.

But the real difference is in the antique mill which the family acquired in 1795 from a local duke who had a monopoly in the region. It sits unobtrusively on a busy street in town, facing a park, behind a simple arched gateway wide enough for trucks. In 1989 Andrés and Paco refitted the old press and began to produce commercially in tiny amounts.

Because of the artisanal approach, their competitively priced oil probably costs ten times more to make than that produced by modern methods. It is better. That it is not ten times better does not seem to worry either brother. A few food writers caught on fast, and fancy markets in the United States and Europe clamored for all they could get. With no advertising, the company was making money, selling all the oil it could produce.

Paco started my tour with what he insists on calling a humble olive-man's breakfast in the decantation room, a shrine to olivedom. At one end of the long white tablecloth, a Serrano ham, complete with shank and trotter, rested on a wrought-iron rack. It was *pata negra*, the best there is, from a free-range mountain pig; the hoof is black rather than white. A clay bowl contained real capers: big green pods like pickled peppers. Those little round things we normally see, Paco explained, are buds of the caper flower. No comparison. Andrés brought in what he calls *huevos a la mala educación*, or ineptly done eggs. They were fried in—what else?—and cut into pieces. Among bouquets of fresh flowers and olive sprigs, there were cheeses, croissants, and pots of quince jelly.

As we sat down, Paco shoveled loaves of bread into an iron stove the duke must have used. "I love the ritual of this," he said, laughing slightly at himself. No one else was laughing. With the warm bread distributed, Paco produced the *pièce de résistance*: two glass bottles of Núñez de Prado.

The first was last year's oil, mature and rounded, with a hint of ripe fruit behind the olive taste and a mild spicy finish. The second was for the real aficionados, a sharp, fresh oil, cold off the press. Rich in fresh polyphenols, it bordered on bitter, with that catch at the back of the palate the Italians call *pizzica*. We slopped both on everything: ham, eggs, bread, capers, cheese, laps, shoes. Much later, somewhat reluctantly, we got up for a look around.

Trucks dump the olives into beveled chutes in the lot outside, and they go underground to the crusher. At first, the brothers washed the olives. It seemed like a good idea at the time. "Later we saw no point in adding all that water to a natural process," Paco said. "The oil is better without it. We use no toxic pesticides and pick directly from the tree. Why wash?"

The olives are ground to mash by 300-ton granite cones, which are tuned by a specialist before each season. They are filed or chiseled for perfect balance and surface. This is an old Roman improvement on the *trapetum*, which crushed with two rounded stones, each the half of a massive granite sphere.

From the crusher, oily paste rides a conveyor to the Núñez de Prados' prized contraption, invented in Málaga last century by the Marquis of Acapulco. It is called a Thermofilter, though nothing approaching heat gets near any part of the process. It won't even warm the building when it is freezing outside.

The Thermofilter consists of two giant stainless steel rollers covered in a tight wire mesh, one atop the other, which lift and turn the paste at a snail's pace. Oil drips from the crushed olives by gravity, strained through tiny holes—50 per square millimeter—and runs out a trough at the bottom to a separate decantation system. This they call *flor de aceite,* the flower of oil. Not pressed, it just runs out by itself. Normally, pressing yields a kilo of oil for every five kilos of olives. One kilo of *flor* takes eleven kilos of olives.

The remaining mash is spread carefully onto *capachos,* the same double-layered *scourtins* used in France. Italians call them *fiscoli,* the name often used in California. Traditional mats are often woven from esparto grass; Tunisians make many of them. New ones are of synthetic fibers. But they are hardly different from the woven mats used at Ekron three thousand years ago.

At Núñez de Prado, a mill hand builds a tower of 120 mats loaded with mash, each placed like a doughnut on a central pillar and separated at intervals by metal disks for stability. The stack is trundled on a trolley to the press. The gasping hydraulic pump pushes up from the bottom, and oil runs down the tower into a spillway to the decantation tubs. It takes nearly an hour to compress by two meters. After each pressing, the mats are painstakingly cleaned so residue does not flavor the new oil.

Apart from folkloric splendor, the archaic press has decided scientific advantages. Modern systems crush the olives, pits and all, and mix in hot water to loosen the oil. If the water is not too hot, this is still considered a "cold press"; olive sellers and oil makers like to stretch reality. Then centrifugal drums spin the oil and water into separate pipes. This causes abrupt chemical change, Andrés insists, just as Max Doleatto did in Flayosquet. It aerates the oil, washes away volatile compounds, and separates the glucosides too quickly. Particles of humidity remain.

There is a price to superior oil, of course. By comparison, a nearby cooperative turns out an excellent oil that qualifies for the same DO label. Two workers there produce thirty times more oil than Andrés can make with a team of twelve.

The cooperative, named Germán Baena, is about as far as one can go to the other extreme. Rows of stainless-steel machinery glisten in the hard fluorescent light. Mill hands in matching coveralls keep watch in a control booth, studying the dancing red numbers and bouncing needles.

With buttons or dials, they regulate water temperature, flow rate, and pressure. Finished oil is piped to storage vats. Spare parts and supplies are trundled around the large open room on noiseless rubber wheels.

Engineers pooh-pooh any molecular-level questions, stressing instead hygiene and efficiency. This battle of old versus new would follow me everywhere along the olive trail, growing steadily more complex. At this early stage, taste and tradition had me squarely on the side of the ancients. The Germán Baena process was no more exciting than canning corn.

As old as it is, the Núñez de Prado mill is so clean that you can, as the cliché goes, eat off the floor. Which is fortuitous, because that is exactly what you do. The new oil, black as overused Shell thirty weight, runs along open gutters. Slowly, it collects in the decantation room.

A dozen interconnected square tiled basins purify the oil, a process that dates back to Roman times. In the first basin, most of the vegetable water and impurities settle to the bottom, and the oil floating on top is piped to a second chamber. Waste water is drained off to be used as fertilizer for the trees. In the second basin, and others afterward, this separation by gravity continues for several days until only pure oil, cloudy and golden, is ready for bottling. *Flor de aceite,* clearer at the start, goes through four chambers before it is ready. Pressed oil takes eight.

To qualify as extra virgin, oil must contain less than 1 percent acidity. Fine Italian oils hover near .5 percent. Núñez de Prado ranges from .09 to .17 percent. This, in itself, means little, since such small variations in free oleic acid do not affect taste. But the low acidity suggests that flavor compounds have not been disturbed.

Acidity level is only part of it. Extra-virgin oil must pass a panel of tasters who grade its taste, aroma, and appearance. On an international scale of nine, an extra-virgin oil must score at least 6.5. For Baena producers, that is too low.

From the beginning, the brothers decided that filtering removed too much of the flavor. "It was a marketing problem," Paco said. "Many people who don't know much about oil like to see a clear liquid. They think that makes it better. But we felt our customers would prefer better oil. Besides, if we were the only ones with cloudy oil, that might set us apart."

From the final decantation basins oil is brought to another drafty chamber for bottling, Paco's domain. For tradition, he decided to put *flor de aceite* in the square-sided stubby half-liter glass bottle that families in Madrid used for bringing home bulk wine. Pressed oil is packed in five-liter tins. Later he also began using a few yellow porcelain bottles of the same shape.

Paco's assembly line looks more like a few dutiful sons helping put up the family preserves. Bottles on a table are filled, corked, and passed along. The label, a small booklet, is tied on by a string that runs under a plastic sleeve designed to prevent leakage. This is applied with an old paint-removing heat gun lashed to the arm of a flexible lamp. Next, someone melts red sealing wax onto the cork and imprints the brothers' seal. The Baena DO shield is glued to the bottle. Finally, the finished flask is numbered in India ink, logged onto the lined pages of a tattered book, and packed with five others in a cardboard box.

Each Núñez de Prado label, in whatever language, carries an invitation to visit the mill. They mean it. Good businessmen, they know that a look at their operation tends to turn casual consumers into faithful devotees. But it is the sort of Old World soft sell that went out with the Industrial Revolution.

Entertaining is done in the decantation room, where breakfast fades into the pre-luncheon apéritif and then high tea follows another round of apéritifs. The wine is Rioja and the sherry is the finest. Salami and cheese mysteriously materialize. The atmosphere is churchlike, and each morning someone puts fresh flowers on the altar, the red-tiled basin containing *flor de aceite*. At the slightest prompting, Andrés dips in a wineglass for ceremonial sampling.

But the real show is a ride to the trees. A two-lane blacktop threads its way into hills the color of red clay. Tucked back on the far rises, stone farmhouses crumble into ruin. Too many people have moved to town in order to earn a better living. Guardia Civil outposts have closed down for economy, and the families that remain are isolated and vulnerable in the remote countryside. Some now drive long distances to visit their olives, leaving ancestral homes to thieves and vandals.

Along the road, passing his neighbors' groves, Paco pointed to the bare earth between the rows of olives. "Herbicides," he said with a disapproving sniff. The brothers had found that over time a diminished use of chemicals meant fewer pests. Nature works that way, but only if everyone around has the same approach.

Most Baena planters have shifted to a refinement Andrés introduced in the 1970s. Before, they planted two shoots together so that twin trunks matured from the same root mass. This was to counter the olive's irksome trait of bearing heavily only in alternate years. But after Andrés changed his method, most now use only one shoot. The crown grows hardier and supports a stronger scaffold of main branches, and also produces more young olive-bearing wood. Careful pruning can keep production relatively stable.

The four Núñez de Prado estates total about one thousand acres.

"We produce four hundred thousand kilos a year and cannot do more," Paco told me. "There is no more land." It is a family problem. His father had eleven brothers; his mother, ten. Altogether, about sixty cousins own huge tracts of land that currently do not produce for the company. "We want them to come in with us, but only if Andrés and I can control the process, he said. "They are all architects and professionals, and they don't see the value in spending so much money to do things the old way. They only think in terms of profit. Who knows? Maybe they are starting to understand."

He did not say it, but the future must cause some worry. Andrés is a bachelor. Paco's son is three. Two other brothers, like-minded but not in the business, have a few children between them. But the oldest son, just in his teens, has not yet made up his mind about olives.

We crossed the Guadajoz River, and the scenery changed. Lush grass grew among rows of handsome trees, all carefully pruned for uniformity and easy picking. Branches spread wide and dipped nearly to the ground. Expert hands had sawed away woody spurs to make room for new shoots. This was Andrés's territory.

"An olive tree has a lifespan like a man's," he explained. "At ten or twelve years it begins to produce. It matures, and its best years are between twenty and forty. After fifty it slows down, and after eighty it declines a lot. When a tree gets to be eighty, we pull it up to plant a new tree. We sell the wood for burning or making furniture."

Later, I mentioned to Paco my anger at allowing, through inattention, runaway vines to choke to death trees that were centuries old. He shrugged. "Nature is death and rebirth. That's the beauty of it."

We found the pickers deep in the grove. None slowed their pace at the bosses' approach. Hands moved in a blur, detaching olives and dropping them into baskets hung around the waist. Paco introduced me to Carmen, who first came to pick as a young woman. This year, her teenaged son had come along to help. Carmen was a two-handed picker; she could strip separate branches as fast as more workers could do a single one. She moved off too quickly for me to ask her last name.

"We believe in encouraging long-term relationships and loyalty," Paco said. "We pay more, but it is better in the end. Did you meet our accountant? His father was with our family for all his career. When he retired, his son replaced him. The packers, millers, all of them are proud of their oil."

Back at the mill, Andrés shot me a conspiratorial look. "I'll show you my secret project," he offered. When no one was looking, we slipped through a camouflaged opening in the back wall. Andrés had set up one of those fancy centrifugal mills, complete with digital read-

outs on a gleaming panel. It seems that a local operator had been buying up the olives they left on the ground, but the brothers did not like
the deal. Instead, they would use the olives for a lower-quality oil, not
sold under their name.

"It's going to make a lot of people mad around here," Andrés said
with a little laugh. "This is the system they use to make their best oil,
and we'll be using it to turn out junk."

We lunched at a tacky hotel, which had one of the finer kitchens in
southern Spain. Paco had arranged for a sampling of a half dozen simple peasant dishes, all with Baena oil. The first was a sort of hearty gazpacho called *salmorejo*. In Andalusia, gazpacho is a hot-weather drink.
Salmorejo is made similarly—a blend of the freshest vegetables on
hand, with no water added—but with extra legumes to make a substantial soup. Other dishes were mixed with veal, pork sausage, cod,
garbanzos, potatoes, eggs, and eggplant. The cook, the Spanish version
of a Jewish mother, dished up each portion as if it were to last us until
pruning time. She hovered nearby to make sure we enjoyed every bite.

I made a try at writing the recipe for *potaje del campo*, a muscular
soup of garbanzos, chorizo sausage (Spanish, not Mexican), and vegetables. It began with sautéing garlic and onions and adding conical sweet
peppers. But she lost me the fourth time she said, "You know . . . ," and
flung out her arms. I should have realized—*potaje* means soup; *campo*
means country. The recipe is the same around our neighborhood: Take
what you have and cook it up for lunch. The only constant ingredient
is olive oil.

After lunch, with some gentle probing, I tried to find out whether
the brothers made much money with their thriving enterprise. Their
production costs were enormous, and their prices were reasonable compared to what some Italian producers charged. Clearly, they weren't
starving—but they were hardly flaunting wealth. Andrés clung faithfully
to his perfectly maintained forty-year-old Mercedes-Benz with the original AM-only radio. Paco had his VW.

"I don't really think too much about the accounts," Paco said. "If
I can live normally, I'm happy."

At 5:15 P.M., we roused ourselves from the table, long after I had
planned to leave for Seville. Light would be fading, and I wanted to see
the groves that were already old when the Romans arrived. "Just one
more little *paseo*," Paco said.

He turned off the highway and wound up a narrow road into the
hills of Baena. We were off to Zuheros, a whitewashed relic of the
Moorish wars, one of those few Andalusian villages that have not
changed in centuries. Ignoring a sign that said NO ENTRY, RESIDENTS

ONLY, Paco inched up a paved donkey track past massive carved doors and balconies with wrought-iron grillwork. We peered through open gates at elaborate tiled gardens. At the edge of the village, we stopped to admire the crumbling stone towers of the alcázar, an old Muslim fort. Then he kept going up the hill.

Soon we rose above the olive line, where the last few trees struggled to survive among thick pines. Switchbacks angled upward until our VW was straining in second gear. Still, we kept going. Paco's running commentary melted into a reverential silence. We climbed on. Suddenly we stopped. I followed Paco down a footpath to a secluded overlook on a rocky outcrop.

Zuheros was a white patch far below. Baena was a pair of hilltop towers and a blur, barely discernible in the distance. From our perch, Paco showed me his view of olive heaven. We saw the entire valley, hill after hill nestled within a ring of low mountains along the horizons. Trees marched up and down in long, straight rows. The failing light flashed silver in some spots. In others it tinted the groves in shades of pink and peach and cobalt blue. And every square inch, except for a few ribbons of roadway and the odd clusters of buildings, was planted with olives.

BLIND FAITH

Faith in food

EDWARD HOAGLAND

Trapped
Descriptive
Both dependant Memories
Thankfull
Eventually Freed

WHEN YOU GO PARTIALLY BLIND, as I did for several years a decade ago, your other senses—hearing, touch, taste and smell—come to the fore. You listen intently to people's voices because the timbre may tell you what their body language used to, and feel the curbstone with your groping feet, reach for the banister at every staircase and detect the presence of a silent stranger in the room by perhaps telepathy or the scent of sweat. You squeeze lemon juice on fillet of sole more carefully, not only so it won't squirt in the wrong direction, but because you're paying so much attention to what the lemon adds.

descriptism Orange juice seemed to have a sunny taste (I could dimly see its color) and certainly a morning feeling, though not as bracingly acidic as a pink grapefruit. I liked eggs sunny-side up for the same reason, and peppered liberally as a visual anchor, with ketchup on the table for its color, even if I didn't plan to use it. I liked salmon, too, for lunch, especially for its color, which my fading eyesight took in longer than the shades of white or gray of sole or tuna. But canned tuna fish was like the very sea: penny for penny, maybe the richest taste of all. You can dress up salmon with hollandaise or cod with tartar sauce, and those are comfortingly delicious, but nothing like as real as tuna's evocation of the sea. Spinach had a Popeye strength of character too. And corn on the cob was childhood-yellow. Peas, nibbled raw, were a vivid, crispy green. I went in for red wine, naturally, to go with my red flannel hash or spaghetti marinara, but once or twice spilled wine on my hash, reaching for what I thought was ketchup, or knocked over my wineglass in front of company, mistaking it for ketchup.

Company, when you're going blind (at my worst I was 20/800— seeing at 20 feet what I ought to have been able to see at 800—or legally blind, times four), is a mixed blessing. You crave it, yet it limns what you are losing because your experiences have diverged so miserably from your friends' and you can't see them and therefore really know how they are feeling: whether they look tense and tired and haven't gotten any sleep lately. You fumble for what to say across the gap and haven't been able to read a paper for months, so you know only the sound-bite news, not real stuff that can he discussed in any detail. They are solicitous, rather as if you were terminally ill. Friendship feels suddenly enclosed in a time frame.

Although grades of steak had never meant much to me, they did now because the tenderness of the expensive cuts enhanced the flavor. I'd have a juicy steak and Boston lettuce with Dal Raccolto olive oil and Modenaceti vinegar. But eating well need not be expensive. There's garlic bread and loaves of sourdough; and grilled ribs with red barbecue sauce; and cherry tomatoes dipped in Russian dressing—when blind, I *did* go in for reds. Or just popcorn, buttered and salted can taste as savory as a $50 meal if you're in the perfect mood for it.

Just to "wake up and smell the coffee" in the morning was something. I liked shredded wheat for breakfast, or Grape-Nuts, though seldom more than oatmeal with maple syrup and light cream. But cooking is dicey when you can't peer into the pot and see how things are doing or look at the clock. You have to guess at measurements and stir clairvoyantly with your spoon, being careful not to burn your hand on the edge of the pot, which, like the food, becomes invisible.

Food is a lifeboat when you can't see, but provisional. You need more in your basket of consolations than just gaining weight. Your mettle is tested in losing the blessing of sight. Your forehead has shut down over your eyes, and, groping along a fence or wall for orientation, you walk and talk and even listen haltingly, struggling for language skills you never thought you'd need, like distinguishing the click of a stoplight at an intersection, the texture of a wind from the west, versus wind from the east. A Girl Scout cookie or a hot dog with ballpark relish is a memory incubator. And memories were the easy part, compared to scrambling to improvise this new existence. What do you do when you wake up and can't read, write or see your partner across the table? Mostly you troll for information at first, beginning with whether your partner slept decently, since her face can't tell you, and what the front page says. Trolling is an appropriate metaphor because it's done blind yet plumbs worlds you need to get a handle on.

Instead of my English muffin, I might butter my thumb—but I did like having muffins because a toaster is so much safer than a stovetop; it was a form of "cooking" I could do. And by switching from marmalade to raspberry jam, I kept my breakfast visible longer. Also enjoyed prunes for the same reason, and V8 juice, so bright-colored and spangled in taste. I wore binoculars around my neck, for recognizing cars that came up the driveway, or gazing at tree shapes, and the scrimshaw on the rising moon. Carrot sticks and orange cheese on melba toast and gazpacho, ruby wine, a lobster and apples for dessert made a fun meal I could see. I didn't much like cranberry juice but appreciated the thought when my partner brought some home, along with lovely apricots or peaches. Affection and sex were pointedly important in not just comforting but rooting me. And I played music every waking hour; anything heartening and directional could make a difference. That is, Bach or Mozart or Louis Armstrong knew where they were going, and in a time of turmoil you could sometimes triangulate from them. My tastes inevitably broadened to more operas, more Baroque and organ music, Gregorian chanting, African music and stride piano and ragtime, as I listened with the sort of focus my eyes had formerly monopolized.

When blind, you appreciate any kindness or diversion and the tinctures of genius that are accessible, but also begin to scrimp as you lose your ability to earn a living. So you do eat more tomato swap, cold beets, acorn squash, red onions and red chowders. As your perimeters narrow, you dodder like Mr. Magoo, always grasping for a handhold or feeling with your toes for where the stairs start; and the tendons of your hobbled legs begin to shrink. Newsstands are only good for Baby Ruths or Butterfingers, and the subway is not a feast of faces, just the decibels. Noise drowns the sounds that would be of more interest. You chew licorice chewing gum and smell the vanilla at an ice cream stand, or hot chocolate, butterscotch, jelly doughnuts, maybe sauerkraut. But the countless spirits shuffling by—telepathy is not enough to register them. I do believe we have a sixth sense, but it has been severely blunted by civilization and was never designed for cities anyway.

I was rescued by civilization, however. Surgery fixed me—a two-month process. And to be lifted from the murk of darkness into blazing sunlight seemed as sudden as a superhero's intervention. I was staggered by the wide world opening before me. Fields as green as salad, clouds like meringue. Or snow, blue water, a red sunset, a purple storm. Children playing. More than joy. Overjoyed.

Body and Soul

CHOCOLATE, CATHOLICISM, ANCIEN RÉGIME

WOLFGANG SCHIVELBUSCH

ALTHOUGH COFFEE SPREAD FAR and wide as the fashionable drink of the seventeenth and eighteenth centuries, it is still easy to determine its gravitational center: where capitalism and middle-class values had most thoroughly penetrated society: in the northwest of Europe—in England, Holland, and France. It was there that medical and literary writings were composed in celebration of the sobering and intellectually stimulating effects of the new beverage; there that the coffeehouse attained a social and economic significance unparalleled elsewhere; and there that coffee became *the* symbolic drink of the bourgeois order.

Much the same can be said of chocolate. At first glance, it too started as a generally fashionable beverage not limited to any particular country. Yet on closer inspection we realize that it too had its specific center of influence, one which lay in diametric opposition to that of coffee— namely, southern Europe, Spain, and Italy, which is to say, in the Catholic world. If we label coffee a Protestant, northern drink, then chocolate must be designated as its Catholic, southern counterpart.

First, though, a word about the distinction between cocoa and chocolate. Cocoa is the name given to the plant and its fruit. Chocolate refers to the product known since the sixteenth century whose chief ingredient is cocoa. Like the substance itself, the name is of ancient Mexican origin. The ingredients from which chocolate is made vary according to taste. As a rule, cocoa, sugar, cinnamon, and vanilla are used. In the seventeenth and eighteenth centuries chocolate was sold in solid form, packaged in bars and cubes. It was consumed in liquid form, dissolved in hot water or milk, often with the addition of wine. Whenever chocolate is mentioned in the seventeenth and eighteenth centuries, it refers to this hot, liquid chocolate.

Chocolate was predestined to be the counterpart of coffee on the basis of its chemical composition. Cocoa, its main ingredient, contains no caffeine, but only a little theobromine, which is comparable to caffeine in its effect, though much weaker. Chocolate does not have a discernibly stimulating effect on the central nervous system—as medical writers in the seventeenth century were quick to note.

Even though chocolate does not have the stimulating effect of coffee and tea, it makes up for this by virtue of its great nutritional value. This is what made it so significant a commodity in the Catholic world. On the principle that liquids do not break fasts *(Liquidum non frangit jejunum)*, chocolate could serve as a nutritional substitute during fasting periods, and naturally this made it a more or less vital beverage in Catholic Spain and Italy.

Yet this was only one aspect of its significance for the Catholic world. The discovery, trade, and consumption of chocolate were quite closely associated with His Most Catholic Majesty—as he was officially known then—the King of Spain. Once the Spaniards brought chocolate back to their homeland from Mexico at the start of the sixteenth century, it would remain an exclusively Spanish phenomenon for the next hundred years, thanks to Spain's monopoly on trade with the New World. (Beyond Spain it was known only in Spanish territories within Italy and the Netherlands.) It was in this century that it acquired its specifically Spanish identity, first as a clerical fasting drink and soon after as a fashionable secular beverage. At the court in Madrid it became a kind of status symbol. From there it inevitably became a standard feature of Spanish courtly style, which in the seventeenth century, in the days before Versailles, was the trend-setter for the rest of aristocratic Europe.

Toward the end of the seventeenth century the French style began to supplant the Spanish (having first assimilated its major elements). One important factor in this transitional period was the marriage of the Hapsburg princess Anna of Austria to Louis XIII in 1615. With Anna, who had grown up in Madrid, chocolate came to the French court; and here it managed to lose its Spanish, clerical aftertaste. It no longer carried associations of Jesuitical gloom, the Inquisition, and the Escorial; instead it simply represented Rococo elegance. It became the drink of the European aristocracy, as much a status symbol as the French language, the snuffbox, and the fan.

Aristocratic society preferred to drink its chocolate at breakfast. Ideally it was served in the boudoir, in bed if possible. Breakfast chocolate had little in common with the bourgeoisie's breakfast coffee. It was quite the opposite, and not only because the drinks were intrinsically different. Whereas the middle-class family sat erect at the breakfast table, with a sense of disciplined propriety, the essence of the chocolate ritual was fluid, lazy, languid motion. If coffee virtually shook drinkers awake for the workday that lay ahead, chocolate was meant to create an intermediary state between lying down and sitting up. Illustrations of the period nicely portray this ideal of an idle class's morning-long awakening to the rigors of studied leisure.

Morning chocolate in the boudoir was as popular a motif for Rococo painting as pastoral landscapes and amorous bed scenes. Chocolate evidently appealed to the playful and erotic spirit of the age. Yet this association of chocolate and eroticism is not only iconographic in nature. According to an old belief that persisted into the nineteenth century, chocolate was an aphrodisiac. "People seek to be fortified through chocolate in order to perform certain duties," as a prudish end-of-the-seventeenth-century text euphemistically puts it.

Thus in this respect as well, chocolate appeared in the seventeenth and eighteenth centuries as coffee's opposite. The latter, as we have seen, was markedly anticorporeal and antierotic. Common wisdom had it that what coffee gave to the mind it took from the body. With chocolate it was exactly the reverse. It nourished one's body and one's potency; thus it represented the Baroque, Catholic acknowledgment of corporeal being as against Protestant asceticism.

The dichotomy was reflected in two types of drinking establishments in late seventeenth-century London. We have already had a look at the coffeehouse—above all, its bourgeois and puritanical character. Apparently, though, other establishments were set up to serve chocolate, the so-called chocolate parlors or chocolate houses. These were meeting places for an odd mixture of aristocracy and demimonde, what Marx would later refer to as the *bohème;* in any case, they were thoroughly antipuritanical, perhaps even bordello-like places.

Wherever we look in the seventeenth and eighteenth centuries, chocolate appears as the status beverage of the *ancien régime,* coffee as a stimulant for the ever more vigorously stirring bourgeois intellect and entrepreneurial spirit. Goethe, who used art as a means to lift himself out of his middle-class background into the aristocracy and who as member of a courtly society maintained a sense of aristocratic calm even in the midst of immense productivity, made a cult of chocolate, and avoided coffee. Balzac, who, despite his sentimental allegiance to the monarchy, lived and labored for the literary marketplace and for it alone, became one of the most excessive coffee-drinkers in history. Here we see two fundamentally different working styles and means of stimulation—fundamentally different psychologies and physiologies.

A final word about the fate of chocolate in the nineteenth and twentieth centuries. It vanished with the *ancien régime*. Or more precisely, it ended its existence as chocolate, continuing as cocoa, which has been drunk in its place since the nineteenth century. The modern cocoa process was developed around 1820 by the Dutchman Van Houten. Most of the oil from the cocoa bean is extracted; thus cocoa becomes less nourishing but far more digestible. In its new form it is a powder. This process put an end to the Spanish tradition of chocolate drinking, in which solid and liquid chocolate were identical. Ever since the nineteenth century the two have gone their separate ways. Cocoa now became a favorite drink in northern and central Europe too, but primarily for children. At the same time, the chocolate bar gained a new significance as a luxury in its own right. By an irony of history it was the two arch-Protestant countries that put an end to the Spanish, Catholic chocolate tradition. Holland became the first major producer of cocoa and solid chocolate in bar form, Switzerland following its lead with the innovation of milk chocolate.

Chocolate and cocoa are not common "adult" luxuries like coffee and tobacco. Cocoa became the preferred breakfast drink for children; chocolate and candy were given to women and children as presents. The former status drink of the *ancien régime* had sunk to the world of women and children. What formerly symbolized power and glory was now in the hands of those excluded from power and responsibility in middle-class society. Bourgeois society, as the historical victor over the old society, made a mockery of the status symbols once so important to the aristocracy. History repeatedly reveals how the self-esteem of the class that loses out is destroyed.

Other status symbols of the *ancien régime* shared this fate with chocolate: for instance, dress. Before 1789 an aristocrat's colorful, sumptuous costume was the expression of social prestige. His goal, if anything, was to present himself like a peacock; whereas for the simply dressed burgher nothing was more offensive and laughable than an association with this bird. Once again, in middle-class society it was children and women who were allowed to wear colorful dress.

What the peacock was for costume, the "sweet tooth" was in matters of gastronomic taste. The lover of sweets differed from the general gourmand or glutton. Middle-class taste, physiologically and by extension aesthetically, abhorred the bright and sweets, favoring somber black garments and bitter foods. In this sense coffee was both black and bitter, the antipode to the aristocracy's light, sweet chocolate—just as, in 1789 in Versailles, the Third Estate with its simple black garb was, politically and chromatically, diametrically opposed to the colorfully dressed aristocracy.

WHY DO I FAST?

WOLE SOYINKA

W

HY DO I FAST? I do not mean, why do I fast now? I have settled that in terms of continuing conflict. But why do I fast at all? Why have I, at any given time, suddenly decided—I must now do without food for some time? Perhaps I ought to settle that in my mind before I am trapped in a fatal demand of my own self-indulgence.

Yes, self-indulgence. A sensual self-indulgence. It is important to separate the area of will-power from the drugged immersion in rainbow-tinted ether. For I suspect that it is the truly sensual that take easily to fasting.

I have read of, but never experienced even a nearness of the sensation of freezing to death. I understand that after a while the body ceases to feel pain, sinks blissfully into sleep. Rest. I think fasting must be like that. It begins with that critical hump which is in fact a very brief passage and occurs during the first three days. The body either succumbs at this point or afterwards condemns the very thought of food. I find it best to provoke this hump as early as possible. When the decision to fast is taken, I dwell on the next meal in my mind, I let my body crave it and I let the food come to me. I am hungry. I open the dishes and sniff, I dwell on the tasting, the mastication, the swallowing. I salivate. I dwell on my body's satisfaction, the heavy body-contented sleep that must follow if I fill my hunger from this plenitude. A fierce protest commences in the pit of the stomach and I let it rage. Armed with the power of my veto, I stand aside and enjoy the violent conflict, waiting for my cue to thump the gavel. The moment arrives and I cover the food with a slow deliberate motion saying: This taste cannot die. I have known it and will know it again. Taste is selectiveness, choice. I am denied choice and thus all taste is rendered non-existent. Pleasure also is choice; it is fulfilment and choice. My existence is a crippled one, it debases fulfilment by restricting fields of fulfilment. To take pleasure in the granted area of fulfilment is self-betrayal. To eat without pleasure is to betray my nature. From now on I will not betray my nature.

Sometimes a day or two later the stomach devils come out again to play. But I view their antics with dispassionate interest. Food cannot tempt me but I wonder sometimes what I would do if I had, within reach, vitamin pills. I do after all entertain fears of the gut-walls collapsing, of unfed enzymes atrophying and dying, of perpetual damages done to the body by excess. I know it is wiser to take a glass of orange juice a day but I am not capable of the compromise. Orange juice is too close to food. Vitamin pills on the other hand do not seem insidious saboteurs of will-power; that test has luckily never come. So I accept only a glass of water each day, sipped at intervals. I ensure that I do not exceed the one glass a day.

The body achieves, of course, true weightlessness. I am blown about by the lightest breeze, by the lightest lyrical thought or metaphor. The body is like an onion and I watch the flesh peel off, layer by layer, layer by layer. And this is the risk, it is this condition that begins the danger of self-indulgence. For, by the fourth day the will is no longer involved. I become hungry for the show-down, the moment when I must choose between death or surrender. I resent even the glass of water and begin to cheat. Each day it gets lesser by a fraction. Once, for a whole day I did not drink at all. In the morning I said, I shall drink at noon. At noon I began to cheat, procrastinating until I decided I shall drink an entire cupful when the sun goes down. I lay in bed until dark, then said, I did not see the sun go down.

What do I do all day? I watch light motes in the air. When eyes are shut a whole universe of colors fills the dome of darkness behind the eyelids. In extreme fasts the open eye is treated to the same display on a lighter, vaster scale. The air is broken up in swirls of colored dots. Each speck of dust in a sunbeam is a fiery planet in the galaxy, its motion sedately plotted, imbued with immense significance. In the muting of sounds which overtakes the senses the mind drifts easily into transcendental moods, wiping out environment, reality, fragmenting slowly till it becomes one with specks of dust in ether.

Only sunsets prove unbearable, for while sounds are muted, colors are intensified, and the sunsets turn raw, cannibalistic, fanged and blooded as if the drooling demon of day is sinking its teeth in the lap of a loud lascivious courtesan, reeking of gore. Not so the storm-clouds with their copper rims and light golden depths hinting of caverns beyond the passages of deities. The stars fade into nothingness; only the silence exists that brought them forth.

Rejoicing, I watch my body waste. I identify but do not prohibit the human satisfaction which comes from the pain and fear, the concern and incredulity in their eyes as the jailers prowl round, on orders to report the slightest hint of weakening. Something in me, a glee I recognize as profoundly human laughs and condescends when a warder stops and says, "Please, this is not possible. You must stop." The Grand Seer enters . . . "I have come to beg you. I ask you to think of your family, your wife, your children." I protest—but I am well and strong. "You cannot see yourself. I can. We all do. You don't know what you look like. You are a living skeleton."

It is strange, but the effect they all have on me is to resent even that cup of water. Each time the Grand Seer has turned up I have thrown the rest away. His concern adds to the growing sense of superhumanity. I need neither drink nor food. Soon I shall need no air.

The hallucinations, the brief fainting spells in which walls, earth and sky move suddenly about me I accept and control. And so I know it is no illusion when one night I detect the motion of a terrestrial object among the stars. Seeking beyond stars into that pool of silence I fasten suddenly on this fluid speck, sedate and self-assured in its predetermined orbit. Another hallucination? The passage was brief since I could only follow its motion through my barred window. Yet I am so certain that I wait again the following day and the next. And remember its identity. A heavenly body but a human satellite. The immensity of the moment—the moment of certainty—becomes imperishable. Locked and barred from a more direct communion, a human assertiveness has reached me through the cosmos, a proud, inextinguishable promethean spark among dead bodies, astral wraiths, failed deities, tinsel decorations in barren space. Sign, probe and question I accept you, incandescent human dare. Extension of my restless eye and mind I claim you and absorb you. I transmit you, pore of my skin, electronic core of my will, prowl . . . prowl . . .

Tenth day of fast. By day a speck of dust on a sun-beam. By night a slow shuttle in the cosmos. Night . . .

A clear night, and the moon pouring into my cell. I thought, a shroud? I have returned again and again to this night of the greatest weakness and lassitude, to the hours of lying still on the stark clear-headed acceptance of the thought that said; it is painless. The body weakens and breath slows to a stop. Gone was the fear that a life-urge might make me retreat at this moment. I held no direct thought of death, only of the probable end of a course of action. I felt the weakness in the joints of my bones and within the bone itself. A dry tongue that rasped loosely in the mouth. I felt a great repose in me, an enervating peace of the world and the universe within me, a peace that truly "passeth all understanding." I wrote . . .

A SLICE OF LIFE

I anoint my flesh
Thought is hallowed in the lean
Oil of solitude
I call you forth, all, upon
Terraces of light. Let the dark
Withdraw

I anoint my voice
And let it sound hereafter
Or dissolve upon its lonely passage
In your void. Voices new
Shall rouse the echoes when
Evil shall again arise

I anoint my heart
Within its flame I lay
Spent ashes of your hate—
Let evil die.

No one came on the eleventh day. I thought the jailer when he peeped in my cell looked wary, even frightened. I mistook the cause. It had happened. It was happening, happening even then. I understood now why the Seer had laid waste their paradise. I understood when they stormed into my Crypt the following day, the twelfth, questioning and threatening. I wedged myself between door and wall for support, seeking to disguise my weakness. It was a long way, a long height from which to cast down my gaze and understand. The sounds, the words, the gestures were plain and yet remote. The presence of strange faces, and the Grand Seer among them concerned me crucially but did not touch me. I saw and pitied his bafflement. They paused often waiting, pauses of increasing desperation. I watched them hang upon my silence yet I could only think, But what is it? What do you want of me? Why should you want of me?

I need nothing.   I feel nothing.   I desire nothing.

Were these new kingdoms which that sage hermit sought, the kingdoms of nothing. Or did he speak, as being replete in his own being, spurning all exterior augmentation?

GOD IN CRUMBS

DOMINIQUE PRÉDALI

FOR CENTURIES, MONASTERIES and convents were bastions of gastronomy. To this day two- or three-star itineraries follow virtually the same "routes of taste" that have connected up monasteries, convents, abbeys and great religious centers since the Middle Ages.

The reputation of these famous centers of gastronomic luxury has never faded. Monks were the researchers, breeders, herbalists and apothecaries of the Middle Ages. At their disposal they had the finest produce, the best-equipped kitchens and the staff best trained in culinary matters. Though they asserted themselves as masters of festive cookery, it was during periods of fasting that their great treasury of cunning and imagination emerged to fullest effect. Monks compensated for the limited choice of produce available with remarkable culinary skill. Since food is a gift of God, it is forbidden to waste it. All the various orders thus became masters at exploiting leftover flour, apples, milk, honey and so on. Some developed or perfected methods of preserving cheese, biscuits, spice bread (in Austria they invented *Oblaten-Lebkuchen,* spice bread on a wafer base to make it keep better), hydromel, cider and wine. At first, spices were added to mask the acidity of the wine, then techniques were discovered to conserve and improve it.

In the austere Middle Ages, no thing could be wasted and leftovers had to be "recycled." This was particularly so with bread, imbued as it was with symbolic values. According to a German legend, the devil collected any crumbs which fell from the table, turned them into burning coals and threw them at sinners roasting in hell. Anyone accidentally allowing crumbs to fall from the table would be punished. The Benedictine rule, which was echoed in the Statutes of Peter the Venerable, the twelfth century abbot of Cluny, clearly states that, at the end of the meal, one of the monks should use his hands, a knife or a brush to care-fully gather up the crumbs and put them in a special basket. The same crumbs were used to make a soup at the end of the week to be eaten hot on Saturday evenings. The same ingredients could be used to make a hum-ble pudding for the poor. A similar tradition has survived in Spain where, on Christmas Eve, they eat *las migas del Niño* (the Crumbs of Baby Jesus).

To this day, in monasteries and the lay world alike, stale bread is not wasted and instead is used to make the sweet fried pancake which the French call *pain perdu* and the Spanish *torrijas de Santa Teresa*. The recipe, which originated in the convents of Castille, is repeated all over Europe with the same ingredients: slices of bread soaked in milk, dipped in beaten egg yolk and fried and sprinkled with sugar and cin-namon. In Sweden it is served with blackcurrant jam. Another, slightly more elaborate variation on the theme is *sopa dourada*, a soup which always features on feast-day menus in Portuguese monasteries. Its sole ingredients are great quantities of egg yolks, syrup and almonds. In France the same dish is called *soupe dorée;* in Savoy it becomes *soupe crute* and in the Creuse region *soupe rousse.*

Stale bread is also one of the ingredients of *mendiant,* a very com-pact sweet pudding originally named *quatre mendiants,* in honor of the mendicant orders: the Augustines, the Carmelites, the Dominicans and the Franciscans. In this recipe the four orders are represented by raisins, hazelnuts, figs, and almonds, the colors of which evoke those of the habits of the respective orders.

Celestial nourishment

Eggs are an inexhaustible source of inspiration in monastic cook-ery. According to popular legend, the ban on eating eggs during Lent, in force since the fourth century, derives from the fact that Christ was pelted with eggs after the flagellation. The ban translated into a surplus of this ingredient in the days following the "lean period." The egg yolk-based confectionery of Portuguese and Spanish convents in the Middle Ages undoubtedly constitutes the most original and creative way of using surpluses or leftovers in recipes that would make a saint swoon.

Why the yolks? Simply because the whites were used to lubricate the rigging of ships and to clarify sherry and sometimes red wine as well. It would have been out of the question to waste all the yolks, so the common practice was to donate them to convents. The nuns had Saracen maids' whose flair and skill with egg yolks and sugar could be harnessed to bake an infinite variety of delicate sweetmeats. It was the Saracen maids who initiated the nuns to the Secrets of Arab confectionery, a direct legacy of the refined cuisine of the aristocracy. For the greater glory of confectionery, these women invented a thousand and one variations on the theme of egg yolks and sugar, adding almonds, coconut, walnuts, cheese, candied pumpkin, milk, flower essences, vanilla, cinnamon and liqueurs, all with sublime delicacy. Some of these creations have disappeared today, but in both Portugal and Spain, the traditional fare of religious festivals survives as a delicious reminder of the Arab presence in the Iberian peninsula.

In Portugal, the names attributed to these specialties sometimes assume religious connotations. This is the case, for example, of the so-called "celestial nourishment" and its several variants. Some are made with almonds, others with cheese. There are also many recipes for what in Spain is known as "celestial lard." These confections are made of egg yolk, syrup and caramel, but none envisages even the slightest amount of lard! The names of these cakes oscillate between the erotic, the amusing and the evocative: "nun's belly," the cinnamon-scented "angel's breasts," "angel fleece"—dainty, pale, round cakes filled with an egg custard, cream and sugar—"damsel's nectar," "sighs," "widow's dessert." The more austere Spanish convents invested their egg yolk cakes with more prosaic names: "almond marzipan" or simply "yolks of Saint Teresa" or "yolks of St. Paul," depending on which religious order baked them. These "yolks" are a sort of deliciously nauseating candyfloss and are traditionally eaten in Castille at Easter or on other religious feast days.

So not all these good old-fashioned customs have been lost. The Spanish Clarissan nuns offer the following tips in a cookbook they once published: "Nothing must be thrown away. Stale bread can be used to make delicious *torrijas*, and with fish leftovers it is possible to make marvelous croquettes." One year when the fruit harvest was a disaster but there were plenty of cucumbers, Father Hugues of the priority of Saint Benoît de Chérence decided to make cucumber jam. The leftovers served to prepare delicious soups, always popular in monasteries and convents because, as St. Teresa of Avila said, "God exists even in a *pot-au-feu.*"

WHAT'D YOU PEOPLE CALL THAT?

NTOZAKE SHANGE

> *Once again, she held the box of cookies in front of me.*
> *I took another cookie but she kept the box there, in the*
> *same place. I took yet another cookie, and another*
> *until the whole box disappeared. "Can you read what*
> *it says there?" she asked, pointing at a line of red let-*
> *ters. "I cannot read American," I said.*
> —EDWIDGE DANTICAT, "The Missing Piece," *Krik? Krak!*

THIS PARTICULAR CHILD WHO ate all the cookies is a character in one of Edwidge Danticat's amazing stories of life in contemporary Haiti and the Haiti of Brooklyn and Miami. Whether we speak or read American, we've had a terrible time taking freely from the table of bounty freedom's afforded the other Americans. I often wonder if the move to monolingualize this country is a push for the homogeneity of our foods as well. Once we read American will we cease to recognize ourselves, our delicacies and midnight treats?

There are moments in our past when I have to wonder how did we celebrate, why, with whom? Not Christmas or Easter or Caledonia's birthday so much as the first night north of the Mason-Dixon line before Sherman's March, or dry pants and shoes at a clean table in the Rio Grande Valley, having outwitted the border patrol at La Frontera. When we are illicit, what can we keep down, what do we offer the spirits, the trickster, *el coyote,* who led us from bondage to a liberty so tenuous we sometimes hide for years our right to be?

Frederick Douglass, the great abolitionist, was reluctant to celebrate the Fourth of July, so we can assume that his famous Fifth of July speech was not followed by racks of barbecued ribs and potato salad. Actually, long before Douglass's disillusion with Independence Day, African-Americans in Philadelphia, the Cradle of Liberty, were wrestling with authorities over who was free to do what. Why would they want to celebrate the American Declaration of Liberation while the Fugitive Slave Act, which allowed the kidnapping of free slaves back to slave states on the word of any white man, was in effect? In Gary B.

Nash's *Forging Freedom* we learn:

> While white abolitionists were withdrawing to the shadows free blacks in Philadelphia continued their political campaign to abolish slavery at both state and national levels, to revoke The Fugitive Slave Act, and to obtain legislation curbing the kidnapping of free blacks . . . Beginning in 1808, when Congress finally prohibited the slave trade, Absalom Jones and other black preachers began delivering annual thanksgiving sermons on New Year's Day, the date of the prohibition of trade and also the date of Haitian independence in 1804. The appropriation of New Year's Day as the black Fourth of July seems to have started simultaneously in Jones' African Episcopal Church and in New York's African Zion Church.

And so, black-eyed peas and rice or "Hoppin' John," even collard greens and pig's feet, are not so much arbitrary predilections of the "nigra" as they are symbolic defiance; we shall celebrate ourselves on a day of our choosing in honor of those events and souls who are an honor to us. Yes, we eat potato salad on Independence Day, but a shortage of potatoes up and down Brooklyn's Nostrand Avenue in July will not create the serious consternation and sadness I saw/experienced one New Year's Eve, when there weren't no chitlins to be found.

Like most American families strewn far and near 'cross the mainland, many African-American families, like my own, experience trans-cross Caribbean or Pan-American Highway isolation blues during global/ national holidays. One Christmas and New Year's my parents and siblings were somewhere 'tween Trinidad, Santo Domingo, and Los Angeles. My daughter and I were lucky enough to have a highly evolved horizontal family, that is, friends and associates from different bloodlines, but of the same spirit, reliable, loving, and alone, too, except for us.

Anyway, this one winter I was determined that Savannah, my child, should have a typical Owens/Williams holiday, even though I was not a gaggle of aunts and uncles, cousins, second and third cousins twice removed, or even relatives from Oklahoma or Carolina. I was just me, Mommy, in one body and with many memories of not enough room for all the toddlers at the tables. How could I re-create the smells of okra and rice, Hoppin' John, baked ham, pig's feet, chitlins, collard greens, and corn bread with syrup if I was goin'ta feed two people? Well, actually one and a half people. She woulda counted as a half in the census. But how we are counted in the census is enough to give me a migraine, and I am trying to recount how I tried to make again my very colored childhood and my very "black" adolescence.

So in all of Clinton-Washington where I could walk with my shopping cart (I am truly an urban soul), there were no chitlins or pig's feet. I remember standing with a very cold little girl right at the mouth of the C train entrance. Were we going on a quest at dusk on New Year's Eve or were we going to be improvisationally nimble and work something out? I was cold, too, and time was not insignificant. Everything I had to prepare before midnight was goin'ta take all night. Back we went into a small market, sawdust on the floor, and a zillion island accents pushing my requests up toward the ceiling. "A pound and a half of pig tails," I say. Savannah murmured "pig tails" like I'd said Darth Vader was her biological father.

Nevertheless, I left outta there with my pig's tails, my sweet potatoes, collards, cornmeal, rice and peas, a coconut, habañera peppers, olive oil, smoked turkey wings, okra, tomatoes, corn on the cob, and some day-old bread. We stopped briefly at a liquor store for some bourbon or brandy, I don't remember which. All this so a five-year-old colored child, whose mother was obsessed with the cohesion of her childhood, could pass this on to a little girl, who was falling asleep at the dill pickle barrel, 'midst all Mama's tales about suckin' 'em in the heat of the day and sharin' one pickle with anyone I jumped double Dutch with in St. Louis.

Our biggest obstacle was yet to be tackled, though. The members of our horizontal family we were visiting, thanks to the spirits and the Almighty, were practicing Moslems. Clearly, half of what I had to make was profane, if not blasphemous in the eyes/presence of Allah. What was Elegua, Santeria's trickster spirit, goin'ta do to assist me? Or, would I have to get real colloquial and call on Brer Rabbit or Brer Fox?

As fate would have it, my friends agreed that so long as I kept the windows open and destroyed all utensils and dishes I used for these requisite "homestyle" offerings, it was a go. I'll never forget how cold that kitchen was, nor how quickly my child fell asleep, so that I alone tended the greens, pig's tails, and corn bread. Though late alone that New Year's Eve, I knew a calm I must attribute to the satisfaction of my ancestors. I tried to feed us.

PIG'S TAILS BY INSTINCT

Obviously, the tails have gotta be washed off, even though the fat seems to reappear endlessly. When they are pink enough to suit you, put them in a large pot full of water. Turn the heat high, get 'em boilin'. Add chopped onion, garlic, and I always use some brown sugar, molasses, or syrup. Not everybody does. Some folks like their pig extremities bitter, others, like me, want 'em sweet. It's up to you. Use a large spoon with a bunch of small holes to scrape off the grayish fats that will cover your tails. You don't need this. Throw it out. Let the tails simmer till the meat falls easily from the bones. Like pig's feet, the bones are soft and suckable. too. Don't forget salt, pepper, vinegar, and any kinda hot sauce when servin' your tails. There's nothin' wrong with puttin' a heap of tails, feet, or pig's ears right next to a good-sized portion of Hoppin' John, either. Somethin' about the two dishes mix on the palate well.

HOPPIN' JOHN (BLACK-EYED PEAS AND RICE)

Really, we should have soaked our peas overnight, but no such luck. The alternative is to boil 'em for at least an hour after cleaning them and gettin' rid of runty, funny-lookin' portions of peas. Once again, clear off the grayish foam that's goin'ta rise to the top of your pot. Once the peas look like they are about to swell or split open, empty the water, get half as much long grain rice as peas, mix 'em together, cover with water (two knuckles' deep of female hand). Bring to a boil, then simmer. Now, you can settle for salt and pepper. Or you can be adventurous, get yourself a hammer and split open the coconut we bought and either add the milk or the flesh or both to your peas and rice. Habañera peppers chopped really finely, 'long with green pepper and onion diced ever so neatly. Is it necessary to sauté your onion, garlic, pepper, and such before adding to your peas and rice? Not absolutely. You can get away without all that. Simmer in your heavy kettle with the top on till the water is gone away. You want your peas and rice to be relatively firm. However, there is another school of cookin' that doesn't mix the peas with the rice until they are on the actual plate, in which case the peas have a more fluid quality and the rice is just plain rice. Either way, you've got yourself some Hoppin' John that's certain to bring you good luck and health in the New Year. Yes, mostly West Indians add the coconut, but that probably only upset Charlestonians. Don't take that to heart. Cook your peas and rice to your own likin'.

COLLARD GREENS TO BRING YOU MONEY

Wash 2 large bunches of greens carefully 'cause even to this day in winter critters can hide up in those great green leaves that're goin'ta taste so very good. If you are an anal type, go ahead and wash the greens with suds (a small squirt of dish detergent) and warm water. Rinse thoroughly. Otherwise, an individual leaf check under cold runnin' water should do. Some folks like their greens chopped just so, like rows of a field. If that's the case with you, now is the time to get your best knife out, tuck your thumb under your fingers, and go to town. On the other hand, some just want to tear the leaves up with gleeful abandon. There's nothing wrong with that, either. Add to your greens that are covered with water either ¼ pound salt pork, bacon, ham hocks, 2–3 smoked turkey wings, 3–4 tablespoons olive oil, canola oil, and the juice of 1 whole lemon, depending on your spiritual proclivities and prohibitions. Bring to a boil, turn down. Let 'em simmer till the greens are the texture you want. Nouveau cuisine greens eaters will have much more sculpted-looking leaves than old-fashioned greens eaters who want the stalks to melt in their mouths along with the leaf of the collard. Again, I add ⅓ cup syrup, or 2 tablespoons honey, or 3 tablespoons molasses to my greens, but you don't have to. My mother thinks I ruin my greens that way, but she can always make her own, you know. Serve with vinegar, salt and pepper, and hot sauce to taste. Serves 6–8.

FRENCH-FRIED CHITLINS

I was taught to prepare chitlins by my third and fourth cousins on my mother's side, who lived, of course, in Texas. My father, whose people were Canadian and did not eat chitlins at all, told me my daughter's French-fried Chitlin taste like lobster. Most of the time you spend making these 5 pounds of highfalutin chitlins will be spent cleaning them (even if you bought them "pre-cleaned," remember, the butcher doesn't have to eat them!). You need to scrub, rinse, scrub some more, turn them inside out, and scrub even more. By the time you finish, the pile of guts in front of you will be darn near white and shouldn't really smell at all. Now you are ready to start the fun part. Slice the chitlins into ½-inch strips and set them aside. Prepare a thin batter with ½ cup flour, ½ cup milk, ⅓ bottle of beer—drink the rest—and seasonings to taste (if you forget the cayenne, may God have mercy on your soul!). Heat 2–3 inches of oil or bacon grease—use what you like as long as you don't use oil that has been used to fry fish—until very hot but not burning (360–375 degrees). Dip each strip into the batter, let excess drip down, and fry until golden brown. Only fry one layer at a time and be sure to move the chitlins around in the pot. After

patting away excess grease with a paper towel, serve with dirty
rice, greens, and corn bread. Or you can just eat them by them-
selves on a roll like a po' boy.

But seriously, and here I ask for a moment of quiet meditation,
what did L'Ouverture, Pétion, and Dessalines share for their victory
dinner, realizing they were the first African nation, slave-free, in the
New World? What did Bolivar crave as independence from Spain
became evident? What was the last meal of the defiant Inca Atahualpa
before the Spaniards made a public spectacle of his defeat? I only ask
these questions because the *New York Times* and the *Washington Post*
religiously announce the menu of every Inauguration dinner at the
White House every four years. Yet I must imagine, along with the surrealistic folk artists of Le Soleil in Port-au-Prince in their depictions of
L'Ouverture's triumph, what a free people chose to celebrate victory.
What sated the appetites of slaves no longer slaves, Africans now
Haitians, ordinary men made mystical by wont of their taste for freedom? How did we consecrate our newfound liberty? Now this may
only be important to me, but it is. It is very important. I need to know
how we celebrate our victories, our very survival. What did we want for
dinner? What was good enough to commemorate our humanity? We
know Haitians are still hungry. Don't we?

I wake each morning to a canvas by Paul Théaud of a woman, with
no body as we understand a human form, walking in a lime green
ocean; she is strolling by a lovely, living coral fish. But there on the
shore is a young boy whose stomach is missing, simply not there. His
face is scrambled with confusion. There is a fish alive, a woman with
no body walking in the sea, and he is on shore with no tummy. What
does it mean? Maybe Bob Marley can answer us, so we don't spend
years in a daze thinking Dred Scott has transmogrified: "Dem belly full,
but dey hungry/A hungry man is a angry man.

No one told me that to be dangerous one had to be ugly as well. No
one told me I had to speak American to know tenderness. Speaking
American ain't necessarily nourishing. I want to know what Grenada's
Socialist prime minister, Maurice Bishop, had for his last meal before
the tiny island's dreams were dashed by American forces in a matter of
minutes. Was there anything for him to eat? Is the Haitian woman without a body heading toward New Orleans where the slave ships useta
land or is she on her way to Guantanamo Bay, or maybe your back
door?

A SPIRITUAL MEAL GUIDELINE

DONALD ALTMAN

EXPERIENCING A SPIRITUAL MEAL in the Buddhist tradition means living and eating in a way that manifests compassion and loving-kindness. By following the suggestions here, you'll bring awareness, liberated consciousness, and wholesomeness to each meal and morsel.

While some Buddhist traditions require exclusively vegetarian meals, others permit meat. The Buddha himself ate meat when it was offered to him. Yet, in what was probably both a practical and compassionate decision, he taught that while it is a sin to kill for meat, it is not a sin to eat it.

Wash the Hands. It is customary in Buddhism to cleanse the hands before eating.

Begin with a Prayer The *Vinaya Pitaka,* or *Book of Discipline,* offers a reflection on food. While it's often recited by monks, anyone can gain value by reciting it before mealtime:

> With appreciation I am going to eat; not to frolic and not to indulge, not to increase conceitedness, and only in order to maintain my body, and prolong life, and to quench hunger, so that I can commit wholesome deeds to benefit myself and to benefit others . . .
> I will benefit by this food in prolonging my life, in leading a wholesome and peaceful life.

You can also consider and reflect upon this prayer during your meal. The fruits of your efforts can create a better attitude toward food, including the ability to overcome temptation, overindulgence, and unhealthy eating habits. One benefit of beginning any meal with a prayer is that it helps you to pause before eating.

Be Attentive. When we are attentive to the needs of others at the dinner table, we show them courtesy, compassion, and respect. Through small acts of mindfulness and thoughtfulness, such as anticipating when someone needs more food or drink, we become centered in the present moment.

If desired, silence can be incorporated into the meal. By maintaining silence we are less distracted and can be more fully aware of such things as how quickly we eat, how well we chew our food, what food we desire, and how much we eat.

Just as during meditation we don't fill up our lungs completely with each breath, we need to leave space in our stomachs when eating. This helps us establish moderate eating habits and, metaphorically lets us transcend our self-limiting behaviors and overwhelming desires. By giving ourselves space—in our stomachs, in our lungs, and in our minds—we can know and experience that there is always room for expansion and growth in our lives.

End with a Blessing and Transmit Loving-Kindness. After the meal, sit silently and respectfully for a moment. Place your palms together over your heart center and say a loving-kindness blessing or grace for others:

> May all beings be free from pain, hunger, and suffering. May all beings live long and be healthy. May all beings receive physical nourishment, well-being, and spiritual awareness through food. May all beings experience loving-kindness and serve others with compassion.

This lets you accomplish two things. First, you bless your food with loving-kindness. This gives your meal meaning and helps your body digest and receive full nourishment from food; it also reinforces spiritual consciousness and healthy eating habits. Second, you transmit loving-kindness to others—a step toward manifesting change in the world.

Should the reflection feel too long or cumbersome, try shortening it and putting it in your own words. Keep the essence of loving-kindness, and of food's purpose to yourself and others.

PRACTICE: NONATTACHMENT AND MODERATION

Savoring food with the senses offers a temporary worldly bliss. Eating food with spiritual awareness offers the potential of a more compassionate world and spiritual bliss. Through nonattachment and moderation we can appreciate and observe food's true meaning.

This simple and elegant inner meal practice takes only moments and can be used before any meal or snack.

Training of any kind requires repetition, so remind yourself to pause and reflect on food's higher purpose at every meal. Do this inner meal practice until reflection at mealtime becomes a new habit—a process that usually takes one to three months, though you will feel the results as soon as you begin this practice.

As you continue on your road to self-discovery you may find that nonattachment and moderation liberate you from overwhelming desire. This may let you step more securely onto the inner meal path.

The first part of this exercise is straightforward: pause before eating. Even if you've been conditioned to pick up the fork and dig in, pause for a moment to focus your inner awareness. Take a few seconds to observe the food and feel what it provides for you in terms of health and well-being. By focusing only on the higher meaning and value of food, you practice nonattachment from your emotional connection to it. Notice what draws your attention to the food before you—its hook, its flavor, its scent. In your mind's eye, make a checklist of those qualities of food that increase your feelings of hunger and greed and desire. For example, you might think, "I am drawn to this food's juiciness," or "I am attracted to the crunchiness and richness of this food." Be patient as you do this, and allow yourself to note these qualities dispassionately— like a detective who is solving a mystery. Later, jot down these qualities in a notebook.

By permitting yourself to experience a "desire-free moment," you slowly break the bonds of attachment to food. If you have a desire or an impulse to eat immediately, just note that in your mind dispassionately, with a sense of nonattachment.

Second, make a point of starting with an empty plate. (If you are eating at a restaurant, it may be useful to ask for an extra plate.) Make it your job—and no one else's—to place just as much food on your plate as you think your body needs. If you want to put more on the plate, just note this desire in your thoughts: "I feel desire for food and want to put an extra helping on my plate." Even if you finish eating a plateful, take a second helping according to what you think your body needs. Try to be aware of when your body has had enough nourishment. If you take only as much as you require, you'll avoid wasting food and overeating.

Third, recognize and be aware of your food choices. Know that you have complete freedom to pick the food that best serves you now. It may help to reflect on food's ultimate purpose—as the provider of your life energy and consciousness. By doing this, you bring moderation into your life and are less likely to abuse a particular food. You are also respecting your life and the value that food brings to it.

But what if you make a less than ideal food choice? Take responsibility for your choices, and know that while you might have fallen short of your ideal right now, you can make a better choice at the very next meal. In this way, moderation teaches us compassion for ourselves.

If you have a hard time feeling the importance of food's ultimate purpose, try to visualize what your life would be like if you didn't have enough food or didn't have the right food for good health. Eventually, you would suffer hunger, be unable to think properly, and become physically weak. All good things in life would lose their luster and become meaningless. Your existence would be consumed by trying to fill this one vital need. Keep in mind—this isn't supposed to make you feel sad or depressed or fearful—that the purpose of this exercise is to allow you to feel the essence of food's ultimate purpose as giver of life and consciousness.

There are many benefits to practicing nonattachment and moderation at mealtime. It bolsters our intuition about what kinds of food we need. It improves digestion. It teaches patience. It lets us avoid wasting food. It gives us a more accurate sense of how much food we require for optimum health—no more and no less. Freedom of food choice brings true liberation from habit, and from such humble beginnings the soul takes wing.

EDIBLE ÉCRITURE

TERRY EAGLETON

THE LINK BETWEEN EATING and writing has a venerable pedigree. Francis Bacon famously observed in his essay "Of Studies" that "some books are to be tasted others to be swallowed, and some few to be chewed and digested." Literary language can be mouth-filling or subtly flavored, meaty or hard-boiled, spicy or indigestible. Words can nourish or poison, and somewhere beneath this figurative equation lurks the eucharistic Word itself, a body which feeds other bodies, a sign which is also a meal. There are anorexic texts like Samuel Beckett's, in which discourse is in danger of dwindling to a mere skeleton of itself, and bulimic ones like Gerard Manley Hopkins's, muscle-bound and semiotically overstuffed. The language of Keats is as plump and well-packed as an apple, while less palatable poets like Swinburne are all froth and ooze. If Dylan Thomas binges on words, Harold Pinter approaches them with the wariness of a man on a diet. Bombast is a kind of verbal flatulence, a swelling which, like the bodies of the famished, conceals a hollowness.

Words issue from the lips as food enters them, though one can always take one's words back by eating them. And writing is a processing of raw speech just as cooking is a transformation of raw materials. One of Roland Barthes' structuralist models, bathetically enough, was a menu: just as a diner selects one item each from the "paradigmatic axes" of starters, entrées and desserts, and then combines them along a "syntagmatic axis" in the actual process of eating, so a literary work chooses items from various repertoires (genres, formal devices, narrative forms) and then goes on to string them together. These are the kind of speculations which send most English critics scrambling for their Helen Gardner. The later, poststructuralist Barthes threw over this model for the delights of semantic indeterminacy, but nothing is more alimentary than the ambiguous. If there is one sure thing about food, it is that it is never just food. Like the post-structuralist text, food is endlessly interpretable, as gift, threat, poison, recompense, barter, seduction, solidarity, suffocation. The ultimate floating signifier for the English is the cup of tea, appropriate for the most diverse occasions.

Food is just as much materialized emotion as a love lyric, though both can also be a substitute for the genuine article. A sign expresses something but also stands in for its absence, so that a child may be unsure whether receiving nourishment from its mother's hands or breasts is a symbol of her affection or a replacement for it. Perhaps a child may rebuff its food because what it really wants is some impossibly immaterial gift of affection, rather as a symbolist poet wants to strip language of its drably functional character and express its very essence. Food looks like an object but is actually a relationship, and the same is true of literary works. If there is no literary text without an author, neither is there one without a reader. The doctrine of transubstantiation, which states that the bread and wine of the Mass become the body and blood of Christ, redescribes physical substances in terms of relationships. A chemist would still identify the consecrated elements as bread and wine, but this for Catholic theology would be as pointless as describing the proffering of a box of chocolates in physiological terms. There is a parallel mystery about writing: how come that these little black marks on the sheet are actually meanings? By what strange transfiguration do arbitrary physical inscriptions come to be the medium of spirit, a matter of human address in the way that random tracks in the sand are not?

Language is at once material fact and rhetorical communication, just as eating combines biological necessity with cultural significance. Hunger-striking is not just a matter of refusing food, as you might refuse a fourth helping of pudding, but a question of not taking food from a specific oppressor, and thus a dialogical affair. Starving here is a message rather than just a physical condition, semiotic as well as somatic. Food is cusped between nature and culture, and so too is language, which humans have as a dimension of their nature but which is also as culturally variable as cuisine. Nobody will perish without Mars bars, just as nobody ever died of not reading *Paradise Lost,* but food and language of some sort are essential to our survival.

Fast food is like cliché or computerese, an emotionless exchange or purely instrumental form of discourse; genuine eating combines pleasure, utility and sociality, and so differs from a take-away in much the same way that Proust differs from a bus ticket. Snatching a meal alone bears the same relation to eating in company as talking to yourself does to conversation. It is hardly surprising that a civilization for which a dialogue of the mind with itself has provided a paradigm of human language should reach its apotheosis in the Big Mac.

Those starved words, gaunt bodies and sterile landscapes of Beckett's dramas may well carry with them a race memory of the Irish famine, a catastrophe which was the slow death of language as well as of one million people. The famine decimated the farm laborers and small tenants, who made up most of the Irish speakers, and using the language in post-famine Ireland rapidly became a symbol of ill-luck. It is possible to read Beckett's meticulously pared-down prose (for which French, he thought, was the most suitable medium) as a satirical smack at the blather and blarney of stage-Irish speech. Beckett hoards his meager clutch of words like a tight-fisted peasant, ringing pedantic changes on the same few signs or stage properties like someone eking out a scanty diet. There is, perhaps, a Protestant suspicion of superfluity here, in contrast to the extravagant expenditure of a Joyce, the linguistic opulence of J. M. Synge or the verbal gluttony of Brendan Behan.

But all that reckless prodigality may itself have a bearing on food, as a form of compensation in the mind for what is lacking in historcal reality. In conditions of colonial backwardness, language is one of the few things you have left; and though even that in Ireland had been put down by the imperial power, words were still a good deal more plentiful than hot dinners. Part of the point of language was to bamboozle the colonialists; indeed the word 'blarney' derives from the Earl of Blarney's doing just that in the reign of Elizabeth I. The linguistic virtuosity of the Irish writers springs partly from the fact that, like Joseph Conrad and many a modernist emigré they are inside and outside a language simultaneously. But it is also a form of displacement, whereby you hope to discover in discourse a richness denied to you in reality.

The most celebrated food-text of English literature is the work of an Anglo-Irish patriot who bitterly recommended munching babies as a solution to his country's economic ills. During the great famine, this may well have happened; as Swift's fellow-Dubliner Oscar Wilde observed, life has a remarkable knack of imitating art. Language in Irish culture, however, is associated less with food, which was hardly much in evidence, than with drink. As drink flows in, so words pour out, each fuelling the other in a self-sustaining process. In fact, apart from the notoriously bibulous trinity of Brendan Behan, Flann O'Brien and Patrick Kavanagh, remarkably few Irish writers have been alcoholics— far fewer than American authors, for whom alcohol seems as much of a prerequisite as a typewriter. There is a fair amount of eating in *Ulysses,* but the novel itself, at least in the view of the critic John Bayley, is impossible to consume, 'sunk in its own richness like a plumcake.' Bayley, with his English distaste for fancy foreign modernists, misses the point that Joyce's work is deliberately calculated to induce dyspepsia. Modernist art was born at much the same time as mass culture, and one reason for its obscurity is to resist being sucked in as easily as tabloid print. By fragmenting its forms, thickening its textures and garbling its narratives, the modernist text hopes to escape the indignities of instant consumption.

It is significant that our word for the use of a commodity—consumption—is drawn from the guts and the gullet. This modern metaphor has a rather more high-toned ancestor: taste. The eighteenth-century idea of taste was partly a way of freeing artistic evaluation from too rigid a consensus: taste was subjective, beyond disputation, a *je ne sais quoi* which refused any total reduction to rules. Just as there was no moral obligation to like rhubarb, so it wasn't a capital offence to turn up your nose at Rembrandt, even if true gentlemen in fact turned out conveniently enough to relish much the same works of art. Similarly, what food you enjoyed was a private, arbitrary affair—until, that is, you tried ordering in your London club the kind of meal they ate in rural Cork. But this gustatory trope made room for individual freedom only at the risk of trivialising art to the status of a sausage, rather as the modern idea of consumption celebrates individual choice while threatening to drain it of value.

Food is what makes up our bodies, just as words are what constitute our minds; and if body and mind are hard to distinguish, it is no wonder that eating and speaking should continually cross over in metaphorical exchange. Both are, in any case, media of exchange themselves. There is no more modish topic in contemporary literary theory than the human body. Writing the body, texts as bodies, bodies as sign-systems: in the thick of all this fashionable Foucaulteanism, there has been strikingly little concern with the physical stuff of which bodies are composed, as opposed to an excited interest in their genitalia. The human body is generally agreed to be "constructed," but what starts off that construction for all of us—milk—has been curiously passed over. There has been much critical interest in the famished body of the Western anorexic, but rather little attention to the malnutrition of the Third World. Perhaps such dwindled bodies are too bluntly material a matter for a so-called "materialist" criticism. One notable exception to this indifference to the politics of starvation is Maud Ellmann's brilliant study *The Hunger Artists*, which concludes with the following reflections:

> [Food's] disintegration in the stomach, its assimilation in the blood, its diaphoresis in the epidermis, its metempsychosis in the large intestine; its viscosity in okra, gumbo, oysters, its elasticity in jellies; its deli-

quescence in blancmanges; its tumescence in the throats of serpents, its slow erosion in the bellies of sharks; its odysseys through pastures, orchards, wheat fields, stock-yards, supermarkets, kitchens, pig troughs, rubbish dumps, disposals; the industries of sowing, hunting, cooking, milling, processing, and canning it; the wizardry of its mutations, ballooning in bread, subsiding in soufflés; raw and cooked, solid and melting, vegetable and mineral, fish flesh, and fowl, encompassing the whole compendium of living substance: food is the symbol of the passage, the totem of sociality, the epitome of all creative and destructive labor.

Ellmann quite properly makes a meal of it. Her paragraph coils like an intestine, the sense slipping from clause to clause like a morsel down the esophagus. As these lines track the processing of food, so they in turn process that subject-matter, by the cuisinary transformations of style, into a delectable feast.

FUNERALS

MIMI SHERATON

M Y MOTHER'S REFLEX REACTION to any special event, joyous or sad, was to call the butcher. A death in the family was no exception. "At least let there be a plate of soup in the house," she said, explaining why she ordered a chicken, and, "At least let there be some meat to slice when visitors get hungry," she added, thus accounting for the pickled tongue or pot roast or roast beef or turkey. Sorrow was bad enough without compounding it with hunger. Sometimes the food was to be left at home if she expected condolence callers, but usually at least some of it went to the house where shiva was being observed.

It was the shiva house—the house of mourning, usually where the deceased had lived—that frightened me as a child. Mirrors were shrouded with sheets, living room furniture was pushed back to accommodate bridge chairs for visitors and the plain wooden crates or the small bare benches sent by the funeral parlor for the immediate mourners to sit on. Those mourners wore stockings or, at most, slippers (since they were not permitted to wear shoes) and black clothes usually with a cut near the lapel, although in later years the cut was made more practically in a strip of black grosgrain ribbon that was then pinned to the clothes. Men did not shave for the seven days of mourning nor did women wear lipstick, no radio or music was played (unusual for a family in which everyone, it seemed, played the piano), and the house was full of visitors from times and places far removed.

Mothers introduced children to long-lost relatives with pride as the children squirmed, and when I was older my mother always admonished me to dress nicely at funerals (but not too nicely) so she could show me off to a distant cousin or aunt. Tears alternated with laughter as funny stories were recalled and photographs of the deceased were passed around, along with others of new and unseen babies and brides.

Most visitors brought food if they had not already sent some. Not only the sorts of things my mother prepared, but lofty soufflé-like sponge cakes fragrant with vanilla, nut- and cinnamon-filled coffee cakes, pounds of delicatessen meats such as whole, garlic-flecked salamis, bologna, liverwurst, peppery sides of pastrami, and whole corned beefs, their glistening fat waiting to be steamed to melting, succulent tenderness. There were jars of soup, boxes of candy, and big, flat baskets that held a kaleidoscopic array of dried tropical fruits wrapped in orangy cellophane, each packed with a little bone or ivory two-pronged fork. There were tins of salted nuts and high steamer baskets of hothouse fruits with big satin bows ("Dopes," my father loved to say. "Don't they know that hothouse fruit has no taste? Who cares if it looks beautiful? What good is it if you can't eat it?" he would ask, as my mother upbraided him for being an ingrate.)

But the most memorable spread was the one laid out immediately after the funeral and burial, again usually at the home of the deceased and at its best when that was my grandmother's house and the family was still large and close together. One such funeral was for her husband (my grandfather), the other for a son (my uncle) who died at thirty-seven. Though his young family lived in Brooklyn, his wife was unable to cope with crowds, food, and the attendant fuss, so the shiva was observed at my grandmother's.

Somehow, magically, one or two of the less immediate family members, or perhaps the neighbors, set out the spread while relatives went to the cemetery, and since all the funerals I remember took place in the morning and in cold or rainy weather, the meal they came back to was more or less a breakfast, with dairy foods and plenty of hot coffee as a welcome restorative.

But before coffee or food, even on empty stomachs, there would be shots of schnapps—rye whiskey thrown down neat with nothing more than a shudder as a chaser, for both men and women, although the latter sometimes sipped theirs down in thirds. The toast "lachaim"—to life—had special meaning at such an event, and that meaning never passed unremarked.

But they also ate to life, starting with the symbolic hard-cooked egg and piece of bread. The table, whether set in kitchen, dinette, or dining room, was covered with the best damask cloth and groaned under the weight of bowls of gleaming silver-blue pickled herring with sour cream and onion rings, ruby fillets of maatjes herring with minced scallions, dishes of coral canned salmon to be served with finely minced Bermuda onion in white vinegar, trays of smoked fish such as whitefish, alabaster sturgeon, satiny sable, all looking as though they had been gold leafed, and paprika-edged smoked carp. Sliced tomatoes and onions dotted with wrinkled, salty black musselines olives, baskets of pumpernickel rye bread, matzohs, bagels, onion rolls, and bialys, dishes with slabs of cream cheese and butter, slices of imported Swiss and buttery Muenster cheese, were all there to be nibbled on while someone at the stove dished up to order eggs, any style, fried or scrambled plain or with lox and onions, or blintzes puffy with cinnamon-sugar cottage cheese fillings that appeared magically from some beneficent relative to be fried crisply brown and topped with sour cream as needed.

Then for the coffee cakes, the crunchy rugelach and schnecken of crisp yeast dough enveloping chewy fillings of walnuts, cinnamon, raisins, and sugar, gold and chocolate marble cake sometimes with streaks of fudge running through it, high sunny cheesecakes, pecan rings and almond braids, streuselkuchen crumbcakes, an endless array of cookies from neighbors and friends, perhaps apple strudels and poppyseed rolls, and more that I have probably forgotten.

With the family grown small, even funerals come infrequently now, and there is no one left to observe shiva. But one cousin and I who share the memory of that funeral food, and feel it a palliative for sadness, usually go to Ratner's after a funeral (now that Rappaport's, our favorite, is closed) and duplicate as best we can some of the standards of the postfuneral breakfast.

The foods eaten at one funeral always recall another—and all recall to me the most memorable circumstances surrounding the funeral of my Uncle Al. He was the big, bald, rotund, jolly favorite of everyone in the family, a happy-go-lucky man who had a hard time making a living and who traveled and lived all over the country to do so, and so was most often away. His visits to Brooklyn always seemed hike holidays, with much card playing, eating, and, way into the night, laughter, always laughter.

His death, which came suddenly and early of a heart attack, really did cause my mother agony. He died in Virginia, but he was to be buried in the family plot on Long Island, so my cousins, his sons, came North with the body, and my mother, in spite of her anguish, helped them with funeral preparations. The first task was to go to a funeral home and order the coffin and arrange for the service, and, inevitably, to bargain for the whole affair. My cousins could afford only $600, but the coffin they liked cost $900, and so my mother took over with the funeral director, who had handled all the family deaths until that time. "Look, Sherman," she said to him, "be smart. Give the kids the coffin they want for six hundred dollars. You know, Sherman, you buried my mother, my father, one brother, now another brother. Be smart, Sherman, and you'll bury me." Sherman eventually thought this made sense and dropped the price $300.

But this was not the end of Uncle Al's funeral, for when the cemetery workers opened the grave he was to occupy in the family plot, they discovered in it a stray leg—my grandfather's leg, which had been amputated many years before he died. In the orthodox Jewish tradition, it was buried in the grave he was eventually to occupy, so that he could go to his Maker Intact. But when my grandfather died, he had obviously been buried in the wrong grave, without his leg. My mother was incensed. "Imagine Morris Breit in his grave all these years without his foot," she said. "I'll sue!"

She never did, though, but saw to it that the gravediggers opened my grandfather's grave and buried his foot before they readied the new grave for my uncle. When all was done, and when she was sure there would be no charge for correcting the error, she let herself go and cried for Uncle Al.

THE PLEASURES OF EATING

WENDELL BERRY

*M*ANY TIMES, AFTER I HAVE finished a lecture on the decline of American farming and rural life, someone in the audience has asked, "What can city people do?"

"Eat responsibly," I have usually answered. Of course, I have tried to explain what I meant by that, but afterwards I have invariably felt that there was more to be said than I had been able to say. Now I would like to attempt a better explanation.

I begin with the proposition that eating is an agricultural act. Eating ends the annual drama of the food economy that begins with planting and birth. Most eaters, however, are no longer aware that this is true. They think of food as an agricultural product, perhaps, but they do not think of themselves as participants in agriculture. They think of themselves as "consumers." If they think beyond that, they recognize that they are passive consumers. They buy what they want—or what they have been persuaded to want—within the limits of what they can get. They pay, mostly without protest, what they are charged. And they mostly ignore certain critical questions about the quality and the cost of what they are sold: How fresh is it? How pure or clean is it, how free of dangerous chemicals? How far was it transported, and what did transportation add to the cost? How much did manufacturing or packaging or advertising add to the cost? When the food product has been manufactured or "processed" or "precooked," how has that affected its quality or price or nutritional value?

Most urban shoppers would tell you that food is produced on farms. But most of them do not know what farms, or what kinds of farms, or where the farms are, or what knowledge or skills are involved in farming. They apparently have little doubt that farms will continue to produce, but they do not know how or over what obstacles. For them, then, food is pretty much an abstract idea—something they do not know or imagine—until it appears on the grocery shelf or on the table.

The specialization of production induces specialization of consumption. Patrons of the entertainment industry, for example, entertain themselves less and less and have become more and more passively dependent on commercial suppliers. This is certainly true also of patrons of the food industry, who have tended more and more to be *mere* consumers—passive, uncritical, and dependent. Indeed, this sort of consumption may be said to be one of the chief goals of industrial production. The food industrialists have by now persuaded millions of consumers to prefer food that is already prepared. They will grow, deliver, and cook your food for you and (just like your mother) beg you to eat it. That they do not yet offer to insert it, prechewed, into your mouth is only because they have found no profitable way to do so. We may rest assured that they would be glad to find such a way. The ideal industrial food consumer would be strapped to a table with a tube running from the food factory directly into his or her stomach.

Perhaps I exaggerate, but not by much. The industrial eater is, in fact, one who does not know that eating is an agricultural act, who no longer knows or imagines the connections between eating and the land, and who is therefore necessarily passive and uncritical—in short, a victim. When food, in the minds of eaters, is no longer associated with farming and with the land, then the eaters are suffering a kind of cultural amnesia that is misleading and dangerous. The current version of the "dream home" of the future involves "effortless" shopping from a list of available goods on a television monitor and heating precooked food by remote control. Of course, this implies and depends on, a perfect ignorance of the history of the food that is consumed. It requires that the citizenry should give up their hereditary and sensible aversion to buying a pig in a poke. It wishes to make the selling of pigs in pokes an honorable and glamorous activity. The dreamer in this dream home will perforce know nothing about the kind or quality of this food, or where it came from, or how it was produced and prepared, or what ingredients, additives, and residues it contains—unless, that is, the dreamer undertakes a close and constant study of the food industry, in which case he or she might as well wake up and play an active and responsible part in the economy of food.

There is, then, a politics of food that, like any politics, involves our freedom. We still (sometimes) remember that we cannot be free if our minds and voices are controlled by someone else. But we have neglected to understand that we cannot be free if our food and its sources are controlled by someone else. The condition of the passive consumer of food is not a democratic condition. One reason to eat responsibly is to live free.

But if there is a food politics, there are also a food aesthetics and a food ethics, neither of which is dissociated from politics. Like industrial sex, industrial eating has become a degraded, poor, and paltry thing. Our kitchens and other eating places more and more resemble filling stations, as our homes more and more resemble motels. "Life is not very interesting," we seem to have decided. "Let its satisfactions be minimal, perfunctory, and fast." We hurry through our meals to go to work and hurry through our work in order to "recreate" ourselves in the evenings and on weekends and vacations. And then we hurry, with the greatest possible speed and noise and violence, through our recreation—for what? To eat the billionth hamburger at some fast-food joint hellbent on increasing the "quality" of our life? And all this is carried out in a remarkable obliviousness to the causes and effects, the possibilities and the purposes, of the life of the body in this world.

One will find this obliviousness represented in virgin purity in the advertisements of the food industry, in which food wears as much makeup as the actors. If one gained one's whole knowledge of food from these advertisements (as some presumably do), one would not know that the various edibles were ever living creatures, or that they all come from the soil, or that they were produced by work. The passive American consumer, sitting down to a meal of pre-prepared or fast food, confronts a platter covered with inert, anonymous substances that have been processed, dyed, breaded, sauced, gravied, ground, pulped, strained, blended, prettified, and sanitized beyond resemblance to any part of any creature that ever lived. The products of nature and agriculture have been made, to all appearances, the products of industry. Both eater and eaten are thus in exile from biological reality. And the result is a kind of solitude, unprecedented in human experience, in which the eater may think of eating as, first, a purely commercial transaction between him and a supplier and then as a purely appetitive transaction between him and his food.

And this peculiar specialization of the act of eating is, again, of obvious benefit to the food industry, which has good reasons to obscure the connection between food and farming. It would not do for the consumer to know that the hamburger she is eating came from a steer who spent much of his life standing deep in his own excrement in a feedlot, helping to pollute the local streams, or that the calf that yielded the veal cutlet on her plate spent its life in a box in which it did not have room to turn around. And, though her sympathy for the slaw might be less tender, she should not be encouraged to meditate on the hygienic and biological implications of mile-square fields of cabbage, for vegetables grown in huge monocultures are dependent on toxic chemicals—just as animals in close confinement are dependent on antibiotics and other drugs.

The consumer, that is to say, must be kept from discovering that, in the food industry—as in any other industry—the overriding concerns are not quality and health, but volume and price. For decades now the entire industrial food economy, from the large farms and feedlots to the chains of supermarkets and fast-food restaurants, has been obsessed with volume. It has relentlessly increased scale in order to increase volume in order (presumably) to reduce costs. But as scale increases, diversity declines; as diversity declines, so does health; as health declines, the dependence on drugs and chemicals necessarily increases. As capital replaces labor, it does so by substituting machines, drugs, and chemicals for human workers and for the natural health and fertility of the soil. The food is produced by any means or any shortcut that will increase profits. And the business of the cosmeticians of advertising is to persuade the consumer that food so produced is good, tasty, healthful, and a guarantee of marital fidelity and long life.

It is possible, then, to be liberated from the husbandry and wifery of the old household food economy. But one can be thus liberated only by entering a trap (unless one sees ignorance and helplessness as the signs of privilege, as many people apparently do). The trap is the ideal of industrialism: a walled city surrounded by valves that let merchandise in but no consciousness out. How does one escape this trap? Only voluntarily, the same way that one went in: by restoring one's consciousness of what is involved in eating; by reclaiming responsibility for one's own part in the food economy. One might begin with the illuminating principle of Sir Albert Howard's *The Soil and Health,* that we should understand "the whole problem of health in soil, plant, animal, and man as one great subject." Eaters, that is, must understand that eating takes place inescapably in the world, that it is inescapably an agricultural act, and that how we eat determines, to a considerable extent, how the world is used. This is a simple way of describing a relationship that is inexpressibly complex. To eat responsibly is to understand and enact, so far as one can, this complex relationship. What can one do? Here is a list, probably not definitive:

    1. Participate in food production to the extent that you can. If you have a yard or even just a porch box or a pot in a sunny window, grow something to eat in it. Make a little compost of your kitchen scraps and use it for fertilizer. Only by growing some food for yourself can you

become acquainted with the beautiful energy cycle that revolves from soil to seed to flower to fruit to food to offal to decay, and around again. You will be fully responsible for any food that you grow for yourself, and you will know all about it. You will appreciate it fully, having known it all its life.

2. Prepare your own food. This means reviving in your own mind and life the arts of kitchen and household. This should enable you to eat more cheaply, and it will give you a measure of "quality control": you will have some reliable knowledge of what has been added to the food you eat.

3. Learn the origins of the food you buy, and buy the food that is produced closest to your home. The idea that every locality should be, as much as possible, the source of its own food makes several kinds of sense. The locally produced food supply is the most secure, the freshest, and the easiest for local consumers to know about and to influence.

4. Whenever possible, deal directly with a local farmer, gardener, or orchardist. All the reasons listed for the previous suggestion apply here. In addition, by such dealing you eliminate the whole pack of merchants, transporters, processors, packagers, and advertisers who thrive at the expense of both producers and consumers.

5. Learn, in self-defense, as much as you can of the economy and technology of industrial food production. What is added to food that is not food, and what do you pay for these additions?

6. Learn what is involved in the *best* farming and gardening.

7. Learn as much as you can, by direct observation and experience if possible, of the life histories of the food species.

The last suggestion seems particularly important to me. Many people are now as much estranged from the lives of domestic plants and animals (except for flowers and dogs and cats) as they are from the lives of the wild ones. This is regrettable, for these domestic creatures are in diverse ways attractive; there is much pleasure in knowing them. And farming, animal husbandry, horticulture, and gardening, at their best, are complex and comely arts; there is much pleasure in knowing them, too.

It follows that there is great displeasure in knowing about a food economy that degrades and abuses those arts and those plants and animals and the soil from which they come. For anyone who does know something of the modern history of food, eating away from home can be a chore. My own inclination is to eat seafood instead of red meat or poultry when I am traveling. Though I am by no means a vegetarian, I dislike the thought that some animal has been made miserable in order to feed me. If I am going to eat meat, I want it to be from an animal that has lived a pleasant, uncrowded life outdoors, on bountiful pasture, with good water nearby and trees for shade. And I am getting almost as fussy about food plants. I like to eat vegetables and fruits that I know have lived happily and healthily in good soil, not the products of the huge, bechemicaled factory-fields that I have seen, for example, in the Central Valley of California. The industrial farm is said to have been patterned on the factory production line. In practice, it looks more like a concentration camp.

The pleasure of eating should be an *extensive* pleasure, not that of the mere gourmet. People who know the garden in which their vegetables have grown and know that the garden is healthy will remember the beauty of the growing plants, perhaps in the dewy first light of morning when gardens are at their best. Such a memory involves itself with the food and is one of the pleasures of eating. The knowledge of the good health of the garden relieves and frees and comforts the eater. The same goes for eating meat. The thought of the good pasture and of the calf contentedly grazing flavors the steak. Some, I know, will think it bloodthirsty or worse to eat a fellow creature you have known all its life. On the contrary, I think it means that you eat with understanding and with gratitude. A significant part of the pleasure of eating is in one's accurate consciousness of the lives and the world from which food comes. The pleasure of eating, then, may be the best available standard of our health. And this pleasure, I think, is pretty fully available to the urban consumer who will make the necessary effort.

I mentioned earlier the politics, esthetics, and ethics of food. But to speak of the pleasure of eating is to go beyond those categories. Eating with the fullest pleasure—pleasure, that is, that does not depend on ignorance—is perhaps the profoundest enactment of our connection with the world. In this pleasure we experience and celebrate our dependence and our gratitude, for we are living from mystery, from creatures we did not make and powers we cannot comprehend. When I think of the meaning of food, I always remember these lines by the poet William Carlos Williams, which seem to me merely honest:

> There is nothing to eat,
> seek it where you will,
> but the body of the Lord.
> The blessed plants
> and the sea, yield it
> to the imagination
> intact.

ISABEL ALLENDE, who was born in Peru and raised in Chile, is the author of *Daughter of Fortune, Aphrodite: A Memoir of the Senses, Of Love and Shadows,* and *The House of the Spirits.* She lives in California.

DONALD ALTMAN, a former monk, is the author of *The Art of the Inner Meal* and *Living-Kindness* and an Emmy Award-winning TV and documentary writer. He lives in Portland, Oregon.

LEON ARON, who was born in Moscow and then emigrated to the U.S., is the author of *Yeltsin: A Revolutionary Life* and *Reshaping Europe,* and editor of *The Emergerce of Russian Foreign Policy.* He is a resident scholar at the American Enterprise Institute in Washington, D. C.

GERALD ASHER, the author of *Vineyard Tales, On Wine* and *The Pleasures of Wine,* is a two-time James Beard Foundation Award-winner. He has been wine editor for *Gourmet* magazine for three decades and divides his time between San Francisco and Paris.

RUSSELL BAKER, a Pulitzer Prize-winning columnist for the *New York Times* Op-Ed page for more than three decades, is now the host of Masterpiece Theatre. He is the author of two memoirs, *Growing Up* and *The Good Times,* and the collections featuring his columns, *An American in Washington* and *Poor Russell's Almanac.*

CHITRITA BANERJI, who grew up in Calcutta, is the author of *Life and Food in Bengal, Bengali Cooking,* and *The Hour of the Goddess.* Her writings on food have appeared in *Gourmet, Granta,* and *Gastronomica.* She resides in Cambridge.

ROLAND BARTHES was one of Europe's major literary figures and the author of several books, which include: *Empire of Signs, A Lover's Discourse, Camera Lucida, Mythologies,* and *The Responsibility of Forms.* He died in Paris in 1980.

WENDELL BERRY has been writing on agriculture, gardening, culture, and politics for several decades. A novelist, poet, and essayist, his books include: *Home Economics, What Are People For?, A Timbered Chair, Jayber Crow, The Gift of Good Land,* and *The Unsettling of America.* He lives on a farm in Kentucky.

ANTHONY BOURDAIN is executive chef at Manhattan's Brasserie Les Halles and the author of *Kitchen Confidential, Bone in the Throat,* and *A Cook's Tour,* also the title of his Food Network show. He is a *Bon Appétit* "Food Writer of the Year."

JULIA CHILD, America's most celebrated cookbook author and TV cooking show host, recently celebrated her ninetieth birthday. Among her many widely-influential books are: *Mastering the Art of French Cooking, The French Chef Cookbook,* and *Cooking with Master Chefs.* She lives in Santa Barbara.

LAURIE COLWIN is the beloved author of *Home Cooking,* a James Beard Foundation Award-winner, and *More Home Cooking,* collections of her *Gourmet* articles. She also wrote the novels, stories, and non-fiction volumes, *Passion and Affect, Family Happiness,* and *Another Marvelous Thing.* She died in 1992.

ELIZABETH DAVID shaped British culinary tastes from the post-war years until her death in 1992. She wrote several influential volumes: *Summer Cooking, English Bread and Yeast Cookery, An Omelette and a Glass of Wine* (her *Spectator* articles), and the posthumous collection, *Is There a Nutmeg in the House?* Elizabeth David also had a kitchen shop near her home in London.

CARA DE SILVA is a writer, food historian, and editor of *In Memory's Kitchen: A Legacy from the Women of Terezín.* Formerly on staff at *New York Newsday,* she lives in Manhattan.

MICHAEL DORRIS wrote *Paper Trail, A Yellow Raft in Blue Water, Morning Girl, Guests,* and *Working Men: Stories.* He died in 1997.

TERRY EAGLETON is an influential English scholar and author of *Sweet Violence, Literary Theory, The Illusions of Postmodernism, William Shakespeare,* and *Criticism and ideology,* and the memoir *The Gatekeeper.* He teaches at the University of Manchester.

UMBERTO ECO, one of Europe's best-known intellectuals, is the author of the novels *Baudolino, The Name of the Rose, Foucault's Pendulum,* and *The Island of the Day Before.* A professor at the University of Bologna, he has written many books on culture, art, and literature through the centuries.

M. F. K. FISHER wrote prose of such intelligence and stylish wit that for more than half a century her books have been regarded as classics of American food literature. Included among them are: *An Alphabet for Gourmets, How to Cook a Wolf, The Gastronomical Me.* She was the editor of *Here Let Us Feast* and Brillat-Savarin's *The Physiology of Taste,* which she also translated. M. F. K. Fisher died in California in 1992.

BETTY FUSSELL is a culinary historian and author of several books, including: *My Kitchen Wars, Masters of American Cookery, Eating In, Food in Good Season, Home Plates,* and *The Story of Corn,* which received the Julia Child Cookbook Award. Her articles on food have appeared in *The New York Times, The New Yorker,* and *Vogue.* She lives in New York City.

ADAM GOPNIK is a staff writer of *The New Yorker* and author of *Paris to the Moon.* He has contributed to several volumes, including *Richard Avedon's Evidence 1944-1994, Parisians, Wayne Thiebaud,* and *Defining Edges.* Adam Gopnik lives in New York City.

JANE GRIGSON was a much-admired British food writer for nearly three decades. She wrote many books, including *English Food, Vegetable Book, Fruit Book, The Mushroom Feast,* and *Fish Cooking,* as well as a regular column for the magazine of the *Observer.* She died in 1990.

MARCELLA HAZAN is the well-known Italian cookbook author who has won several James Beard Foundation Awards for her *Essentials of Italian Cooking, Marcella Cucina,* and *The Classic Italian Cookbook.* Her home is in Venice.

EDWARD HOAGLAND has published several volumes of travel and nature writing and essays, including *Compass Points, The Courage of Turtles, African Calliope, Tigers & Ice,* and *Redwolves and Black Bears.* He teaches at Bennington College and lives in Vermont.

JAY JACOBS was the restaurant critic for *Gourmet* magazine in the years 1972-1986 and also the author of *A Glutton for Punishment, New York à la carte, Gastronomy,* and *The Eaten Word.* He lives in New York.

FREDERICK KAUFMAN wrote the text for *Manuel Alvarez Bravo: Photographs and Memories.* His writings on art, photography, film, and cultural issues have appeared in *Harper's, Aperture,* and other national periodicals.

JANE KRAMER is European correspondent for *The New Yorker* and author of *The Politics of Memory, Unsettling Europe, Lone Patriot,* and *Off Washington Square.* When she is not working abroad, she is at her home in New York City.

MAXINE KUMIN is a novelist and poet whose *Up Country* received the Pulitzer Prize. Among her other titles are: *Always Beginning, Nurture, The Designated Heir, In Deep,* and *Women, Animals, and Vegetables.* She has lived for many years in New Hampshire.

CORBY KUMMER is the author of *The Pleasures of Slow Food* and *The Joy of Coffee,* and recipient of the M. F. K. Fisher Distinguished Writing Award from the James Beard Foundation. A senior editor of *The Atlantic,* he is based in Boston.

RACHEL LAUDAN is a historian and author of *The Food of Paradise: Exploring Hawaii's Culinary Heritage,* which received the Jane Grigson Award and Sophie Coe Prize from the Oxford Symposium on Food and Cooking. She makes her home in Mexico.

NIGELLA LAWSON is the author of *How to Eat: The Pleasures and Principles of Good Food* and *How to Be A Domestic Goddess.* Television series based on *Nigella Bites* and *Forever Summer* have been shown in England and the U.S. Popular on both sides of the Atlantic, her articles appear in the *New York Times* and *Gourmet* as well as the *Sunday Times* of London and *Guardian.*

BONNIE MARRANCA is the author of two collections of essays, *Ecologies of Theatre* and *Theatrewritings,* which received the George Jean Nathan Award for Dramatic Criticism, and the editor of *A Hudson Valley Reader, American Garden Writing,* and *Conversations on Art and Performance.* A former Guggenheim Fellow and Fulbright Scholar, she lives in New York City.

DAVID MAS MASUMOTO is the author of *Harvest Son, Epitaph for a Peach, Planting Roots in American Soil,* and *Four Seasons in Five Senses.* He is a third-generation farmer who grows organic peaches and grapes near Fresno, California.

JAY PARINI is a poet, novelist, biographer whose books include *Some Necessary Angels, The Apprentice Lover,* and *Benjamin's Crossing,* and editor of *The Columbia History of American Poetry.* He teaches at Middlebury College and lives in Vermont.

MICHAEL POLLAN is the author of *Second Nature, The Botany of Desire,* and *A Place of My Own,* whose frequent writings on food, the environment, and gardening have appeared in *The New York Times Magazine.* A former editor of *Harper's,* he lives in Cornwall Bridge, Connecticut.

EMILY PRAGER is a novelist and author of *A Visit from the Footbinder and Other Stories, Eve's Tattoo, Wuhu Diary, Clea and Zeus Divorce.* She lives in New York City.

DOMINIQUE PRÉDALI is the author of *Recettes Religieuses, Les Prédateurs de la Santé,* and *Les Dessous de l'Agroalimentaire.* Also a painter and sculptor, she lives in France.

FRANK PRIAL has been writing the *New York Times* "Wine Talk" column, which he created, for more than three decades. A Chevalier of the French Legion of Honor, he is the author of *Decantations,* a Gourmand World Cookbook Award-winner, and *Wine Talk* and former host of New York's WQXR wine program.

CLAUDIA RODEN, who was born in Cairo, has written *The Book of Jewish Food,* which received the James Beard Foundation Award, *Invitation to Mediterranean Cooking,* and *A Book of Middle Eastern Food.* A recipient of several European food prizes and England's Food Writer of the Year Award for her articles in the *Observer Magazine* and *Daily Telegraph,* she lives in London.

MORT ROSENBLUM is the author of *Olives,* a winner of the Jame Beard Foundation Award, *The Secret Life of the Seine,* and *A Goose in Toulouse and Other Culinary Adventures in France.* An Associated Press special correspondent and former editor of the *International Herald Tribune,* he lives in Paris and Provence.

WOLFGANG SCHIVELBUSCH is a German historian and sociologist whose studies include: *Tastes of Paradise, Disenchanted Night,* and *The Railway Journey.*

PAUL SCHMIDT translated plays from French, Russian, and German, including *The Plays of Anton Chekhov,* Rimbaud's *A Season in Hell,* and *The Collected Works of Khlebnikov.* A poet and historian, he also wrote *Meyerhold at Work* and acted in The Wooster Group's *Brace Up!* before his death in 1999.

NTOZAKE SHANGE is a poet, novelist, and playwright whose writings include the award-winning theatre work, *For Colored Girls Who Have Considered Suicide/ When the Rainbow is Enuf, IF I CAN COOK/You Know God Can, Sassafras, Cypress and Indigo,* and *A Daughter's Geography.* She lives in Florida.

MIMI SHERATON is the author of *The Bialy Eaters: The Story of a Bread and a Lost World, From My Mother's Kitchen,* and *The German Cookbook.* A former *New York Times* food critic, her articles on food and restaurants appear in *Vanity Fair, Condé Nast Traveler,* and *Food & Wine.* She lives in New York City.

MARY TAYLOR SIMETI is the author of *On Persephone's Island* and *Pomp and Sustenance: Twenty-Five Centuries of Sicilian Food.* She was born in New York City but has lived for many years in Sicily.

CHARLES SIMIC is a poet whose books include *The World Doesn't End,* which received the Pulitzer Prize for Poetry, *Jackstraws, Looking for Trouble, Hotel Insomnia, The Book of Gods and Devils, Unending Blues.* He teaches at the University of New Hampshire.

NIGEL SLATER is the author of *Real Fast Food, Real Cooking,* and *Real Food,* also the title of his British television series, in addition to a memoir, entitled *Toast.* Winner of the Glenfiddich Trophy and the André Simon Award for cookery writing, he publishes a weekly column in the *Observer* and contributes to the *Observer Food Monthly* supplement and *Sainsbury's Magazine.*

SUSAN SONTAG is one of American's most well-known literary figures whose many books include the novels, *In America,* which won the National Book Award, and *The Volcano Lover,* several plays, short stories, films, and the essay collections, *Where the Stress Falls, On Photography,* and *Illness as Metaphor.* She is also a recipient of the Jerusalem Prize. Susan Sontag lives in New York City.

WOLE SOYINKA is the Nigerian poet, playwright, and novelist who received the Nobel Prize for Literature in 1986. His works include *Death and the King's Horseman, Kongi's Harvest, Mandela's Earth and Other Poems, The Man Died: Prison Notes.*

JEFFREY STEINGARTEN is the author of *The Man Who Ate Everything,* a Julia Child Cookbook Award title, and *It Must've Been Something I Ate.* He has received many awards from the James Beard Foundation and was honored by the French as a Chevalier in the Order of Merit for his writings on French gastronomy. The food critic for *Vogue,* he lives in New York City.

SARA SULERI, who was born in Pakistan, is the author of *Meatless Days* and *The Rhetoric of English India.* A founding editor of the *Yale Journal of Criticism,* she teaches at Yale University.

SALLIE TISDALE is the author of *The Best Thing I Ever Tasted,* a James Beard Foundation Award-winner, *Lot's Wife, Talk Dirty to Me,* and *Stepping Westward.* A frequent contributor to national periodicals, such as *The New Yorker, Harper's, New Republic,* and *Esquire,* she lives in Oregon.

JOHN THORNE is the author of *Pot on the Fire,* a James Beard Foundation Award-winning title, *Serious Pig,* and *Outlaw Cook.* He writes the lively "Simple Cooking" food letter, named after one of his books, with his wife and frequent co-author, Matt, from their home in Northampton, Massachusetts.

CALVIN TRILLIN has been on the staff of the *New Yorker* for more than three decades and is the author of many books, which include: *Travels with Alice, The Tummy Trilogy, Uncivil Liberties, Floater,* and *To Soon to Tell.* He has also performed at the American Place Theatre in one-man shows of his own work. Calvin Trillin lives in New York City.

ALICE WALKER is the Pulitzer Prize-winning author of *The Color Purple, In Love and Trouble, Her Blue Body Everything We Know, Anything We Love Can Be Saved,* and *In Search of Our Mothers' Gardens.* She lives in California.

ALICE WATERS is the owner of the widely-admired San Francisco restaurant Chez Panisse and author of *Chez Panisse Café Cookbook*, *Chez Panisse Fruit*, and *Fanny at Chez Panisse*. She is also founder of Chez Panisse Foundation which supports educational and food-related projects.

JOSEPH WECHSBERG, born in Moravia before emigrating to the U.S., was a writer and musician. Among his many books on food, travel, and music are: *Blue Trout and Black Truffles*, *The Cooking of Vienna's Empire*, *The Waltz Emperors*, *Verdi*, and *The Danube*. He died in 1983.